Social Science Research and Public
Policy-Making: A Reappraisal

Social Science Research and Public Policy-Making: A Reappraisal

Edited by D. B. P. Kallen, G. B. Kosse,
H. C. Wagenaar, J. J. J. Kloprogge, M. Vorbeck

Proceedings of the International SVO Workshop on Educational Research and Public Policy-Making organized by the Foundation for Educational Research in the Netherlands (SVO) under the auspices of the Secretary General of the Council of Europe

SVO Foundation for Educational Research in the Netherlands (SVO)

A publication under the auspices of the Secretary General of the Council of Europe

NFER—Nelson

*Published by The NFER-Nelson Publishing Company Ltd.,
Darville House, 2 Oxford Road East,
Windsor, Berks. SL4 1DF.*

First Published 1982
© *Foundation for Educational Research in the Netherlands (SVO),
1982*
ISBN 0-85633-246-1
Code 8131 021

*All rights reserved. No part of this publication may
be reproduced or transmitted, in any form or by any
means, without permission.*

*Typeset by Cambrian Typesetters
Farnborough, Hants*

**Printed in Great Britain by
Unwin Brothers Limited, The Gresham Press, Old Woking, Surrey
A member of the Staples Printing Group**

*Distributed in the USA by Humanities Press Inc.,
Atlantic Highlands, New Jersey 07716 USA*

Contents

Preface   1
C.W. van Seventer, Director of the Foundation for Educational Research in the Netherlands (SVO)

Editorial Introduction   4

Social Science and Public Policy-Making in the 1980s   7
Major Findings of the SVO Workshop Educational Research and Public Policy-Making
H.C. Wagenaar, D.B.P. Kallen, G.B. Kosse

CONTRIBUTIONS
(Invited Papers and Summaries of Criticisms and Discussions)

  1. **Introductory Article**   21
    A Cloud of Unknowing: Social Science Research in a Political Context
    H.C. Wagenaar (Foundation for Educational Research in The Netherlands, SVO)

  2. **Social Research and Public Policy at the National Level**   32
    N. Caplan (Center for Research on Utilization of Scientific Knowledge (CRUSK), University of Michigan, U.S.A.)
      Criticism and Discussion   49

  3. **The Contribution of National Surveys to Achievement to Policy Formation**   55
    W.B. Dockrell (Scottish Council for Research in Education, Edinburgh, U.K.)
      Criticism and Discussion   71

vi   *Contents*

4. **An English Summary of Two Dutch Articles on Research as a Learning Process and Policy as a Learning Environment** 79
   Wanted: An Adequate Interface between Policy and Research 86
   A.D. de Groot (University of Groningen, The Netherlands)
   Futures Research and Public Policy-Making: A Context of Use for Systems Theory and Gaming 94
   Appendix 121
   J.H.G. Klabbers (Futures Research Unit, University of Leyden and Social Systems Research Group of the University of Nijmegen, The Netherlands)
   Criticism and Discussion 127

5. **Educational Research and Policy-Making in France** 130
   L. Legrand (Professor at Louis Pasteur University, Strasbourg and Former President of the Institut National de la Recherche Pédagogique, France)
   Criticism and Discussion 138

6. **The Sectoral Principle in Swedish Research Policy** 141
   and
   The Impact of Policy-Oriented Educational R & D 153
   I. Marklund (Swedish Governmental Commission on Educational R & D, University of Uppsala, Sweden)
   Criticism and Discussion 176

7. **Action and Knowledge from a Cognitive Point of View** 185
   M.T. De Mey (Institute of Logic and Epistemology, State University of Gent, Belgium)
   Criticism and Discussion 196

8. **Evaluation Research: Political and Organizational Constraints** 199
   and
   The Functioning of Policy-Oriented Research within some Major Innovatory Programmes in Dutch Education 224
   J. Sheerens (Foundation for Educational Research in The Netherlands (SVO)

9. **On the Effectiveness of Educational Research** 255
   P. Suppes (Institute for Mathematical Studies in Social Sciences, Stanford University, U.S.A.)

10. **A New Federal Policy for Disseminating Educational R & D in the United States** 271
    M. Timpane (National Institute of Education, Washington, U.S.A.)

11. Policy Research in the Context of Diffuse Decision-Making	288
C.H. Weiss (Graduate School of Education, Harvard University, U.S.A.)	
Presentation	305
Criticism and Discussion	314

Special Sessions   323

Special Session One: What can policy-makers and subsidizing agencies learn from two decades of social science research in a political context?   325
Chaired by Professor W. Mitter
Special Session Two: Research into the interplay between social science research and policy making in the 1980s: inventory and prospects   338
Chaired by Professor T. Husén

Appendixes

A. Address Directory	346
B. About the Editors, Invited Authors and Critics	357
C. Bibliographies, Unsolicited Papers and French Texts	371
D. Special Interest Group (SIG)	374

The Workshop reported herein was sponsored and organized by the Foundation for Educational Research in The Netherlands (SVO). However, the opinions expressed do not necessarily reflect SVO's position or policy, and no official endorsement by the Foundation for Educational Research in The Netherlands (SVO) should be inferred.

Preface

Ever since the mid-sixties governments in most Western countries have increasingly looked to the social sciences for rational support in articulating, implementing and evaluating policies in many areas. This has resulted in a progressively tighter interlocking of social science research and public policy-making.

As the volume of policy-oriented research mounted, however, so did feelings of unease about its rationale. To date no more than scattered instances are on record of research having had an immediately demonstrable impact on public policies. The initial sanguine expectations that the social sciences would provide a solid groundwork on which to base policy decisions and evaluations have not been fulfilled. SVO, the Foundation for Educational Research in The Netherlands, is almost daily confronted with this dilemma in its own domain, which is being appropriated more and more by research geared to educational policy-making.

At the same time, however, a key objective of our Foundation, and of comparable institutions abroad, has always been to foster the contribution that scientific research can make towards resolving the problems confronting practitioners and policy-makers alike both within the educational system itself and in its wider social context. In the Foundation's view, this contribution cannot be meaningfully enhanced by one-sidedly tailoring research still more closely to the needs of policy-makers. Rather it can be argued that optimal benefits in terms of rational support and evaluation of educational policy and practice will ultimately accrue from stimulating a vigorous growth of the social sciences themselves. Furthermore, it is important for the realization of our goal to strive to develop deeper understanding and more effective cooperation between policy-makers and researchers.

These and related considerations have prompted our Foundation to engage in a searching reappraisal of the relations between social science research and public policy-making in general, and of the role of policy-oriented research in education in particular. To this end, our Foundation organized an international symposium, entitled SVO Workshop 'Educational Research and Public Policy-Making', held on 20, 21 and 22 May 1981 under the valued auspices of the Secretary General of the Council of Europe.

The aim of the Workshop was to review in detail the main problem areas outlined above and to attempt to draw conclusions about the proper functioning of policy-oriented research. Renowned experts from the three domains most closely involved — i.e. social science research, policy-making and the sphere of interplay between these two domains were invited to the Workshop, as well as delegates from the member states of the Council for Cultural Co-operation (CCC) of the Council of Europe. Our attempt at comprehensiveness was reflected in the composition of the symposium's Panel of Critics who also took part in discussions. Since the Workshop was intended to provide an opportunity to examine specific problems within a variety of contexts, our Foundation sought out experts from the relevant domains each of whom was known to represent a different point of view. The Panel reviewed the invited papers before the Workshop began and took part in the discussions following the authors' presentations, making contributions based on their own experiences in research contracting and policy-making.

The wide range of interests represented at the Workshop should help to ensure an optimally effective dissemination of its findings. We hope this will achieve two things. First, that policy-makers may be encouraged to promote, systematically and on the basis of international and interdisciplinary exchange, the fundamental conditions for sound and critical policy-oriented research. Second, that there will be an improvement in the basic organizational structures in social science research which will better and more realistically meet public expectations. We hope that this book will give a major impetus to continued study of a subject that is of general importance to modern society, on both sides of the Atlantic. The Special Interest Group (see Appendix D) launched during the Workshop might in future become an effective vehicle for such a combined, international and interdisciplinary effort.

The discussions and papers focused mainly on the field of educational research and public policy. However, the findings presented in this volume are not restricted to this field. The diversity of experience and depth of knowledge reflected in the contributions make this book valuable reading for social scientists in many different disciplines, especially those engaged in policy-oriented and/or government-commissioned research. I hope that this searching reappraisal of fundamental issues will prove equally helpful to executives of policy-making agencies in examining or formulating their own assumptions about the role social science plays, and is able to play, in policy-making.

Our Foundation is greatly indebted to the members of the Editorial Committee, the Netherlands Ministry of Education and Sciences

J.J.J. Kloprogge), the Council of Europe's Section for Educational Research and Documentation (M. Vorbeck, who also chaired the Workshop) and the European Cultural Foundation (D. Kallen) who so generously cooperated with SVO both in organizing the Workshop itself and in delimiting and structuring the subject matter, and to our executive staff members G.B. Kosse and H.C. Wagenaar who undertook the greatest part of the editing work for this volume. Furthermore I would like to express my appreciation to Isabel Fornari for the many ways in which she relieved the editors from burdensome details and for her indispensable help in preparing the manuscript for publication. Last but not least, our Foundation wishes to express its gratitude to the authors and to the members of the Panel of Critics for their balanced presentation of theory, findings and implications by which they improved the basis for an effective linkage of social science and public policy-making.

In conclusion I should like to draw the reader's attention to the bibliographies and other documents listed in Appendix C, all of which are available from SVO. Among them there are the French translations of the contributions in this volume.

The Hague, The Netherlands
September 1982

C.W. van Seventer
Director of the Foundation
for Educational Research
in The Netherlands (SVO)

Editorial Introduction

Social Science Research and Public Policy-Making: A Reappraisal contains the contributions to a symposium organized by The Foundation for Educational Research in The Netherlands (SVO) under the auspices of the Secretary General of the Council of Europe. SVO, as the major Dutch funding agency for commissioned policy-oriented educational research in The Netherlands, considered that the time was right for a reconsideration of the established place social science research had won over the past twenty-five years. The increasing demand for a clear demonstration of the value of social science research, for evidence of visible and practical return from substantial national investment, called for a re-examination of the interplay of social science and policy-making. The claim that social science research — in particular educational research — can provide a scientific basis for both policy and practice has been disputed by researchers, practitioners and policy-makers alike. Concern over the gap between research and policy-making has increased sharply over the last decade due, in part, perhaps to the economic crisis which has affected, in varying degrees, most countries throughout the world. The questions have been put in many different ways, but they come down to an expectation of immediate and practical benefit. Each of the various groups involved tends to view the situation differently and has different solutions to offer. Practitioners complain of the isolation of researchers and recommend improving communication on both sides, together with better dissemination and implementation efforts. Governments, on the other hand, propose a close customer-contractor relationship as a solution, implying both active initiation of research by the authorities on problems of their own choosing, and more direct control. Researchers themselves, especially those involved in 'research on research' and writers on the philosophy of science, locate solutions in greater insight into the proper function and nature of research and its social context. A distinction is often drawn between research operating within the constraints of the existing system and research which criticizes or challenges it. The former is often seen as helpful by practitioners and policy-makers; the latter as a threat. In democracies as we know them, there is and certainly has to be a place for both types.

Although research can perform a quite direct, short-term, practical function in helping practitioners to find solutions to specific problems, and supplying policy-makers and administrators with information on which to base their decisions or to legitimate existing policies and practices, the impact of research is more often indirect and long-term. Carol Weiss has described this kind of impact as the 'enlightenment' function of research, while Nathan Caplan has referred to the 'conceptual use' of social science knowledge.

There is an abundance of literature on the impact of research on policy and practice, which is very often presented in the context of evaluation and implementation of innovations. To review all this would have been a difficult task and the organizers of the Workshop chose instead to focus on a redefinition of the questions asked so far, since these falsely imply a linear model of impact and a rational model of decision-making. The papers brought together here are written from such diverse perspectives as the philosophy of science (De Mey and Suppes), utilization research (Caplan), decision-making (Weiss) and dissemination policy (Timpane). Other contributions concern actual cases of research contributions to policy-making within different organizational and geographical constraints (Dockrell, Scheerens and Marklund), develop new views on the nature of social science research and the way policies come into being (Klabbers), or search for ways to improve the interface between the two communities involved from the standpoint of a learning process (de Groot).

The book begins with a summarized report on the findings of the Workshop concerning linkage, utilization and public policy-making. While exploring current views on these topics, more questions are asked than answered. But there is an important new dimension to these questions. They provide the reader with the opportunity to examine his or her own assumptions about the contribution of research to policy-making at all levels. Furthermore, the report brings together the issues and experiences raised by the critics during the discussions following the presentations of the contributing authors.

A paper by H.C. Wagenaar, 'A Cloud of Unknowing' presents a comprehensive approach to the subject of social science research and public policy-making, and was written as an introduction to the Workshop. There then follow the invited papers in alphabetical order of the authors' name. Where relevant, a summary of the criticism and discussion following the presentation of a paper has also been included. Together with the two Special Sessions these summaries contain vivid illustrations of the fact that the processes in policy decisions, in educational practice and research are far too complex for simple guidelines to indicate how the three should interrelate. The editors therefore refrained from drawing up a list of clear cut recommendations. However, many generalizations and findings of the participants are presented, and in this way the book itself is an illustration of one of its major conclusions, that research provides a background of data, empirical generalizations and ideas that affect the way we think about problems. To enable the reader to acquaint himself more fully with the main issues in the relationship between social science research and policy-making, a series of appendices give relevant literature and the names and addresses of those in universities and elsewhere who are involved in tackling these issues.

The Editors

Social Science and Public Policy-Making in the 1980s:
Major Findings of the SVO Workshop Educational Research and Public Policy-Making

H.C. Wagenaar, D.B.P. Kallen, G.B. Kosse

1. Introduction

The use of social science research in public policy has a flavour of rationality, as *Weiss* remarks in her contribution to the Workshop. Governments are keen to invest in the knowledge industry, partly of course for what it has already proved to yield, but also from a deep-rooted sense of rationality which is found permeating the whole of our Western society. In the sixties the social sciences — other than economics which was already comfortably installed — managed to integrate themselves into the scientific establishment by becoming an institutionalized component of government policy-making. Research was held to enhance the efficacy of government policy, and, from that time on 'almost every major policy initiative in health, social services and education was attended by formal systematic evaluation of the effects of the policy' (Weiss). Researchers, for their part, felt that by carrying out research for social policy programmes they were contributing to the development of the welfare state: 'an ideal opportunity to combine research practice with social conscience', as *Weiss* put it. However, complementary motivation does not inevitably lead to a fruitful relationship. Even by the early seventies researchers and policy-makers alike had already begun to feel uneasy about the impact of policy-oriented research programmes. It was becoming obvious that results from this type of research were having hardly any perceptible influence on policy decisions. The recent severe cuts in the social science research budgets seem to demonstrate that this type of research has to be looked on as a product of the welfare state rather than its manager. Knowledge utilization became a subject for symposia and government committees.

But how evident, after all, is the under-utilization of social science research? Various participants in the SVO Workshop (*Suppes, Weiss*) found no difficulty in supplying examples of extensive, incontestable impact both on society and on government policy. Perhaps, as *Wagenaar* suggests in his introduction to the Workshop, it is the presuppositions that underly our notions about the correct use of the social sciences that are wrong. This is not in itself an original remark but careful scrutiny of these presuppositions did prove greatly to enlarge our concepts of the nature of policy generation and the social sciences and, in general, of what knowledge is and how it is acquired. The question of knowledge utilization goes much further than the mere practical problem.

In the context of the Workshop organized by the SVO, policy-makers, researchers and research managers discussed the utilization in public policy-making of social sciences knowledge. All aspects of the question already mentioned came under discussion in a series of sessions which the participants characterized as 'important', 'provocative', 'stimulating' and 'highly successful'. This report contains the main lines of thought as they appeared in the written papers, reviews and their oral presentations and during the discussions. It goes without saying that much has had to be omitted but this account is meant particularly for readers with a wide general interest but little time to spare. More detailed information can be found by consulting other parts of this volume.

One of the theses put forward during the Workshop was that the impact of social science research occurs not so much at the level of concrete research results but rather at the conceptual level. It is above all the ideas produced by the social sciences which influence the opinions and vision of the user. The editors of the proceedings hope that this volume will lend support to this thesis by contributing to the formulation of ideas on the subject of a good and productive relationship between the social sciences and society.

2. Utilization of social science knowledge. The missing link

The way a question is put predetermines its solution. The problem that confronted researchers in the seventies was that the results of applied social science research were being used by policy-makers much less than had been expected. Almost as a matter of course the resultant question was cast in technical terms: by what means can a bridge be constructed between the knowledge producer, or researcher, and the users of that knowledge, mainly policy-makers. In other words, as *Caplan* says, 'A gap is hypothesized between knowledge producers and users, and, based on the understanding of the gap, means are offered to effectively link the two', and he points out that this question arose largely out of research on the spread of agricultural innovations (Caplan).

The 'gap-theory' was extremely popular, not least because it held out prospects of easily-managed technical solutions to the utilization problem. It offered itself as a paradigm to researchers and government committees anxious about the limited social yield of policy-oriented social science research. Various different participants gave examples of government commissions whose specific task was to produce recommendations for efficient dissemination of research results to potential users. *Marklund*, for example, provided a detailed account of the work of the Swedish School Research Committee. The Swedish government, disappointed by the scarcity of useful results emanating from the educational research it had financed, instructed the Committee to search for ways and means of bringing research and development closer to everyday school problems. The solution was couched in terms of dissemination of results. Even though in many cases research had quite certainly had a demonstrable impact on education policy and practice, the Committee concluded that dissemination of results was the most neglected aspect of the research process. 'Even projects which are well planned in all other respects often lack a considered dissemination strategy' (Marklund). In consequence the recommendations made by the Committee in order to improve the situation, varied from the establishment of special funds or project budgets for dissemination activities to the use of a multi-media approach in order to reach various different groups of users.

Timpane, in turn, described the dissemination programme set up by the National Council on Educational Research, the policy-making board of the American National Institute of Education (NIE). The Council asserts that dissemination is so complex that, in spite of considerable research on practice improvement, much is still unknown and *Timpane* commented that the organization of an institutional system for dissemination was still only fragmentary (Timpane). However, one of the most striking aspects of the NIE report is how the concept of dissemination has broadened over the years. In the fifties dissemination was thought of as 'a natural consequence of good research', in the sixties as a structured strategy with the object of making R & D results accessible to the lay user, but now it is described as part of an innovatory activity which must envisage increasing the user's problem-solving capacity. The Council's recommendations mirror this development for alongside the expected insistance on things like 'capacity building to strengthen field capabilities to disseminate', and 'coordination to provide improved use of existing capabilities', strong emphasis is laid on strategies for 'organizational renewal and professional growth'.

The aims of dissemination activities certainly seem to have expanded a good deal, now comprising not only diffusion of results but also going much further to include their beneficial application to solving practical problems. But the user's heuristic strategies include not only research results but also social knowledge and practical experience: in other words the traditional linkage or diffusion model with its connotations of an active transmitter and a passive receiver has given place to a model in which the user occupies the central place as an active, inquiring, problem-solving entity. This, it must be concluded, if we look back over the Workshop, is the vision which, implicitly or explicitly has provided the dominant theme throughout the discussions.

In the light of such a view the linkage or gap-filling theory seems no longer adequate to explain the under-utilization of social science knowledge. *Caplan's* paper contains an elegant critique of linkage theories. On the basis of his own earlier research, he comes to the conclusion, that the presence or absence of a gap between researchers and policy-makers makes hardly any difference to the actual use of research results. In Finland, for example, a relatively small community with intensive contact between both groups, 'the level of knowledge application to matters of public policy' was scarcely higher than in the USA where such contacts were far more scanty. *Caplan* concludes that communication of social science knowledge to policy-makers is clearly much more complicated than the attractively simple gap-filling theories suggest and is affected strongly by all sorts of attendant factors such as 'the nature of the policy problem, the type of information involved and the position of the user in the organizational hierarchy'. By way of illustration he points out how the utilization of social science knowledge varies according to the importance attached to the policy problems concerned.

Caplan's 1975 study on the use of social science knowledge by upper-level executives showed that 'approximately 90% of reported uses of social science research were associated with day-to-day policy issues of limited significance' (Caplan). At this level data from research was used directly in testing the applicability of already established programmes or to monitor the administrative process. The data in question were generally collected by internal research bureaus. This *Caplan* calls the instrumental use of knowledge.

The picture changes in the case of decisions with a greater range, 'important matters which affect the nation as a whole' (Caplan), where results of empirical research seldom play a decisive role. In the process leading up to a decision of this type, opinions are formed by a diffuse process during which information culled from various sources somehow crystallizes into a definite attitude towards the policy problem. *Caplan* remarks that, in such situations, the most important sources of information are the mass media (newspapers, radio, television) and informal contacts inside and outside the policy-making organization. Knowledge-utilization by these means cannot be pinned down to a single, isolated event, as the linkage-theories seem to suggest, but appears to involve a process which takes place over a longer period of time during which the information used is subject to many influences and modifications. This leads *Caplan* to speak of information having a life-cycle within an organization. In his opinion, study of the assimilation of information by policy-making organizations is essential to the understanding of the relationship between the social sciences and public policy.

(On this subject various participants in the Workshop drew attention to the importance of informal contacts as means of affecting behaviour. *Timpane*, for example, quoted from a study on decision-making in the

American Congress, from which it appeared that personal contacts exerted by far the greatest influence on the decision-making process, whereas evaluation and research studies occupied the very lowest place in the hierarchy of factors contributing to a decision. This led *Timpane* to conclude that, at least for politicians, 'human testimony is most often a dominant factor in the interpretation of information' (Discussions). *Husén and Dockrell* also found that, particularly in small communities, informal networks were of crucial importance to the process of decision-making. The apparent conflict between this conclusion and *Caplan's* data about the restricted influence of contracts between researchers and policy-makers on knowledge-utilization, is one among the many examples of the complexity of the subject.

Weiss' description of the utilization of social science knowledge by policy-makers agrees with *Caplan*'s on many points. Cases of research results having an immediate and direct influence are few and far between, but *Weiss* observes that, on a conceptual level, there is considerable influence. Rather than making a rational impact on clear-cut decisions, 'research provides a background of data, empirical generalizations and ideas that affect the way that policy-makers think about problems'. The effect of this form of influence is that: 'It influences their conceptualizations of the issues with which they deal, it affects the facets of the issue that they consider inevitable, it sensitizes them to new issues, etc.'. In short, 'it's the ideas coming from research that have an impact' (Weiss).

Ideas move elusively. Once again it becomes apparent that it is through popular and informal channels that conclusions from social science research spread most readily. Policy-makers are seldom able to point to a specific study or research report as the main influence governing their decision.

Weiss uses the term 'enlightenment' to cover this diffusion of ideas through the issue of current social notions. Ideas change the way in which problems are expressed and provide the goals envisaged by society. Little by little policy-makers come to use terms of reference derived from the social sciences. But, as *Weiss* hastens to add, social scientists can hardly expect the enlightenment theory to fuel a renewed sense of confidence within the profession. In itself enlightenment contains no guarantee of quality, for as much attention will be paid to what is merely fashionable or unconsidered as to what is dependable and workmanlike. Furthermore, as *Weiss* remarks in one of the background documents for the Workshop, research 'elaborates rather than simplifies'. The results of research often succeed in introducing added complications and nuances and are quite likely to be contradictory, which is hardly surprising because the problems of society are, by their very nature, complex, many-sided and contradictory in their implications. Research can provide more insight into the play of forces in a community but the implications for policy-making are much less clear.

12 Social Science Research and Public Policy-Making

Without calling in question its value, *Weiler* points out what he terms an element of cognitive dissonance in the enlightenment view. There are other reasons for the poor impact of social science research on policy. We are obliged to admit that much policy-oriented research is quite simply useless: 'conceptually or methodologically flawed, poorly executed or all three'. Thus, even when policy-makers have adopted the language of social science, this does not always work out as an advantage and uncritical use of social science concepts reduces their selective force. The researchers themselves tend to make optimistic promises, caught up as they are in the mechanism of a free research market, and the customers, whose expectations are constantly being raised, then suffer from chronic disappointment. Researchers hardly ever impress upon their clients the natural limitations of their profession; the actual yield to be expected compared with realistic costs. Both *Caplan and Weiss* explain the new view of knowledge-utilization with reference to the diffuse, elusive character of political decision-making but *Weiler* argues that even if it were an entirely rational process, research results would still be of little effect for the reasons given above. He fears that too great an enthusiasm for the enlightenment model may blind us to a number of bitter truths about contract research.

The separation of instrumental from conceptual use of knowledge has a number of important implications for the organizational position of policy-oriented research. *Weiss* suggests differentiating such research according to type. Short-term research on clearly-defined policy problems, which does not necessarily require the collection of original data and which has immediate relevance for the user, is best done by analysis units within the organization itself. The main aim of this type of research, which *Weiss* calls policy analysis, is the synthesis and analysis of available data and it provides an important means of organizational learning. Traditional linkage and dissemination strategies seem to be very effective at this level, the problem being, according to *Caplan*, that the notion of use which is generated by such instrumental application of information will not stretch to accommodate major issues, that is, issues of radical importance that will continue to confront society for many years to come. What is needed here is reflective research with a long-range view, research in the academic tradition. This is described by *Weiss* as policy research and is best carried out outside the government machine in independent institutions and in the universities, where the necessary critical distance and detachment can best be achieved. *Husén* adds that such fundamental research has yet another essential function which is to provide a training ground for young researchers. There must be an infrastructure of fundamental research in order to keep the intellectual powers of a society up to scratch.

This discussion on the influence of social science research on public policy-making began by considering the simple and obvious question of how the gap between researchers and policy-makers could best be bridged. Various Workshop participants showed that in view of the fact that there was as yet extremely little proof of research influencing policy decisions at all, the question was oversimplified and perhaps not sufficiently well-defined. So-called linkage or gap-filling theories, with their suggestion of a direct linear relation between research results and policy decisions, do not fit in with the complex nature of the decision-making process. *Weiss*, in particular, showed that the relationship is actually much more subtle or even problematic: policy-making and the social sciences can be said to occupy two angles of a triangle with society as a whole at the apex. Both research and policy-making are component parts of a greater entity, society at large, and as such, subject to its inherent forces. Already the gap-filling theory was being reformulated as the initial question of how to communicate research knowledge to policy-makers gave way to *Weiss*' more profound inquiry as to how the wisdom of policy-making can be improved and whether and how social science can play a part in improving its quality.

Reformulating a problem first of all involves detachment from the presuppositions underlying it. The new question has vast implications for the study of knowledge-utilization. It concentrates first of all on policy-making and organization. The linear view rested on strong assumptions about the nature of policy-making, but many participants pointed out the problem nature of these assumptions in the light of everyday reality. It would appear that the nature of the policy-making process and the specific organizational structure in which it takes place are potent factors determining the use made of social research. Chapter 3 goes more deeply into this question.

But the implications go even further, touching on the very nature of social science research itself. If both policy-making and research belong to the larger entity of society as a whole, research can no longer be thought of as a detached, independent and objective source of cool, certain judgment on practical matters. Research, just like any other human activity, is clearly prey to the forces in society and is constantly obliged to perform the bootstrap operation of attempting to discover the precise influence which such forces wield. Chapter 4 shows that some Workshop participants were expressly interested in elucidating this question and thus in exploring the nature of social science research and the status of its results.

3. Policy, organization and decision-making. The politics of knowledge-utilization

Rational theories of policy-making envisage a largely linear process, starting with a careful examination of the pros and cons of various alternative courses of action and culminating in an optimal decision. But such a description of the case assumes, among other things, that decision-making takes place within fixed limits of time and space, is goal-oriented and that the forces moulding the decision can be clearly demonstrated; yet all this is far removed from reality. *Weiss* sees the policy-making process far more as a cumulative affair, involving contributions from many people who continue to follow out their myriad small-scale routines or come up with *ad hoc* solutions, only half-conscious of the consequences, all of which ultimately adds up to something we call policy. Even upper-level policy-makers quite often complain that they themselves are not making decisive choices but merely operate in the small margins that remain when the administrators or judiciary have finished making their decisions. She illustrates this with a long list of the sort of activities which inadvertently contribute to policy-making: reliance on custom and implicit rules, improvisation in the face of unexpected problems, negotiation, imitation of techniques used by colleagues, reactions to the unforeseen consequences of previous decisions, and so forth. The process of decision-making in a political context goes on in an aimless, diffuse way in harmony with the fluid political reality in which it is immersed. In a democracy, the political process is not linear but involves a whole system of continuous adjustment and negotiation resulting in decisions which are usually compromises between conflicting interests of various sectors of society. There is a special rationality attaching to politics which, as *Ringeling* has emphasized, somehow has to steer a course between the Scylla of political downfall and the Charybdis of upsetting the balance of society.

In such a view research is ascribed its rightful position as one of the factors influencing the policy-making process. As *Weiss* insisted once again during the presentation of her paper, 'social science has no monopoly of knowledge and insight' which, from an ethical viewpoint is hardly a matter for regret. Seen in the light of our Western tradition of democracy there is little to be said for the ideal of a monolithic meritocracy, enthroning Science as the jealous guardian of knowledge. A diffuse decision-making process demands a diffuse absorption of knowledge (Weiss). The effect of the social sciences on policy comprises the combined impact of large numbers of studies over long periods of time.

(During the Workshop many participants emphasized that the way in which research knowledge is used can only properly be understood in the light of a valid conception of the policy-making process. Much of this discussion was occasioned by *Klabber's* paper on 'Futures Research and Public Policy-Making'. This project is an interesting attempt to apply systems theory to policy-making situations. A computerized model of the Dutch education system enables policy-makers to see the consequences of various different policy options. The new element in the project is that simulation and gaming aspects are combined in order to cope with the uncertainty inherent in policy development. Groups of interested parties involved in a certain policy take part in a simulation game during which the computer confronts them, there and then, with the policy implications of what has been negotiated.

Although *Klabber*'s explanation of the technique of interactive simulation aroused a lot of interest, a number of participants had strong doubts about its practical value. *Timpane*, for example, thought that the amount of the policy-maker's time that the gaming technique consumes would, in itself, prohibit its use in everyday decision-making. Both *Eide* and *Timpane* also suggested that the technique, although appropriate to policy problems of a numeric-economic character would have only limited application to controversial, normative problems. Yet a third related objection was that because a computerized model of the education system was being used, there was a danger that the importance ascribed to any issue in a policy-making situation, might come to depend on whether the relevant data happened to be available.)

It will be apparent that the utilization of research knowledge is not an isolated event but a long process influenced by heterogeneous forces in the political spectrum. *Caplan* suggested that knowledge introduced into an organization has a life-cycle during which it is used, forgotten and rediscovered, usually undergoing considerable modification on its way. As he explained, this is not a fortuitous or unpredictable process, for the fate of particular items of knowledge is closely determined by their importance to the organization. Numerous studies of the adoption of innovations have repeatedly shown that new knowledge has to be converted, reinvented or 'sanitized' before it becomes acceptable to its user. For most organizations control of information is important because new knowledge may upset the balance necessary to the organization itself, but with proper control it is perfectly possible to 'deal with the organizational difficulties which ensue when an idea, innovation or new finding is detected' (Caplan). It may appear to the observer that the user is simply rejecting the knowledge whereas in fact, behind the scenes, it has had real impact and a feverish hunt is on hand for means to adapt the policy to fit, within certain sacred political and organizational limits. This is why there is a time-lag for acceptance of new knowledge and only after the passage of years is its effect discernible in the form of an alteration in policy the occasion for which is already forgotten.

However convincing such a general description of the political and organizational context of policy-orientation may be, the fact remains that actually carrying out research while tossed on the waves of current politics can be frustrating. Some European participants had interesting comments to make on this subject. *Scheerens* gave an account of a piece of evaluation research by which he had attempted to attribute the vast problems which confront certain policy-oriented research programmes to the specific nature and organization of the Dutch government policy on educational innovation. He concluded that there was a serious discrepancy between research, which was empirical and rational, and policy-making, which was incremental and ideological, in which the burden of the innovation fell upon the individual schools concerned. Although the phrasing of the innovatory policy had a rational flavour and the official implementation strategy was couched in terms like experiment, goals and evaluation, the main objectives were largely from a humanistic-psychological interpretation of the world. Consequently, and especially at a local level, research with its empirical-rational approach sometimes met with unconcealed hostility because it was seen as damaging to the innovation process.

Organization can have a decisive influence on the role played by research. *De Groot* and *Kallen* both pointed out the peculiar corporative structure of public policy-making in The Netherlands with its combination of an excess of advisory committees and a strongly centralized decision-making apparatus. This seems to be the result of religious differences which traditionally give rise to what *de Groot* terms: 'a high degree of social cleavage', in The Netherlands. The combination appears to have been fatal in the case of policy-oriented research. Research planning was endlessly discussed in numerous advisory committees but not one of these bodies, not even the SVO which has statutory control of finance for educational research, had sufficient powers to get a research programme quickly and efficiently off the ground. The minister took a budget decision on each and every separate project which led to enormous delays in the start of a number of pieces of research. The conclusion which *Scheerens* and *de Groot* drew from the situation in The Netherlands was that under certain conditions the conduct of policy-oriented research can be easily frustrated. A good deal of research is quite simply bad, as *Weiler* said, and no appeal to the diffuseness of the spread of knowledge should blind us to this fact, but at the same time we must realize that without minimal financial and organizational support there would be no research at all.

The separation of research from policy implied in most utilization theories is perhaps a somewhat artificial or even misleading distinction. Policy-oriented social science research undoubtedly has a political dimension, as was made clear in an impressive presentation by *Legrand*, and in this dimension it is research that is the more vulnerable. In his survey of French educational research over the last 25 years, *Legrand* plainly demonstrated how, in an autocratic government system, independent educational research often elicits deep suspicion and is met with active antagonism. His message, also publicly subscribed to by the Spanish participants, was that independent, critical research is possible only in an open pluralist society, or, to be more precise, is itself characteristic of such a society. With the support of *Mitter, Legrand* went as far as to claim that a democratic state has a duty to stimulate research critical of its own policy: 'In a democratic state one is duty bound . . . to allow different approaches to be explored and different or divergent results to be published and discussed, not only to demonstrate their veracity, but to give a clearer idea of the ethical assumptions underlying them. A process of this kind is essential to democracy' (Le grand).

4. Fundamental questions. The act of knowing

Unexpected difficulties sometimes reveal the preconceptions upon which our idea of the world is based. It is the obstinate and persistent problem that lays bare the truths and ideals by which we have tried to make sense of the world around us. Of course the social sciences are relevant to society but when, contrary to our expectations, their counsel is all but ignored by the policy-makers, we are bound to re-examine our original notions of science and society and the relation of one to the other. What makes the question of knowledge-utilization a fascinating one is that it leads on, almost as a matter of course, to basic questions of epistemology and policy whose implications range far beyond the practical importance of usable research results.

Large areas of the social sciences, especially within the empiricist tradition, rest on the assumption that every event is consequent upon a preceding event or that every event has a sufficient determinant cause. *Suppes*, however, in his opening speech, made it clear that even a superficial description of a straightforward human activity like talking or driving a car, shows that strict determinism is hopelessly unsuitable when it comes to explaining such a phenomenon. Analysis in terms of determinant causes explains only part of the phenomenon, at the most. So, according to *Suppes*, causality should be understood in a probabilistic rather than a deterministic way. Discussions of the probabilistic nature of causality touch on the fundamental principles of science and may appear to be far removed from the troubles afflicting applied social science research, but if once the explanatory basis of the social sciences is wrongly apprehended, then the way is open for misleading conceptions about the effectiveness of these sciences in society. *Suppes* thinks that one of the most important tasks of the social sciences is to explore 'to what extent a theory of probabilistic causality can be developed in a given domain and when to accept results that are as good as can be expected'.

What appears to be yet more fundamental to empirical social sciences is that they are deeply rooted in certainty. The essence of the empirical method, based as it is on systematic perception of objective facts, is that it holds out the promise of certitude. But modern psychology has undermined the objectivity of sensory perception and modern philosophy has revealed the positivist epistemology of the empirical social sciences as a contemporary manifestation of old Cartesian rationalism. Perceptions are not passive registrations of the outside world but are actively selected from the chaos of stimuli that surrounds us. In our acts of perception we endue the world with a meaning in harmony with the expectations and aspirations with which we go to meet it.

The crucial notion here according to *De Mey*, is 'context'. Merely to understand simple but in some degree ambiguous units of information (such as the word 'arms'), it is necessary to know the context in which they appear. (As for example in Thomas Hood's everlasting song: 'Ben Battle was a soldier bold, And used to war's alarms; But a cannon-ball took off his legs, So he laid down his arms!') In most cases, however, the context is not an objective fact but a construction of the perceiver himself. His ideas, intentions or 'conceptual frameworks' make up the personal context which gives meaning to his world. *De Mey* speaks of the cognitive view which is 'the theory of perception which emphasizes the production of expectations on the basis of a world model to such a degree that intake of input can be seen as almost entirely restricted to a few points of control, and to filling in parameter values. Within such a view *perception* is, to a large extent, the product of *imagination*: the few points of intake of information only safeguarding it from becoming *illusion* by tying imagination to "reality" ' (De Mey). (Italics as in the original).

For the positivist approach to science the most important implication is that perceiver and 'fact' can no longer be regarded as strictly separate systems. Subject and object are inextricably entangled because the object is seen as included in the subject's conceptual framework.

Rein carried this implication into the field of the relation of research to policy-making. Policy-oriented research always starts from a number of cogent implicit assumptions. First of all social science knowledge is portrayed as independent of policy. 'There is an antithesis between knowledge development which takes place in society among laymen and policy-makers and knowledge that is developed by research' declared *Lövgren*. All this springs from a strict separation between knowing and doing. The policy-maker is someone who does things and receives information from the scientist who is the person who knows things. Knowledge precedes action. But, as we have seen: 'there are no facts independent of the theory that organizes them' and in social science theory the action element plays a dominant role. According to *Rein* concepts such as 'unemployment' or 'poverty' can hardly be separated from the political context in which they function. Their specific meaning is determined by the information user's beliefs and intentions regarding the type of labour market he thinks suitable or the best solution to the problem of poverty. Concepts in the social sciences contain a concealed policy-programme or, even more strongly: analytic concepts are themselves policy concepts and are derived from a coherent position of the policies behind them.

Rein combines these factors into the concept of 'frame' which 'brings together and interprets theory, fact, value, interests and action'. Frames determine not only the orientation of political programmes but also and just as much, the research questions which are formulated in their context. Policy-makers and researchers operate inside the same frame.

One of the most intriguing aspects of the cognitive approach is the centuries-old question of the role played by action in our thinking. The world of science admits to a strict dualism and sense of the consequences of action upon knowledge, but *Rein* has already shown that the relationship between the two is much more subtle and intricate. Action components seem to be an essential element in our knowledge of the world and to play a decisive role in guiding the process of knowledge-assimilation. *De Mey* describes action as a generic source of ideas, basing this proposition on Piaget's theories of developmental psychology. In a fascinating series of experiments Piaget showed that young children can readily learn a simple manual trick, seem to understand how they are to perform it, but when asked to explain what is happening are quite unable to do so. The children have a rough conceptual scheme which guides their actions but has little explanatory value. Their ideas about the physics of the situation are substantially inferior to the level of their performance, concludes *De Mey*. The highpoint in Piaget's results is that he also shows that by continually following out the effect of their actions the children gradually acquire a better cognitive grasp of the situation. *De Mey* suggests that the conceptual scheme is slowly but surely filled out and refined 'by balancing two systems: one to account for the actions of the subject, one to account for the effects on the object'. This description contains a miniature of the process of research, for hypotheses are tested by their effects on the outside world.

But the crucial element in this account is the action component; this is the objective we keep in mind, shaping our interest and guiding our interventions in the outside world; producing the results which we all, researchers and policy-makers alike, look back on and attempt to comprehend.

5. Social science and public policy-making. A future of decline?

As many governments seek to cut expenditure, the social sciences find themselves going through a difficult period, for it is they who are the easiest victims and fall first under the axe. However, tragic and short-sighted this may prove to be, it cannot be denied that, with hindsight, much of the policy-oriented research in recent years must be described as an appanage of the affluent society, a pleasing ornament to the welfare state rather than an essential ingredient of human happiness. And now galloping technology and worldwide economic instability are striking at the very roots of our protected society, directly threatening the economic position and future prospects of millions of citizens, and casting sombre shadows of the Christian-humanist ethos which has formed our ideals of welfare. The social sciences seem to be a small vessel indeed in such a hostile ocean. Providing policy-makers with the exact parameters of their programme, however important in itself, contributes little to solving such major issues. Now even the well-tried remedies themselves are being weighed in the balance and found wanting.

Yet it is in such circumstances that the social sciences can play a far more extensive and effective role than they have done in the recent past. One of the messages emerging from this Workshop was that the social sciences may not always act directly on decisions, as such, but on the frame of discourse and the terms of understanding. Their essential impact lies in redefining the problem. What is put forward here as a conclusion should perhaps be taken in the future as an imperative. The task of the social sciences is to scrutinize the definitions and solution-strategies of our problems in the light of changing circumstances. It is precisely at times like these that the policy-makers charged with the responsibility of running our society may not like to see their assumptions challenged. The researcher, in turn, may find it painful to redefine his economic and political position and to accept that he cannot always expect a place in the highest councils of the land. But in a democratic society, science can have no master but only a public to whom it is responsible. As the last ten years have shown, perhaps in a somewhat negative sense, it is only as a crritical and independent force that the social sciences can be effective and earn the long-term respect of those they serve.

INTRODUCTORY ARTICLE

A Cloud of Unknowing: Social Science Research in a Political Context*

Henk C. Wagenaar, Foundation for Educational Research in the Netherlands

> The fate of an epoch which has eaten of the tree of knowledge is that it must know that we cannot learn the *meaning* of the world from the results of its analysis, be it ever so perfect; it must rather be in a position to create this meaning itself (Max Weber).

On 20, 21 and 22 May this year, the Foundation for Educational Research in The Hague is organizing an international symposium on Educational Research and Public Policy-making. Before an invited audience from the Netherlands, the other member states of the Council of Europe and a few other countries, some 70 experts — researchers, policy-makers and specialists in the sphere of interplay between the domains of research and of policy-making — from a variety of countries will spend three days exchanging ideas on this important and topical subject. In the context of the literature on 'knowledge-utilization', 'the political realization of social science knowledge', and 'social science research and public policy-making', to name only a few labels, this introduction to the programme looks at some of the main problems and dilemmas which the Foundation daily encounters in its role as the financier of applied educational research in the Netherlands. It is not intended that this introduction should influence the course of the discussion during the symposium itself. The pragmatic approach adopted in defining the problem areas is of course not the only way to deal with the complex question of knowledge utilization; indeed, the symposium programme proves the contrary. It is hoped that by means of intensive and varied discussion the symposium will help to clarify the relationship between policy-making and social research — a relationship which has been plagued by misunderstandings and mistaken expectations — and in so doing will aid both policy-makers and researchers.

Since around 1973 the social sciences have enjoyed the undivided attention of the Dutch Government. When Den Uyl's coalition government

---
*This text served as an introduction to the programme of the Workshop.

took office, its declaration of policy marked a shift of emphasis from public affluence to private well-being, as a result of which the authorities began to take an increasing interest in the social sciences. Policy in such areas as housing, transport, education, health, the environment and young offenders was henceforth to be based on academic research, and the 1974 Science Budget — the government's annual multi-year plan for scientific research — accordingly contained the announcement that the government intended to encourage research aimed at providing rational support for public policies. In the matter of educational research, the government took an important step forward with the publication in 1975 of the discussion document 'Contours of a future education system in the Netherlands', which set out plans for a radical restructuring of the education system and expressly stated that educational research was an essential component in this process. In 1975 only 17 per cent of the budget of the Foundation for Educational Research was spent on research for the Ministry of Education, whereas now the figure is nearer 50 per cent. Contract research on behalf of the government has become a minor industry. A cynical observer might wonder to what extent this ambitious programme has been inspired by the numerous social scientists who have entered government service since the 1960s, a fact which in itself constitutes an example of the impact of the social sciences on society.

Internationally speaking, the Netherlands was somewhat late with these developments. In the United States, for example, the debate about the impact of the Westinghouse/Ohio evaluation of the Headstart project or the ethical implications of Project Camelot, was already in full swing by 1970, but we seem to have caught up since then. Here, as in other Western countries, the present mood is one of deep disillusionment about the ability of the social sciences to help solve policy problems or the problems of society as a whole. In the Netherlands, moreover, this disillusionment is accompanied by serious doubts about the quality of applied research in the social sciences. The Minister for Science Policy noted in a policy document on the subject, published in 1978, that the results of such research were under-utilized by government and that there was a gulf separating researchers and civil servants. From the Minister's purview as policy director his remedy was predictable and has been much criticized in academic circles: research was to be tailored even more closely to the government's needs.

In educational research too, initial enthusiasm was followed by surfeit. Practically all of the ambitious and costly research programmes set up on behalf of the innovation policy referred to above fizzled out through a combination of bureaucreatic inertia, impenetrable jargon and reluctance on the part of the schools, leaving thousands and tens of thousands of pages of research reports to gather dust in ministerial archives. At present the Foundation is carrying out an evaluation study of its own in order to try and establish what results these research programmes actually produced and why they failed. (*Cf*. Scheerens, 1981.) Although the final results of the study are not yet known, the picture is already a dismal one: at every organizational level and at every stage of the research and policy-making process there are serious problems, some of them typically Dutch (because of researchers' repugnance to any hierarchy of competence in research) while others are inherent in the nature of social research in a political context (discrepancies between the requirements of those commissioning the research and what researchers are actually able to achieve).

It will be apparent that there is a crisis in relations between the social sciences and government policy. But it should be asked whether the present disillusionment is not just as much a blanket response as was the initial optimism. Our views about what should be regarded as a problem are determined by the values and presuppositions underlying the way we look at social reality. Whether the results of social research may be said to be under-utilized depends on what one one understands by utilization. In the last ten years, especially in the United States, there has been a wave of research into the influence of social research on policy. The results, as is usual in the social sciences, are far from unequivocal. But one thing is clear: knowledge-utilization is a complex concept and is subject to various interpretations.

The generally accepted belief about the importance of social research for government policy — generally accepted, that is, by policy-makers, researchers and users of research results, at least in the Netherlands — is that through direct application of the results, research helps to solve social and/or political problems. Weiss speaks of this view of research as the 'problem-solving model', which she defines as follows: 'The model is (. . .) a linear one (. . .). Here the decision drives the application of research. A problem exists and a decision has to be made, information or understanding is lacking either to generate a solution to the problem or to select among alternative solutions; research provides the missing knowledge. With the gap filled a decision is reached' (Weiss, 1979). And: '(. . .) it is usually assumed that the specific study commissioned by the responsible government office will have an impact and that its recommendations will affect ensuing choices' (*ibid*.). The problem-solving model is the standard model for knowledge-utilization and is based upon a number of deep-rooted and, as we shall see, somewhat naive assumptions both about the nature of knowledge in the social sciences and about the character of policy and policy-making. The bulk of research into knowledge-utilization in recent years has concentrated on demonstrating the untenability of these assumptions. The standard model for knowledge-utilization is based on the presumption, usually implicit, that social research is capable of making decisive pronouncements and providing certain knowledge about social and cultural issues. This presumption arises in part from the conviction, prevalent particularly among researchers, that more and better research will ultimately lead to a consensus on concepts, theories and pronouncements; it also arises partly from the deep-rooted emotional yearning for certainty which is common to all mankind. However, there are various reasons for questioning its validity and these get at the roots of the development of the social sciences.

Firstly, according to the modern philosophy of science there is no form of knowledge — not even scientific knowledge — which can aspire to absolute certainty. In order for such certainty to be attained there would have to be an ultimate foundation, an Archimedean locus from which it would be possible to prove 'that all true propositions are true and possibly that all false ones are false' (Albert, 1976, p. 27). However, as Albert demonstrates, like Popper before him, such a foundation would be unacceptable on logical grounds, and it would be arbitrary to assert that a particular piece of knowledge was true on such a basis. For the continuation of the argument it is important to note that even 'factual' observations are incapable of providing the ultimate foundation required.

All perception is guided by expectations and/or beliefs, personal theories about the assumed or desired interrelationship of phenomena in the world. Observation only takes on significance in the light of these expectations and beliefs so that the distinction between hard fact and uncertain theory is at the very least disputable. Every factual observation is 'impregnated with theories', as Popper says. (*Cf.* Popper 1972, p. 93 *et seq.*) The proponents of Critical Rationalism in the philosophy of science abandoned the search for certain knowledge and hence gave a consistently pursued 'fallibilism' a central place in their theories (*Fallibilismus*, Albert, 1975, p. 36). Even the most successful theories, even the apparently most certain knowledge, contain weak spots and can in the long run be refuted, at least in part, and replaced by better knowledge, i.e. a better theory which offers a more satisfactory explanation. According to Critical Rationalism, all theories and hypotheses are only temporarily 'true', namely for as long as no better ones are available. It is not difficult to see that the fallibilist view of human knowledge could be unwelcome to policy-makers, who have a practical job to do and prefer to act from a position of certainty.

While the above arguments suggest that scientific statements in general are uncertain, the social sciences as a rule are moreover noted for the absence of even temporary consensus about results and statements. In the case of the applied social sciences (and educational research in particular), Cohen and Garet (1975) adduce two reasons for this. In the first place, much applied social research relates to the consequences of major social innovations, the aims of which are generally so vague, the treatments so weak and the number of unknown, interfering variables so great that it is no wonder that attempts to measure the effects tend to produce confused and contradictory results.

In the second place, the various disciplines within the social sciences, and even the various schools of researchers within a single discipline, commonly work with different terms of reference, different methodological designs and different statistical techniques, so that it is often very difficult to set about a comparative interpretation of results. Their own study, like that of Cohen and Weiss (1977), illustrates the paradox that years of research using increasingly refined methodology to investigate the effects of education and racial problems in education have produced practically no definite results or conclusions. Cohen and Garet conclude that 'improving applied research has produced (...) knowledge which is no better by any scientific standard, no more authoritative by any political standard and often more mystifying by any reasonable public standard' (Cohen and Garet, *op. cit.*, p. 33).

This is a bitter pill for the researcher, the policy-maker and the taxpayer, but perhaps the expectation that social research could ever produce indisputable knowledge is rather naive. Man has only limited financial, temporal and cognitive resources with which to grasp the complexity of social reality, as Lindblom and Cohen (1980) write, and the moral they draw from this is that the search for conclusive knowledge is illusory, that in order to solve practical problems Man — or the policy-maker — must make use of every kind of knowledge he can obtain, for example experience (ordinary knowledge) and learning through action (interactive knowledge), and that for this reason the results of social research should be regarded as just one policy input among others. Research is only one of various ways of human learning, but one which, amidst other forms of obtaining knowledge, occupies a special position because of its objectivity, its susceptibility of control, its dependence and reliability. One last question here is to what extent the limited utilization concept prescribed by the standard model conflicts with the democratic decision-making procedures on which our mixed and complex Western societies are based (*Cf.* Rein, 1980).

The second and probably the most natural assumption of the standard utilization model is that policy-making consists of separate decisions. This assumption is ultimately derived from the classic model of rational decision-making: '1. Faced with a given problem; 2. a rational man first clarifies his goals, values or objectives and then ranks or otherwise organizes them in his mind; 3. he then lists all important possible ways of — policies for — achieving his goals; 4. and investigates all the important consequences that would follow from each of the alternative policies; 5. at which point he is in a position to compare consequences of each policy with goals; 6. and so choose the policy with consequences most closely matching his goals' (Lindblom, 1968, p. 13). The rational decision is taken at stage 6, while it is at about stage 4 that research results enter the decision-making process. However, it is highly questionable whether policies are in fact formulated by means of such clearly localized decision-making as this suggests. During her research into the use of research in federal policy, Weiss (1980) made the surprising discovery that, almost without exception, the policy-makers she interviewed reacted with surprise and discomfort to questions containing the word 'decision'. The questions contained an implied expectation that policy-makers must constantly make decisions, but this was apparently at odds with the experience of the respondents. It seemed that policies came into being incidentally, as improvised responses to problems which suddenly loomed up, as unforeseen consequences of previous action, or as the result of numerous smaller steps taken by many different people which gradually came to exclude certain alternative policy options.

The idea that separate and demonstrable decisions are taken is an idealized rational reconstruction of this process. Thus Weiss' findings are in accordance with the major policy models which came into being in the 1950s in reaction against the classic model of rational decision-making; in the latter models policy is construed as a series of small adjustments without clearly defined aims, seeking primarily to maintain the *status quo* ('incrementalism', Lindblom, 1968), as the result of routine procedures carried out by administrative organizations, or as the outcome of negotiations between various rival factions in the management process (Allison, 1969). However, the belief that research should concentrate exclusively upon the decisions which policy-makers will have to make in the future is as natural as it is persistent. A proposal which the Foundation for Educational Research recently put forward for evaluating policy on the new middle school is an example of this in that, at the instigation of government and parliament, it concentrates entirely on the decision which parliament will have to take in 1985 as to whether or not to comprehensivize secondary education in the Netherlands. It follows from this that the proposed evaluation would from the first have built-in limitations as to its scope in view of the ongoing heated controversy surrounding the middle school concerning its overall aims, normative orientation, teaching objectives, innovation strategies and employment aspects as well as the value of the current innovation experiments. Any research in this area which is focused exclusively on the future decision and takes no account of the various streams of public feeling on the subject between now and 1985 runs the risk of producing irrelevant or outdated results at the crucial moment.

The above-mentioned study by Cohen and Garet contains a second attack on the concept of policy with which the standard model operates. As well as being a series of actions, policy is also, and perhaps primarily, a set of ideas and beliefs about society. Policy is, in the words of Cohen and Garet, a 'grand story: a large and loose set of ideas about how society works, why it goes wrong and how it can be set right' (*op. cit.*, p. 33). Dutch Government policy on educational innovation again serves as an example. What at first sight appears to constitute a far-reaching structural reorganization of the education system will be found upon closer examination to be above all an impenetrable tangle of sociological theories concerning the origins of social inequality, ideas about personal growth borrowed from the humanist school of psychology, and theories of innovation based upon German pedagogical writings which regard as taboo any form of change imposed from above; all of this being propped up by a visionary, progressive-idealistic view of society. In other words, every policy has an ideological nucleus which is likely to render its proponents all but immune to counterevidential research results. Cohen and Garet conclude from this that it is just as pointless to assume that applied research consists of separate and independent studies as to assume that policy consists of separate and independent decisions. As confirmed by the case studies quoted, policy is influenced not by individual education projects but by research *programmes* and *traditions* — series of consecutive projects which exert a gradual influence not upon the decisions of policy-makers but upon their ideas.

It is obvious what conclusions should be drawn from the above: the standard model is based upon incorrect premises and therefore gives too limited a picture of knowledge utilization. The relationship between research and policy-making is more complex and more varied than the model would have us believe. But if the results of social science research do not directly affect the decisions of policy-makers, what are the real facts about knowledge utilization? Weiss offers the following possibilities: general guidance ('finding evidence of needs and problems and gaps or shortcomings in existing services'), ritual or symbolic utilization ('a ceremony to satisfy requirements for rational procedure or scientific gloss') and above all, overall learning or 'continuing education' (Weiss, 1980, p. 395). The social sciences influence the way in which policy-makers see social reality: 'The concepts and theoretical perspectives that social science research has engendered (. . .) permeate the policy-making process' (Weiss, 1979). Weiss sums up all this as the 'enlightenment function' of research, and most authors who have written about this subject recently agree that the most plausible of knowledge utilization is along these lines — i.e. that the social sciences influence policies or society in this diffuse, generalized, unpredictable fashion largely at the conceptual level. Realistic as it is, the enlightenment model at the same time reveals certain objections to the present system of contract research.

Firstly, the enlightenment model does not correspond to the predominantly empiricist tradition of applied social research. Weiss *et al.* rightly emphasize that what percolates through from the social sciences to society is above all theories, concepts and the like — the organizing principles of thought. This makes the enlightenment model an indictment of the usual course of events with contract research, since efforts to ensure that research produces results with the maximum utility for policy-making tend to result in the research being tailored carefully to the existing policy. This means that the terms in which the policy-maker defines his problem (which also incorporate his norms, values, prejudices and blind spots) are transferred to the terms of reference of the research, with the result that it may not be of any use outside the specific situation which interests the policy-maker on this occasion.

An even greater danger is that the research results may confuse rather than enlighten, owing to the absence of an interpretative framework. Albert points out that the idea of strengthening the direct relationship between research and the practical sphere in order to increase the relevance of the social sciences is based upon an underestimation of the importance of comprehensive theories which go beyond specific practical problems. 'It is precisely this kind of theory, which is primarily constructed for its capacity to explain phenomena and yield pure knowledge, that has again and again proved itself useful in solving specific practical problems, even though its applicability to such problems could not have been foreseen' (Albert, 1976, p. 72). Theories are the currency of scientific progress, and to ignore the central role of theory-building in scientific research is to open the door to ignorance and stagnation.

The enlightenment model also highlights a second objection, or at least a bias against the generally accepted view of knowledge utilization and, *mutatis mutandis*, against the normal way of studying this subject, *viz.* the implicit assumption that research influences society rather than *vice versa*. It is indeed astonishing that while there are so many studies of the impact of research on policy, there are so few of the impact of policy on research. Cohen and Weiss' study of research into racial problems in education is one of the few examples. But whereas the authors show in some detail how research into the race problem interacts with ideas about this problem current among the public at large, they do not go on to describe the consequences of this for the relationship between research and society, being 'puzzled by the difficulty of devising any evaluative criterion' (*op. cit.*, p. 80).

There are enormous difficulties in defining this relationship effectively, taking into account all the epistemological, sociological and axiological implications. It is a problem which can only be glanced at here. But it is absolutely essential to define the relationship, both for purely intellectual reasons and for the practical reason that part of the under-utilization of social research may be attributable to the inability of the social sciences to adopt a sufficiently autonomous position, i.e. to detach themselves sufficiently from the prevailing views about all manner of social questions. If research is 'part and parcel of social enthusiasms' (Cohen and Weiss, *op. cit.*, p. 75), it is difficult to suppose that the significance of the research will extend beyond these social enthusiasms.

The most striking aspect of the problem of the relationship between the social sciences and social and political reality is that the answers which already exist are constantly allowed to sink into oblivion. As early as 1904, Max Weber gave an analysis of this problem in the long essay which he wrote when he became editor of the famous journal *Archiv für Sozialwissenschaft und Sozial-politik*, and this analysis, which even now it would be hard to equal in depth and thoroughness, contains the principal points which have been taken up by others since. After Max Weber, a whole generation of philosophers and theoretical sociologists disseminated and developed his ideas (e.g. Talcot Parsons, C. Wright Mills and in our own times particularly Hans Albert, who has been quoted above), but it seems that many social scientists are unaware of them. Weber's main thesis is that it is impossible to make an entirely objective analysis of society, i.e. an analysis which avoids taking into account the prevalent norms and values. The very choice of particular social or policy-making problems as subjects for research is determined by *a priori* assumptions and attitudes. This goes largely unnoticed because the language in which these problems are described is itself imbued with certain norms and values. Such concepts as educational innovation, social inequality, motivation and curriculum development, which are the currency of educational research in the Netherlands are not neutral technical concepts but imply aims or even a complete ideological programme; they cannot be separated from the context in which they are used (*cf.* Rein, 1980, p. 361). An example may help to clarify this.

In the coalition agreement on the strength of which the present government came into power, it was laid down that decisions as to whether or not to comprehensivize secondary education will be based on a scientific evaluation of the current middle-school innovation experiments. In the plan for this evaluation, designed by a special advisory committee appointed by the Minister of Education, the emphasis was on the 'transferability' of the middle-school experiments. This is one of the standard terms used when talking about the middle school, and it cannot be properly understood unless one is familiar with the policy directors' ideas about the planning of large-scale social innovations. What these ideas amount to is that it is not considered right to 'impose' innovation from above; rather, the changes should be carried out by those in the field, and it is in this context that the term 'normative-re-educative model' is used. In order to achieve this, a number of motivated schools were selected to seek to transform themselves into middle schools with the aid of extra facilities. These are known as the 'middle-school experiments', but this term is misleading in that they may more accurately be called demonstration projects. The experiments are regarded as the first step towards the general introduction of comprehensive education, and their primary purpose is to demonstrate the viability of the middle school. This purpose also extends to the evaluation plan. In spite of all the rhetoric about rationality, the evaluation was not intended to produce an objective assessment of the results of the experiments but to collect experiences which would facilitate their transfer to other schools. SVO was highly critical of what it considered an immunizing tendency in the proposed evaluation of the middle-school policies and designed its own evaluation plan emphasizing an objective comparison between the yield of the middle-school experiment and traditional secondary education.

The problem of the intrusion of values into the social sciences cannot be solved by means of an illusory attempt to banish values entirely from the research process, although this has been the strategy preferred by the Anglo-American empirico-scientific tradition; the answer is rather to state as clearly as possible the normative basis of the research. The next step, and one which Weber saw as one of the most important tasks of the social sciences, is to analyse the values thus revealed, to trace their history, to think out and if necessary criticize their consequences, and particularly to ascertain their influence on the development of the social sciences. Only then can the social sciences really enlighten, as instruments of criticism and reflection in a complex and constantly changing society.

References

ALBERT, H. (1968). *Traktat über kritische Vernunft*. Tübingen.
ALBERT, H. (1972). 'Theorien in den Sozial-wissenschaften.' In: ALBERT, H. (ed.). *Theorie und Realität. Ausgewählte Aussätze zur Wissenschaftslehre der Sozial-wissenschaften*. Tübingen. (Dutch translation).
ALLISON, G.T. (1969). 'Conceptual models and the Cuban missile crisis,' *American Political Science Review*, 63, Sept., 3, pp. 689—718.
COHEN, D.K. and GARET, M.S. (1975). 'Reforming educational policy with applied social research,' *Harvard Educational Review*, 45, Feb., 1, pp. 17—43.
COHEN, D.K. and WEISS, J.A. (1977). 'Social science and social policy: schools and race.' In: WEISS, C.H. (ed.) *Using social research in public policy-making*. Lexington (Mass.): Lexington Books, pp. 67—90.
LINDBLOM, Ch.E. (1968) *The policy-making process*. Englewood Cliffs, N.J.: Prentice-Hall.
LINDBLOM, Ch.E. and COHEN, D.K. (1979). *Usable knowledge. Social science and social problem solving*. New Haven, Conn.: Yale University Press.
NETHERLANDS, MINISTERIE VAN ONDERWIJS EN WETENSCHAPPEN. (1976). Contouren van een toekomstig onderwijsbestel; discussienota. (Contours of a future education system in the Netherlands, summary of a discussion memorandum).
POPPER, K.R. (1972). *The Logic of Scientific Discovery*. London: Hutchinson.
REIN, M. (1980). 'Methodology for the study of the interplay between social science and social policy,' *International Social Science Journal*, 32, 2, pp. 161—8.
SCHEERENS, J. (1981), The functioning of policy-oriented research within some major innovatory programs in Dutch education. Invited Paper prepared for presentation at the SVO international workshop on Educational Research and Public Policy Making. The Hague.

WEBER, M. (1949). ' "Objectivity" in social science and social policy.' In: WEBER, M. *The methodology of the social sciences*. New York: Free Press, pp. 49–112.
WEISS, C.H. (1979). 'The many meanings of research utilization,' *Public Administration Review*, Sept.–Oct.
WEISS, C.H. (1980). 'Knowledge creep and decision accretion,' *Knowledge, Creation, Diffusion, Utilization*, 1, March 3, pp. 381–404.
WRIGHT MILLS, C. (1970). *The Sociological Imagination*. Harmondsworth: Penguin Books.

Social Research and Public Policy at the National Level

Nathan Caplan – The University of Michigan

The last several years have witnessed a marked increase in commitment to the use of research-based knowledge in matters of public policy at the national level. Research studies and reports on utilization during these years have shown a remarkable increase in numbers as well as in importance. The number of persons actively engaged in knowledge transfer activities, the number of conferences, the degree of interest by potential knowledge user and producer groups, and the fact that government funding agencies ask for dissemination and utilization plans as part of formal grant applications are all indicative of increased recognition of the significance of utilization. Utilization has at least reached a takeoff point and may now be properly considered as a movement.*

The attention now given to utilization is long overdue. But the fact remains that utilization as a discipline or as a set of activities in its own right is by no means securely established – either in terms of a mass of coherent knowledge, an organized body of persons working to coordinate and advance its cause, opportunities for training or career gain, or through a set of well-calculated governmental science policy decisions at the national level designed to increase and regulate the availability of funding for utilization research and practice programmes. Consequently, it remains a difficult and risky undertaking to offer advice on how to improve the level of utilization, particularly in matters of government policy. Nonetheless, some lessons have been learned.

As a result of recent empirically-based studies, it has become evident that even with the increased production of policy-relevant knowledge and improved technological procedures for transfer and dissemination,

---

*These developments in knowledge use have gained greatly from the interest shown by European nations. My experience in working with European countries has left me with the belief that they may be well ahead of the United States in such matters. Having engaged in research on utilization abroad, I am also convinced that some of the best and most systematic uses made of US-produced social science information in public policy decisions occur outside of this country.

the frequency of use and impact of knowledge has not increased substantively. Simply because information is timely, relevant, objective and given to the right people in usable form, its use has not been guaranteed. Thus, the 'intelligence' value of the information conveyed does not directly relate to its utilization. Obviously, utilization is not a simple process. Bureaucratic, ethical, attitudinal, and social considerations take precedence over the value of information in its own right, and that is probably the way it should be. After all, social problem-solving is a political process and it is neither desired nor expected that it should be otherwise. Nonetheless, within the political context social science research can be expected to be used more often and more wisely. My purpose here is to highlight some lessons learned about utilization from recent studies and to present my own re-thinking of some of the issues involved.

National Academy recommendations on research utilization in education policy

Recently the National Academy of Science (NAS, 1981) published a report on the role of programme evaluation research in the determination of education policy in the United States. The Academy was requested by Congress to assemble a panel of experts to prepare the report with a view to meeting information needs among upper-level officials in the US Department of Education. I served as a member of the panel. My experience in research and education policy derived from a study in which I found that of all major government agencies, the Office of Education was most likely to fund policy-related research, and at the same time, least likely to use it (Caplan, 1976). I do not mean to imply that this is good or bad. The uncritical use of results is certainly inadmissible especially in view of the quality of impact assessment studies during the early 1970s, but such findings are indicative of the problems associated with the sponsorship production and use of policy-related research. A section of the NAS report is addressed specifically to recommendations on utilization and is of immediate relevance to the purposes of this conference. As a member of the panel I can share with you that there was great difficulty in preparing these recommendations and, even then, it was not a section of the report characterized by a high level of consensus among panel members. Nonetheless, a set of recommendations were agreed upon and included in the report and I will share them with you here. Not only are they relevant to the conference, but they provide a springboard for the remarks to follow. The six recommendations pertaining to utilization are as follows:

Recommendation I. The Department of Education should test various mechanisms for providing linkage between evaluators and potential users.

Recommendation II. The Department of Education should institute a flexible planning system for evaluations of federal education programmes.

Recommendation III. The Department of Education should establish a quick-response capability to address critical but unanticipated evaluation questions.

Recommendation IV. The Department of Education should ensure that evaluations deal with topics that are relevant to the likely users.

Recommendation V. The Department of Education should ensure that dissemination of evaluation results achieves adequate coverage.

Recommendation VI. The Department of Education should observe the rights of any parties at interest and the public in general to information generated about public programmes.

Recommendation VII. The Department of Education should give attention to the identification of 'right to know' user audiences and develop strategies to meet their information needs.

Each recommendation was followed up by narrative on implementation. For example, with regard to the first recommendation the Committee recommended that the Department consider the establishment of a special unit within the Department, outside, or both, for the purpose of studying, developing and evaluating knowledge transfer. The purpose of such linkage units would include activities such as:

Providing translation of research reports in language appropriate to intended audiences.

Sponsoring or conducting research on information transfer, communication and obligation.

Development of techniques for the synthesis, storage and retrieval of evaluation studies on a continuing basis.

Developing and institutionalizing research data on a day-to-day basis.

A detailed discussion of this and other recommendations can be found in the report. What I would like to discuss here are thoughts on one recommendation, the first recommendation, and to examine its underlying premise, namely, the importance of linkage between knowledge producers and users and how it may best be achieved.

Audience issues

Before discussing linkage and knowledge transfer I would like to call attention to the fact that this first recommendation mentions 'potential' users and that considerable attention is given in the remaining recommendations to issues pertaining to a variety of potential user audiences.

From the very outset of our discussions of utilization recommendations, the issue of audiences: Who are the primary, secondary users, specialized constituencies and stakeholder groups, right-to-know groups, the media; what are the problems in identifying these audiences; how do you determine their information needs; which have proprietary rights and which have limited proprietary rights, and, how can relevant information be provided to each of them in situationally appropriate language? These audience issues were raised early and remained on the table as, if not *the* issue, certainly the most pervasive issue for all discussion that followed. The audience issue raises tough questions which are both political and technical in their implication and, at least in the United States, it seems to me that no constructive discourse on the utilization, the public policy use, of federally sponsored research can be carried out without this issue being faced openly and squarely. Yet, once raised, the difficulties of effective utilization of research findings becomes infinitely more complicated once the audience targets for knowledge use extend beyond those government policy-makers in their traditional command and report relationships who are specifically charged with formulating and implementing education policy.

Linkage and gap-filling solutions

The substantive significances of this first NAS recommendation rests with the idea of linkage. For the sake of expediency, let us think of linkage as involving the transfer of knowledge from researchers to only one audience group, namely, government officials in policy-influencing roles. The underlying assumption is that routine day-to-day methods of communicating among those who generate knowledge and those who have use of that knowledge constitute the main barriers to effective utilization. This position attempts to explain non-utilization in terms of the relationship of researchers and the systems in which they operate to policy-makers and policy-making systems. In many ways the argument is similar to that which C.P. Snow makes in *The Two Cultures* to explain the gap between the humanities and the hard sciences. Usually people who hold this position argue that social scientists, particularly researchers and policy-makers, live and operate in separate worlds with different and often conflicting values, different reward systems. Government policy-makers are action-oriented, practical persons concerned with obvious and immediate dilemmas. By contrast researchers don't like to be pressed for time and are more likely to concern themselves with esoteric issues.

A gap is hypothesized between knowledge producers and users and, based on the understanding of the gap, means are offered to effectively link the two. It is argued by some that the gap between the knowledge producer and the policy-maker needs to be bridged through personal relationships involving trust, confidence and empathy. Others, however, see this gap as something apart from cultural differences. They stress conflict over who determines the ends of policy, often seen as an important factor that keeps the social scientist and policy-makers apart. Some feel that the spectre of misuse of knowledge by political power tends to widen the gap, and still others, particularly those who argue the need for 'linking' mechanisms, see the gap as a consequence of the failure to introduce research-based knowledge in usable form into the policy-making process at the key points where it will most likely be used.

Emphasis on linkage techniques in utilization practices derived from research on communication and the spread of innovations (Katz and Lazarsfeld, 1955; Rogers, 1962; Rogers and Schumacher, 1971). Conceptualization and theoretical discussions of the position as it applies to education can be found in Havelock (1971).

There is no question in my view that 'gap-filling' theories of utilization are the most common ones found in education and it is no surprise that the National Academy Committee should embrace this interpretation of the problem and address it as its first recommendation.

Is there really a gap? What is its significance?

Basic to the linkage approach is the assumption of a communication gap between producers and users. At least in the US there is strong evidence that such a gap, or what Carol Weiss has labeled the 'great divide', does really exist. In a study I directed (Caplan et al., 1975) over two hundred upper-level federal executives in policy-influencing positions in the US were carefully questioned to determine if they were in contact with an influential network of scholars, or participants in an 'invisible college', with expertise in social science fields relevant to the respondents' area of policy responsibility. Responses to these items showed that no such liaison exists and that contact, formal or informal, between social scientists and upper-level decision-makers is rare. Later, Poppen (1978) obtained responses to the same set of questionnaire items for US social scientists involved in policy-relevant research and also concluded that a gap exists between knowledge producers and users. More recently, however, in a study I helped to conduct for the OECD (Caplan, 1979) government officials were on a first name basis with researchers in areas of their policy responsibility and were familiar with their work — our government respondents were able to provide phone numbers and arrange contact with outside experts. Yet, the level of knowledge application in Finland to matters of public policy was no greater than that found in the United States. So, while it may be tempting to conclude that the lack of direct contact with knowledge producers may have special significances for utilization, there is certainly no guarantee that the absence of such a 'gap' will necessarily promote utilization.

Furthermore, apart from the existence of the gap and its possible significance, there are good reasons to question the possible efficacy of this approach based on recent government experiences. While the logic of the linkage approach may have its appeal, there is no strong evidence to support its success. In fact results may be to the contrary. Efforts to improve utilization in education through the establishment of RD&D (research, development, and diffusion) labs were premised on the assumption that knowledge transfer through specialized institutional arrangements would be effective. Unfortunately, there have been no careful evaluations of these efforts and present opinion as to their success depends upon whom one talks to about which particular RDD group. It simply does not follow from tested evidence that an alliance of social scientists and policy-makers mediated through knowledge transfer agents is the panacea which will produce relevant research and allow translation of the results of scholarly analysis into practical policies. The notion that more and better contact may result in improved understanding and greater utilization may be plausible, but there are also conditions where familiarity might well breed contempt rather than admiration. In the policy arena the problem of achieving effective interaction of this sort necessarily involves issues along ideological as well as technical lines.

Further, it is unlikely that any single system for linking producers and users could be applied broadly. Effective linking arrangements depend upon the nature of the problem and context in which utilization is embedded. A better understanding of utilization — under-utilization, non-utilization, premature utilization and over-utilization — would seem necessary to successful knowledge transfer.

My own view is that the gap-filling function does make good sense, but it is often too simplistically formulated or too simplistically applied to be effective. What was learned from early research on communication in the spread of innovation by agricultural extension agents in their efforts to persuade farmers to use hybrid seed corn may well apply to knowledge transfer under those circumstances, but it does not apply as directly to the governmental policy setting as some would have us believe. There is a marked tendency for utilization people to talk about the transfer of all types of knowledge as if the same principles applied universally. That is, that the transfer, whether of technological or medical innovations, social inventions, craft skills or policy-relevant research, occurs in a similar fashion. There may be important similarities but there are also important differences and at least in so far as knowledge in the policy arena is involved, the differences are very important.

So, it is unlikely that any single system for linking producers and users could be applied broadly. Linking arrangements may depend upon the nature of the problem, the type of information involved and the position of the end user in the organizational hierarchy. Differences in the significance of the policy decision under consideration will be used here to illustrate the importance of giving attention to these additional considerations before attempting to link the producer and user communities. Moreover, such differences will also be used to make another distinction which is important in understanding utilization, namely, the difference between *instrumental* and *conceptual* uses of information.

Micro-level problems: instrumental utilization

In my study of upper-level executives, approximately 90 per cent of reported uses of social science research were associated with day-to-day policy issues of limited significance, usually involving either small segments of the population or the user's own organization (Caplan *et al.*, 1975). At least one-third and possibly as many as one-half of these applications involved administrative policy issues pertaining to bureaucratic management and efficiency rather than substantive public policy issues (Caplan, 1976). Most often the primary purpose of such knowledge application was to test the acceptability of already established programmes and policies, or to measure progress or retrogression with respect to the success of such efforts. Because of the narrow scope represented by these decisions, they can be thought of as 'micro-level' decisions. Three-quarters of the data used in micro-level decisions was produced in-house or commissioned under contract by the using agency. Finally, the data used were ordered by the decision-maker for a specific purpose. Thus, knowledge application at this level involves the use of data ordered by the end user, produced by the user's agency and most often applied with a view to improving management of the agency's internal operations.

This type of use represents the straightforward reaction of the agency's utilization system to some obvious realities. Most of the policy-related information needs in any governmental agency are of this sort, and it is valuable to know that such decisions are often premised on empirically-based knowledge. Moreover, such instrumental applications need not mean that the issues involved are necessarily trivial. The major problem is that preoccupation with knowledge application of this type leads to a technological conception of knowledge use which dominates thinking about utilization and how it may be improved. Caplan (1974), Weiss (1976), and Knorr (1975) have all recognized the prevalence of what may be called 'instrumental' utilization.

Most information transfer procedures based on gap-filling theories are best suited for policy decisions involving instrumental application. However, the major problem in utilization is not how to increase the amount of instrumental application. Either by producing its own data or by contracting for information, government appears to have available the information deemed requisite for dealing with micro-, intermediate- and administrative-level issues. Linkages between researchers and those in the middle-level bureaucratic positions of the agency have been established, and such linkages are apparently functioning adequately in knowledge applications involving micro-level decisions.

The greater problem arises from the fact that scientific knowledge use in public policy is not fully realized because of this emphasis on only the most practical aspects of its value. Further, emphasis on this instrumental type of application leads to a conception of utilization possibilities which is entirely different from that necessary to deal with macro-level issues. Information gathered and applied instrumentally results in an image of reality too narrow to provide a suitable foundation on which to premise decisions involving the more important policy issues.

Macro-level problems: conceptual utilization

Although the federal executives studied participants in deliberations involving the use of scientific information in micro- and intermediate-level policy issues, they also deal with macro-level decisions. Approximately ten per cent of the instances of knowledge applications reported by respondents involve important policy matters which affect the nation as a whole. At this level, only rarely is policy formulation guided by concrete, point-by-point reliance on empirically-grounded information alone. This is not to deny that many respondents cited the use of specific social science research studies in discussing important decisions, but such information was usually only one of many sources used. Rather than relying upon any single piece of information, the final policy decision was likely to depend upon an appraisal of scientific (hard) and extra-scientific (soft) knowledge from a variety of sources. Both types of knowledge are combined conceptually, resulting in a judgment or a perspective which is then applied broadly to decisions involving problems at the macro-level range.*

The importance of conceptual utilization is evident from responses to the following item from our questionnaire: 'On the basis of your experiences in the federal government, can you think of instances where

---

*The *generalizability* of the knowledge-based perspective is important to keep in mind. Not only does information used in this way have more 'power' in the sense that its application involves issues of national priority, but it also has an added dimension over instrumental-type applications in that it can be applied to a variety of issues beyond the routine boundaries of what is considered social policy. It is applied in policy matters that have social *consequences*, a fact which virtually involves it in all major public policy consideration.

It is also worth noting that knowledge used in micro-level decisions is amenable to empirical study and, in consequence, the kind of knowledge use about which we

a new program, a major program alternative, a new social or administrative policy, a legislative proposal or a technical innovation could be traced to the social sciences?' It should be noted that this item did not specify that the respondent limit his or her answer only to applications involving empirically-grounded research findings. The 82 per cent of the respondents who replied 'yes' to this question were asked to be specific and to provide examples. Among the approximately 350 examples given, the policy areas represented ranged widely. They were as likely to be of a technological or medical nature as they were to involve strictly social policy issues. To illustrate, the following decisions were offered as examples: To establish highway construction projects; to select particular diseases, such as sickle cell anemia and cancer, for major governmental research funding; and, major programmes to 'humanize' service delivery programmes. All of these and many more programmes involving governmental actions of considerable national importance were in some way credited by the respondents to information from the social sciences, yet rarely were they able to cite specific knowledge sources.

Such decisions involving conceptual use of knowledge appear to result from combining two basic approaches to problem-solving. First, policy-makers gather and process the best available information they can obtain to make an unbiased diagnosis of the policy issue. They use knowledge in this way to deal with what may be called the 'internal logic' of the problem. Next, they gather information regarding the political and social ramifications of the policy issue, to deal with what may be termed the 'external logic' of the problem. To reach a policy decision, they finally weigh and reconcile the conflicting dictates of the information. Thus, more so than in the case of instrumental utilization, the inquiry process involved in conceptual utilization depends upon the properties of the individual rather than upon those of the bureaucracy.

Whereas the policy-makers studied generally relied almost exclusively upon routine agency sources of information for reaching decisions regarding micro-level issues, they were eclectic in their use of information for decisions involving issues of greater consequence. In addition to government reports and staff supplied-information typically relied upon so heavily for micro-level decisions, the macro-level decisions were influenced by information acquired independently by policy-makers from

---

know most. It can be studied because the purpose for which it is gathered can usually be specified in advance and it is usually possible to trace the utilization process as a set of sequentially linear and predictable input-output processing steps. Further, because of the character of such application, it is possible to measure whether or not intended use occurred. Unfortunately, however, because instrumental application lends itself to empirical study, it receives attention at the expense of other uses of knowledge (e.g. conceptual utilization) whose effects are less predictable, but whose impact on policy may be considerably greater. Conceptual utilization as described here generally goes unrecognized or at best is referred to obliquely in the empirical research on utilization.

diverse sources external to government — sources such as newspapers, books, professional journals, magazines, television and radio. At least 50 per cent of the respondents studied mentioned each of these as important sources of 'social science' information. Rarely, however, were such sources cited when respondents were questioned on the use of 'empirically-grounded' information. Thus, when dealing with policy matters of lesser importance, the respondents appear to have relied almost exclusively on agency sources for information; when dealing with macro-level policy issues, they acted more independently in gathering, organizing and analysing knowledge perceived as relevant.

Regardless of the scientific merit of this knowledge-based perspective, which plays such an important role in conceptual utilization, the fact is that these respondents exhibited great sensitivity to informal sources of information bearing on social issues and contemporary social reality. Further, while this perspective may include the use of agency-supplied, empirically-based knowledge, the strong impression is that more general forms of social science knowledge (soft knowledge) are important far more often in upper-level policy decisions that specialized scientifically premised (hard) knowledge typically provided through routine channels of information.

So, the connection between knowledge producers and users has to be thought out carefully if efforts to improve utilization based on a linkage approach are to succeed. To couple existing knowledge and the production of new knowledge to user needs requires collaborative arrangements which must be congruent with the nature of the utilization problem and the existing system of inquiry used to acquire and process information. The problems encountered in macro-level and micro-level decision-making illustrate the relevance of the linkage theory perspective to the needs of upper-level government officials in dealing with public policy issues which affect the nation. While the potential for improving utilization at this level of social problem-solving is great, such arrangements will be unlikely to succeed if premised on the technological (i.e. instrumental) conception of knowledge use which now dominates utilization theory, research and action. The theory has led to 'linkage' efforts which may have increased the quantity but not the quality of utilization. Such arrangements may be appropriate for the use of application-oriented empirical findings to micro- and administrative-level problems, but they are likely to be inappropriate in dealing with meta-level problems. Collaboration at this level must be concentrated upon dealing with issues which involve more general problems, the formulation of the problem, assisting the policy-maker in knowing what he or she has to know, and, finally, an understanding of which aspects of the problem are to be decided on the basis of data-based knowledge and which ones are to be decided on the basis of non-research knowledge.

One difficulty with linkage theories is the stress on knowledge impacts as if they were isolated events producing one effect. In addition to different types of impacts discussed above, knowledge is used and re-used. Utilization rarely occurs as an isolated event. More often it is an iterative process — another important aspect of knowledge use which rarely receives attention.

Life-cycle knowledge impact

Research and thought in utilization has concentrated on an input-output model, in expectation of immediate and direct impacts, despite obvious evidence of the gross discrepancies between what goes in and what comes out. Utilization is a process, i.e. input-*throughput*-output, a process greatly influenced by the function of information to organizational interest until recently. 'Throughput' remained ignored in the utilization literature — possibly because of oversight, possibly due to unwillingness to abandon the belief that utilization in the policy-making arena is a rational, sequentially linear process. In short, a single or multi-factor variance model rather than a process model, dominated thought, research and practice.

Rather than viewing knowledge use as a one-shot, time-limited occurrence, it should be reconceptualized as an iterative process. Information flows through an organization: It may have multiple, not single effects; it may be used and reused; and most important, its substance or 'message' may actually be changed or 'converted' as it is used and reused. Thus, it can be said that knowledge has a 'life-cycle' within an organization: it both endures and changes. A life-cycle approach by definition encompasses more than 'input-output' stages. Once attention is given to the 'throughput' stage, organizational variables become preeminent over the customary variables such as timeliness, relevance etc. In short, the life-cycle perspective coupled with the context of the using organization forces us to examine knowledge use in non-traditional ways which hold potential for throwing light on a dimly understood organizational process touching on such varied concepts as 'organizational memory' (Schon, 1971) and 'latent and manifest functions' (Merton, 1968).

Utilization as a conversion process

There is evidence scattered throughout the knowledge utilization literature that organizations do indeed react to new knowledge, but they react in ways heretofore unrecognized by knowledge utilization researchers. A sizeable number of diverse investigators in diverse settings have independently noted and described under difficult names a similar throughput activity associated with utilization. What follows is a sampling of that literature and its possible importance.

Drawing on research in the area of mental health, Manning and Rappoport (1976) wrote an article entitled 'Rejection and Reincorporation: Case Study in Social Research Utilization'. They conclude that the reception of ideas depends on a process through which ideas are first rejected before they are ultimately accepted.

Larsen and Agarwala-Rogers (1977) wrote an article with the noteworthy title 'Re-invention of Innovative Ideas: Modified? Adopted? None of the Above?'. The authors concluded that a large 'proportion of ideas were not adopted as suggested, but were adapted, or re-invented'.

Rein (1979) describes an analysis by Robert C. Cole (n.d.) on inventive work structures in Japan, Sweden and the United States. Cole concludes that ideas are 'sanitized' before they are incorporated into practice, that is, they become administratively acceptable in the new setting.

Based on their experience with innovation adoption in public health and municipal government, Munson and Pelz (1979) stress that time is needed to allow for 'internal redesign' of innovations. Holzner and Fisher (1980) discuss knowledge 'transformations'. They relate such change to the 'relevant frames of reference' of the using agency.

In 1977 Robert Yin wrote a report on the implementation of innovative practices in municipal government titled *Changing Urban Bureaucracies: How New Practices Become Routinized*. 'Routinization' describes the settling in of innovation into the day-to-day operation of municipal government required before utilization becomes evident. Yin also argued for the importance of a process approach to the research on utilization and the adoption of innovations.

Rogers (1978) actually employed such an approach in the investigation of innovations in computerized information systems and in the area of urban transportation (Dial-A-Ride). He and his colleagues concluded that a 're-invention' phase was essential to the adoption of these innovations. Their definition of the term is worth noting:

> ... the degree to which innovation is changed by the adopter in the process of adoption and implementation after its original development. We stress that reinvention is a matter of degree; the ultimate in reinvention would be the independent generation of a new idea that someone else had already created. The range of reinvention that we studied is much less than such parallel invention (p. 3, Chapter 12).

Rogers states that the insight to focus on re-invention was gained from an article by Charters and Pellegrin (1972) who recognized a similar phenomenon in studying the adoption of an educational innovation in different schools. These authors conclude that 'the innovation was to be invented on the inside, not implemented from the outside'.

This statement coincides closely with the empirical findings on knowledge use in public policy formulation in which Caplan *et al.* (1975)

found that over 90 per cent of the social science knowledge reportedly used by upper-level government officials in the US was either produced or funded by the using agency. Later, Caplan and Barton (1978) examined the actual use of social indicator data by federal executives who had earlier expressed interest in having such data available. The source of these data was another government agency, the Office of Management and Budget (OMB). These respondents did not use such data as anticipated on the basis of their previously expressed interests. They did not apply the data to deal with substantive policy responsibilities. The data did have an influence, however, on science policy decisions: various agencies in which these officials worked subsequently collected and reported their own indicator data. Caplan and Barton (1978) speculate that power over the control of information is more important that its use, i.e. the 'bureaucratization' of information is more important to the using agency than the substantive 'message' value of the information conveyed.

The replication of the federal executive study in Finland (Caplan, 1979b) yielded further evidence of 'bureaucratization'. When interviewed in a formal setting respondents reported that Erik Alardt's Cross-Scandinavian Social Indicator Study had not produced a major effect on social science thought and policy decisions in Finland (Finland ranked lowest on both subjective and objective SI measures when compared with Sweden, Denmark and Norway). In informal discussion with these same officials, however, recognition of the importance of Alardt's findings was acknowledged. That is, within the workings of the government bureaucracy there was a keen awareness of the 'message' conveyed by these cross-national social indicator findings: the results were attended to and considerable thought had been given to the improvement of Finland's comparative quality-of-life standing. It is likely however, that the political importance of this research will not be officially acknowledged until the government agencies are confident that the nation's perceived quality of life has improved over its earlier showing.

To the outsider, it may appear that no use is being made of the knowledge during this period. The using agency, however, maintains a sustained awareness of its 'message' but will delay acting on it so long as use constitutes a greater organizational risk than nonuse. To summarize, the evidence on knowledge conversion presents serious practical and conceptual challenges requiring study of the inner workings of organizational and bureaucratic processes, rather than the mere comparison of input-output measures.

It is a basic contention here that utilization does occur more often than we are led to believe, but that it occurs in ways which are untapped by the all too common input-output research models employed in utilization research. Bureaucratic, ethical, attitudinal and social considerations frequently take precedence over the intrinsic value of the information. The determinants of utilization appear to be embedded in a complex organization process wherein knowledge must first be 'converted' before it can be used. If studied from the inside, it can be expected to be found that agencies are attentive to and use scientific findings informally and that such use takes place in ways which have gone unrecognized by utilization researchers. This brings us to a final point which touches on the reasons for the long lag between knowledge inputs and their public use, and the organizational significance for that lag.

Bureaucratic control and knowledge use

One of the major problems in designing effective utilization policies and programmes stems from naive expectations about what the user or using agency *ought* to do with research findings. Based on assumptions about rationality, we anticipate certain types of impacts, and where they do not occur, we are quick to presume that there has been no impact. We do so in spite of the fact that impacts may indeed occur, but in ways that may differ greatly from our expectations. Weiner *et al.* (1977), in a paper on the impact of programme evaluation in education, talks about three varieties of influence: appreciative, symbolic and allocative. The allocative impact closely matches what persons concerned with utilization think 'ought' to occur:

> Included in this category are discrete, authoritative actions concerning changes in program budgets; formation and enforcement of regulations; modifications of organizational structure; and decisions about expansion, continuation, or cancellation of specific program components.

Thus, allocative influence occurs in situations where evaluation information leads directly to programmatic changes or to decisions to make no changes. The 'allocative influence' category deals with direct impacts linked to assumptions about organizational priorities. Those priorities are assumed to be tied directly to the stated mission of the agency — when, in fact, the function of knowledge may serve a very different goal, namely, the preservation and enhancement of the organization. In short, from the organizational standpoint, the control of information may be far more important than its use. So, to an outsider following a model of rationality based on 'allocative influence', the nonuse of research may make no sense because most of us hold the view that new information is always wanted and that the reduction of ignorance by any amount is desirable. We cherish the opportunity to learn and find it difficult to understand why potential users do not leap at the opportunity to be informed. What we may fail to see is that the agency understands only too well the implications of the findings and that from the standpoint of bureaucratic rationality more is to be gained from the control of the information rather than suffer the consequences of its immediate organizational implications.

A government agency can be aware of the immediate mission-related utility of information, but still not use it because, instead of reducing uncertainty, the new knowledge may increase uncertainty. Organizations, agencies of government, possibly individuals are made uncomfortable when they learn something that affects their day-to-day, business-as-usual, routines. In order to make effective and quick use of relevant scientific information, the using agency must be resilient and 'error-embracing', that is, willing to face the turbulence, perturbations and political costs caused by the introduction of new knowledge. Thus nonuse is viewed as a form of risk avoidance when use could threaten organizational stability. If this view is correct, then the function of a time lag in information use is to allow the agency opportunity to deal with the organizational difficulties which ensue when an idea, innovation or a new finding is first detected.

So, returning to the Committee's first recommendation, even if organizational arrangements and practices can be achieved so as to produce successful knowledge transfer through linking arrangements, the pacing of that knowledge into actual use will have to take into account the adaptive innovations and capacity of the agency using the information.

Linkage efforts and their possible success

Knowledge transfer agents, or whatever we choose to call such persons, will have to care about the problem they are engaged to help solve. It means that they must involve themselves deeply enough in that problem to see it in the context in which it arises. They must be able to assess the appropriateness of all means available for its solution, research-based information being only one such means. Effective application of knowledge often means solutions that break away from approaches which implicitly maintain the problem by proceeding from socially acceptable — even sacred — assumptions about how people ought to behave. In the sphere of education, utilization is complex because of the legal, ethical, political and administrative difficulties involved.

How can effective utilization be accomplished? It probably will proceed best if it is pursued by a group of individuals representing different combinations of roles and skills, located in an institutional arrangement that allows them to take into account practical factors affecting both the production and use of knowledge. Thus, there is a point where utilization and social action are distinguishable. This closeness of utilization and action calls for a type of commitment to problem-solving that carries with it tremendous implications in terms of reward structure, professional identity and the like. It may mean turbulence, risk and serious dilemmas because if taken seriously the most important uses of knowledge challenge the legitimacy of established bureaucratic inactions.

I am personally convinced that the ways and means to extend the range of knowledge that government pays attention to lie outside the formalities of scientific communication and social science activities as traditionally defined by university and private sector organizations. Effective knowledge transfer, however, will not be achieved if based on simplistic linkage or transfer models premised on the *pot-pourri* of factors which abound in the literature. The probable outcome of such an approach will be an overload of irrelevant knowledge packaged in unusable form. A better idea would be to base utilization practices on an understanding of the role of information in bureaucracies and the bounded rationality which guides its use.

Bibliography

CAPLAN, N. (1978). 'The Use of Social Statistics by Federal Executives in Policy Decisions in Education.' In: *Setting Statistical Priorities*. National Research Council, pp. 75–88.

CAPLAN, N. (1978). 'Utilization and The Better Mousetrap Theory,' *APA Monitor*, Dec.

CAPLAN, N. (1979). Social Science Utilization in Finland. (To be included in OECD report.)

CAPLAN, N. and NELSON, S. (1973). 'On Being Useful: The Uses of Psychological Research on Social Problems,' *American Psychologist*, 28(3), pp. 199–211.

CAPLAN, N., MORRISON, A. and STAMBAUGH, R. (1975). *The Use of Social Science Knowledge in Policy Decisions at the National Level*. Ann Arbor: Institute for Social Research, The University of Michigan.

CAPLAN, N. and BARTON, E. (1978). 'The Potential of Social Indicators,' *Social Indicators Research*, 5, 4, pp. 427–56.

CHARTERS, W.W., Jr. and PELLEGRIN, R.J. (1972). 'Barriers to the Innovation Process: Four Case Studies of Differentiated Staffing,' *Education Administration Quarterly*, 9, 1, pp. 3–14.

COLE, R. (n.d.) The Diffusion of New Work Structures in Japan, Sweden and the United States. Mimeograph.

DOWNS, A. (1967). *Inside Bureaucracy*. New York: Little Co.

HAVELOCK, R. (1971). 'The Utilization of Educational Research and Development,' *British Journal of Technology*, 2, 2, pp. 84–96.

HOLZNER, B. and FISHER, E. (1979). 'Knowledge in Use: Considerations in the Sociology of Knowledge Application,' *Knowledge*, 1, 2, pp. 219–244.

KATZ, E. and LAZARSFELD, T.S. (1955). *Personal Influence: The Part Played by People in Mass Communications*. New York: Free Press.

KNORR, K.D. (1976). 'Policy-Makers' Use of Social Science Knowledge: Symbolic or Instrumental?' In: *Proceedings of the First International Conference*, Society for Social Studies of Science. Ithaca, N.Y.: Cornell University.

LARSEN, J. and AGARWALA-ROGERS, R. (1977). 'Re-invention of

Innovative Ideas: Modified? Adopted? None of the Above?' *Evaluation*, 4, pp. 136–40.

MACK, R.P. (1971). *Planning on Uncertainty*. New York: Wiley-Interscience.

MANNING, M.T. and RAPPOPORT, R. (1976). 'Rejection and Reincorporation: Case Study in Social Research Utilization', *Social Science and Medicine*, 10, pp. 459–68.

MUNSON, F.C. and PELZ, D.C. (1980). Innovating in organizations: a conceptual framework. Ann Arbor: Institute for Social Research, The University of Michigan. Unpublished manuscript.

NATIONAL ACADEMY OF SCIENCE (1981). *Program Evaluation In Education*. Committee on Program Evaluation in Education. Washington DC.

POPPEN, P. (1968). 'Social Scientists' Attempts to Influence Public Policy', *SPSSI Newsletter*, 148, pp. 10–12.

REIN, M. (1979). 'Methodology for the Study of the "Interplay" between Social Science and Social Policy.' A paper prepared for UNESCO Conference on the Utilization of Social Sciences, Surinam.

REIN, M. and WHITE, S.H. (1977). 'Can Policy Research Help Policy?', *The Public Interest*, 49, pp. 119–36. Fall.

ROGERS, E. (1978). 'Re-Invention During the Innovations Process.' Chapter 12 in RADNOR, M., FELLER, I. and ROGERS, E. (eds.) *The Diffusion of Innovations: An Assessment*. Evanston, Ill: Center for the Interdisciplinary Study of Science and Technology, Northwestern University.

ROGERS, E. and SCHUMACHER, F. (1962). *Communications and Innovations: A Cross-Cultural Approach*. New York: Free Press.

WEINER, S.S., RUBIN, D. and SACHSE, T. (1977). Pathology in institutional structures for evaluation and a possible cure: Stanford Education Consortium, School of Education, Stanford University. Unpublished paper.

WEISS, C.H. (1977). 'Research for Policy's Sake: The Enlightenment Function of Social Research', *Policy Analysis*, 3, 4, pp. 531–45.

WEISS, C.H. and BUCUVALAS, M.J. (1977). 'The Challenge of Social Research to Decision Making'. In: WEISS, C.H. (ed.) *Using Social Research in Public Policy Making*, pp. 213–34.

WEISS, C.H. and BUCUVALAS, M. (1978). *Truth Tests and Utility Tests*. New York: Columbia University Center for Social Sciences.

YIN, R. (1980). *Studying the Implementation of Public Programs*. Golden, Colorado: Solar Energy Research Institute.

CRITICISM AND DISCUSSION

Note by the editors: as Caplan's paper had not been reviewed before the Workshop, only the discussion following its presentation is summarized here.

1. General

Caplan's exposition of knowledge transfer through the use of linkage or gap-filling measures concerned in particular the effectiveness of such arrangements. His analysis and findings generated much discussion and comparison of linkage arrangements in several of the participating countries. These are summarized in section 2 below. Caplan's treatment of two kinds of knowledge utilization — instrumental and conceptual — was seen as an extremely fruitful conceptualization. The distinction was considered an effective tool for questioning existing and future linkage efforts, while at the same time shedding considerable light on the inner workings of bureaucratic organizations.

2. Comparative findings

There are apparently *trends* in the use of research. As *Weiler* pointed out: 'There are trends in the extent to which decision-making communities are willing to embrace research, and this creates a context for receptivity. The atmosphere in which research is regarded is very often an important determinant of the extent to which there is willingness for the decision-making community to use it.' Weiler described the changing trend in the US as 'a period of enormous excitement about the possibilities of research followed by tremendous disillusionment, when research did not produce the hoped for results'. Weiler felt that at the moment 'we are moving into a period of some balance, where people are beginning to talk rationally to one another again about what research can really produce'. The same cycle appeared to exist in many European countries, although not all countries are in the same phase of the cycle.

Mitter pointed to another strong trend: the growing influence of government on educational research in many European countries. Participants of the Workshop unanimously agreed with Mitter that this growing influence made it difficult for research to 'defend its scientific character'. Opinions differed widely, however, on whether a strict separation of the two domains is required and fruitful for policy-oriented research. The following section (3) elaborates on this.

Husén suggested that prospects for the utilization of research results were generally brighter in small countries than in large federal countries such as the US and Germany, since communication between researchers and policy-makers is relatively easy in small countries. *De Groot* disagreed with this. He stressed that the issue was not a communication gap in itself but *how* this gap was to be bridged. Caplan's findings about utilization frequencies in Finland where no such gap existed (*cf*. Caplan's paper) support De Groot's view. However, neither Husén nor De Groot specified the time span they had in mind when making their points.

The utilization of research by policy-makers appears more complicated in countries where decision-making is largely decentralized. *Vorbeck* mentioned Switzerland as an example of a highly decentralized power structure, with local authorities deciding their own educational policies. Vorbeck said that Federal authorities were in general more open to the research world, but that their influence on education matters was small whereas the local authorities who actually shaped education policies had hardly heard about research. *Mitter* pointed out that decentralization at local level was often paralleled by attempts at centralization by federal authorities, particularly as far as documentation and information facilities were concerned. Central agencies acquired considerable power in this way. This made it difficult to decide at whom research should be directed. 'Who is the policy-maker?', Mitter wondered, adding that one might say that in many cases the Minister (at federal or state level) is . . . 'only the formal head of policy making bodies which are influenced increasingly by teachers' unions, parents' associations, service agencies and others'. His observations were in line with Weiss' description of the diffuse ways in which policy is formed. *Vorbeck* observed that in small countries, in particular, the *teacher* associations are important policy-makers. However, teachers did not appear to be very receptive to research. *Timpane* enlarged upon this aspect: 'The training of educators pays precious little heed to the notion that a spirit of inquiry ought to pervade their professional lives. Dan Lortie analyzes in persuasive detail how little the teacher is prepared, intellectually and psychologically, for a life of inquiry with respect to his or her professional performance.' Timpane regarded this as the 'greatest weakness on the demand side . . . of our information economy. Moreover, whatever professional incentive to inquiry there might have been is often driven out by the contextual realities of teaching..' Timpane warned that 'correcting the technical imperfections of our information economy will not handle this problem', a point repeatedly stressed by Caplan.

Kjell Eide felt that, where the US was concerned, it was 'probably a good thing that research is often neglected by politicians. Research is then part of the nature of things.' He pointed out that problems of utilization and under-utilization were tackled in quite a different fashion in the US than they were in Europe, where there had been '15 or 20 years of intensive discussions, at a philosophical and political level' on subjects ranging from 'rationality' and 'knowledge growth' to 'theory and practice'. In his view the US had largely escaped that phase. Eide concluded: 'I think that has created real problems in communication. It now seems that we need a kind of Columbus in reverse to discover Europe and its scientific developments over the past 20 years.' Later on Weiss volunteered to be one of these Columbuses and stressed the importance of a greater exchange of ideas. SVO's initiative in launching an international Special Interest Group (SIG) for this purpose was welcomed as an excellent communication channel.

Note by the editors: More information about European developments in 'knowledge use' are to be found in De Mey's paper and the summary of the Special Session devoted to prospects for the 1980s.

3. Linking two systems: interface problems

Caplan's paper was based on the premise that there are two separate systems involved: research and policy-making. *De Groot* questioned whether this assumption applied to all countries. Like Kallen, he did not believe this to be the case in, for example, the Netherlands, where 'there is such an osmosis between research on the one hand, and policy preparation on the other, that any clear distinction is impossible'. If, indeed, there were two separate systems, linkage made sense. But, as *Ingrid Eide* pointed out, linkage might cause other gaps to widen. She argued that effective linkage might be considered unwelcome by the 'people in the educational system itself: teachers, students and their parents'. A linkage between research and politics would be seen as 'solidifying an alliance that many people already perceived as being too strong'. *Caplan* agreed with her. Referring to the opening remarks in his paper about the 'audiences' of research, he stressed that 'historically at least, everyone has gained from research with the exception of those who have been subjected to analysis'. He agreed with the need to disseminate information to all relevant groups, particularly those immediately affected. But how such optimal dissemination could be achieved was not known. Caplan felt, however, that this was a 'very promising area for utilization'. That this was a view shared by many participants was clear from the many remarks made during discussions on the location of power in policy-making (see section 2 above). *Mitter* even felt that research reaching these groups — he spoke of 'groups at the microlevel' — would become an increasingly important issue in the near future. *Vorbeck* pointed out that the same view had been expressed by several European researchers in the context of the evaluation of innovatory projects at a Council of Europe Workshop in Montreux.

Several participants mentioned a number of the *negative side effects* of existing linkage arrangements. *De Groot* considered 'middle men' a poor solution for bridging the gap between the two sides involved. In the Netherlands this solution had resulted in a situation of 'many middle men who are neither the one nor the other, who confuse the issues and are also confused about their own roles'. *Lövgren* agreed. In his view, the professional identity of researchers was jeopardized, in particular, by arrangements whereby researchers were very closely linked to the policy making bodies (as was the case in Swedish sectoral research; *cf.* Marklund's paper and presentation): 'Middle men very rapidly become socialized into the values of the department and this causes some very difficult problems in their relationships with their colleagues'. Conversely, *Ringeling* remarked that socialization worked the other way round as well. In this he followed Weiss' notion of the enlightening function of research. *Caplan* stressed that direct contact between the two sides did not seem to work very well, or at least it did not at the moment: in fact, it often bred contempt. His recommendation was to create separate institutions to promote knowledge transfer, as was being done in the Federal Republic of Germany (*Note by the editors*: Caplan was referring to the so-called *Fachinformationsstellen*, which collect, document and disseminate information in a particular field).

4. Resistance to utilization

Caplan observed that we all seem to have a certain 'unwillingness to be put to scrutiny'. This resistance, particularly among teachers, was described by *Timpane* as resulting from a 'lack of preparation for a life of inquiry with respect to their professional performance'. Caplan considered this a general phenomenon, and hypothesized that at the root of this resistance was a need 'to be certain', which was considered more important than 'to be right', especially where a person's career was concerned. His illustration made this clear. In the field of medicine, gastric freezing as a cure for ulcers persisted for something like six years, despite continuous evidence that there was no difference between experimental and control groups. 'By writing about it as if it were true, you build a social system around it and thus "certainty" is achieved and maintained.' The same unwillingness to use new information overtly was described by Caplan in his paper when dealing with the 'organizational control' of information.

Weiler considered the resistance of policy-makers to the utilization of research to be a healthy trend:

> The history of insight that has been provided by educational research is not so encouraging as to inspire confidence that research is always the best way of solving problems. In fact, some concepts and ideas in education arose in the first place from a misunderstanding of the way progress was to be made. I am thinking in particular of the research and

development model for transferring knowledge and information, which was itself based on a misunderstanding of how research and development really worked. When that model was applied to education, the misunderstanding was compounded. So, it is very often the case that the policy-making community is in the position of saving researchers from their own folly.

Weiler observed, moreover, that the research community had its own knowledge-utilization problems, one of which was the reverse of the one mentioned above: 'The research community is not always open to knowledge about how policy is made and how research can be useful'. *Mitter* pointed out another factor which stood in the way of knowledge utilization within the scientific community: the discipline-boundedness of research knowledge. The researcher is confronted with outcomes of different disciplines with different languages, different methods, thinking structures and philosophies. Understanding was further complicated by the fact that different disciplines attached different meanings to the same word. 'It is the terminology, apart from the other issues, which lays the foundation for a great number of misunderstandings', Mitter concluded.

Vorbeck raised the issue of the status of research findings, pointing out that groups who 'were not happy with the research that was presented to them created their own research . . . contesting the official research'. In such a case the main value of the 'official' research apparently was in causing others to challenge its relevance and validity. This brings us back to the issue of the different rationalities held by the research and the policy community; an issue which had been touched upon by De Groot and Husén earlier and which was implicit in Caplan's treatment of 'bureaucratization of information' in his paper.

Vorbeck believed that research institutes were quite often a powerful lobby, and that the researchers themselves created confusion at the policy level, so that people could no longer distinguish decisive research results from the lobby's view on what should be done. *Ringeling* strongly supported the rights of researchers to act as a pressure group, in the same way as any other group in a democratic society. *In 'T Veld-Langeveld* seconded this and expressed her view that to act as a pressure group 'does not mean that the researchers are interested parties who deliberately provide us with ideologically distorted results. . . . One can be very scientific and objective, while acting as a pressure group at the same time.' *Note by the editors*: In section 5 of the discussion following Weiss' presentation, In 't Veld-Langeveld states in some detail her ideas on how ideological distortion can be prevented.

5. Defining 'utilization'

Caplan pointed out that sometimes 'utilization' may not be apparent but has occurred nevertheless. 'The function of information can be understood in terms of the substantive information value as well as in terms of its bureaucratic significance.' His paper speaks about information producing a series of effects, not just a single effect. 'Information follows a life cycle, it is used and re-used, in ways that are often unpredictable. . . . New information may well produce a higher degree of uncertainty within an organization. . . . Up to the moment when the organization gains control and ownership of that knowledge, utilization does not become obvious.' Caplan thinks that knowledge transfer procedures will not be successful until they take this aspect into account. Hasty conclusions about non-use often fail to take into account the information life cycle described. Caplan's paper discussed this aspect in some detail in dealing with the *process* concept that should guide utilization research. The term 'utilization' is too ill-defined to serve for ascertaining the extent to which knowledge is actually used. Caplan pointedly illustrated this by reminding the Workshop of the case when, several years ago, the Director of the National Institute of Education (NIE) was asked to name ten things that the NIE had done and which had proven to be useful and worthwhile. 'We remember the painful spectacle of that Director being unable to respond', Caplan recollected, commenting that the question, as posed, was too broadly phrased and thus rather unfair: 'The concrete examples of what I would consider instrumental utilization were requested, and that was really almost the meanest possible question in the context of government policy at a national level'. *Timpane*, who was at NIE eight years later, agreed and pointed out that the question still cannot be answered unless the kind of utilization envisaged is specified.

Note by the editors: Arguably, Caplan's conceptual utilization of knowledge will come most to the fore in the diffuse **decision-making** processes described by Weiss (*cf.* her paper and section 4 of the **related** criticism and discussion). More about this topic is to be found in Wagenaar's introductory article.

The Contribution of National Surveys of Achievement to Policy Formation

W.B. Dockrell — Scottish Council for Research in Education

The issue for this Workshop is how educational research can contribute to the formation of policy. There are those who argue that the primary contribution of research is to the shaping of the climate of opinion. Certainly much research makes its impact by its contribution to the concensus, to the general feeling that exists within the informed community. There are however, questions to be asked about this argument. The first question is whether research findings do in fact contribute to the climate. Are they simply used if they happen to fit the existing climate and ignored or forgotten if they do not? A second question is whether research which appears to make an impact does so or whether it is the climate of opinion which determines the interpretation that the researchers place on their findings. Research findings do not exist in abstract. They are the constructs of researchers. The researcher sees through a filter, through a set of expectations. Research which is cited as having contributed to the climate of opinion consists often of conclusions in harmony with the existing presuppositions of the author and a climate of opinion which may not be general but is that of an intellectual elite.

This particular approach has become popular with the growing disenchantment that we see on both sides of the Atlantic with the contribution that research and evaluation can make to specify policy decisions. It may be a strategic withdrawal to previously prepared positions. A safe retreat for the academic. It is not however a satisfactory answer for the politician or administrator who is asked to provide millions of pounds or dollars or guilders. He may legitimately feel that he wants more for the public's money than that.

The contribution of this paper to the discussion is a presentation of a case study. The example of research selected is a national survey of achievement. There are several reasons for choosing this particular example as a case study. The first one is that so much time, effort and resources are being devoted internationally to surveys. National or regional surveys are being carried out or planned in many countries. The best known are the American NAEP studies and the state-wide assessment programmes in a number of American states. In Europe a number of such studies have been launched in England and others are being planned or discussed elsewhere. The last round of IEA surveys involved 26 nations (Walker, 1974). The next round of surveys which is currently being planned will involve many more though the exact number is not yet certain. The survey therefore is an example of one kind of prominent research activity.

The second reason for choosing it was that the particular surveys discussed were examples of good educational research. That is, they were carefully planned and meticulously carried out. The third reason is that the studies did produce valid findings. Much research of all kinds including educational research leaves us very little wiser than we were before we began. That is not something to be surprised at, or something to be concerned about. It is to recognize the limitations of the human endeavour. In this particular case however, valid findings were produced.

Another reason for choosing these studies is that their findings had relevance at various levels. Relevance to administrators, to teachers and to parents. A fifth reason for selecting these studies is that their findings are relevant to general issues and not simply to particular local and temporal questions. If it is argued that good research will inevitably contribute to general thinking then these studies can serve as an empirical test for that hypothesis. Finally, these surveys are important because they show the advantages and the limitations of survey work, what can be learned from surveys and what cannot.

The Scottish system

The Scottish educational system is like the English system in some respects, in that it divides responsibility between the central agency, the Scottish Education Department, and the local education authorities. The system is described in the booklet, *The Educational System of Scotland* which states that the education authorities, 'are required to ensure that there is adequate and efficient provision of school education for children in their areas.... They are responsible for the curriculum taught in their schools, head teachers normally exercising that responsibility on their behalf' (p. 21).

The Central Government on the other hand, 'generally oversees the planning of school provision by education authorities and matters such as staffing, curricula, teaching methods, equipment, attendance and support of pupils . . . (it also) prescribes the requirements for entry to teacher training on the advice of the general teaching Council for Scotland' (p. 21).

There is therefore a division of responsibility between a central authority which has a supervisory and a guiding role and local authorities which are responsible for the context of the curriculum and the methods of teaching. There is no centrally prescribed curriculum, no list of approved textbooks. Such a system permits a great deal of diversity and indeed there is a substantial variability among Scottish primary schools. In these circumstances it is more difficult to monitor standards of achievement than in more centralized systems where expectations are more precisely defined.

Nontheless it was believed that there was sufficient consensus for generally applicable tests to be devised and administered.

The 1953 Scottish Survey

There had been previous nationwide surveys involving the application of intelligence tests in 1932 and in 1947, and it was accepted that valuable information had been obtained about variations in intelligence. As the first report on the surveys, *The Scottish Scholastic Survey 1953*, states 'It was thought that equally useful knowledge about the spread of the scholastic attainment of pupils could be found from the results of a similar national survey involving educational tests' (p. 17). Among the useful knowledge that it was expected that the survey would gather was information about 'the amount of acceleration and retardation in the schools system (that is, grade skipping and grade repetition). The relative educational standards for urban and rural schools and of different sizes of schools and of schools organised on individual as compared with class methods' (p. 17). If there were more specific objectives than these for the survey they are not stated in the report.

Tests of arithmetic (mechanical and reasoning) and English (usage and comprehension) were administered to 76,121 ten-year-olds (all those born between the 1st of July 1942 and the 30th June 1943) except those 'thought by their teachers to be unable to tackle with any hope of success tests primarily designed for normal pupils in their age group' (p. 21). The report explains why the particular age group was chosen, records the tests and reports in detail the sample.

It was not thought necessary to justify the content of the test except in the most formal sense. The curriculum as it existed was taken as a given. 'The tests set were restricted to what was assumed to be common to the schemes of work of all the areas' (p. 83). There was none of the careful sifting of aims and content that now takes place. Attention was however given to an issue that still is contentious. In order to overcome 'the fear that comparisons between the results of schools or of separate authority areas would be made as the result of the investigation. An assurance . . . (was) given that the survey results will be published in a form in which no such comparison would be possible' (p. 18).

The results were given in full and informative detail and a substantial number of conclusions were drawn. 'In the first place it has been shown that a scholastic survey on a national scale is possible' (p. 185). That in itself is important since nearly 30 years later there are still a number of countries where no national survey has been attempted and where there is considerable doubt about the feasibility of such surveys. 'The survey has also shown the difficulties of which the principal one is the diversity of work normally professed by an age group. At the ten year old level chosen for the survey this was particularly evident in the subject of Arithmetic where the complicated British tables of money, length and weight were introduced in different ways at different times in different areas' (p. 185).

The report goes on to say wisely that 'it will be folly to attempt to standardise curricula in this field until it has been shown that one method is superior to others' (p. 185). This quotation highlights two issues for those considering national surveys today. The first is the great variation in test score which reflects not long-term differences in level of attainment but short-term consequences of different teaching methods. The second is the danger of a backwash in the schools. If there are standard assessments which are administered nationally it may be assumed that these define a national curriculum. Even in a decentralised system schools will be under pressure to adopt this putative national curriculum. This is a fundamental issue which is discussed in more detail later.

A number of general conclusions were drawn. The usual sex differences were noted: 'boys and girls attained approximately the same standards in mechanical Arithmetic while the boys were superior to the girls in Arithmetical reasoning. In both tests of English the girls were superior to the boys. . .' (p. 151).

'The association between tests score and type of area (city, large town, small town, rural) was slight and for practical purposes the average performance by pupils in each of the four types of area was the same' (p. 155). A similar conclusion was drawn about differences in the ten regions, 'While there are variations in the attainment in the four tests the total attainment does not vary greatly from region to region' (p. 158). Nonetheless an inspection of the data indicates that scores from pupils in the Edinburgh and Dundee areas were generally high and the scores of those from the Glasgow area were generally low.

A careful analysis was made of the performance of left-handed children and the conclusion that was drawn was that the superiority of the right-handed group was probably a real one but was so slight as to be insignificant from the educational point of view.

The report turned next to the question of class size. It was careful to draw attention to the various factors that might be involved and rightly concluded that 'it will be apparent that there is no regularity about the results . . . It does not follow that size of class has no effect on attainment. The conclusion to be drawn is rather that it will be difficult to obtain definite conclusions on this topic with an experiment which is not specifically designed for the purpose' (p. 162).

On the impact of school size an issue which is still relevant in the United Kingdom and doubtless elsewhere the conclusion was 'the performance of the pupils in these schools (smaller) was on the whole as good as that of pupils in larger schools. In particular pupils from one teacher schools reached the same standard as those attained by pupils in schools with more than six teachers' (p. 168).

The difficulties which the authors had pointed to in drawing conclusions about curriculum (referred to above) did not deter them.

The panel dealing with Arithmetic arrived at very specific conclusions.

> Division by factors is undesirable in the primary schools . . .
> More attention should be paid to the lay-out of short division sums . . .
> There is need for standardising the notation used in recording the time of day by the clock. The panel recommends that for written expression it should be in the form 8.50 a.m. Use of written working in Arithmetic facilitates accuracy. Further use of working is helpful to a teacher in diagnosing a pupil's difficulties . . .
> A standard practice is required for recording remainders in division . . .
> The final point . . . question of the use of English. It was evident that the various aspects of teaching Arithmetical problems required further consideration e.g. the need for accurate reading of the question and for noting units used (p. 186).

The panel dealing with the English tests arrived at equally definite conclusions.

> The tests in English usage demonstrated the need for persistent oral practice in accepted speech forms and a restrained use of pencil and paper exercises for occasional testing . . .
> Reading as a thought-getting process seemed insecure. It is possible that acquaintance with forms of verbal testing and the common use of reading textbooks with exercises make it all too easy to suppose that pupils working through a series of questions have understood what they are reading. The tests in this survey showed unmistakeably that many pupils dealing as well as they could with details have not first grasped the general meaning of what they had read (p. 187).

A survey which had begun with primarily structural objectives had been used to draw mainly curricular conclusions.

The 1963 Scottish Survey

The second survey was reported in *Rising Standards in Scottish primary schools*. The objectives were apparently no more detailed than those of the earlier one. The report simply states that it was decided to conduct a second survey because 'it was hoped that besides indicating any changes in attainment that might have taken place in the ten intervening years a new survey might give some indication of the possible effects of new teaching methods' (p. 17).

The same tests were used as had been used on the previous occasion. Apparently the earlier tests were thought to be entirely satisfactory since they were not revised at all. The test booklets were surplus stock from the 1953 survey. On this occasion however, a stratified random sample of 5,209 pupils was tested, not the whole age group.

The answer to the question which was the basis of the second survey had been given in the title of the report, *Rising Standards in Scottish Primary Schools*. 'Between the 1953 and 1963 surveys the changes in score in each of the four tests have been in an upward direction. The sizes of the gains are about 1/3rd of the standard deviation of the distribution of scores or roughly the gains that will be made in six months by an average ten year old pupil' (p. 85). The study however, looks not only at general differences. The changes are related also to levels of ability, sex, types of area, region, sizes of schools, aspects of the tests and so on. 'The gains have been made by pupils at all levels of ability, by boys and girls to the same extent, in all regions of the country and in all sizes of schools . . . while performances on some items show greater improvement than on others the gains have been spread over nearly all of the items of the test. They are attributable partly to greater speed in response and partly to greater accuracy when the responses have been made' (p. 85). The researchers dismiss test sophistication as a possible cause of these changes.

They then go on to look at specific instructional and administrative arrangements. The retention of attainment tests (previously used universally for selection for secondary education), the use of the Cuisenaire method, provision of libraries in schools, the effects of shortage of teachers, and left-handedness. Their conclusions on these issues vary. 'Areas still using attainment tests at the transfer stage show gains about twice as large as those in other areas' (p. 85). 'Little or no association was found between attainment in the Arithmetic test and the use of Cuisenaire methods' (p. 85). 'Higher attainments in the English test go with greater provision of school libraries' (p. 85). They go on to point out cautiously 'a cause and effect relationship cannot be assumed; both of these results could be due to a common third factor' (p. 85). One wonders equally whether a common factor could not have been responsible for the relationship between use of attainment tests and achievement. On the question of the shortage of teachers they conclude 'no association has been found between attainments and the shortage of teachers' (p. 85), but again caution rules the day and the report points out 'the sample data provide only scanty information on this point' (p. 85).

The committee were hesitant however, to make the same kinds of comments on teaching as had been made ten years earlier. For the most part they simply drew attention to the items where there had been changes and those where there had not. A few points however, were made. 'Computational errors still persist. Fractions are still being treated by some pupils by rote and long division is still insecure. The concept of zero as a place-holder is unfamiliar to many pupils' (p. 128).

In English some of the deficiencies noted ten years earlier were less conspicuous. 'Pupils were reading with more skill and becoming more independent in their thinking about what they read' (p. 128). They could not however, resist drawing special attention to a specific point. 'A disappointing feature for Scots was that the Scots poem showed the least gain of any section. Printed Scots is becoming completely unfamiliar to Scottish children' (p. 128). (It remains completely unintelligible to English adults.) In the detailed comments on the responses to the Scottish poem it was noted that Scots words were becoming even less familiar than they had been ten years earlier. 'Kye might as well have been a foreign word. The popular error was key followed by sky. Other suggestions (most of them not unreasonable) were pigs, horses, sheep, crops, corn, wheat, hay, children, keys' (p. 100). The authors go on to comment perhaps despairingly that 'All right may have been an interpretation of O'Kay' (p. 100). 'To the majority the Scots forms were not intelligible, and from the errors in other words not dialectical it was obvious that a large number did not begin to understand what the lines were about. Neither did they have the benefit of hearing them read or spoken. The 1953 comment is reiterated. "When one considers the extent to which Scots of some kind is spoken and understood one can only conclude that Scots in print is completely unfamiliar to ¾ of the pupils of this age group . . . it would appear desirable to include some printed Scots among the reading material for Scottish children"' (p. 100).

The surveys were carefully designed, meticulously conducted, reported comprehensively and many conclusions relevant to policy were given. What impact did they have?

General issues

Before turning to that question which is the major one for this paper it is worth noting some issues which were given less attention then than they would be given now.

In more recent studies, the National Assessment of Educational Progress in the United States for example, more thought has been given to the content of the tests than in Scotland or at least more of the effort put into deciding the content of the test has been recorded. Objectives are defined which have to be acceptable to the subjects specialists, teachers and thoughtful adults. The items are chosen not to spread those taking the examination for selection purposes but rather are intended to indicate what proportion of the age group has mastered a particular aspect of the subject.

As with all criterion-referencing there is a problem of validity and in this case content validity is determined by a lengthy process of review involving the three groups of specialists referred to above. The National Assessment results indicate the proportion of the age group reaching the pre-defined criteria. These results are reported in lengthy bulletins which are prepared by the NAEP which attempt to interpret the meaning of test results and not simply to report them.

The scope of the Scottish tests was limited to what could be accomplished in 2½ hours. There was not matrix testing such as Carlson (1980) describes in California where the complete battery consists of 1,020 items. 'The long test battery means that it is possible to assess a much wider array of skills and concepts than would otherwise be possible' (p. 14). In the Scottish survey, as noted above, tests were restricted to what was assumed to be in common and could not cover the many alternatives of content and method that can be covered in California.

Nor were there any attitudinal measures. The Scottish survey could only show what pupils in different sizes of schools achieved not what attitudes were developed. Did school libraries result in more extensive reading and greater pleasure in reading as well as in higher attainment? The Scottish pioneers did not set out to gather such data.

Even more fundamental questions were left unanswered. The first task in a survey is to define the aspects of school work which are to be assessed. At the primary level should assessments be related to the traditional division of arithmetic and English as in the Scottish survey or should they be interdisciplinary and focussed on the child's ability to solve problems drawing on all the experiences that the school provides? Do we want to know whether a pupil has acquired the basic skills allowing him to tackle particular problems or do we want to know whether he has also learned to apply the skills in a realistic situation?

There may be a sharp distinction between the words a child can decipher, those which he can interpret and those which he can use. In arithmetic there may be a gap between a pupil's ability to recite number facts and to use his understanding of those numerical relationships.

The Scottish pioneers did not ask as we would today why do we teach children arithmetic or reading? What effects do we expect them to have on pupils when they have become adults? Are we moving to a society where the standards required of a minority will be far in excess of what we conventionally defined as literacy or numeracy and relate to an ability to absorb complex ideas presented in a variety of media and ability to think mathematically about a range of problems. And, where the standards required of the majority will be limited to the ability to find Page 3 of the *Daily Mirror* and to calculate the stake money for a football pool entry?

Appropriate standards required in a future society have to be defined and this is not an issue that can be burked by taking refuge in the use of established tests. What applied to tests of English and arithmetic in the Scottish studies applies to surveys of science and social studies. Do we merely wish children to be able to reproduce a series of facts, formulae and theories or to understand the scientific method? Is there a purpose to teaching about the Battle of Bannockburn, if so what is it and how can it be assessed?

Impact

When we turn to the question of impact we must first ask what we can expect such exercises to achieve.

As noted above the objectives specified for the Scottish Scholastic Surveys were very limited. What information was sought is defined but the use that could be made of it is not. A later and considerably more detailed statement is made in a leaflet. *Why, What and How*, produced by the English Assessment of Performance Unit. The purpose of monitoring, it says, is to provide national information, not only to describe the current position but also to record changes as they occur. Further, such information would both help determine policy including the making of decisions about the employment of resources. They would also help teachers in planning the balance of pupils work in schools, without attempting at national level to define detailed syllabus content. Moreover, the outcomes of the tests were expected to make parents, employers and others concerned better informed about the achievement of schools.

There are three sets of objectives: to provide information about matters of general policy, to provide information for teachers and to make parents, employers and others better informed. The Scottish Mental Survey provided information relevant to each of these objectives. I will look at the recommendations that refer to each of these issues in turn.

General policies

Much of the information at the national level was primarily of negative value. The differences among pupils in different types of areas (cities, large towns, small towns, other areas) could be dismissed. There was therefore no need to redeploy resources from or to any of these types of area. There was, for example, no need to concentrate the resources on the cities or the rural areas. Needs if they existed were specific and not related to type of area. The same is true of the geographical regions. The survey produced no evidence of regional differences and therefore no argument for redeployment of resources. There was no argument for more schools, more teachers or more instruction materials in one part of the country than in another. Educational priority areas such as those established in the 1970s could not simply be defined in terms of general types or in terms of geographical region. Much more specific information than that was needed and therefore much more focused intervention.

Another apparently negative piece of information but one still relevant to policy, both national and regional, was the finding that pupils from smaller schools attained practically the same standards as those in larger schools. 'In particular, pupils from one teacher schools reached the same standards as those attained by pupils in schools where there were more than six teachers' (p. 189). Since the publication of the reports, we have experienced, in Scotland, in England and no doubt elsewhere, the closing of small one- and two-roomed rural schools. The evidence of the survey made it perfectly clear that such action was not justifiable on the basis of pupil achievement. The arguments for these changes which proceeded on a massive scale in the 1960s and 1970s has to be on the basis of cost or other social values.

The second survey produced more and equally valuable information for the formation of policy. It showed that gains in achievement were greater in those areas where the local authority continued to make use of a battery of attainment tests on the completion of primary schooling. An obvious inference would be that the existence of a formal external assessment of this kind has beneficial effects upon the attainment of pupils. The information about library provision in primary schools has equally important implications. 'Pupils in schools with libraries of various types have made higher scores in the English test than pupils not having these facilities' (p. 80). While as noted above the researchers are cautious, they do go on to conclude 'nevertheless the association shown between possession of a library and the high performance on English tests is suggestive' (p. 80).

The process of policy formation is one that is not easily unravelled but there is no evidence that even one small school was spared because of the findings of the research. Certainly I have not seen it cited during the debate that has taken place over the last ten years and which continues today. The arguments for closing small schools are predominantly economic though the social development of the children is also mentioned and occasionally fears, apparently misplaced, are expressed about academic achievement. The protagonists of the schools usually advance community values and the deleterious effect of travelling on their side.

The impact of the finding on the use of attainment tests at the end of primary schooling is clearer. All authorities have now abolished them in spite of the evidence that their use was positively related to improvements in attainments. I have found no evidence that the provision of school libraries has been based on the findings of the scholastic surveys. In the present period of retrenchment I have seen no reference to the importance of maintaining the school libraries because of their anticipated effect on achievement in English. As far as I can see the recommendations which had relevance to national policy have been ignored. Why was this?

In a recent analysis by the Rand Corporation of the contribution of evaluation to policy, *Educational Evaluation in the Public Policy Setting*, a number of points were made that relate to this issue. The authors point to timeliness, costs and values as important factors.

If the evidence from surveys is to help determine national policy then the information provided must speak to contemporary concerns. It is unlikely that accidental evidence gleaned in the process of the survey and simply recorded in technical reports will have any influence. Specific information from explicitly focused studies must be produced at the appropriate time.

The information from survey studies is partial and may therefore be misleading. Perhaps the administrators who abolished attainment testing in spite of the survey evidence were right. A notion of what primary education is meant to achieve is not adequately defined by formal tests. Any advantage accruing to schools from use by the authority of attainment tests may well be outweighed by other more negative effects on the curriculum of the schools. As the Rand Corporation report points out 'Studies that use a single outcome score to judge the relative value of programmes without regard to different programme goals or approaches are of little value. Large scale summative evaluations should be reconceptualised . . . (to) present carefully justified judgements about the relationship of programmes to changes in educational treatments that may be affecting children' (p. 84).

As the authors of the 1953 report wisely point out 'an analysis of the effect of class size has yielded no clear conclusions. It appears that an investigation of this topic would require a specific design in which the accepted principles for organising classes would be altered for the purposes of the experiment' (p. 168). This is a conclusion which might well have been applied to other findings about school size, school libraries or the use of external examinations. Administrators were rightly sceptical of conclusions based exclusively on formal tests of arithmetic and English and which could not take into account a full range of contextual variables. More focused studies related to the effects of particular administrative arrangements are necessary to provide a balanced picture for the guidance of policy makers.

Teachers' planning

What contribution did the surveys make to the second set of objectives? That is, what help was available to teachers for planning the balance of pupils' work?

Teachers have two interests. The first is in the standards of their own pupils compared with those in other similar schools, as with wages our reference groups tend to be local and individual rather than national and general. It is a question of each teacher defining for himself what standards are appropriate in his circumstances, finding out whether his pupils are reaching those standards and taking the appropriate action.

The teacher's other interest is what he should teach and how he should teach it. National surveys cannot help any individual teacher to decide what teaching scheme should be used next year, nor how it should be used and still less the balance of work for particular pupils.

The specific advice to teachers in the scholastic survey illustrates these limitations. Did many schools cease division by factors, or pay more attention to the layout of short division sums or provide persistent oral practice in accepted speech forms as a result of the publication of these findings? If they did, how many teachers would now think that was good advice? As with more general issues the specific recommendations relate to a particular perception of the purposes of school which is not now so widely held.

Even for those who do accept the assumptions of the authors, how would a particular teacher know whether the more attention which it is held should be paid nationally to the layout of a short division sum applies to his class? If he was already providing more attention than the average should he provide not more but perhaps less? Is it likely that those already giving 'considerable attention to the layout of short division sums' would feel strengthened in their conviction and provide even more? Would those not giving sufficient attention have overlooked this point in the recommendations of the report?

Findings from national surveys may or may not apply to any particular teacher and whether any teacher will take account of them will depend very much on their own values and their own perceptions of their current practice. In the case of the standardized notation for the recording of time of day the survey merely indicated variation in practice. The panel's choice of a particular form arose not from the survey but from their own general experiences. Information which will be relevant to specific questions cannot for the most part be satisfactorily obtained from a national survey.

A teacher's decision about the emphasis to be given to layout in teaching arithmetic is more likely to be based on his own experience of the situation around him than on any information that the nation as a whole did well or did badly in this respect on a general test. Individual teaching decisions are not made on the basis of general tests but on the basis of specific information which relates to the teacher's own objectives in the circumstances in which he is operating.

The general trend of the report is towards a greater standardization of curriculum and method. It is difficult to see, how it could be otherwise. A few quotations will illustrate the point. 'Examination of the errors demonstrates forceably the need for persistent oral practice of correct forms and usages . . . Although pencil and paper must be used for testing this kind of usage, it is not the best medium for teaching' (p. 106). 'The use of the apostrophe . . . is not taught . . . the correct form should be shown and explained' (p. 107). 'It would appear desirable to include some printed Scots among the reading material for Scottish children' (p. 100).

The advice may be good or bad but the conclusion is clear. Either one has a national curriculum which includes those elements which the authors thought were important or one maintains the traditional British division of responsibility, placing trust in the professionalism of the teachers. The position of the authors of the report is akin to that of St Augustine when he prayed 'Lord make me chaste – but not just yet'. The report says that 'it would be folly to attempt to standardise curricula until it has been shown that one method is superior to others . . . If it were possible to determine a standard order to teaching . . . these contributions would be useful contributions to teaching' (p. 185) – but not just yet.

The authors of the survey wanted their cake and halfpenny as well. They wanted to have in effect a national curriculum but did not recommend so directly nor did they recommend any mechanism for establishing or enforcing it. Perhaps because they anticipated rightly that any such recommendation would meet overwhelming objection from the teachers' organizations.

In the case of the recommendations which were relevant to classroom practice, the authors of the report failed to grasp the nettle and draw the conclusion that was implicit in most of their recommendations i.e. there should be a national curriculum. If there was not to be a national curriculum then the recommendations were to individual teachers but as suggested above they were not a form which provided useful guidance to individual teachers.

Information for parents, employers and others

When we turn to the third issue, that of making employers, parents and others better informed, there are again a number of problems. Information about the current position and/or changes is a recurring concern of those involved in administration, of educational researchers and occasionally of those with a more general interest in the schools such as employers and academics. There are occasional flurries of interest in the national standards with headlines in the national press but they are usually followed by a period of quiescence. The former British Prime Minister, Mr Callaghan, started 'a great debate' on standards in education. Little is heard of it now. Instead interest is focused on the effects of reduction in public expenditure.

The call for information about contemporary standards sounds reasonable enough but it is not at all clear what use this information has. There is for example, considerable American evidence that standards of candidates for the College Entrance Examinations have been dropping steadily in recent years but since nobody knows why, there is not much that can be done about it.

Recording changes as they occur is less obviously compelling on analysis. It seems self-evident that we should monitor standards over time as a sort of quality control but what use can be made of such general information? Such findings are important because they correct false impressions. It is easy to believe that standards are falling. Two or three experiences with shop assistants who cannot perform simple arithmetic accurately and quickly would convince the casual observers that standards are low and indeed falling. Yet the data from the surveys I report and from later surveys indicate that virtually all school leavers have a high level of facilities in rote arithmetic.

Similar important, if negative, findings were produced as part of a recent study of the primary schools (HM Inspectors of Schools, 1980). These surveys demonstrated that the standards of achievement in the schools in arithmetic and reading were high and indeed in most aspects higher than they had ever been. This meant that the inspectors in their part of the report could go beyond the sterile arguments about falling standards in the basic skills to look at what primary education ought to be concerned with. *When Rising Standards in Scottish Primary Schools* was published ten years ago however, it was not exactly a best seller. Noone seemed to want to know. Perhaps the problem lay in the title. Would a book entitled 'What has Happened to Standards in Scottish Primary Schools' have sold better?

It is arguable that what parents and employers and others need is not more information of a general kind about standards but a better understanding of what it is that schools are setting out to achieve and how particular activities fit into these objectives. Employers need to know, as a basis for discussion with educational authorities, what arithmetic the schools are trying to teach and what communication skills are being taught. Parents need to know that apparently random play activities in Primary 1 or field studies in Secondary 4 are carefully thought out parts of an overall programme making a specified contribution to children's learning. They also need to be reassured that the schools their own children attend are providing the same opportunities as are available to others. Surveys of national standards will not inform them on either of these points.

There are circumstances when national surveys can be useful for national policy-making. These are mainly when the national conscience is agitated by a specific educational issue. If there is concern about standards then national surveys may play some useful role in providing empirical evidence. Even then as demonstrated by an article by the secretary of the

Scottish Confederation of British Industry (national association of employers) demonstrates, there may be a tendency among the protagonists in the debate to question the survey evidence (*CCC News*, No. 2).

Surveys may also have a publicity value in some circumstances. The publicity given to a series of surveys on reading standards contributed to the atmosphere which made the establishment of the Bullock Committee acceptable.

Dissemination

How did the Council expect to affect practice? The reports that they published were highly technical and were presumably addressed to the research community. Mulkay, when drawing the familiar distinction between pure and applied research asserts that for pure research 'the audience for results consists of other researchers who are working upon the same or related problem and have judged the adequacy of the results by means of scientific criteria' (p. 95). That audience is interested in the extension of scientific knowledge. Where the findings are expected to 'have useful practical consequences' (p. 95), other criteria apply and other kinds of communication are appropriate.

The Committee made a conscious attempt to reach at least two of the audiences referred to above by means of an abridged report called *The Attainments of Scottish Ten Year Olds in English and Arithmetic*. It was published 'in accordance with their policy of making research findings available in compact form to teachers, parents and others' (p. 2). This report consisted largely of the two tests and the technical material. It did have a chapter devoted to general results where the major findings about sex differences, different types of area, different size of class, different sizes of school and the significance of left-handedness were reported. However, the information of significance for teachers is buried in the analysis of the test scores. Even the briefer report explicitly designed for the lay audiences seems to have been written with rather more than half an eye to the research community.

Caplan, Morrison and Stanbaugh outline three utilization theories which seek to explain problems of communication between the social researcher and his audience. The 'knowledge-specific' theories try to explain lack of use of social science knowledge as a consequence of the nature of the information itself and the research techniques employed. The 'two communities' theory explains failure to use research in terms of the relationships of the researcher and the research system to the policy-maker and the policy-making system. Finally, the 'policy-maker constraints' theories argue that failure to use can best be understood from the standpoint of the constraints under which the policy-maker operates, for example, his need for concise information in a short period of time. In the case of the Scottish surveys all three sets of problems existed. The reports were addressed to the research community and not presented in a form which was likely to attract the attention of any one of the lay audiences to which the conclusions were presumably addressed. 'The research is focussed on understanding and fails to provide necessary action frame-work' (p. X).

While the Committee were anxious to draw attention to the practical implications of their findings, they seem to have no thought to 'key points where it will be most likely to be used' (p. XI), thus maintaining the barrier between the two communities. Nor do the researchers seem to have taken into account the constraints on the policy-makers, the extent to which other factors must determine the decisions actually taken.

The reports as distinct from the conclusions do not seem to have been addressed to the relevant audiences and were hence likely to get lost in the theoretical literature rather than reaching those who were in a position to use them.

Conclusions

What can we learn from the Scottish experience? Our French colleagues have a reputation for pithy comments. You may know that when in 1918 Wilson produced his fourteen points, Clemenceau commented, 'le bon Dieu was satisfied with ten'. I am afraid I can measure up to neither. I have only seven. First, if we wish to be listened to, at least in the short run, we must speak to policy-makers about the issues that concern them when they concern them. Second, we must recognize that our contribution to the discussion is a partial contribution. There are other considerations, economic, social, political, which may over-ride our findings, no matter how conclusive we think them. Third, what is sought is usually knowledge of specifics which is relevant to particular local circumstances. Studies on the grand scale may be interesting to researchers and utterly uninformative for policy-makers. What they require are focused studies which provide information about particular issues. Fourth, it may be necessary for us to sacrifice some of our academic purity to provide information which will be of help for policy formation. Fifth, national tests will inevitably have some curriculum backwash and will involve pressure towards a centrally determined curriculum no matter what we may wish. Sixth, if we wish to influence classroom practice our findings must, in Eaker and Huffman's phrase, be not only statistically tested but also classroom tested. Finally, administrators, politicians, teachers, parents and employers will not take us seriously as we take ourselves.

Bibliography

ASSESSMENT OF PERFORMANCE UNIT (1977). *Why, What and How*. Department of Education and Science.

ASSESSMENT OF PERFORMANCE UNIT (1978). *Monitoring Mathematics.* Department of Education and Science.
CAPLAN, N., MORRISON, A., and STANBAUGH, R.J. (1975). *The Use of Social Science Knowledge in Policy Decisions at the National Level.* Institute for Social Research, University of Michigan.
CARLSON, D., (1980). 'Statewide Assessment in California',*Cadermos de Pesquisa*, December.
DEVEREUX, A. (1979). 'What is Education For – An Industrialist's View', *CCC News*, 2, February.
EAKER, R. and HUFFMAN, J. (1980). Interview in *Communication Quarterly*, 4, 1.
GREAT BRITAIN. H.M. INSPECTORS OF SCHOOLS (1980). *Learning & Teaching in Primary 4 and Primary 7.* London: HMSO.
MULKAY, M.J. (1977). 'Sociology of the Scientific Research Community.' In: SPIEGEL-ROSING, I. and De SOLA PRICE, D. (eds) *Science, Technology and Society*, Sage Publications.
PINKUS, J. (Ed) (1980). *Educational Evaluation in the Public Policy Setting.* Rand.
POLLOCK, G.J. and THORPE, W.G. (1979). *Standards of Numeracy in Central Region.* Scottish Council for Research in Education.
SCOTTISH COUNCIL FOR RESEARCH IN EDUCATION. (1963). *The Scottish Scholastic Survey, 1953.* University of London Press.
SCOTTISH COUNCIL FOR RESEARCH IN EDUCATION. (1969). *The Attainments of Scottish Ten Year Olds in English and Arithmetic*, University of London Press.
SCOTTISH COUNCIL FOR RESEARCH IN EDUCATION. (1968). *Rising Standards in Scottish Primary Schools.* University of London Press.
SCOTTISH EDUCATION DEPARTMENT. (1977). *The Educational System of Scotland.* Scottish Information Office.
SUMNER, R. (Ed) (1977). *Monitoring National Standards of Attainment in Schools.* Windsor: NFER.
WALKER, D.A. (1976). *The IEA Six Subject Survey.* John Wiley & Sons.

CRITICISM AND DISCUSSION

Note by the Editors: The first section of this chapter contains only a summary of Dockrell's oral presentation which means that a great deal of the presentation's liveliness is lost. However, the major points are presented. This appeared to be necessary, because the discussions were geared to this information which is not present in the paper itself.

1. Abridged oral presentation

I chose this example (*note by the editors*: Dockrell refers to his paper about the contribution of surveys to policy-making) for a number of reasons:
1) The first one is because so much time, effort and resources are being devoted to surveys internationally. The last round of IEA surveys alone involved 26 nations. The next round, which is now under way, will involve many more. That is apart from the kinds of surveys that are being conducted in many individual countries. 2) Secondly, I chose it because it seemed to me that this was an example of good educational research. Good in the sense that it was carefully planned and meticulously carried out. 3) The third reason was that it did produce valid findings. That sets it off from a good deal of educational research. Many of the studies that we carry out leave us very little wiser than we were before. That is not something to be surprised at or something to deprecate but simply teaches us to recognize the limitations of the human endeavour. 4) They had various levels of relevance. The title of the survey's second volume is *Rising Standards in Scottish Primary Schools* and with a title like that, one would have expected the teaching force to read it and cheer. However, few people bought it. That is rather puzzling. What is it that makes a good piece of research not acceptable? My guess is that good news is no news, to reverse the common saying. Good news does not make as much impact as bad news. 5) The fifth reason for selecting these studies is that they are relevant to general policy issues. They seem to serve in some sense as an empirical test of Weiss's hypothesis, that if we go on doing good research, in time people will beat a path to our door because our mousetrap is better. I do not believe the empirical evidence we have supports the hypothesis. The evidence was not only ignored, but the actions taken were the reverse of the conclusions drawn from the data. 6) The sixth point is relevant to a distinction between research which is directed to general policy issues and research directed to teachers. In the scholastic surveys there were findings which were directly relevant to teacher issues. Yet, these were not implemented either. The example I take of policy issues which were not implemented was that on small schools. The evidence the surveys turned up was that small schools were no less effective than schools with six or more teachers. We have gone on closing small schools at an increasing rate. On the teacher side, one of the comments made was that although virtually all the children in the school speak, not English but Scots as their natural language, Scots is not taught at all in the schools. This is something that was found deplorable in 1953, 1963, 1973 and no doubt will be in 1983 and if I could see into the future, I would make a bet on 2003. 7) Finally, I chose it because it shows the advantages – what can be learned from surveys – and the limitations of surveys. The con-

clusion I draw from that is that we must relate the research procedure we follow to the particular issue we are faced with.

My first concern (in the paper written for this Workshop) was with getting knowledge; my second with using knowledge. What conclusions can we draw from these surveys:

First of all, as far as administrators are concerned, it seems clear to me that the evidence we offer has to be relevant to the issues of the day. Knowledge does not live on in the system. Reaching teachers is a complex and difficult activity. The people who carried out the research published not only two technical reports, but also a special book which was addressed to teachers. The problem seems to be that the information gained at the survey level was not applicable by any individual teacher. Furthermore, although the information was addressed to parents as well, it seems that national survey data are rarely of interest to them. Parents only seem to want to know whether the particular school their child is going to is a good school.

Secondly, it should be stressed that researchers should be concerned about the contribution they make to the climate of opinion. Related to this, it is important to note that we see things through a filter, through a set of expectations and a set of patterns. When I think of research which has apparently contributed to the climate of opinion, it has been in harmony with the Zeitgeist.

Thirdly, it seems to me that our evaluations, our surveys, can be effective in correcting biased impressions, in undermining prejudice. An example of correcting biased impressions is the case of rote arithmetic. My impression and that of most other people is that the general level of skill in manipulating figures in Scottish school leavers is low. The data we have, however, indicate that virtually all our school leavers, 98–99 per cent of them, leave school with a high level of facilities in rote arithmetic.

Some final remarks about research influencing policy via informal networks. Of course, I know there is multiple causation. But, nevertheless, it seems to me that political educational policy decisions are sometimes of the clear-cut type. This is especially the case in small unit contexts. For example, when I was in Alberta – geographically large, but small in numbers – I was quite astounded to be taken before a committee of cabinet, where we made a submission about provision for the maladjusted. There was at that time no provision within the province for maladjusted, emotionally disturbed, children. We argued the case, we produced what evidence we had and they asked questions. The meeting took an hour or so, and the Premier turned to his colleagues and said: 'Well, I take it then we are agreed. We will start such institutions.' Within three years there were more than 20 institutions within the province. That was a clear decision, clearly taken. All kinds of other influences had gone into that decision, of course. But there was a point at which a decision was made. Another example of how perfectly clearly a decision was made is the case of the examination structure at 16-plus in Scotland. The point is that, in smaller units at least, one can see actual policy decisions having been made. How does this happen? It seems to me that informal networks are crucial to the decision-making that has gone on. I was surprised to hear that Finland does not seem to fit in this pattern. We are aware of the importance of informal contacts between researchers, administrators, civil servants, directors of education etc. The informal exchanges of information at parties, in the bar, and especially in one's club usually result in a formal arrangement, and a research project is launched. That is possible because we are a small community, and we are essentially located in a single city.

It does seem to me that if informal networks matter, then it can only be those people who participate in them, who can contribute to them. This is my explanation for the fact that the studies which I quoted failed to show effective informal network influence. My hypothesis would be that my predecessor was a teetotaller. That is, he did not drink and consequently did not share in and participate in this kind of informal network.

2. Criticism and discussion

2.1. Human testimony – informal networks

The issue of 'informal networks' and their impact on policy decisions drew much attention. *Timpane* considered human testimony of crucial importance. He reminded the Workshop of Robert Andringa who at the time was a congressional staff member in the US House of Representatives. Andringa listed in priority order as he had perceived them, in Congress amongst the politicians, those factors which influenced decisions. At the bottom of the list of eleven came evaluation and research studies. But the top of the list was dominated by human factors: persons whom the Congressman encountered, the leading factor being a colleague in Congress who knew the issue. The second on the list was a local educator from the constituency who happened to be a friend or an acquaintance, and so the list went on. *Weiler* stressed that teachers and school administrators follow exactly the same pattern as Andringa described for politicians and federal bureaucrats. 'They are not, by and large, interested in the written word. It is more common for them to change their behaviour on the basis of some piece of information that they glean from a close colleague, ordinarily in face to face communication.' Weiler pointed out that such a behavioral change must come about as a result of a trust relationship that policy-makers, practitioners and administrators have with other individuals who are facing what they perceive to be the same practical problems that they face, 'and they do not think, perfectly appropriately, that researchers face those problems on a day to day basis'. *Husén* explicitly seconded Weiler's observation that a trust relationship is at the basis of human testimony influencing policy. Husén referred to his work in a group charged with the task of producing a plan for the development of an educational system in Botswana up to 1990. The acceptance of the recommendations was 'very closely related to the possibility of having regular meetings with the Cabinet and Parliament members'.

Although Dockrell was not advocating 'informal networks', but merely described how they happen to work in one particular context, it was pointed out that in a highly pluralistic society (like the US, for example) such networks can be seen to be extremely exclusive and inequitable.

2.2. Receptivity to the use of research

At variance with Dockrell's observation that 'research which apparently contributed to the climate of opinion, is in harmony with the Zeitgeist', was *Timpane*'s elucidation of Coleman's contribution to policy:

> Let us say first of all that Dr Coleman is a first class sociologist and empiricist, and one of the brightest persons studying education anywhere, certainly in the US. If one were to look back over his career of 20 years, it should be stressed that he has had the courage as a citizen, as well as a scholar, and the wit, to take head-on four consecutive major policy issues in the US. When he did his work on equal education opportunity in 1965, on youth in 1972, on re-segregation and white flight in 1976, and when he did his work on public and private schools in 1980, he was in every case, a social scientist who was well ahead of the political process, forcing the political process to confront issues.

Timpane considered it would be worthwhile using such controversial and confrontational models of the use of social science research in policy making to a much greater extent than is the case at the moment.

Legrand pointed out that evidence in many cases does not lead to changes in the actual policy of the time if this evidence does not accord with what the inspectorate would like to see. In other words, the 'Zeitgeist' influence on decision-making can be located quite often in certain sectors of the governmental machinery; in this case the inspectorate. Legrand illustrated his point with the case of spelling and history teaching:

> For 50 years now, they have had national surveys in France, which always turned up meagre spelling results. The recommendation to implement other, more effective teaching methods never got a chance, since the Inspectorate first of all never wished to believe the evidence and, secondly, feared that other methods might lead to even lower

spelling results. Another example is the teaching of history in France. Several studies showed that the young French pupils understood very little of all the history that they were being taught. But these facts are simply not taken into account since the government authorities want French children to know all the dates of their country's history. So, if research produces evidence which is not acceptable to the inspectorate or other authorities, they simply ignore it.

Of course, one should not forget that an important characteristic of France's national policy style is its high degree of centralization of power, which might explain this situation to some extent. Other references were made to what Weiss states in her paper concerning political rationality which takes precedence over the value of information in its own right. After all, problem-solving is a political process 'and it is neither desired nor expected that it should be otherwise', says *Caplan*. The crucial point in all this, according to *Legrand*, is that there are conflicting values at stake.

2.3 Surveys and national policy

Before presenting the Workshop's findings on the place surveys occupy and deserve to occupy in policy-making at the national level, it should be stressed that the Workshop discussed surveys of one very special kind only. In the words of *Weiler* these are: 'surveys to be used to identify problems, to see where there might be an opportunity for policy intervention, not so much to give us good information about how to solve those problems, but at least to tell us the problems exist, and to highlight an area where some form of policy might be appropriate'. Weiler went on to explain that other types of surveys 'that research organizations such as mine do, have to do with obtaining empirically-grounded theories about how things work in complex organizations'. These should not be confused with the first group mentioned above.

Timpane and others agreed with Weiler that to state the obvious, 'the purpose of surveys is by and large to generate hypotheses, to sharpen the question or to illuminate a trend or development for the debate, rather than to provide the answer to the debate'. However, this function is not without communication difficulty. Timpane illustrated this with a recent case: Recently,

> the US National Assessment of Educational Progress reported its most recent round of results on reading performance in the US. There was some modest improvement in basic reading skills, with some particular improvements noted amongst blacks and correlatively in the Southern portion of the US. But there was not much improvement in higher

order performance and the comprehension of reading, and some feeling that the performance in comprehension was not as good as performance on more basic reading skills. The *New York Times* and the *Washington Post* covered this story on the same day; in fact it was front page news, the first time the national assessment has ever made front page news of the *Times* or the *Post*, as far as I know. The *Post* headline said 'Black Student's Reading Improves' and then went on to tell the story. The *Times* headline said 'Students Cannot Understand What They Read' or words to that effect. Two leading newspapers gave diametrically opposite billing to those results. This story puts in a nutshell quite a lot of our communication problems.

Mitter underlined this and pointed out that the role of the mass media in communicating research results had received little attention so far in utilization studies. This is important to keep in mind since a considerable part of national policy-making relies on what Caplan called the 'conceptual use' of research results by top officials and policy-makers. Such conceptual use appeared to a great extent to rely on information provided by the mass media. However, *Dockrell* had already made clear that 'good news is often no news' to the media, while at the same time (see paragraph 2.1. above) human testimony makes more impact than written information. Dockrell illustrated this quite convincingly as far as the impact on the public was concerned. In the case of proposals for the revision of the examination systems, a national report was produced, and it was agreed to make it as public as possible: up and down the country school councils organized parents' meetings at which someone spoke about it . . . . and we did a study of the impact of the reports, one part of which an analysis of the correspondents in the newspaper columns 90 per cent of whom proved to be practising teachers. Dockrell concluded: 'As far as we could see, we did not provoke a discussion of issues among the non-professional public but even the professionals – in our case the teachers – are not easy to interest in research matters (see paragraph 4 of the discussion following Caplan's paper).

Heene suggested that the audience might be much more receptive to the findings of surveys if these were preceded by a more explicit public discussion of the goals to be achieved. There would then also be a better chance of the findings being implemented. The existing procedure for the IEA surveys – where every country has a national planning committee whose composition may vary from country to country – does not pay enough attention to this aspect. Heene implied that surveys could have a greater influence in shaping policies than is the case now.

Husén enumerated a series of cases in which IEA surveys had strong policy repercussions: language of instruction in Botswana, regional differences in Italy in achievement and available resources in schools over there, and reading in Hungary. Husén added that examples could easily be multiplied, but warned that surveys alone could never lead to the shaping of new policies. There is no such direct linear connection, and surveys 'have to be followed up with other types of more focused research'.

In relation to Legrand's remarks (in paragraph 2.2. above) concerning the decision-making power of the Inspectorate in France, the Workshop discussed the localization of policy decision-making at the national level. Seemingly somewhat contrary to Weiss's description of the ways most policies come into being (see her paper and the discussion following it), *Dockrell* reported that in Scotland 'few decisions are made on political grounds, the majority of decisions being made by administrators rather than by politicians'. He considered the personal contacts between researchers and such administrators (see the discussion about informal networks) of great importance for relating research results to these centers of power and authority.

Weiler pointed out that in the American setting a great deal of policy-making in education at present resides in the American judicial system. The use of social science research to influence policy made by the courts was thought to be considerable. Weiler adds:

> To my knowledge, there is no precise parallel to this in European countries. Certainly in the US direct policy has been made as a result of social science testimony. Perhaps the most famous example is the 1954 Brown versus the Board of Education Supreme Court decision, which first made official the unconstitutionality of segregation in the US, and which was based in large part on social science research testimony.

Mitter stated that he did not know of such clear examples in European countries although experts are consulted frequently by European courts.

An English Summary of Two Dutch Articles on Research as a Learning Process and Policy as a Learning Environment

A.D. de Groot – University of Groningen

1. In spite of differences in aim, function and form of the two articles in question – one[1] was a critical review of a Ministerial policy proposal[2] in a weekly periodical; the other[3] an invited address to a plenary meeting of the Royal Netherlands Academy of Sciences and Humanities – both carried the same *basic message*.

First, if scientific research itself is considered as a, hopefully exemplary, learning process, it can be seen to be aimed at an output of socio-culturally valuable *collective and public learning effects*.

Second, these learning effects do not consist solely of the two well-known categories that can be roughly labelled as 'new knowledge' and 'new instruments'. In addition to the effects of pure and applied science that are eventually stored in libraries, and/or given substance in tools and products of cultural instrumentation, an often ignored third category must be taken into account. This third type is that of the personal *learning effects in the individual participants in research activities*: acquired knowledge and experience, know-how and habit formation, that are primarily stored in individual memories. In an indirect sense these learning effects can also be considered as 'collective and public' in nature, in that researchers are supposed to make them available to others. In fact, there is a tacit understanding that researchers – in our time mainly on the community payroll – will share with others the considerable know-how they have personally acquired beyond what they have put on paper or given shape in instrumentation. In practice they disseminate their personal experience almost continually: not only through their personal example but in teaching, discussions, and interviews, by contacts in the corridors of conferences, etc.

Therefore, whenever the output of research activities is to be evaluated or estimated in advance, this third category of learning effects must also be taken into account.

Third, and more important, it is clear that the socio-cultural value of the output of *future* research efforts will depend very much on the then available *supply of competent researchers*. Since research competence must be learned largely through doing research, it is also clear that the quality of this supply hinges on what those then available researchers will have learned individually from previous experience.

Fourth, it is useful to distinguish here between two different types of environmental inputs that are instrumental in the learning process. Next to learning from such *factual inputs* as are provided by the materials and outcomes of research activities proper, the stimulation and conditioning, the critical feedback, and the example provided by the *human environment* must also be considered: 'learning through co-specifics' as an ethologist would put it. The latter inputs appear to be particularly important in producing and shaping certain learning effects of the third category, such as the development of personal insights and attitudes as well as habit formation, beyond what transpires from sober scientific reports and results.

Fifth, the argument — fairly self-evident up to here — becomes more pointed when attention is focused on scientifically and/or socio-culturally '*negative*' personal *learning effects*. It must be noted that inadequate sub-programmes in a researcher's professional repertoire — e.g., biased knowledge, one-sided experience, defective methods, in short, 'bad' intellectual habits — may be learned, and are often learned, in the same way as are adequate sub-programmes — e.g., constructive insights, useful know-how, attitudes (problem-handling routines) of objectivity, and of openness-of-mind, that is, 'good' intellectual habits. It is true that serious, well-trained, and intelligent researchers will not contaminate their repertoire by incorporating sub-programmes of which they clearly see the defects. However, as we know, not all researchers are perfectly trained and intelligent as well as perfect in their seriousness of purpose. Moreover, one-sidedness may go unobserved, bias may be hidden; and, last but not least, resistance against the pressure of a human environment that is less than perfect in competence or in scientific independence (or in both) may be hard. In any case, the possibility of negative learning effects from research practice must be taken seriously.

Sixth, from these considerations the general conclusion is drawn that it will be *fruitful* to consider and *to study research settings as learning environments*; learning environments primarily for researchers but also for participating, or otherwise interested bystanders. Such studies, conducted from the learning point of view, should be helpful in attempts to improve research practice in any field where such improvement is felt to be needed. In spite of the fact that a substantial and useful body of knowledge on human learning is available, this point of view appears to have remained neglected to a remarkable extent. In planning, policy and innovatory decision-making — not only with regard to the function of research, for that matter — the learning effects which are likely to be produced in participants by such changes in limiting conditions (format, interrelationships) as result from proposed measures are rarely taken into account in anything like a systematic manner.

Seventh, *in the area of educational innovation* in particular it should be worthwhile to look at existing conditions and policy measures by which research settings are shaped (organizationally), and can be seen or anticipated to work (psychologically) as learning environments.

2. So much for the general argument as expounded mainly in the 1980 paper.[3] Furthermore, in both articles the argument is sustained and illustrated by the description of certain readily observable inadequacies of existing learning environments.

First, according to current complaints about social science research in general and educational research settings in particular, *three types of shortcomings* are distinguished. The three types also correspond roughly to three approaches to human learning processes:

1. ineffectiveness or malfunction of the formal and informal *reward system*;
2. insufficiency of the *critical* ('Forum') *function* in the corresponding scientific communities;
3. suboptimal utilization of *leadership* — in the form of supervision, inspiration and example — for learning purposes.

Second, in the present situation in the Netherlands *one complex factor in the social climate* is considered as a cause underlying and perpetuating all three types of shortcomings. This presumed cause may be typical of small democracies in general; in any case, there is some agreement that it — among other factors — hampers sound developments in this country.

Briefly, this country shows, to quote the political scientist Lijphart[6] 'an unusually high degree of social cleavage', not only in the number of religious groups, political parties and factions, but also in schools of (social) thought, and splinter groups, down to individuals. These groups and individuals find it hard to cooperate in communal goal-directed enterprises. On the other hand, they have learned the art of peaceful coexistence[4] — on a *bourgeois-egalitarian basis*. It has often been said that it is good to live here, provided one does not want to achieve too much, let alone excel.

In the last 10 to 15 years these egalitarian tendencies have been strengthened by the anti-authoritarian mood of the day: they are reflected in political programmes, and have resulted in official conceptions and laws as well as unofficial opinions, all strongly emphasizing the (social) security of the individual and his (equal) rights. It appears that in some respects the case for equality has been overstated to the detriment of adequate recognition of differences in competence and intellectual achievement. In any case, in the present social climate, *rewards* (and in particular honours) for achievement (1), constructive *criticism* to promote achievement (2), and *leadership* based on intellectual achievement — even in its function of promoting that of others (3) – have become more 'suspect' than they already were. Even at the universities and in social scientific research settings generally, where selection by and training for the best possible achievement are indispensable, our egalitarian tendencies appear to impair the learning environment.

Third, in particular in the 1978 paper,[1] attention was drawn to a somewhat related but more specific problem in the Netherlands: that of the alleged *apeliefde* of the Ministries and government agencies, generally, for the social and behavioural sciences. The Dutch word *apeliefde*, literally, means 'monkey-love' and refers to the myth(?) that monkey mothers are given to cuddling and hugging their young almost to the point of suffocation. The term is used, in general, to denote 'unwise parental affection' and, in particular, possessive maternal love which provides an unfavourable developmental and learning environment for the young.

The social context of the criticism (1978) can be sketched briefly – and in somewhat oversimplified terms – as follows. When, in its policy-making or innovating activity, a government agency feels the need for support from research, it hopes to obtain answers to the questions from which the need springs. These questions tend to be either in the nature of requests to deliver plain, mostly statistical facts – hardly a task for a researcher – or questions that are phrased too indeterminately to be answered straightforwardly. If then an outside researcher (university department, research institute) is contracted, his, partly uninteresting and partly vague, terms of reference will induce him to rephrase the problem and design the set-up according to his own research views and interests.

This situation – in other words: *an insufficiently worked out*, and agreed upon, interface between the two worlds – may lead to designs that are shaped much more by the current methods and existing needs of the discipline (and school) in question than by the original needs of the contractor. For instance, at the risk of exaggerating a little: sociologists will produce theoretical generalizations, psychologists measuring instruments, and educationists educational precepts. Since such supplies do not fit the demand, both parties tend to feel dissatisfied – an internationally well-known and generally recognized problem.

Fundamental differences of opinion, however, exist on the question of how to solve this problem organizationally. In the Ministerial policy proposal[2] to which the 1978 paper[1] was a reaction, the position was taken – supported by a few authors – that:

1. government-instigated policy research is a specific kind of research which requires *a methodology of its own* – to be developed in cooperation with contractors, and outside the sphere of influence of the traditional academic methodology;

2. one recommendable way to improve the interface between contractor and client (researcher) is that of strengthening the organizational connection between the two by *incorporating the researcher* into the contractor's organization — i.e., by locating the basis from which he develops his project design and carries out his research *within the government department in question*;

3. increasing the research effort (funds) in line with the conception *sub (1)* and the organizational structure described *sub (2)* is *a means of promoting the quality of social science* research in general.

In the two critical papers, then the main contentions were:

sub (1): The claim for a separate methodology is both ill-founded and dangerous, the danger being that it creates a new interface problem instead of solving the old one.

sub (2): This new interface problem — which was not even mentioned in the government proposal[2] — is greatly aggravated if the researcher's home base is located in the department. The more securely he is 'nested' there, the harder will it be to find sound solutions to problems of scientific quality control, and of establishing a sound learning environment. Other rewards are likely to replace those of independent critical thinking (see *sub (3)* below), and the indispensable benefit of scientific feedback provided by discussion and peer criticism as well as those of advice and leadership by top scientists become much more difficult to reap.

sub (3): If the policy of a relative increase in the volume of directly government-funded — and ministry-controlled — research is presented as a way of promoting the social sciences, then such a policy is rightly labelled one of *apeliefde*: unwise parental affection, of a 'possessive mother' government towards her (adolescent) social science 'child'.

3. The obvious pitfall in handling governmental contract research is contamination of the reward system. In particular if the researcher is 'nested' as described above or, generally, if he is not sufficiently protected and supported by an independent research institute with a reputation at stake, then the reward system inherent in his environment is likely to be politically slanted.

This means, for example, that rejection or drastic transformation by the researcher of a poorly formulated problem as proposed by the contractor is unlikely to be welcome. Nor are outcomes of an agreed research project that run counter to envisaged policy decisions likely to be gratefully received by the contractor. Since the government and its officials want results with which something 'can be done' politically, the researcher is likely to see his efforts appreciated only if his outcomes provide a positive implementation and/or support of the existing political plans. It must also be noted that good researchers in particular show themselves to be well aware of the limitations of their conclusions by conscientiously stating these limitations. However, they make it all too easy for the participants in the ensuing political discussion to play down or discard unwelcome outcomes. In fact, it appears that it is not research quality but only 'positive support' that is rewarded – not solely by gratefulness, but also by sympathy, influence and possibly by further research grants.

This argument is by no means intended to blame politicians for their political way of thinking. Its only purpose is to present three conclusions. First, in the type of situation considered here, the organizational problem of how to structure the interface between the world of politics and that of rational, independent scientific reasoning and research is not properly solved. Second, as a result, the reward system in the learning environment is seriously contaminated. Third – and this is a critique of government, in particular of the Ministry of Science Policy – the consequences of this biased learning environment for present and future research quality, and thus for the practical utility of research efforts, are greatly underestimated.

4. The latter underestimation is apparently caused by another, more general one. The extent to which the *motives* of ministers, politicians, and government officials in calling for research may differ from those of competent researchers is rarely realized. Here, again, our simian metaphor applies, with its connotation of 'possessive' or at least dubious love, based on motives other than those of the best interests and individual identity (development, future competence) of the love object.

For what reason do Ministers and Ministry officials want research carried out? Quite often, an obvious motive appears to be that an authority wants to be in a position to state, either in Parliament or in some other official context, *that* he has initiated a research project on a certain issue, preferably a project 'actually in progress'. Why is this a desirable position? Because such a statement creates confidence, or confers status, or keeps the opposition at bay, or enables both to postpone a decision to a more favourable time, or meets a demand from the field (e.g. the teaching professions), or keeps researchers at work. Politically, each of these motives and certainly the last two, may be of real interest. However, if this is how 'mother' government primarily looks at research, then she can hardly maintain that she is mainly interested in the objective outcomes which good research can provide, much less claim that her primary concern is to promote the social sciences *per se*.

5. In its most inclusive formulation, our specific learning environment problem is: How to structure, in terms of organization, the interface between the two worlds? This question cannot be answered here (compare, however, Scheerens' exposition), but a few closing remarks are in order.

First, to expand our metaphor a little further, the counterpart of the world of 'mother' government can be said to be that of 'father' science –

who enjoins on the researcher his own high standards of competence and of being unbiased, independent and critically-minded. As hinted at the outset, it must be noted that in particular in the social sciences this paternal world of theory-guided, conclusion-oriented, and to a large extent 'pure' research does not provide an ideal learning environment either. If the aim is to breed highly competent researchers able to design and carry out investigations that meet criteria of high quality as well as of practical relevance for policy, planning, and ongoing innovation, then a purely 'paternal' education will not work either. It is understandable, therefore, that 'mother' government has a tendency to shield her children from the influence of 'father' science.

Or to put it less whimsically: the interface problem with which we are concerned here is hard to solve. A researcher must *learn* to steer clear of alluring anchorages to either side. Moored at one, he will learn how to do theoretical or laboratory research that is likely to remain socio-culturally sterile; moored at the other, he will learn how to do 'applied research' which because of its scientific weakness is unlikely to provide a sound basis for decisions, much less for generalized conclusions. However, it must be possible to chart a course that will take him beyond these beckoning havens, or in other words, to organize an interface between the two worlds which functions better than the ones proposed thus far. In attempting this, it appears wise to define this 'better functioning' primarily as: functioning better as a learning environment.

Second, it must be noted that, as presented here, the problem of the learning environment has been simplified. Apart from the mother and father in our metaphor there are also other children who want to impose their wishes on the learning researchers. Or, to drop the metaphor: In most research settings in the social and behavioral sciences there are third party interests at stake, in addition to the needs of the sponsor and the requirements of sound methodology. In educational innovation projects in particular, the picture is complicated by the fact that the workers in the educational field must be ready to cooperate, but will also insist on a say in the proceedings.

This issue — not treated in the two pages reviewed here — prompts the following considered opinion. In view of the high complexity of the problem even when only two parties are involved, it appears necessary that the role of third parties is strictly confined to the stages of designing and concrete planning of the research set-up. The cooperation of those in the field must be ensured in advance even if this requires a highly detailed explanation of what is expected, but any say in ongoing research activities is best ruled out beforehand. Or, to formulate the conclusion negatively: research set-ups that are open-ended as regards field cooperation and other field influences are certain to lead to inconclusive results. Worse still, they create a learning environment for all participants in which 'negative' learning effects are likely to prevail.

Notes

[1] DE GROOT, A.D. (1978). 'Apeliefde voor de gamma-wetenschappen,' *Intermediair*, 14, 35, September 1st 1978.

[2] Ministeriële Nota Wetenschapsbeleid: *Meerjarenplan Sociaal Onderzoek en Beleid*. Tweede Kamer der Staten-Generaal. Zitting 1977–1978, 15043 nrs. 1–2. Den Haag: Staatsdrukkerij 1978.
English summary available:
Ministerie van Onderwijs en Wetenschappen
Medium-term plan for social research and policy; summary, ed. by the Information Department of the Minister for Science Policy.
(Den Haag,) Government Printing House, 1979.
10 pages.

[3] DE GROOT, A.D. (1980). *Onderzoek als leerproces: over optimalisering van de leeromgeving van onderzoekers*. Rede gehouden in de Verenigde Vergadering van de beide Afdelingen der Koninklijke Nederlandse Akademie van Wetenschappen op 29 maart 1980. Amsterdam: Noord-Hollandsche Uitg. Mij.

[4] Typically, the nineteenth-century *schoolstrijd* (denominational versus state school education) in the Netherlands ended – if it has really ended – in a 'pacification' on a basis of equal state funding.

[5] Jaap Scheerens. Evaluation Research: political and organizational constraints;
Invited paper for the SVO international Workshop 'Educational Research and Public Policy Making' organized by the Foundation for Educational Research in The Netherlands; The Hague, 20–22 May 1981.
Foundation for Educational Research in the Netherlands (SVO), 1981.

[6] A. Lijphart. *The politics of accommodation: pluralism and democracy in the Netherlands*. Berkeley: University of California Press, 1968.

Wanted: An Adequate Interface between Policy and research Some More Comments – A.D. de Groot

After reading a few other papers submitted to this Workshop and after reconsidering my own contribution, I would like to make a few additional comments. I hope that these comments will serve the purpose of improving our understanding of the situation in this country – as a case from which perhaps something more general can be learned.

1. A few qualifications and some background information with regard to my own paper: in that paper, the leading point of view was that

research is, or is aimed at, *learning* — learning in a double sense and in two respects: learning something about the world, but also: learning how to do research, i.e. how to do it better, hopefully; and: individual learning as well as collective learning.

My prime motive for choosing this point of view should be clear: dissatisfaction with the learning environment, with the learning conditions under which many educational researchers are working, and learning; dissatisfaction in three respects: rewards, feedback and leadership — with both 'father' science's and 'mother' government's establishments. I felt, and I feel, dissatisfied in particular by the way in which in this country the *interface problem* is handled. Organizationally, this problem has been poorly solved, in my opinion — if it can be regarded as 'solved' at all.

Other reasons for some special attention to the aspect of the learning environment for educational researchers are that it locates where and suggests how, in principle, improvements in the relationship between policy-makers and researchers can be initiated. That this is so was exemplified by the discussion of the *apeliefde* theme: when policy-makers by their organizational embrace of researchers narrow down the latter's learning environment, they are certain to make a suboptimal use of what research can do for them, and they work against that badly needed 'learning how to do research better'.

2. Since the *apeliefde*-theme is only one, specific, sub-problem of the interface problem, some words must be said about other sub-problems that were not mentioned as such in the paper.

The term *interface*, to begin with, has been chosen on purpose. The point is that in using it the presupposition is made that *there are two clearly distinct systems*, each of which is well developed and relatively independent of the other one. Each of the two systems — or 'cultures' or 'partners' — is implicitly supposed to have its own objectives, points of view, standards of quality, modes of operation, and its own approaches and methods. This raises the question of whether this supposition is fulfilled — for instance in the case of the Netherlands.

It must be noted that in Carol Weiss's excellent paper this is taken for granted as regards the United States. In particular, the existence of a full-blown, and relatively independent 'father's' system is taken for granted; that is, a loosely organized but, even so, somewhat hierarchically ordered system where some scientific excellence, sufficient non-partisan expertise and high level research competence are readily available. There is of course no room for any doubt that this condition is fulfilled in the US; where, for instance, *Standards for Educational Evaluation* are being published by a nationwide committee of top experts, where the National Academy of Sciences has a Committee of Program Evaluation, and where from other centres recommendations pertinent to evaluation and policy research are requested by the Congress and the Department of Education, and brought out — see for instance, the April 1981 issue of *Educational Researcher*.

However, the fulfilment of this condition — indispensable for an adequate solution of the interface problem — may be questionable in the case of other countries.

As regards Sweden: since Torsten Husén describes the main issue of this Special Session as one of 'communication problems' between 'two partners' he, too, appears to imply that for his country our condition is fulfilled. His way of treating the subject suggests, again implicitly, that there *are* two reasonably independent and full-blown systems: 'partners', whose main, or even, only, difficulty is that they have communication problems.

However, from Denis Kallen's comments on Dr Weiss's paper, in the case of the Netherlands a rather different picture emerges. He points out that in this country 'decisions are much more "pre-cooked" in advice and consultation structures before research is called upon'. He even finds that 'there is such an osmosis between research on the one hand, and a policy preparation and implementation on the other, that any clear analysis is impossible' — that is, analysis of the way decisions come about and in particular are or are not influenced by research. One more quotation: 'The "diffusion" that the paper (Kallen again refers to Carol Weiss) describes is hence omni-present, even in the persons that are involved in the process'.

In their main tenor, I cannot but endorse these statements. It seems worthwhile, however, to rephrase and amplify them a little. In other words, then, the policy and the scientific research points of view can hardly be disentangled. Members of the many advisory committees, and government officials as well as researchers often tend to take responsibilities for, and positions in, both policy and research matters. The decision processes, those regarding the setting up and management of research projects included, tend to be diffuse all over. At least, they are largely left to the interactions in the socio-political process between existing — and, quite often, newly created — boards and committees. Furthermore, the fact that most of the committees and boards are advisory bodies only, of mixed composition — field representatives, educational system experts, officials, and, in some cases, research experts — has two consequences. First, their advisory influence depends to a large extent on majority opinions and on the anticipated political backing for those opinions. Second, as a matter of course, advisory bodies can always be overruled by the Minister. This means that the way in which decisions come about — again, decisions on research matters included — is rather heavily politicized, and, in the last resort, centralistic. In some respects, government policy, with its host of low-power committees, reminds one of the Roman strategy of *divide et impera*.

In any case, the picture of two relatively independent partners who, in their attempts at problem solving and decision making by rational analysis and negotiations, have communication problems only, does not apply to our situation. I do not share Kallen's pessimism that 'analysis', and thereby systematic improvement, 'is impossible', but I feel that his succinct description of the Dutch situation is adequate. It may also fit, at least partially, the situation in other countries.

3. What in the Netherlands has been and is being *done to the interface problem* can be formulated in terms of a policy, or *a strategy*. The present situation is, of course, largely a historically grown one. It has grown out of government policy over many decades; namely a policy of, so to speak, 'mixed advisory committeeism' that has been the traditional response of Dutch governments to the reality of our 'high degree of social cleavage'. Over time we have learned very well to *coexist* in powerless committees, but we have not learned very well how to arrive at communal decisions, by means of well-designed, rational and democratic, decision-making procedures.

Even so, in spite of those historical roots, the actual procedures followed in this country with regard to policy research can be viewed, and are often rationalized in fact, as an attempt at solving the interface problem. It is 'solved' – in inverted commas, or, maybe rather 'dissolved' – by what can be called a 'diffusion strategy', that is, one supported by arguments. It will be clear that I do not approve of such a strategy – with its inherent role confusion, as I see it – but the arguments must be mentioned.

First, what is being done corresponds in part to the oldest conception of community democracy as well as to more recent conceptions of democratization policy. I am referring to the notions of grassroots democracy, egalitarianism, participation of all interested parties in all matters of potential social consequence to them. As we know, conceptions of this kind had a strong popular support in the late sixties and the early seventies. In the Netherlands, these conceptions were welcomed at the time, rather as an extension and strengthening of our traditionally bourgeois-egalitarian sentiments; they were incorporated into quite a few new laws and regulations, and they penetrated into, and are still with us in, both establishments: that of 'father' science and that of 'mother' government. The argument is that this is as it should be.

Second, the maintenance of a decision-making procedure that guarantees an 'equal' advisory say to every interested grouping in every question it may feel concerned with, each in its own committee, provides an outlet, and at least, the possibility of having some influence – this in spite of the fact that the resulting recommendations are likely to be compromises already, and that they are easily overruled.

Third, this latter property of the decision-making procedure – *little delegation, centralism* after the diffusion – is often defended by the argument that after all the Minister bears the parliamentary responsibility. Therefore, he must have the freedom to choose his own option. This freedom, then, is guaranteed best by a policy preparation that divides experts and field representatives over a host of mixed advisory committees, that produce a host of different recommendations that do not commit the policy-maker. Therefore, if such freedom is considered a prime good, more important than that of maximizing the quality of governmental decisions by structured, bipartite negotiations between two grown-up and independent partners — again Husén's term — then the present procedure of diffuse policy preparation and centralistic decision-making can be defended as a strategy.

In brief, the higher the *social entropy* in the policy preparatory system, the more freedom the Minister will have.

4. This view of the way in which the interface problem is 'solved' in the Netherlands, namely, by a policy of, first, egalitarian democratization, and second, ultimate centralization, appears to fit in particular the phenomena mentioned at the end of my paper and described more fully in Jaap Scheerens's contributions. I refer to the fact that evaluation research projects with regard to educational innovation tend to be planned, and subsequently contracted in very broad outline only; so that what actually will be done is left partially open-ended. To a quite considerable extent this is left to the unprogrammed interaction of the individual researchers with the pertinent officials and workers in the educational field. The result is that the cooperation of field workers in fact depends on their approval *ad hoc* of the researchers' propositions. So, again, everybody has a say, right down to the grassroots level, even in the setting up and actual management of research activities.

It is obvious that this way of handling projects that are dignified by the name of 'research' runs counter to all official precepts of the 'father's' establishment. In such projects 'negative' learning effects are likely to prevail, and outcomes are almost certain to be inconclusive. Even so, the procedure has defenders — on the basis of the arguments just mentioned: this *is* democratic participation, with an outlet and some potential influence for everyone; and the freedom of the policy-maker is guaranteed.

In fact, nothing is easier than discarding the outcomes, if any, of such projects whenever they do not fit present policies; whereas outcomes that happen to fit can always be quoted.

My personal opinion will be clear. In such environments the temptations that tend to pervert the learning processes of both research workers and policy-makers abound.

5. At this point a reaction of disbelief is to be expected: 'But, well-trained researchers are not that easily seduced, let alone perverted, are they? Are not they more likely to leave this type of work, or, more constructively, to protest and to seek support from persons in their institutes or schools — in general, in that "father's" establishment?'

It is true that other reactions occur; even important learning effects can be observed occasionally: learning how *not* to do research. The problem is, however, that not all persons appointed to do educational research are well-trained; and that this whole 'father's' establishment itself — the study of education as a discipline through university training and scientific output — has some severe weaknesses. If it were strong enough it could be a partner that would be listened to in the same way as, for instance, trade unions (that cannot be 'diffused') are in fact listened to. Such strength is lacking, however — not primarily from a shortage of talent but from a lack of structure and a lack of unity on matters of principle.

That is to say that it is not only the temptation of pleasing 'mother' government — who holds the purse — that tends to weaken the standards of impartiality, objectivity and quality; it is not only the rewards researchers can collect by also 'seating themselves in the policy-maker's chair' (as we say in Dutch) — i.e., by not avoiding being biased — that tend to impair their learning process. At least two other causes of the weakness of the researchers' culture as a partner can be discerned.

Very briefly, then: The first factor has been hinted at already. Our traditional *egalitarianism*, along with the effects of the democratization movements of the late sixties and early seventies, has severely weakened the hierarchy of scientific research competence, and it has *inflated the notion of expertise*.

There is a tendency — and, in addition, there are a few laws in which this tendency has been legitimized — to consider all university-trained persons as equals, not only as human beings and professional workers, but also in judgmental competence. In universities all professors and assistants in a scientific discipline are considered members of a mini-scientific community in which there should be little or no hierarchy. One problem with this, in itself idealistic, notion is that the entrance requirements have been set too low: every graduate holding the equivalent of a master's degree can be a member. In a country where, in general, leadership is not particularly popular, such equality tends to discourage intensive teacher-student relationships and, again, to increase social entropy. Outside the universities one effect is that graduates inexperienced in research are considered all too often fully-fledged experts, whose judgments are of equal weight to those of real experts. At the Department of Education where the problem of how to define an 'expert' appeared difficult to solve I have heard the following operational definition: 'An expert is a person who is or has been appointed as such'. Such a definition is not particularly helpful if the goal is to distinguish and to make use of real competence and excellence.

The second weakness in the 'father's' establishment is best described as *methodological alternativism*. In spite of the fact that there are many good behavioural science methodologists in this country, who consider methodology as a discipline, or an art, or a profession, that serves the main purpose of preventing unfruitful research designs from being adopted and erroneous conclusions from being drawn from research outcomes, 'alternative methodologies' — in fact a *contradictio in adiecto* — are being propagated, and not without influence. What alternativists do amounts to this: They maintain that 'the' traditional, scientific methodology is one-sided, and biased in favour of the *status quo*. They label it the 'empirical-analytic methodology', consider it so to speak as a church, next to which another, equally important, alternative church can be built on entirely different principles. They do not deny that among these principles a few ideological *a priori's* are operative; but they are not bothered by this fact since they accuse the 'empirical-analytic' methodology of being socio-politically biased, too.

The social effects of accepting this way of thinking are clear: they undo the legitimacy of the 'traditional' criteria of impartiality, objectivity and quality that should be basic in the 'father's' establishment. In the Netherlands a good deal of such alternativism is found: in some university departments, some institutes for educational research, and even in the way of thinking of government officials ... and policy-makers.

6. In sum, the interface problem for educational policy research, or, the communication problem of Torsen Husén, has not been properly solved in this country. Moreover, it cannot be properly solved since there are not two full-blown, independent systems. There is too much diffusion and role confusion to reliably locate and define the plane where the contacts occur and the communication problems are to be solved.

If the Dutch situation and current procedures are viewed as resulting from a strategy of diffusion, then that strategy may appear to have some merits: many participate in policy preparation, coexistence and compromise are ensured, and so is the policy-maker's (the Minister's) freedom. However, apart from the fact that, in the last resort, the decision-making is highly centralistic and, consequently, the preceding participation only seemingly democratic, the strategy has very serious disadvantages. With this strategy, the quality of decisions hardly benefits from what educational research and expert advice can contribute. Moreover, by providing a detrimental learning environment for researchers — but also for policy-makers and field workers — the development of research competence and of educational science is not promoted but hampered.

In the present diagnosis, next to 'diffusion', the term 'social entropy' has emerged as a key word. Diffusion, role confusion, advisory committee-ism, egalitarianism, inflation of 'expertise' and alternativism, all these phenomena increase social entropy — that is, they undo or weaken existing, reasonable, social structures without replacing them by other, equally reasonable structures. Clearly, measures that have that effect cannot promote but are likely to hamper good, democratic problem-solving and decision-making in complex fields such as that of educational innovation.

7. Where to go for therapy? The general *direction* is clear: a decrease of social entropy is called for. The first *priority* should be for measures by which the roles of the two partners, policy-makers and researchers, are

disentangled and redefined. I shall not here propose any such measure. Only three comments – 'musts', as I see them – are in order. First, the obvious agent for taking such measures is the policy-maker, that is 'government'. Second, in policy preparation relevant organization experts should be consulted; third, the point of view of the learning environment, and in particular the reward system, must be taken into account. It must be possible, then, to design a few very simple organizational measures in such a way that all concerned are rewarded – and not punished – by consistently implementing them.

Futures Research and Public Policy-Making: a Context of Use for Systems Theory and Gaming

Jan H.G. Klabbers, Futures Research Unit, University of Leyden and Social Systems Research Group, University of Nijmegen.

Abstract

In this paper futures research is described as the development and application of a methodology in order to gain more and better insight into possible and desirable futures of social systems, and the way they can be reached. In futures research six stages are distinguished, which together constitute the so-called macro-cycle. Within this cycle a micro-cycle is defined. In the context of the micro-cycle, characteristics of normative systems are described. Special attention is given to the method of interactive simulation, which is not only an analytical instrument but also a communication tool. Finally, the background, organization and first stage of a project dealing with the Dutch educational system are outlined taking into account the methodology described in the first part.

1. Characteristics of futures research

Futures research, as an organized activity, is about two decades old. It is claimed as a branch of operations research, of systems analysis, and several other multidisciplinary approaches such as management science, policy science, research and development planning, corporate planning, value analysis etc. Within our own perspective, we prefer systems theory as a frame of reference for futures research. There are several reasons why systems theory is suitable and fruitful for studying historical, current and future behaviour of social systems (1, 2, 3):

1. Systems theory offers a frame of reference to integrate the various aspects of our social environment. It offers a basis for interdisciplinary research.
2. Systems theory is problem-oriented. Existing or potential situations that may require action are identified, sometimes only tentatively.
3. The systems approach, as a concrete activity in which particular

methods and techniques are applied, is policy-oriented. The main responsibility of those engaged in futures research is providing all necessary information for policy formation and policy-making.
4. The systems approach is pragmatic. Although methodology is applied as rigorously as possible, models appropriate to the problem should be chosen leaving room for judgment and intuition.
5. The systems approach is future-oriented. Policy-making implies anticipation of future events. Considering the complexity of most issues, and the great variety of possible futures of social systems, a range of alternative solutions, to cope with complexity and variety through time, should be provided.

As previously stated, we will direct our attention to futures research of social systems i.e. organizations, institutions and societies. In this context we see futures research as the development and application of a methodology in order to gain more and better insight into possible and desirable futures of social systems, and the ways they can be reached.

Two aspects are central in this description: preview of the future, and ability to shape the future. In this paper we will discuss both aspects in more detail.

2. Stages of futures research

Amara, president of the Institute for the Future (California), distinguishes the following features of the futures field (4):

— Visionary: integrative and strategic with a temporal focus seldom less than five years, and usually twenty or more years into the future.
— Analytical: multidisciplinary and methodological with special emphasis on explicitness in forecasting, modeling, scenario building and related activities.
— Participatory: problem and implementation oriented with particular attention to the social and political dimension of planning.

Subsequently he describes five basic functions in the futures field, which combine the three features stated above:

1. *Goals formulation.* This function includes issue or problem definition, future-image creation, and alternative futures generation. It is directly related to the visionary component of the futures field.
2. *Methods development.* This function includes the development of a body of explicit knowledge for surveying the future. This function stems from the analytical or research component of the futures field (together with function 3).

3. *Applications*. Amara points out that one of the practical objectives of the futures field is to provide inputs to planning and decision-making processes by helping to expand the range of useful alternatives, to evaluate future consequences of such alternatives, and to structure programmes of intervention or action. This function may or may not involve the application of formal methodologies.
4. *Coupling*. This function is related to the process of assimilation of results of futures research by intended users – individuals, groups or organizations. The objective is to influence individual perceptions, behaviour, and attitudes.
5. *Implementation*. This includes the interventions and actions actually undertaken to realize the objectives of a plan. At the same time it provides the information feedback that may lead to adjustment of goals, development of new methods, or the initiation of modified programmes of action (4 and 5 indicate the participatory components of the futures field).

Amara visualizes these functions diagrammatically as vertices of a pentagon. He points out that at least in the futures field the 'Goals-Methods' link, the 'Application-Coupling' link, the 'Coupling-Implementation' link, and the 'Implementation-Goals' link are either weak or nonexistent or even not yet charted. The link between 'Methods and Applications' is best established as it represents the relatively well-developed research arm of the futures field. We see the strengthening of existing links as the major challenge for the futures field.

For our purposes we will consider these five functions as the main steps in problem-oriented research of social systems, including futures research. They form a cycle in which futures research is embedded as part of a broader process of social change. This cycle represents the accumulation, although not linearly, of knowledge, skill and experience within the scientific community.

In taking into account the policy-making process, too, it is not enough to describe one side i.e., the scientific endeavour, as the only or main link with policy-formation and decision-making. Lindblom and Cohen (5), Caplan (6, 7, 8), Weiss (9, 10), and Rein (11) have made it quite clear that the process of assimilation of results of research by the public policy-making system is far more complex and diffuse than it is usually considered to be in the academic literature on decision-making.

Weick (12) mentions three basic processes of organizing behaviour i.e., enactment, selection and retention. They serve as fundamental stages in the processing of information to and from the environment of social systems. In this regard the findings of Mitchell (13) comply with the theory of Weick. Mitchell, in discussing an empirical study of social science utilization among state legislators, distinguishes four phases of decision-making:

- articulation (enactment)
- aggregation (selection)
- allocation (retention)
- oversight (feedback retention-enactment)

He points out that social science research serves distinctive intellectual and social functions during the four policy-making stages. (It is assumed that the term 'intellectual and social functions' has the same meaning as Rein's notion of 'knowledge and action' (11).

During the articulation phase, social science serves primarily the conceptualization of the policy issue (enactment) and group building within major interest groups. Utilization of social science knowledge during the aggregation phase is more concerned with problem-solving and coalition building. During the allocation phase the main impact of social science is related to evidence assessment and persuasion. Finally, when the legislative oversight phase starts social science is mainly involved in evaluation studies and criticism is being mobilized.

One of the major consequences of this study, in our opinion, is, that depending on the phase of the policy-making process, different methods of inquiry have to be developed and applied. This implies that, at least in principle, the cycle mentioned earlier will have a phase specific content. The implication is that the policy-making process itself is an input for and even a function of the futures field in particular and of social research in general. The phase of the policy-making process identifies the policy issue, which then becomes the input for the problem definition in more strictly scientific terms.

As a result, the coupling of (futures and social) research and policy-making can be summarized as follows. (See Fig. 1.)

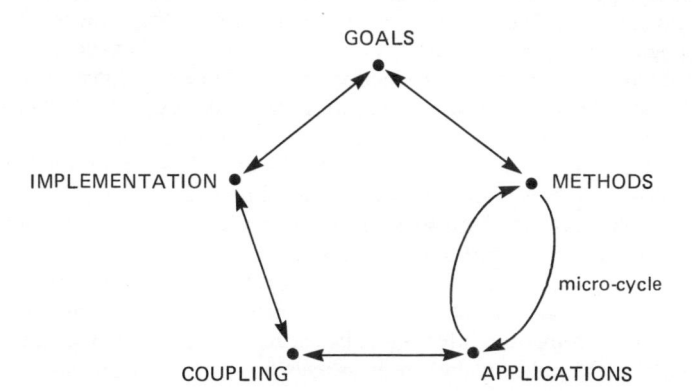

Figure 1: Functions of the Futures Field

For including the subsequent phases of a policy-making process a hexagon is more appropriate (see Fig. 2). The functions of research have been generalized to include all scientific research suitable for the policy-making process. The 'Goals' functions has been replaced by issue or 'Problem Definition' etc. This hexagon will be called the Macro-cycle.

Figure 2: Macro-cycle of policy-oriented research

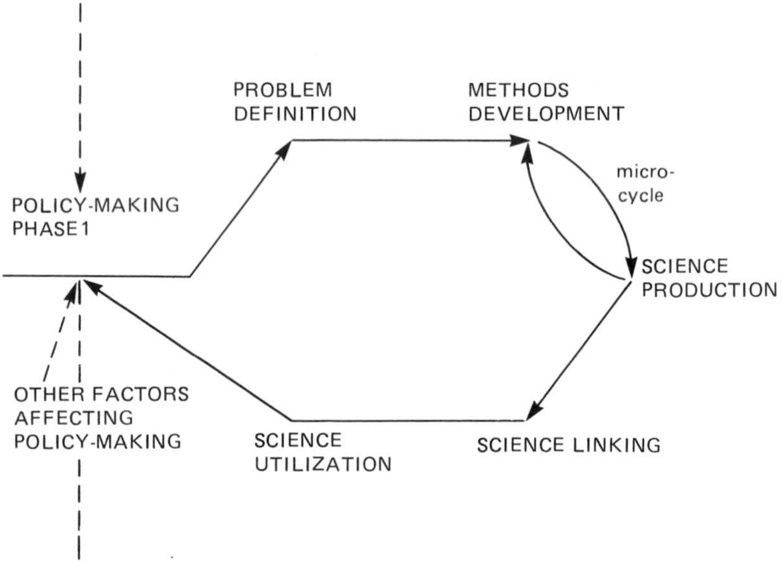

```
                    PROBLEM          METHODS
                    DEFINITION       DEVELOPMENT
                                                    micro-
    POLICY-MAKING                                    cycle
    PHASE 1
                                                    SCIENCE
                                                    PRODUCTION

    OTHER FACTORS
    AFFECTING
    POLICY-MAKING   SCIENCE          SCIENCE LINKING
                    UTILIZATION
```

Finally, to incorporate Mitchell's findings, the phase specific macro-cycle has been connected with the subsequent stages of the policy-making process (see Fig. 3).

In terms of people involved, it is reasonable to assume that in each of the six steps, different people will contribute to the progress of the endeavour. They will differ with respect to motivation, knowledge, skill, experience and responsibility. Looking at the link between 'Methods development' and 'Science production', it is possible to distinguish another cycle. This cycle is called the empirical or model cycle. It includes the processes of abstraction, deduction, and realization. In the context of this paper this cycle will be called the 'Micro-cycle' (time scale one to two years). It represents mainly basic and applied research.

We will start by discussing the micro-cycle to show the underlying principles and to point out conditions for the fruitful embedding of research in the policy-oriented macro-cycle. The central theme for discussing the micro-cycle is the development and use of simulation and gaming to improve the interface between research and policy-making, and to improve the policy-making process itself.

Figure 3: Coupling of macro-cycle with phases of the policy-making process.

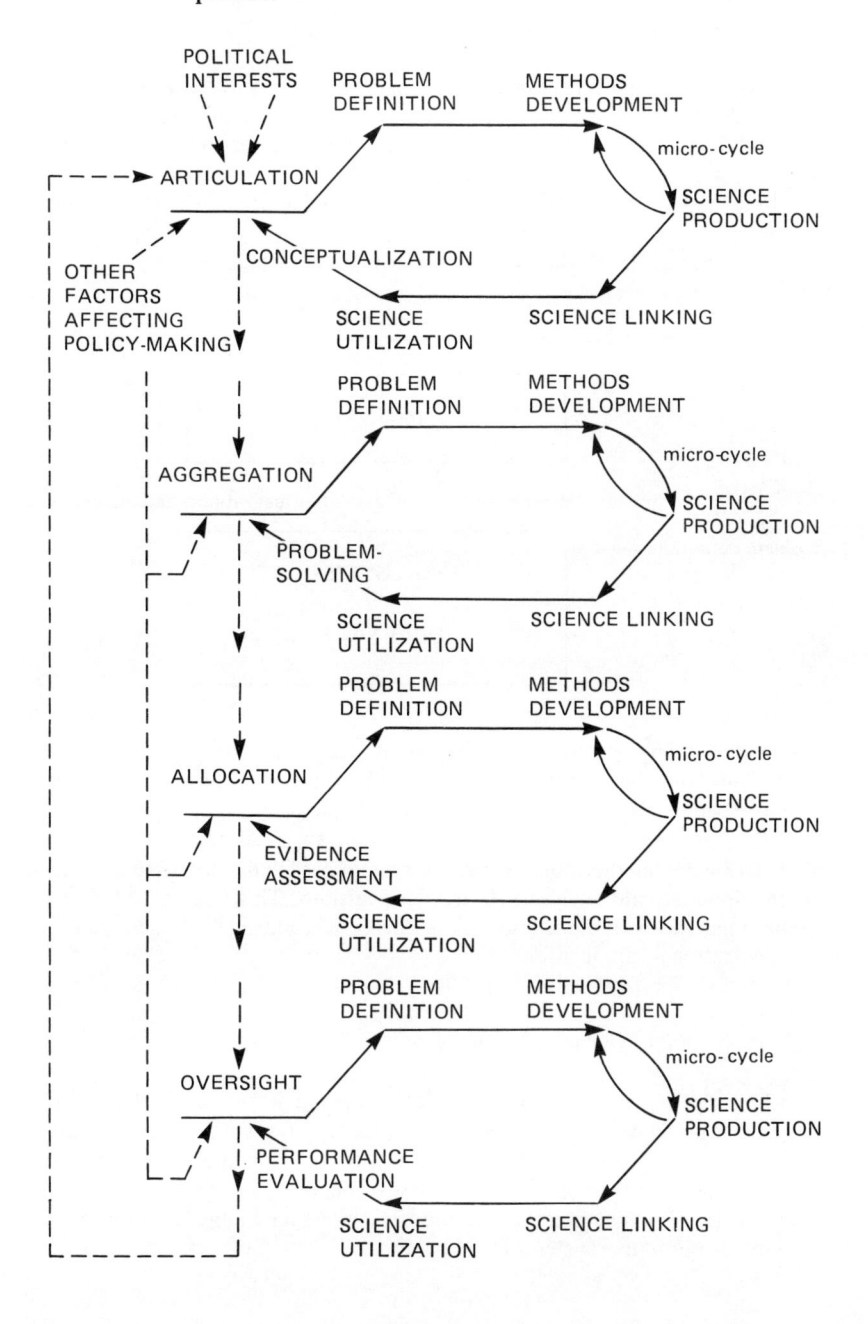

3. The micro-cycle

3.1. Model building in general

In section 1 it has been pointed out that we will apply systems theory for the study of social systems. Elsewhere we have amply discussed systems methodology (1, 3, 14, 15, 16). In this section we will summarize the most important characteristics. As mentioned before, the model cycle consists of three stages (see Fig. 4): (1) abstraction; (2) deduction; (3) realization.

Figure 4: Model cycle or empirical cycle = micro-cycle

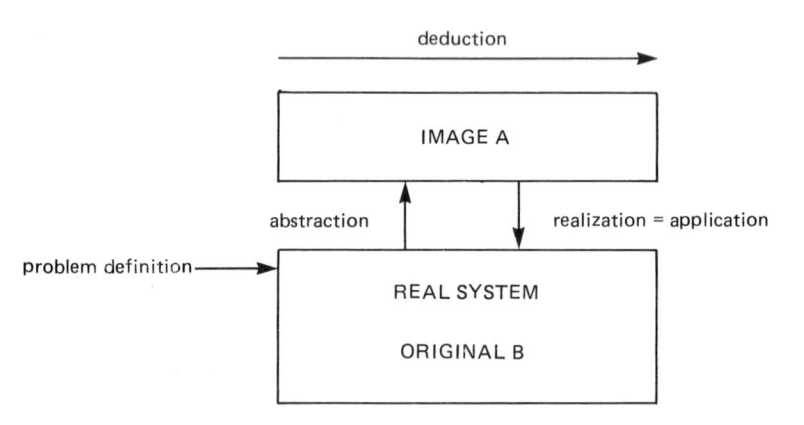

```
                          deduction
            ┌──────────────────────────────────┐
            │            IMAGE A               │
            └──────────────────────────────────┘
                  ▲                  │
           abstraction        realization = application
                  │                  ▼
problem definition ┌──────────────────────────────────┐
      ────────────▶│         REAL SYSTEM              │
                   │         ORIGINAL B               │
                   └──────────────────────────────────┘
```

While developing a model, an image A is designed from the original B. Depending on the problem definition, it is possible to decide which variables and relationships can be mapped into the image system. This selection procedure for choosing the relevant variables is defined as the abstraction. After the model or image system has been constructed, it can be manipulated and analysed to draw conclusions. This stage is called the deduction. The next stage is to verify the conclusions. This stage is called the realization or application.

3.2. Model building of social systems

This description of the model cycle leaves open a whole range of systems A, that can be used as an image, or model, of system B. As we are particularly interested in methodological aspects of analysis and synthesis of social systems from the point of view of planning and decision-making, we will restrict ourselves to the models belonging to the class of goal-seeking or normative systems (see Fig. 5).

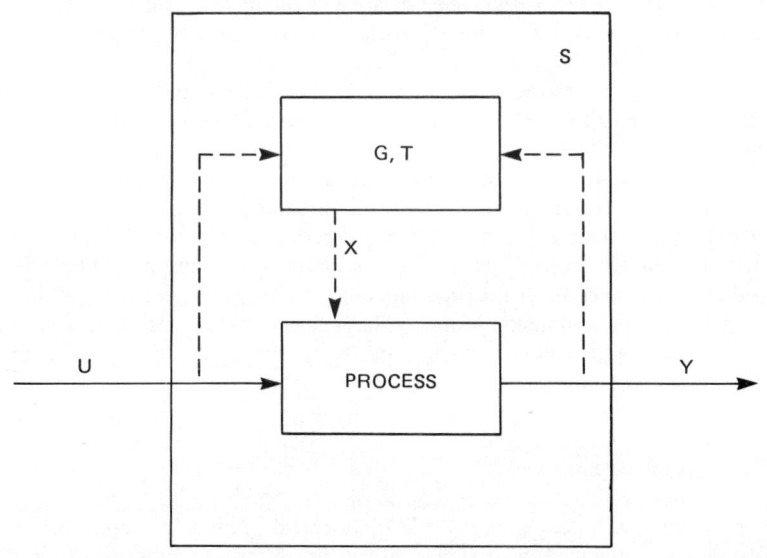

Figure 5: Normative system

[Diagram: System S containing G,T block connected via X to PROCESS block; U input as disturbance, Y output]

X : Control inputs
U : Disturbance

The behaviour of a normative system is defined by two mappings (17, 18, 19, 20):

$$G: X \times Y \longrightarrow Q;$$
  G is the goal function
$$T: U \longrightarrow \Pi(Q);$$

T is the satisfaction function, U is the disturbance set influencing the system. X is the control set, Y the output set and the product of both sets X×Y is the set of ordered pairs $\{(x,y,) \mid x \in X, y \in Y\}$. The function G is a mapping of this product set on the set Q, the value set. For each $u' \in U$ there is another $x' \in X$ such that the value of the goal function $g(x', y') = q'$ is an element of the satisfaction domain defined by T, i.e. $q' \in T(u')$. This implies that for each disturbance $u' \in U$ the system behaves in such a way that the performance, evaluated by G, is within the domain as defined by the satisfaction function T.

System S of Fig. 5 defines the characteristics of image A of Fig. 4.
  Between the original system B and the image system A a rule of corres-

pondence has to be established. This implies that important characteristics of real social systems (original B) have to be included in the image system A. In our view two features of social systems have to be taken into account: (1) complexity; (2) uncertainty.

Complexity is related to the large number of aspects that have to be considered, their interrelationships, and the many different ways in which the system can be described.

Uncertainty is a consequence of our lack of knowledge about certain aspects of the system involved, of the unpredictability of specific future events and of factors such as value judgments and political actions. In order to deal with these factors, models of social systems should be open both to influences from the environment, and to influences from within, caused by decision-making and policy-making processes. Uncertainty about systems behaviour depends partly on its complexity, partly on environmental conditions.

3.3. Hierarchical approach

For dealing with 'complexity' the hierarchical approach is appropriate. The system involved is divided into subsystems (decomposition into subsystems), which will be described and analysed subsequently. Partial solutions of subsystem problems are integrated (coordinated) by a hierarchy of decision problems in order to reach a general description and a general solution.

Applying the hierarchical approach, Mesarovic *et al.* (17) distinguish three aspects in the hierarchy of systems:

1. Strata or levels of abstraction
2. Layers or levels of decision complexity
3. Echelons or levels of action priority, i.e. organizational levels

The result of this type of decomposition of a complex system is a multi-level system with, for each level, a number of goals, i.e. a multi-level, multi-goal system.

Generally three different strata are distinguished, i.e. a casual stratum, a decision-making stratum, and a norm stratum (see Fig. 6).

The causal stratum is related to that system of activities through which the input-output processes are accomplished, e.g. material flows representing money, people, etc. In the decision-making stratum several layers can be distinguished, e.g. a goal, a policy, a strategy, and/or an implementation-layer. Finally the norm stratum is related to norms and values and the way these govern the decision-making process. Higher levels in the hierarchy deal with global and long-term decisions, while the lower levels deal with more specific and short-term decisions. Both the decision-making and the

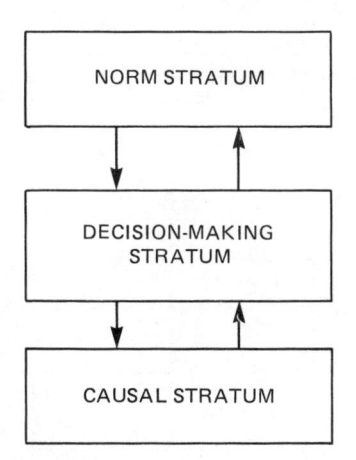

Figure 6: **Strata of a social system**

```
┌─────────────────┐
│  NORM STRATUM   │
└─────────────────┘
     │      ▲
     ▼      │
┌─────────────────┐
│ DECISION-MAKING │
│    STRATUM      │
└─────────────────┘
     │      ▲
     ▼      │
┌─────────────────┐
│ CAUSAL STRATUM  │
└─────────────────┘
```

norm stratum define the purpose of the system and consequently the system responds to influences from the environment and to influences from within the system. The causal stratum and partly the decision-making stratum can be described by mathematical models which can be simulated on a computer.

3.4. Interactive simulation

In order to be able to deal with 'uncertainty', the system described in a hierarchical way, is embedded in a so-called 'interactive simulation'. The way the strata (see Fig. 6) are mapped into an interactive simulation is shown in Fig. 7.

The most interesting characterictic of interactive simulation is that man and computer cooperate during the evolution of the system. The interactor, who can choose from a number of alternatives, observes the systems behaviour which is the result of his decisions and the structure of the causal model. After each time increment its behaviour is evaluated and if the system does not respond according to desired conditions, decisions are adjusted for the next time increment. Interactors integrate available knowledge, adapt to changing conditions and make decisions based on their knowledge, skills, norms and values. The computer program performs the logical numerical operations in a fast and efficient way. In the integrated set-up of interactive simulation man and computer represent the image system or model of the real system.

In the context of policy-oriented futures research of social systems it is important to realize that planning decisions result from complex inter-

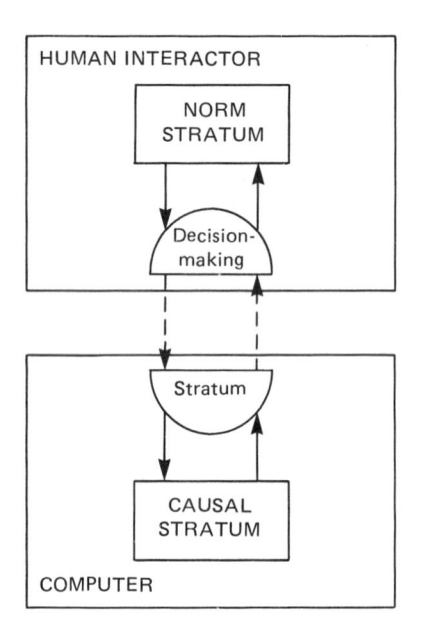

Figure 7: Diagram of interactive simulation

```
┌─────────────────────────────────┐
│ HUMAN INTERACTOR                │
│        ┌──────────┐             │
│        │  NORM    │             │
│        │ STRATUM  │             │
│        └──────────┘             │
│           │    ▲                │
│           ▼    │                │
│        ╱ Decision- ╲            │
│       ╱  making     ╲           │
│                                 │
└───────────┼────▲────────────────┘
            │    │
┌───────────┼────┼────────────────┐
│           ▼    │                │
│        ╱ Stratum ╲               │
│                                 │
│           │    ▲                │
│           ▼    │                │
│        ┌──────────┐             │
│        │  CAUSAL  │             │
│        │ STRATUM  │             │
│        └──────────┘             │
│ COMPUTER                        │
└─────────────────────────────────┘
```

actions among several groups of actors. These groups have different objectives, different modes of organization and operation, different perceptions of reality, and different degrees and kinds of power to shape events (21). Because of this quality of social systems we thought it appropriate to integrate interactive simulation with gaming simulation. Gaming simulation has proven to be a flexible approach in dealing with groups of people engaged in very different activities. With regard to the hierarchical approach mentioned earlier, gaming simulation integrated with interactive simulation enables the development of multi-echelon structures of social systems. It brings the characteristics of the image system closer to reality. Against this background we would like to stress that the method of interactive simulation integrates all-computer simulation, with strong emphasis on a rational and calibrated approach, and gaming, which is more susceptible to an intuitive and uncalibrated approach of social systems.

We are now in a position to describe the micro-cycle as shown in Fig. 4 in more detail. The description of social systems as summarized above will be used as a frame of reference. (For a more elaborate description see (16.).)

3.5. Development of an interactive simulation/game

An interactive simulation/game is developed in three stages (see Fig. 8):

1. Development of the simulation model
2. Embedding of the simulation model in an interactive simulation
3. Embedding of the interactive model in a game

Each stage provides a product that can be analysed in its own right. Stage-specific goals are listed below.

1. Goals of all-computer simulation are more related to analysis of social systems at the techno-economic level, emphasizing the quantitative aspects.

2. Goals of man-computer simulation incorporate the prior goals but also include more qualitative aspects of individual human behaviour such as transfer of information and skill concerning dynamic characteristics of the simulation model in interaction with individual strategies, the study of individual values and norms, and exploration of ways of coping with complex phenomena.

3. Goals of gaming incorporate the prior goals but are also related to interaction in and between groups; to human organizational aspects; and to communication, social learning and policy formation.

Figure 8: Structure of interactive simulation/game

stage 3:
interactive simulation/game

stage 2:
interactive simulation

stage 1:
simulation model

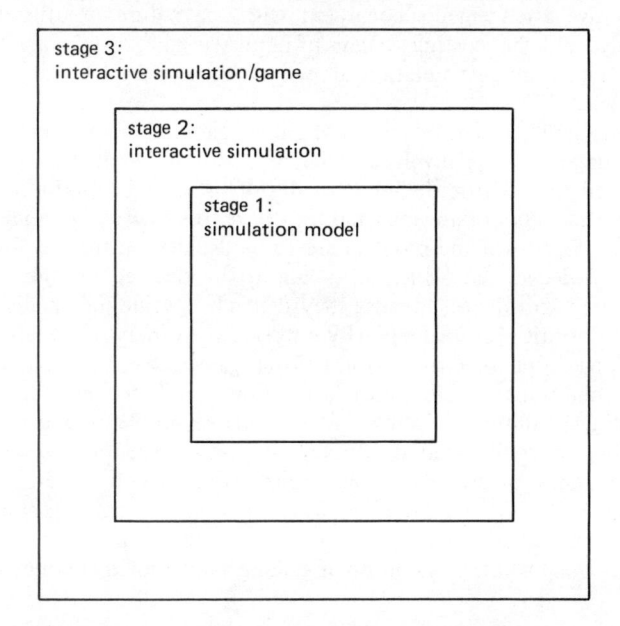

The development of an interactive simulation starts with the problem identification (problem definition) and ends with an interactive simulation/game. This instrument can be used to make deductions at three levels: (1) at the level of the simulation model; (2) at the level of the interactive simulation; (3) at the level of the interactive simulation/game. With this instrument it is possible, in a participatory mode of policy formation and planning, to engage all persons involved in policy dialogues, informed by research. A policy dialogue is a discussion about policy problems, causes, impacts and options (13).

Given these ideas related to the micro-cycle, we can now continue connecting the micro-cycle with the macro-cycle.

4. Embedding the micro-cycle in the macro-cycle

When the link between methods development and science production is considered from the point of view of design and use of simulation and gaming, in dialogue with a client-system, we have available a flexible and powerful tool that can be embedded in the policy-oriented macro-cycle. This is especially suitable in the context of important policy matters affecting a nation as a whole, to be dealt with by upper-level policy-makers.

In this regard gaming/simulation is not only able to provide specialized scientifically premised knowledge, but also and mainly to provide collaborative arrangements congruent with the nature of utilization of knowledge and the existing systems of inquiry used to acquire and process information. Gaming/simulation allows for the conceptual utilization of knowledge.

Through involvement in a series of gaming/simulations, with participants representing all groups involved in the policy-formation process, situations are created that mirror the complexities of the actual situation, assisting the policy-makers in knowing what they have to know, and in understanding which aspects of the problem are to be decided on the basis of data-based knowledge and which ones are to be decided on the basis of non-research knowledge, because they depend on value judgments and/or political priorities for example. (By stressing the variety of use of gaming/simulation, from rigid-rule to free-form games, we have paraphrased certain conditions of knowledge utilization mentioned by Caplan (6).)

Gaming/simulation is able to elucidate problem-solving, policy formation, and policy-making through the new conceptualization that it either provides or stimulates. We realize very well, however, that the potentialities of this methodology have been only partially explored and used in this regard. In the case presented later in this paper, we are exploring the possible ways of use of gaming/simulation in a policy-making context.

Now we will direct our attention to some general notions about policy-making and social systems to provide a frame reference for embedding the micro-cycle in the macro-cycle. Starting the macro-cycle with 'Problem definition' (see Fig. 2), it is important to realize that the level of policy-making is crucial to the issues involved and the way knowledge will be used i.e. either instrumental or conceptual utilization.

We assume that upper-level policy-making deals mainly with long term issues. Amara (4) mentions for example future image creation as part of the visionary component of futures research. Political ideologies belong to this domain. Dror (23) uses the term metapolicy-making. It includes:

1. processing values;
2. processing reality;
3. processing problems;
4. surveying, processing, and developing resources;
5. designing, evaluating, and redesigning the policy-making system;
6. allocating problems, values, and resources;
7. determining policy-making strategy.

On a long term basis social systems are ill-defined and poorly structured. Middle level, bureaucratic policy-making, dealing with issues on a shorter term basis than upper-level policy-making, tends to have a narrower scope. Caplan (6) states that knowledge application at this level 'involves the use of data ordered by the end user, produced by the user's agency and most often applied with a view to improving management of the agency's internal operations'. Utilizations of knowledge at this level are seen by Dror as implying:

1. suballocating resources;
2. establishing operational goals;
3. preparing a set of major alternative policies;
4. preparing reliable predictions of the significant benefits and costs of the various alternatives;
5. comparing the predicted benefits and costs of those alternatives and identifying the best;
6. evaluating the best opinions and deciding whether they are good or bad.

By shortening the timescale i.e. the time horizon for policy-making, the structure of the social systems becomes increasingly well-defined. Policy-makers focus more on improving management of the internal operations and are thus trying to reinforce or even optimize the parameters of the existing structure.

High- or upper-level policy-making in its turn tends to be less inward directed, and is more open to information from the environment of social systems and thus more apt to establish new structures to cope with changing conditions or a changing political context.

Let us assumed that a research project is set up to provide information (knowledge) to be utilized for policy-making. Now it will be clear, also from insights gained from the links between research and policy-making (see Figs. 2 and 3), that it is important to know:

1. For what level of policy-making will the results (instruments) be suitable i.e. upper- and/or middle-level of policy-making?
2. In what phase will the policy-making process be when the product of research becomes available?
   (the product can be: one or more interactive simulation/games; results from statistical analysis etc.)

Depending on the level and phase of the policy-making process, the first step of the macro-cycle will have a quite different content and meaning.

As a consequence the start and progress of designing an interactive simulation/game may be rather different. The final product may be very different as regards form and content. As a result the linking and utilization of knowledge will probably follow different routes. However, the methodology discussed in section 3, dealing with the micro-cycle provides the necessary flexibility for adapting the system.

From the point of view of the two levels of policy-making the need for knowledge may be caused by very distinct 'interpretative contexts' — Michael (24) points out that the interpretative context is formed by the beliefs, policies and programmes at the different levels in the social system. It determines what is important in the (enacted) environment, and consequently what is important within the system to respond to it. Because of this it is selective and value-laden.

Looking at question 1, let us assume that the macro-cycle is started with the problem definition at the middle level of policy-making. It seems reasonable to assume that the structure of the social system involved is considered to be set. Because of the ongoing administrative and information processing activities, more decisions tend to become a matter of routine. As policies and programmes are rather well-defined within that structure, the interpretative context has also been established fairly well.

Looking at such a social system from the point of view of the strata mentioned earlier (see Fig. 6) it is also reasonable to assume that the causal stratum and in part the decision-making stratum are well-defined. An interactive simulation/game based on such a system follows fairly fixed procedures for designing and conducting the game, in accordance with the real situation. Such an interactive simulation/game will be classified as a rigid-rule game. The aim of a rigid/rule game in general is improving or reinforcing the existing structure of the social system, independent of whether the game is used for educational, research or practical purposes.

Next let us assume that the macro-cycle starts with problem definition at the upper-level of policy-making. At this level the structure of the social system involved is assumed to be poorly defined. Policy-making at this level is concerned with establishing notions of acceptable structures and arranging procedures and conditions for the society of tomorrow. The interpretative context is only vaguely known (fuzzy), and so consequently are the 'ins-and-outs' of the system. We consider the structure of none of the strata well-defined. An interactive simulation/game based on such a situation follows a fairly open procedure for designing and conducting the same, also in accordance with the real situation. Such an interactive simulation/game will be classified as a free form game or frame game. The aim of a free form game is to establish a right or satisfying structure, whether for educational, research or practical purposes. Through the use of a frame game or a free form game the interpretative context of the social system, for the long term, may be established.

In both situations mentioned above, it should be stressed that the systems approach and the method of interactive simulation are methods of inquiry rather than tools *per se*.

As for the two questions mentioned earlier, we will now consider question 2, i.e. the possible connection between the phase of the policy-making process and the possibly fruitful use of an interactive simulation/game (see also Fig. 3). During the articulation-phase, the macro-cycle should provide knowledge to enhance the conceptualization of the problem. In this respect the design and use of free form games seems to us the most appropriate. During the aggregation phase when groups involved focus on problem-solving, rigid rule games seem to be more suitable. It should be stressed that in both cases the gaming aspect i.e. communication within and between groups of policy-makers is most important. When a policy-making process enters the allocation phase, rigid rule games will be useful, but emphasis may be placed more upon the simulation part of the game for example to perform cost-benefit analysis. If gaming/simulation is applied in the context of policy-making to us its use seems most suitable during these three stages.

Looking at the macro-cycle, see Figs. 2 and 3, we would like to elaborate on one feature of gaming/simulation that is important for linking and utilizing knowledge and insights from the game to the user, i.e. policy-making system. One of the main results of systems research in general, and gaming/simulation in particular, is that the research team develops a systems view or *Gestalt* in which the relation between state description (structure) and process description (function) can be clearly articulated. A major problem is how that systems perspective can be communicated to the user, who usually lacks the time, skill and/or motivation to become familiar with the 'image system' i.e. the model and its behaviour. To make the linking and utilization as effective as possible, an interactive simulation/game should allow for the following functions (25):

1. Educational function, including
   - demonstrational function, i.e. concepts, principles, methods etc.,
   - training functions, i.e. training skills, teaching (social) problem-solving,
   - motivational function i.e. involving people in the educational process;
2. Research function – formulation of theories – including
   - heuristic function,
   - verification function,
   - formalization function;
3. Operational function, including
   - analytical function, i.e. analysis of organizational structure, policy-making processes, etc.,
   - planning function,
   - experimental function, i.e. experiments with elements of the planning process.

In this regard, interactive simulation/gaming is not only an instrument for analysis, but at the same time an instrument for communicating a systems perspective in a client- rather than method-oriented mode. This will be illustrated as follows.

In an interactive simulation/game participants become directly involved in simulating a part of social reality. Participants as well as the computer imitate (simulate) a particular social system. Doing this is for the participants not only a matter of cognitive skills, but also of exchanging prior experience and knowledge, based to some extent on intuition and beliefs. While interacting with the computer, participants also communicate with each other, within and between groups. Every participant and every group involved develops an image of the system, relying both on instrumental and conceptual information. Because of social interaction during the game, the image of the system is much richer, and has more gradations, than would be the case after reading a 'technical report' of the research. After reading a technical report, there is still no guarantee that the user (policy-maker) has gained experience in using the respective information and knowledge, and that he knows how to translate the results into long range policies or daily decisions. To us it seems like reading about how to drive a car, which may be a necessary but insufficient condition for actually driving a car to reach a specific goal or destination. In this context an interactive simulation/game is more suitable. At the middle level of policy-making it means better insight into the qualities of the existing structure of the social system, at the upper level of policy-making it means better insight into the qualities of new structures and their possible consequences for members of the system i.e. citizens, professional policy-makers, action groups etc.

As the body of knowledge of social systems consists of both scientific and commonsense knowledge, interactive simulation makes it possible to confront them with each other. The more fruitful this confrontation is with respect to social problem-solving (of which policy-making is a part) the more effective will be the linking process.

At this stage in the cycle a plan of actions and interventions can be drawn up to create better conditions within the existing structure, or to design acceptable new structures for the future. In doing so the linking and utilization function are connected to each other.

The macro-cycle as presented above represents research as a process of continuous learning, evaluation and modification, although this does not imply that it is a linear, sequential process. With regard to policy-making however this observation does not apply most of the time. Different contexts, different political paradigms will arrange and shape reality in different ways. The findings of research can be fruitful in one context, threatening in another.

5. Summary

In the foregoing an outline has been drawn of policy-oriented research based upon a theory of social systems. Interactive simulation/gaming has been presented as a flexible method of inquiry and as a mode of communicating complex social phenomena enabling to be included both instrumental and conceptual utilization of knowledge. The macro-cycle has been discussed as a frame of reference for connecting research and scientific knowledge to the subsequent phases of the policy-making process. Emphasis is placed upon the design of instruments for policy-formation and policy-making.

In the following section a research project is introduced that is in progress at the moment. In this project the general ideas, (software) tools, and experience of social systems research outlined above, are being applied. The design, organizational structure and progress made since its inception in September 1980, will be described.

6. Case: a study of the Dutch educational system (preliminary report)

In this section we will discuss briefly the design of the product, its background, its organization, and its progress. As the project has not been running for long, we are only able to discuss the first step in the macro-cycle i.e. the link between problem definition and method development.

In the Netherlands governmental policy-making has been subdivided into distinct societal sectors. Different ministries are responsible for each of the sectors. It is being recognized however that the current sectoral division is not the most suitable to deal with all circumstances. Not all societal problems fit neatly in existing compartments. Policy-making within each sector has to take into account two problem areas. One is related to the complex internal structure of each sector, the other to the environment of each sector i.e. the other sectors. Policy-makers realize that they lack insight into the functioning of each of the sectors, and the way they are interrelated. What is missing is a so-called (societal) systems perspective (1). Policy-makers have started looking for research to enhance and support policy-formation and implementation. Many of them however are disappointed by the contributions of the social sciences. A number of suggestions have been made to improve the relationship between social science research and public policy-making. Analysis of many of the problems and measures to improve the existing situation form part of the following categories:

— research,
— policy-making,
— interface research/policy-making.

Research

Analytical thinking is still a dominant force in the area of scientific research. Ackoff (26) points out that it is a natural complement of the doctrine of reductionism i.e. the mental process by which anything to be explained is broken down into its component parts. Accordingly the organization of scientific research consists of sub-subdisciplines studying the properties of the parts independently. Phenomena related to the behaviour of the parts are described within the frame of reference of a particular subdiscipline. Synthesis of partial knowledge from subdisciplinary research into an integrated body of knowledge is lacking. The way scientific research is budgeted reinforces this situation.

As a result social science research is too much research- and method-oriented. Therefore it is too little conclusion- and decision-oriented. Several governmental committees, surveying the situation, have formulated the following complaints about the social sciences: (27)

1. Frequently results of social science research cannot be generalized.
2. Most research is of little relevance: important problems are not being investigated adequately, or not studied at all.
3. Fundamental and applied research are out of touch with one another.
4. Research is too descriptive.
5. Research focuses too much on methods and techniques with only marginal attention being paid to the problem itself.

Conclusion: the contributions of the social sciences to social problem-solving are inadequate!

Policy-making

Policy-formation faces the following difficulties:

1. Because of the pressure coming from society, policy-makers are inclined to direct their attention to *ad hoc* problems, without asking themselves whether they are looking at symptoms or fundamental problems. They tend to be 'snowed under', and lack the time for reflection. Research based on such a problem-identification will have the same *ad hoc* characteristic.
2. Government policies are not 'stable' for long periods of time (28). New coalitions, changes in the economy, changes in public opinion cause adjustments and shifts in the policy-making processes. Traditional empirical research is not well equipped to adapt to these changes. Once a project has started, it unrolls according to a fixed plan without checking whether the plan is still appropriate.
3. Policy-makers tend not to make explicit their assumptions about the system within which they are working. This hampers communication. Information that does not fit into the implicit frames of reference is excluded.

These problems apply to all sectors, including the educational sector. As the educational system in the Netherlands has changed dramatically in the last fifteen years, the load placed upon policy-makers in this sector has increased considerably. What is lacking is a comprehensive view of the educational system. This not only hinders the development of a long-term government policy, but also the development of any long-term research policy for educational research.

Interface research/policy-making:

Problems at the interface result mainly from differences in expectations between the two sides (29). Even when expectations correspond, there is still a communication gap. The two parties use different languages i.e. different concepts and different ways of reasoning, with respect to the same problem area. The two parties have different ideas of the realizability of research. Proposals to facilitate communication between research and policy-making do not take account of the distinction between the role of researcher and policy-maker or the appropriate form of knowledge transfer. Researchers produce reports, and also comment upon and illustrate them in discussion. Reports are often bulky, and written in highly technical language. Even if the policy-maker takes time to study a report thoroughly, two problems arise:

1. On the basis of the text, the policy-maker must reconstruct the image the researcher had in mind.
2. After reconstructing this image, he must be able to transfer it to his own situation. He must be able to estimate how the results, if implemented, would alter the dynamic characteristics of the system. Instruments to facilitate and improve the process of understanding are usually not provided with the technical report.

Conclusion: the quality of the interface research/policy-making, and thus communication between representatives of both groups, is insufficient. In this context, the aim of the project is:

1. To provide a comprehensive view, based on scientific research of the educational system which will be easily accessible to policy-makers.
2. To develop an instrument that will show policy-makers the possible consequences of intended policies.
3. To develop an instrument that can make explicit different conceptions of the educational system.

To recapitulate on both the macro- and micro-cycle, interactive simulation will be used, with emphasis on its heuristic nature for problem-oriented research.

Project organization

The project organization consists of the following groups:

1. the research team;
2. a steering committee;
3. an advisory committee;
4. the financier.

THE RESEARCH TEAM
The project team consists of a project coordinator, a software specialist, mainly responsible for development and application of the method of interactive simulation, a specialist in developing quantitative mathematical models, and a specialist in qualitative mathematical models. If necessary, *ad hoc* specialists can be contracted on a short term basis.

A STEERING COMMITTEE
The steering committee is composed of the highest level of professionals within the government. Its main task is to formulate the problem at the start of the project, and to be responsible for dissemination and implementation of results.

AN ADVISORY COMMITTEE
The advisory committee consists of representatives from the staff of members of the steering committee. During the course of the project the advisory committee provides a forum for discussion on the content of the model(s), and policy options available. The committee is mainly responsible for the linking process.

THE FINANCIER
The project is financed by the Foundation for Educational Research in the Netherlands (SVO) and by the Foundation for the Advancement of Futures Research (BEWETON) for an initial period of two years.

First stage: Linking problem definition with methods development

During this stage two approaches have been used (15):

1. a top-down approach;
2. a bottom-up approach.

Both approaches take into account the way social systems are described (see Fig. 6) and the mapping of such a description into the design of an interactive simulation/game (see Fig. 7). The frame for the design process is presented in Fig. 9.

THE TOP-DOWN APPROACH
Since its start in September 1980, considerable effort has been put into identification of current and future bottlenecks with respect to the educational system, its internal dynamics and one relevant environment i.e. the labour market. The project team assumed that it was reasonable to start with the problem definition at the upper level of policy-making, in view of the composition of the steering committee. From the point of view of the frame of an interactive simulation/game, the main focus was on the subject matter (see Fig. 9). An adapted version of the delphi-technique was used to identify and describe important issues related to current and future developments of the educational system as seen by the members of the steering committee. After arranging the information provided by the steering committee, six problem areas or major issues were identified from which one had to be chosen. The search for the most suitable problem area was facilitated by the bottom-up approach.

THE BOTTOM-UP APPROACH
Whereas the top-down approach starts with the vertex 'problem definition', the bottom-up approach starts with 'methods development' (Fig. 2). From this point of view it was important to gain insight into the available

Figure 9: Frame of interactive simulation/game

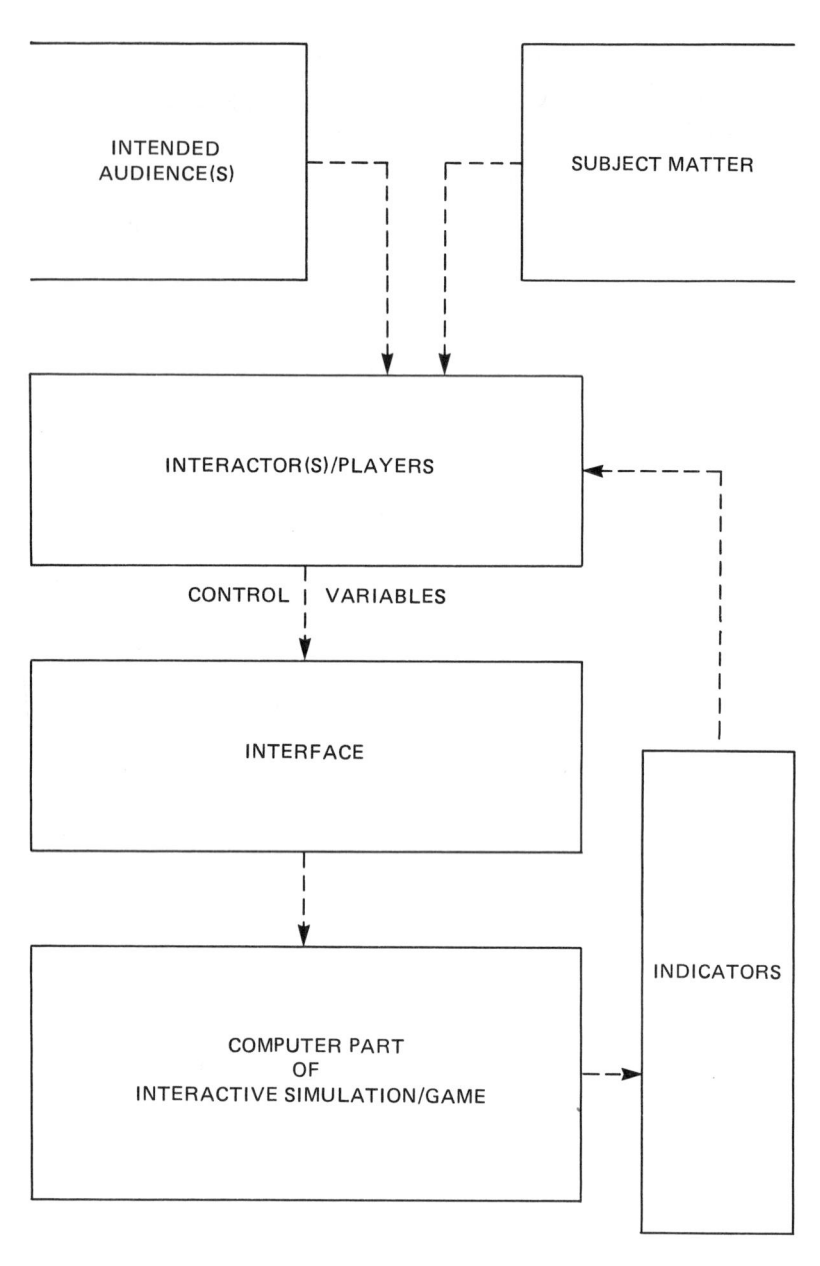

```
┌─────────────────────┐        ┌─────────────────────┐
│                     │        │                     │
│     INTENDED        │───┐  ┌─│   SUBJECT MATTER    │
│    AUDIENCE(S)      │   │  │ │                     │
│                     │   │  │ │                     │
└─────────────────────┘   │  │ └─────────────────────┘
                          ▼  ▼
              ┌───────────────────────────┐
              │                           │
              │   INTERACTOR(S)/PLAYERS   │◄──────┐
              │                           │       │
              └───────────────────────────┘       │
                    CONTROL │ VARIABLES           │
                            ▼                     │
              ┌───────────────────────────┐       │
              │                           │       │
              │        INTERFACE          │       │
              │                           │       │
              └───────────────────────────┘       │
                            │              ┌──────┴──┐
                            ▼              │         │
              ┌───────────────────────────┐│INDICATORS│
              │                           ││         │
              │     COMPUTER PART         ││         │
              │         OF                │┘         │
              │ INTERACTIVE SIMULATION/GAME├──►      │
              │                           │         │
              └───────────────────────────┘─────────┘
```

educational data, to see from what data-base model development could begin. As both the Netherlands Central Bureau of Statistics and the Netherlands Central Planning Bureau participate in the steering committee, access to and cooperation with both bureaus has been most fruitful. In November and December 1980 a first interactive model was designed, running on a PDP-11, describing the flow of students through a number of types of schools. Some interesting results, showing some bottlenecks emerging over time, have been fed back to the steering committee. In terms of the frame (see Fig. 9), the bottom-up approach started with the specification of the computer part and the description of the indicators relevant to the behaviour of the educational system.

The process of coupling both approaches over time resulting in the specification of the design of the interactive simulation/game is shown in Figs. 10–13 (see appendix). It is important to note that the definition of the subject matter, i.e. issue or problem definition, was the last step in the specification for the design of the interactive simulation/game.

PROBLEM AREA

The problem area on which the project will focus is the introduction of the comprehensive school system in the Netherlands in this decade. This structural change on which a political decision will be made around 1984/1985 is causing many, and sometimes, hot debates not only on purely educational but also on political and ideological matters. With regard to the introduction of the comprehensive school it is expected that by early 1983 policy-making will be in the aggregation phase, see Fig. 3. The expected results from this project i.e. the INTOM-interactive simulation/game, will, we hope, be utilized to deal with some of the following problems:

- Will a one-track or a two-track educational system be appropriate, i.e. one comprehensive school or a comprehensive school with parallel options offered by the current system?
- Will there be a change in the demand and supply of teachers as regards quantity and qualification?
- What costs will be involved with regard to personnel, school buildings, etc.?

During the development stage of the interactive simulation/game new problems will certainly emerge with regard to the introduction of the comprehensive school. We hope to be able to adapt the progress of the research as much as possible to these circumstances.

As several distinct audiences will engage in simulation and gaming sessions, either independently or in joint sessions, the interfacing of these groups of players with the computer part will be amenable to last minute adjustments, depending on the needs of the groups of players and/or the purposes of the project team in running a particular session.

7. Concluding remarks

Because of the problems related to the interface research/policy-making (see section 6), a straightforward problem definition should not be expected. Rather, a laborious search will be required. Three key questions can help in this respect: (1) What are the model specifications i.e. what are the relevant input, output and control variables? (2) What are the intended audiences? (3) What is the subject matter (see Fig. 9)? As interactive simulation/gaming acknowledges three levels of use (see Fig. 8), three intended audiences can be distinguished who will look at the subject matter from different points of view.

It is assumed that 'problem definition' is partly a process of increasing awareness of the characteristics of the system involved. The more explicit are the assumptions underlying the interactive simulation, the better the instrument is able to promote discussion of the problem definition, future-image creation etc.

The iterative process of problem definition and method development, presupposes that the latter is flexible. The modelling process should be seen as an unfolding process. One of the most crucial conditions for meeting this requirement is that the software for adjusting the structure of the model and its database should be flexible, without requiring specialist skill in interactive communication with the computer.

The members of the steering committee who are not used to the technicalities of computers should also be able to use the interactive simulation without difficulty. One of the main efforts of our research since 1974 has been the development of the method of interactive simulation in such a way as to meet this standard (30, 31). Although it may seem superfluous, it should be stressed that an interactive simulation/game is a flexible instrument to improve the policy-making process. It will never be a replacement for policy-making. Finally, the more policy-making takes place in a climate of 'interactive planning' (26), the more fruitful will be the approach discussed in this paper.

References

1. KLABBERS, J.H.G. (1980). *The future as a game.* (in Dutch). Leyden: University Press.
2. BOUCHER, W.I. (1977). 'Introduction'. In: BOUCHER, W.I., *The Study of the Future: An Agenda for Research.* Washington DC: US Government, Printing Office, Superintendent of Documents.
3. KLABBERS, J.H.G. (1975). 'General System Theory and Social Systems: a methodology for the social sciences'. *Ned. Tijdschrift voor de Psychologie*, 30, pp. 493–514.
4. AMARA, R. (1977). 'The Futures Field: Functions, Forms and

Critical Issues.' In: BOUCHER, W.I. *The Study of the Future* (see ref. 2).
5. LINDBLOM, C.E. and COHEN, D.K. (1979). *Usable Knowledge: Social Science and Social Problem Solving.* New Haven, Conn: Yale University Press.
6. CAPLAN, N. (1981). Social Research and Public Policy at the National Level. Invited paper for the SVO-Workshop on Educational Research and Public Policy Making, May 20–22, 1981, The Hague, The Netherlands.
7. CAPLAN, N. (1980). 'What do we know about knowledge utilization?' *New Directions for Program Evaluation*, 5, pp. 1–10.
8. CAPLAN, N. (1976). 'Social Research and National Policy: what gets used, by whom, for what purpose, and with what effects?' *International Social Science Journal*, XXVIII, 1.
9. WEISS, C.H. (1981). Policy Research in the Context of Diffuse Decision Making. Invited paper for the SVO-Workshop on Educational Research and Public Policy Making, May 20–22, 1981, The Hague, The Netherlands.
10. WEISS, C.H. (1980). Three terms in Search for Reconceptualization: Knowledge, Utilization, and Decision-Making. Paper prepared for Conference on Political Realization of Social Science Knowledge, Vienna, Austria, June 18–20.
11. REIN, M. (1980). 'Methodology for the study of the interplay between social science and social policy,' *International Social Science Journal*, XXXII, 2.
12. WEICK, K.E. (1979). *The social psychology of organizing.* London: Addison Wesley.
13. MITCHELL, D.E. (1980). 'Social Science Impact on Legislative Decision Making: Process & Substance', *Educational Researcher*, 9, 10.
14. KLABBERS, J.H.G. (1975). 'Interactive Simulation: on-line interaction between man and machine for the study and management of social systems', *Informatie*, 17, nr. 10, pp. 535–60.
15. KLABBERS, J.H.G. (1979). 'The process of modelbuilding and analysis of social systems,' *Progress in Cybernetics and Systems Research*, IV. Washington DC: Hemisphere Publ. Corp.
16. KLABBERS, J.H.G., VAN DER HIJDEN, P.P., HOEFNAGELS, K. and TRUIN, G.J. (1980). 'Development of an interactive simulation game: a case study of DENTIST,' *Simulation and Games*, 11, 1, pp. 59–86.
17. MESAROVIC, M.D., MACKO, D. and TAKAHARA, Y. (1970). *Theory of Hierarchical, Multilevel Systems.* NY: Academic Press.
18. MESAROVIC, M.D. (1967). General Systems Theory and its Mathematical Foundation, IEEE Conference, Boston, Mass. (11–13 October 1967).
19. MESAROVIC, M.D. (1968). 'Systems Theory and Biology-View of a Theoretician.' In: MESAROVIC, M.D. (ed.) *Systems Theory and Biology.* NY: Springer-Verlag.
20. MESAROVIC, M.D. (1972). 'Conceptual basis for a mathematical theory of general systems', *Kybernetes* 1, pp. 35–40.

21. HALL, P. (1980). 'Great planning disasters. What lessons do they hold?' *Futures*, 12, 1, pp. 45–50.
22. LAMSON, R.W. (1978). Policy dialogues: a key to solving the problems we face while increasing America's capacity for self-government. Washington DC: National Science Foundation.
23. DROR, Y. (1968). *Public Policy Making Reexamined.* San Franscisco: Chandler.
24. MICHAEL, D.M. (1975). On growth and the limits of organizational responsiveness. Limits to Growth '75 Conference, October 29, The Woodlands, Texas.
25. STAHL, I. (1980). The use of operational gaming as an aid in policy formulation and implementation. Collaborative Paper CP-80-6, IIASA, Laxenburg, Austria.
26. ACKOFF, R. (1974). *Redesigning the Future.* New York: Wiley.
27. Planning Social Research and Policy-making. (in Dutch). Documents for the Second Chamber, session 1977–1978, 15 043, nrs. 1–2.
28. Reports of the Committee Educational Research, and the Committee Social Research in Dutch).
29. FOUNDATION FOR EDUCATIONAL RESEARCH IN THE NETHERLANDS (1976). Programming Educational Research: a frame of reference for the programming of research in the context of the goals of the Foundation. (in Dutch). SVO/Staatsuitgeverij, SVO Publications 1.
30. VAN DER HIJDEN, P.P. (1978). 'The Method of Interactive Simulation', *Proc. of the 1978 UKSC Conf. on Computer Simulation, Chester, England.* Guildford, Surrey, England: IPC Science and Technology Press.
31. VAN DER HIJDEN, P.P. and KLABBERS, J.H.G. (1978). Report of the project Interactive Simulation, Social Systems Research Group, University of Nijmegen, SSRG 78 10, The Netherlands.

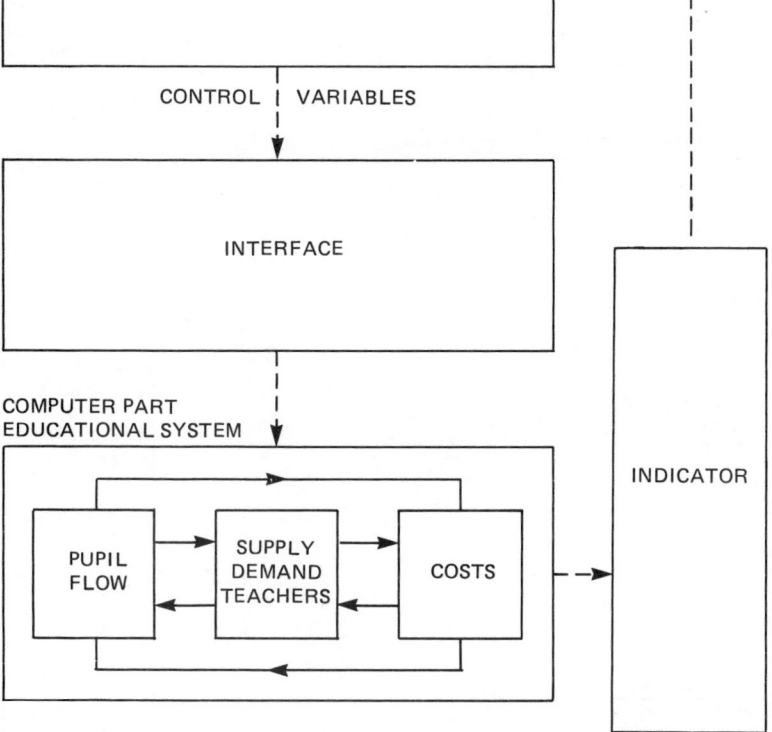

Appendix: Subsequent phases in the specification of the interactive simulation/game dealing with the Dutch educational system

Figure 10: Structure of simulation model

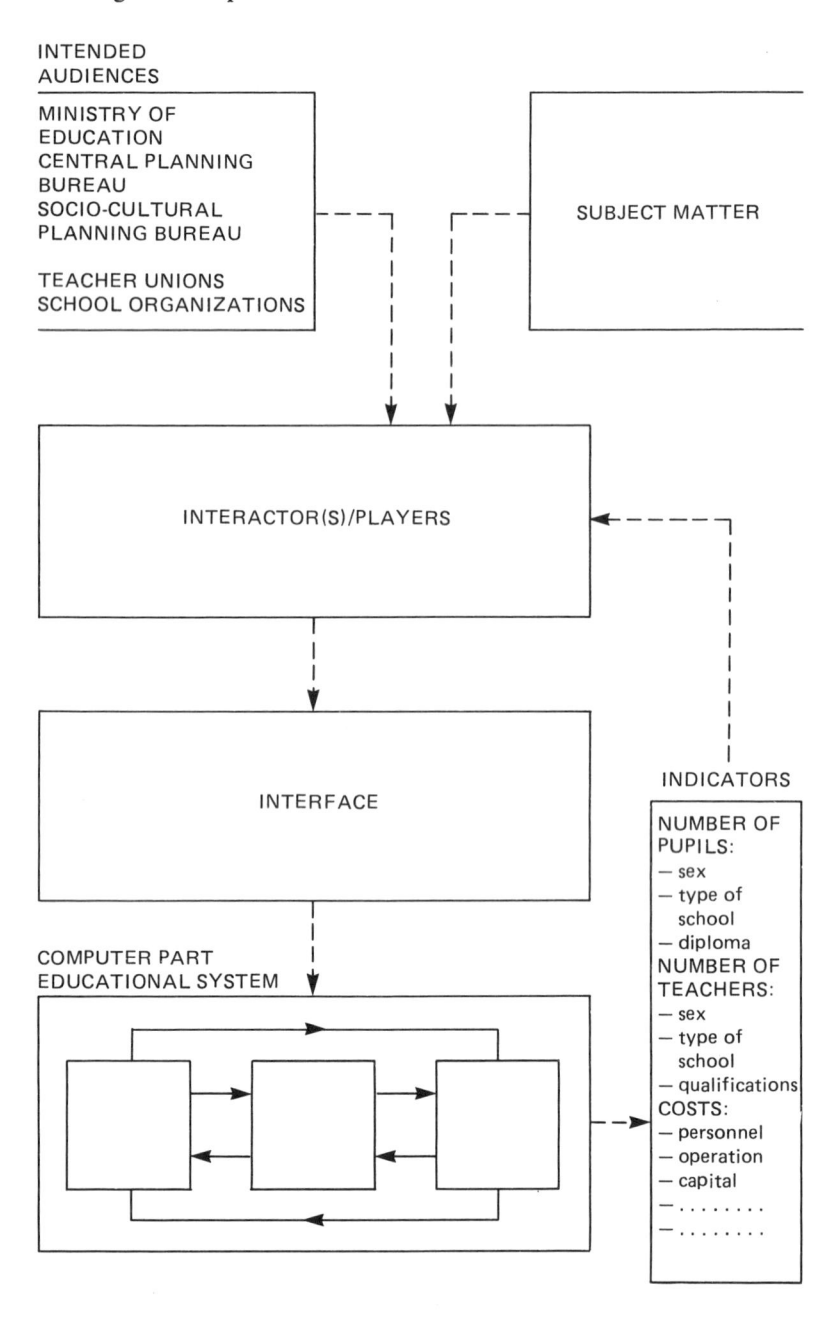

Figure 11: Specification of intended audiences and indicators

INTENDED AUDIENCES

MINISTRY OF EDUCATION
CENTRAL PLANNING BUREAU
SOCIO-CULTURAL PLANNING BUREAU

TEACHER UNIONS
SCHOOL ORGANIZATIONS

SUBJECT MATTER

INTERACTOR(S)/PLAYERS

INTERFACE

COMPUTER PART
EDUCATIONAL SYSTEM

INDICATORS

NUMBER OF PUPILS:
— sex
— type of school
— diploma
NUMBER OF TEACHERS:
— sex
— type of school
— qualifications
COSTS:
— personnel
— operation
— capital
— ....
— ....

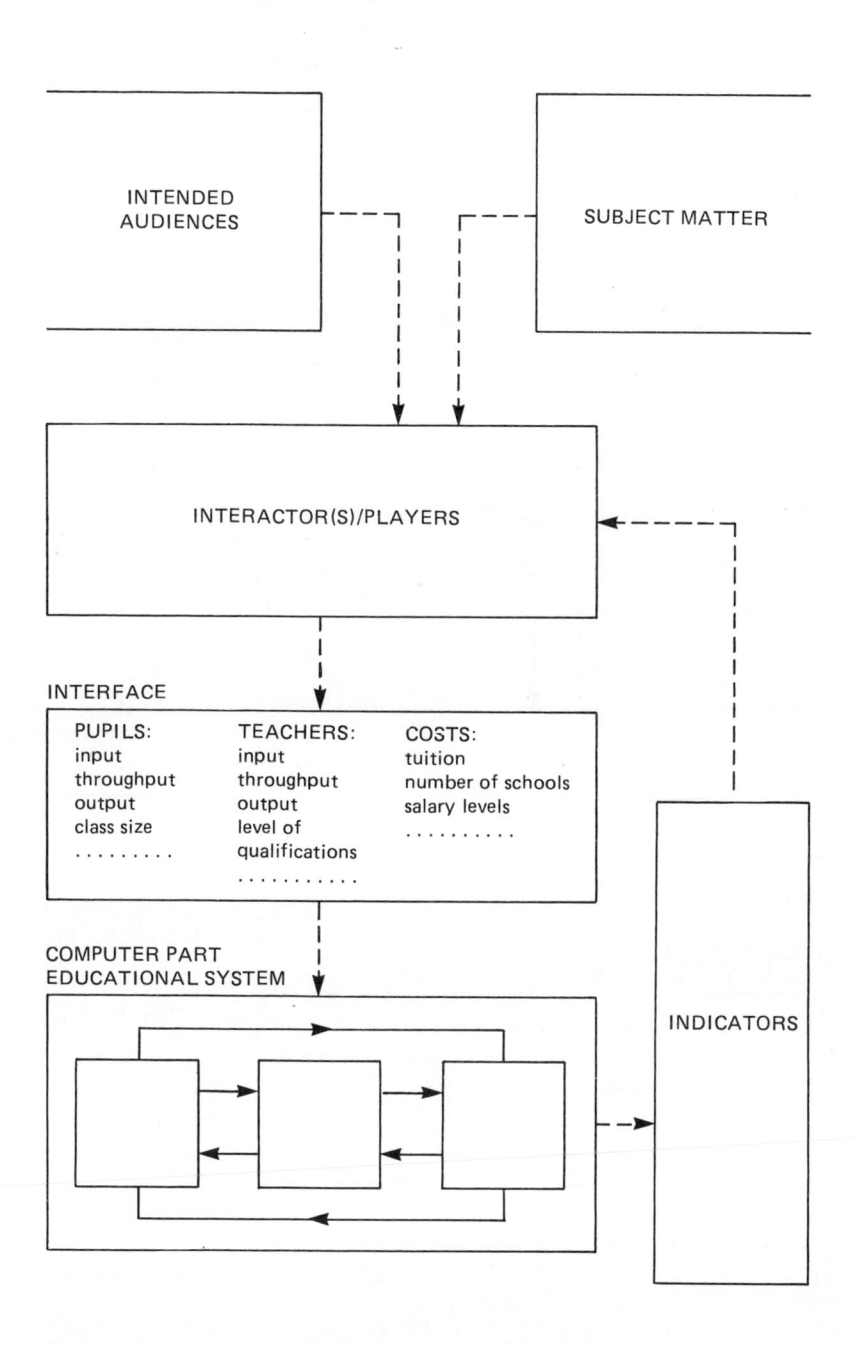

Figure 12: Specification of interface

Figure 13: Specification of subject matter

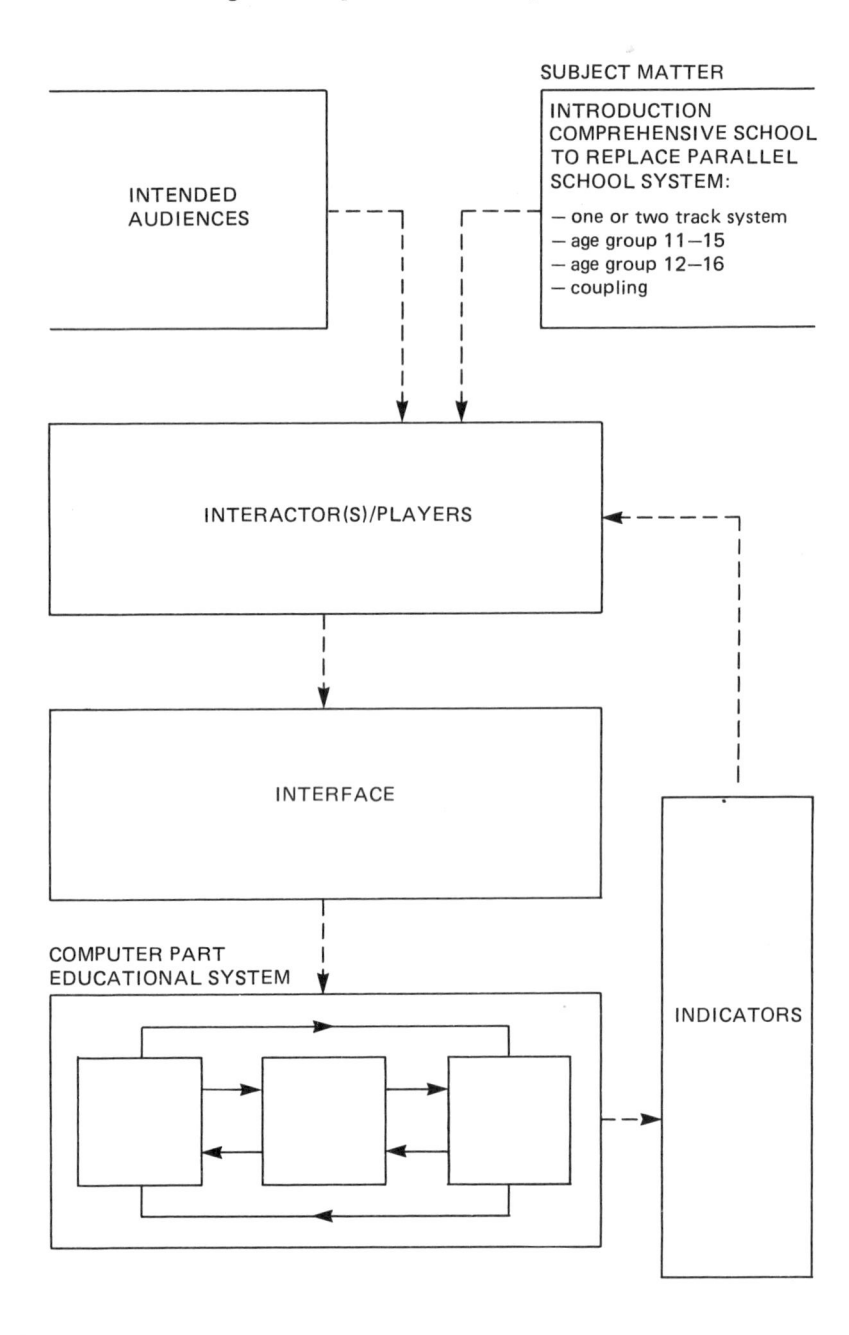

SUBJECT MATTER

INTRODUCTION COMPREHENSIVE SCHOOL TO REPLACE PARALLEL SCHOOL SYSTEM:
— one or two track system
— age group 11–15
— age group 12–16
— coupling

INTENDED AUDIENCES

INTERACTOR(S)/PLAYERS

INTERFACE

COMPUTER PART EDUCATIONAL SYSTEM

INDICATORS

Statements

1. The aim of middle-level policy-making is more in the nature of optimizing the parameters of the existing structure, while the aim of upper-level policy-making is more directed to establishing new structures.
2. Gaming/simulation should take into account these levels of policy-making. An operational game is more suitable for middle-levels of policy-making, a frame game is more suitable for upper-levels of policy-making.
3. A client i.e. policy-maker usually lacks the time, skill and/or motivation to become familiar with the simulation (model) and its behaviour.
4. An interactive simulation/game is not only an instrument for analysis, but also an instrument for communicating a systems perspective in a client rather than method-oriented mode.
5. After reading a technical report, there is no guarantee that the user (policy-maker) has gained experience in using the respective information and knowledge, and that he/she knows how to translate the results into long range policies or daily decisions.
6. Policy-making and planning are processes of continuous, although not linear, incremental learning, evaluation and modification. Policy-makers are willing to take advantage of scientific knowledge of social systems to improve the policy-making process.
7. Synthesis of partial knowledge from subdisciplinary research into an integrated body of knowledge is lacking. The way scientific research is budgeted reinforces this situation. It especially hampers progress and utilization of the social sciences.
8. The quality of the interface research/(public) policy-making, and thus of communication between representatives of the two groups, is insufficient.
9. Problem definition is partly a process of growing awareness of the characteristics of the system involved. The more explicit are the assumptions underlying the interactive simulation/game, the better the instrument is able to stimulate the discussion on problem definition, future image creation etc.
10. Interactive simulation/gaming facilitates the combining of analytical and interactive problem-solving. It elucidates problem-solving (policy-making) through the new conceptualization that it either provides or stimulates (see: LINDBLOM, C.E. and COHEN, D.K. (1979). *Usable Knowledge*. London: Yale University Press; p. 77).

CRITICISM AND DISCUSSION

Note by the editors:
The method of 'interactive simulation gaming' appeared somewhat of a novelty to many participants. Most speakers said they found Klabbers' exposé difficult to comprehend, largely because of its abstract presentation. Klabbers' oral introduction dealt satisfactorily with most of these objections. His lecture is included in this volume in a new improved version which incorporates most of the original text.

1. Essential characteristics of interactive simulation

Klabbers' oral presentation during the Workshop clarified some essential aspects of Interactive Simulation: It is amongst other things a communication device and to a lesser degree a planning procedure. Klabbers stressed that he 'did not expect an interactive simulation as such, to be a replacement or a direct tool for planning itself'. He sees it much more as 'something like a communication or pre-decision tool, an instrument for assessment, for diagnosis, rather than for planning'. Furthermore, it was stressed that interactive simulation is a combination of quantitative and qualitative modelling. 'The qualitative or, one might say "conceptual aspects", are mainly included by means of the players involved in running the game.' The players 'integrate available knowledge, adapt to changing conditions and make decisions based on their knowledge, skills, norms and values'. The quantitative data are stored in the computer. In Klabbers' paper (par. 3.3.) it becomes clear that man and computer cooperate in such a way that players are confronted with possible consequences of intended policies, while at the same time their conceptions with regard to the (in this case educational) system become explicit. Klabbers feels that this combination of quantitative aspects with gaming aspects 'is a better representation of reality than is a major model itself, because it integrates also the evaluation of human beings in interaction with data'.

Klabbers' project 'development of an interactive simulation model for the Dutch educational system' was commissioned by the Foundation for Educational Research in the Netherlands (**SVO**) and the Dutch Social Science Council (**SWR**) of the Royal Academy of Arts and Sciences. It was set up with three goals in mind: to provide a comprehensive view of the educational system, to develop an instrument that offers policymakers and other interested parties the opportunity to show possible consequences of intended policies, and, third, to develop an instrument that can make explicit different conceptions regarding the educational system. With these three goals in mind, Klabbers and his co-workers have concentrated on one important projected policy in the Netherlands; the comprehensivization of secondary education. He expects to present the final results of this project in 1983.

2. Scepticism

Several policy-makers and research directors expressed a certain scepticism. *Timpane*'s remarks can be seen as representing the Workshop's general feelings towards Klabbers' project and approach: 'First of all, I take the paper to be explanatory, the very beginning of thinking about a possible interactive process. It is, in its present format, very abstract with respect to specific educational issues and it may be more useful for some issues than for others, more useful in some decision-making contexts than in others. At this stage it might also be an educational or a professional development tool. But decision-makers and the nature of decision-making would have to be a good deal different from what I have experienced for this approach to be fully successful. Let me be specific. It will be very *difficult to ensure the participation of decision-makers*. The time involved, at least in the US, in working through the many necessary iterations would be prohibitive. It is legendary in the US that the decision-maker is best influenced by a friend, or a trusted colleague ... who can write or diagram fastest and most clearly on the back of an envelope, while walking down the hall from the office to the legislative chamber. It is the uncommon decision-maker who is able or perhaps disciplined enough to devote the time that is required by this technique. This may differ from country to country, though.'

Timpane subsequently questioned the use of *the term 'decision-maker'*: 'We use the term decision-maker, and assume that it has a common meaning amongst us. We might want to question that rather carefully, because the decision-maker implied by Klabbers' paper has quite a different ability to make commitments of time, than many decision-makers I know.' In section 2.3. of the discussion following Dockrell's paper in this volume, *Dockrell* points out that the 'majority of decisions are being made by administrators rather than by politicians (in Scotland, that is). This is a striking observation against the background of Timpane's question concerning the meaning of the term decision-maker. In these two particular cases, it seems that the term as used by Timpane referred to legislators, while Dockrell was thinking of administrators. In line with a recommendation put forward by many participants, it seems necessary to define essential terms in literature bearing on the interplay between the social sciences and policy-making.

The *frankness of expression* of the decision-makers in an interactive simulation game was questioned by Kjell *Eide, Heene* and *Timpane*. The latter expressed his doubts about the policy-makers' candour by questioning an assumption underlying Klabbers' work. Timpane did *not* think that decision-makers were always interested in the solution of a problem (as Klabbers seemed to assume): 'Timing is of essence, after all, in politics and it is very often the case that the decision-makers' preference will be not to decide, or to make the least possible decision'. Timpane wondered how that particular reality of political decision-making would work in an interactive system. *Klabbers* responded by pointing out that an interactive simulation game demonstrated how people might behave in reality: 'When you have several policies and you see how people deal with them, you may expect that this also can happen in reality and it gives you a fair idea of what your intended policy might turn out to be'. (See Murphy's law.)

The *applicability* of Klabbers' interactive simulation game received much attention. Kjell *Eide* raised the question whether such a game was adequate for dealing with matters like education. He states: 'Systems analysis — with which I have been working quite a lot during 20 years as an educational planner — derives from physics, mechanics and regulation theory. It has a built-in assumption that one is dealing with dead material that can be posted in certain ways, influenced by all sorts of external influences. One regulates these influences in order to make sure that the desired outcome is realized.' Eide doubted whether this approach would be possible if the material under question had a will of its own, had a purpose and was a participant in the process itself. However, Eide added to this that the combination of gaming and simulation in Klabbers' approach might be a solution to this problem.

Timpane mentioned a series of issues for which Klabbers' approach might be applicable: 'For example, the issue of comprehensive schooling, reduced enrolment and the reallocation of resources within a series of democratic constraints; the adoption of technology in an education system might be another example'. Some issues were also mentioned by him as unsuitable, for example, desegregation and bilingual education. *Klabbers* countered Eide's and Timpane's remarks by pointing out that 'every model, whether it is a simulation model or an interactive simulation game, has limited applicability. The methodology can be used, however, for quite different areas of application. It can be applied in the area of economic aspects of education, but also in the classroom as games and simulations for education. For example, language teaching games do already exist and are being used. In the design of the interactive simulation game as presented here, the main focus is on the macro-aspects of the educational system. This restriction is a result of the particular set up of the project. It is not a feature of the methodology.' (*Note*: 'Systems Analysis' in the strict sense as used by Kjell Eide seems to be distinct from the systems theoretical approach as presented by Klabbers.)

A final reservation was put forward by *Vorbeck* and Kjell *Eide*. They made clear that this highly technical procedure is often presented in such a way as to obscure its real value. The language used is too technical for most readers. This is a serious problem when one wants to construct an instrument for people who are by definition no experts in this field. Even the name given to this method of assessing possible consequences of policy options — 'Futures Research' — has a rebarbative effect. Vorbeck even suggested to the Workshop that this unfortunate choice of name was the reason for the fact that, five years ago, the Council of Europe's Division for Long-term Planning and Futures Research was abolished. (*Note*: The design of an interactive simulation game is 'user friendly'; this implies that no technical language is used. This facilitates the application of the method as a communication tool.)

3. Some advantages

Several participants stressed that the most important aspect of Klabbers' interactive simulation game was the way it forced researchers and others to engage in a *synthesis* of their knowledge which is — according to Timpane — a very important activity most people almost never engage in voluntarily or without an outside stimulus.

Rein emphasized another aspect by drawing attention to the fact that Klabbers' instrument is a *tool of inquiry*. According to him, this method is an excellent way of specifying research and policy questions (rather than a 'tool for decision-making'). *In 't Veld-Langeveld* found this aspects an essential feature. On the basis of eight years experience with 'futures research' in the context of her membership of the Advisory Council on Government Policy (WRR) in the Netherlands, she felt that Klabbers' gaming device 'was helpful in showing the policy-makers and researchers, as well as other parties concerned, the consequences of policy options'. *Husén*, finally, stressed the effective ways in which Klabbers managed to bridge the communication gap which existed between researchers and policy-makers.

Educational Research and Policy-Making in France

Louis Legrand — Professor at Louis Pasteur University, Strasbourg and Former President of the Institut National de la Recherche Pédagogique, France

The objective of this paper is, on the basis of the particular case of my country, France, to identify the general problems of educational research insofar as they concern decision-makers.

1. *In education, the concept of research covers a variety of fields* involving very different processes:

1.1 On the one hand there is scientific research proper, which deals with observed educational facts, seeking first to establish exactly what they are, then to explain them by means of constants or causes. There are two possible approaches to this kind of research: macroscopic studies falling within the scope of sociology of economics, or the two organically linked. This applies, for example, to studies of the social efficiency of education (studies of training patterns and profiles in the light of available jobs; the study of pupils who go down a year and why they do so; comparative studies of different systems of school organization in relation to democratization or economic development etc.). Evaluation studies belong to this category. Education may also be studied at a more restricted level, e.g. that of the age-group or even that of the individual learner; in this case, the approach is predominantly psychological, although other, related sciences may be involved (psycho-sociology of relationships, psycho-linguistics, etc.). In all cases, what typifies scientific research of this kind is that it takes into account the specific character of education, which is that it presupposes objectives and hence values. The translation of these objectives into observable and, if possible, measurable facts is one of the fundamental elements of such research.

1.2 On the other hand, there is research leading to intervention in the education system to change it so as to enable the set objectives to be better achieved or other, newly-affirmed objectives to be achieved. This involves various forms of experiment, which may be quite far-reaching in the case of development research, or less so in the restricted situations of action research. Experiments on curricula or structures are the most common.

2. The situation in France in the last 20 years

Secondly, I should like to recapitulate important developments in the French education system in the past 20 years. This period has been marked, in France as in other countries, by a whole series of innovations in structure and content. As regards the structure of education, the outstanding developments have been the raising of the school-leaving age in 1959, the introduction of *còlleges d'enseignement secondaire* in 1963 and the harmonization of general and technical upper secondary education. As a result, primary schooling has been reduced to five years and comprehensive education has been introduced at the lower secondary level, first as a streamed system, then as an unstreamed system with unresolved difficulties for low-ability pupils aged from 14 to 16. The result is a massive increase in the numbers of pupils and teachers (roughly speaking 10 million pupils in 1965, 12 million in 1980).

As regards the content of education, the primary curriculum has been reorganized in keeping with its new function of preparing all pupils for the same intermediate studies. Between 1970 and 1980, new mathematics, French, science, physical education and arts syllabuses were published. In secondary education, the mathematics and then science syllabuses were substantially recast. Modern languages syllabuses were transformed. Education in technology and manual skills was introduced at lower secondary level. The short technical courses were considerably developed and the syllabuses transformed.

All these changes were clearly ideal material for educational research. But what happened in practice?

3. The role of educational research in these innovations

It is impossible to answer this question simply in view of the nature of the innovations and the length of the period under consideration. What is potentially interesting in this case study is precisely the very noticeable changes in ideas and practices over the past 20 years.

As regards structural changes, broadly speaking it may be said that educational research as such had very little influence on the fundamental decisions of the 1959 reform. Admittedly, a knowledge of economic studies, particularly those of English-speaking authors, was instrumental in the decision to raise the school-leaving age and to introduce the *collèges d'enseignement secondaire.* The works of Jean Fourastier and Jaccard inspired the politicians and technocrats who drew up the 1959 reform. The need to remove the geographical and social obstacles to economic growth was probably the reason for the two basic measures: the raising of the school-leaving age and the introduction of lower secondary schools. It should be pointed out, however, that this technocratic decision coincided with what was then a major international trend and, furthermore, that it was an extension of political thinking during the Resistance and of the 'Langevin-Wallon' Plan which grew out of it. The call for democratization from one section of public opinion was combined here with the interests of economic development, which was regarded as a necessity in the aftermath of the Second World War. Of course, some research and experiments preceded and accompanied the major decisions: in particular descriptive research carried out by the Institut d'Etude du Travail et d'Orientation Professionnelle (Professor Reuchlin), which was the first official research body to be called upon by the decision-makers. But it is difficult to assess the exact impact of these studies on the transition from primary school to the first year of the secondary schools existing before the reform. Similarly, experiments had been conducted in some départements with combined first and second years in secondary education, the 'new classes' of which were to become pilot schools. Yet these experiments were of a qualitative nature. The same was true of the experiments concerning one of the most original features of the *collèges d'enseignement secondaire*: the so-called transition classes, the introduction of which was preceded by experiments in several classes in each département. It is worth dwelling on these 'experiments' for a short while, as they are indicative of a persistent trend in France where innovation is concerned. The Ministry is currently adopting the same approach in its study of remedial instruction, a vital element in the latest reform, known as the 'Haby' reform.

When an experiment of this kind is begun, the decisions on the changes in question have already been taken by the responsible bodies. These decisions have been formulated, at the request of the political authority, by private commissions composed mainly of inspectors-general, or, at any rate, chaired by an inspector-general and including teachers and administrators chosen by the Inspectorate-General. These commissions draft texts and the purpose of the ensuing experiment will be to iron out the practical difficulties. This process remains a matter of trial and error. Monitoring and assessment are carried out by inspectors, and result in reports put together during short sessions organized by the Inspectorate-General. There is nothing here which could reasonably be termed 'scientific experiment': no concern to describe conditions and attitudes, no measurement of performance, no attempt at objective explanation. The presumed objectivity is that of the inspectors-cum-observers.

Furthermore, when there is a desire to impart some momentum to innovation and to monitor it more closely, as was the case in the 'new classes' experiment, these tasks are entrusted to a team which is set up for that purpose in the Ministry itself, and whose term of office depends on that of the officials promoting the reform. Their period of office, however, is often short, being dependent on that of the Minister who appointed them. As a result, the teams never have the time to complete the task assigned to them. This unfortunate state of affairs is explained by the absence of specialized institutions and, further still, by official ignorance of the services which such institutions can perform.

Having been drawn up and implemented in this way, the major innovations of the 1959 reform gradually went adrift without any action being possible to set them back on course. Thus the 'guidance' system, the cornerstone of the reform, was gradually transformed into a rigorous selection system. This was further compounded by the reform in the teaching of mathematics, which was also diverted from its original purpose. The only critical studies of the phenomenon were those of individual sociologists motivated by political protest, although this in no way detracts from the value of their work.* But the government is not the originator of these studies. Once a reform has been decided on in France, anyone wishing to take an objective look at it arouses suspicion. It must succeed at all costs. In other words, its shortcomings must be concealed. This is the authorities' usual attitude to *a posteriori* evaluation studies. As we shall see, this attitude has recently shifted, among political leaders at least, who now commission follow-up studies on the reform introduced (from the Ministry of Education's Data-processing and Statistical Research Department – SEIS). Yet the reports produced in this way are confidential. Special permission must be obtained to have them published. Thus the practices of industrial research departments are transposed to the field of education.

From 1965 and especially 1968 onwards, a second phase began, with the Institut Pédagogique National playing a gradually expanded role. In fact, this development occurred outside the official system, and sometimes against it, under pressure from the grassroots, in particular teachers' associations, who used the Institute to goad the hierarchy into making the changes which they considered essential, particularly as regards curriculum content.

The absence of specialist teams at the Ministry at that time no doubt explains this takeover, which was to last ten years.

The work consisted almost entirely of large-scale experiments with new content, methods and structures, mainly in primary and lower secondary schools. These experiments were to play a decisive role in the development of official attitudes and the formulation of the programmes and instructions which have been issued over the past decade.

In view of their peripheral origin and, to begin with at least, their highly

---

*Cf. Beaudelot-Establet (1972). *L'école capitaliste en France.*

qualitative nature, as well as the large number of associated fields and the ultimate concern for objective evaluation, these experiments probably constitute an original amalgam which cannot be fitted into the traditional categories, being neither conventional curriculum research nor action-research. The term 'development-research' has been used to describe them. The process needs to be described in greater detail.

First of all, these experiments are based on the previous or simultaneous work of national representative commissions. In France, in the early 1970s, a number of major commissions were set up to discuss ways of reforming the content and methods of primary and secondary education: the Lichneroviz Commission for mathematics, Rouchet and Emmanuel for French, and Laguarrigue for science. The proceedings of these commissions were published. Texts were drafted and teams of teachers were given the task of experimenting with them in primary teacher-training colleges and in experimental secondary schools attached to a university for the last four years of compulsory education. The Institut Pédagogique was responsible for coordinating and evaluating the operations. Local team leaders met quarterly. The decisions on specific experiments were taken on a collegial basis and the work was divided accordingly. The final evaluation involved collecting coordinated objective data on the basis of tests, surveys etc. The data was stored at the Institute and processed by computers where necessary. Publications followed in a limited collection entitled *Recherches pédagogiques*. The reports were sent to the Ministry and Inspectorate-General.

The originality of this approach, which in many respects resembled that of traditional experiments was that it called upon the creativity of local teams, which from the very beginning were expected to make the results of the research known in initial training and permanent education. The teams of mathematicians were the basis for mathematics research institutes, newly-formed university bodies which used secondary teachers partly relieved of their normal duties for research and permanent education activities in lower and upper secondary schools. Gradually the Ministry, which showed interest but was alarmed at an operation partly outside its control, began to set up teams of its own which were more directly controlled by the Inspectorate. It also sought to set up an evaluation department within its own statistical department. This was the start of the decline of the Institut Pédagogique, which, from 1975, as a result of successive structural reforms, was gradually cut off from the grassroots and deprived of the support of the major commissions, which had been disbanded.

At the same time, the authorities sought to take over the innovations which had been brought about in this way. Yet, in so doing, they whittled them down by removing what they felt was harmful. They entrusted responsibility for drafting new instructions to the inspectorates, whose former prerogatives were restored. This led to neutralization of those innovations which the hierarchy had not helped to bring about.* Simultaneously, the gradual elimination of the local research teams and the neutralization of the mathematics research institutes removed what had been the mainstays of the previous system. We are now witnessing a widespread return to the past, with the innovations that were introduced being openly criticized by the highest state authorities.

As for innovation, or what remains of it, it is now under the direct control of the Ministry and has gradually returned to the conventional style of experiments monitored qualitatively by the inspectorates. Better still, some innovations actually conflict with the most outstanding contributions of earlier research (the possibility of widely diversified classes). The Institut Pédagogique survives as a body for fundamental research on specific projects. It is now virtually cut off from the training colleges and experimental schools.

As regards scientific research proper, France for a long time failed to recognize the specific character of education. The Centre National de la Recherche Scientifique has no educational science section. Research on the education system in the past 20 years has been conducted within the framework of conventional branches of study: psychology, sociology, economics. We do, however, have some outstanding results to our credit, especially in sociology with the work of Boudon and Bourdieu. Psychological research in the educational field has focused mainly on guidance (IETOP) and rehabilitation (Wallon, then Sazzo and the educational psychologists). Educational science has only recently been introduced at university (1967). The present Minister has recently shown that its existence is by no means accepted and secure (by the withdrawal of many course approvals). This explains the isolated and confidential nature of the many research projects which are nevertheless being carried out here and there in France: resources are very limited and the official education system stands in the way of university researchers wishing to work in schools.** An active association has been formed on the initiative of Gaston Mialaret within the framework of the French-Language International Association for Experimental Pedagogics.

To date, education science as such has only very rarely played a part in policy formation. The authorities seem to ignore its existence when they are not actually contesting it. The recent reorganization of the Institute is presented as the expression of a desire to bring fundamental research and decision-making more closely into line, but this entails the takeover and bureaucratic control of innovations already introduced, and ultimately their decline. Only the future will tell exactly what this development

---

*See in particular the new grammatical nomenclature for secondary education and the new history syllabuses for lower secondary schools, published by CNDP, 29 rue d'Ulm, Paris.
**Revue Française de Pédagogie (INRP) publishes the results of the most outstanding research projects and a list of doctorate theses in educational science.

means. The Ministry's Data-processing and Statistical Research Department has finally set up a large research department to follow-up educational reforms. The results of its surveys, which are beginning to be published, look interesting.*

4. General considerations emerging from this survey

4.1 Empirical educational research has not yet gained real acceptance in France. This depressing fact invites an explanation. Reasons may be advanced in the form of hypotheses.

4.1.1 Teacher training remains strictly academic. For the vast majority of contemporary Frenchmen, teaching remains a personal art. It is sufficient to know your subject well to teach it. The primary teacher-training colleges themselves have been staffed with untrained secondary teachers to teach future primary teachers the theory and practice of education. The needs of this kind of training have, however, led an appreciable number of training college lecturers to take an interest in educational research, but it is no accident if this research is centred almost entirely on curricular innovations inspired by developments in university curriculum content (mathematics, French, science). The problems of learning and the learning environment have only arisen recently as a secondary consideration.

4.1.2 Educational research is confused with innovation. As such, it arouses suspicion among the majority of the teaching profession, who regard it as mere fantasy, and among the authorities, who are sensitive to its dissident and political character. The considerable increase in innovations after 1968 confirms the authorities in their view. To their way of thinking, innovation should serve the official policy, not contest it.

4.1.3 The French hierarchical system is hostile to educational research, which it regards as an arrogation of the power to innovate and evaluate. The independent institutes and universities cannot enter schools without special permission from the hierarchy. In theory, they have no business there.

4.1.4 Ministerial officials are recruited increasingly from the administrative colleges. Accordingly, they are aware of educational phenomena only to the extent that they affect the economy. They are suspicious of educationalists who attach importance to values and whose demands entail unnecessary expense. Educational research is regarded as the quintessence of such unrealistic attitudes.

---

*Published by SEIS, Ministère de l'Education.

4.2 Positive aspects

The experience gained from over ten years' work at the Institut Pédagogique and the results of the development research conducted there show the effectiveness of a process which joins the centre and the periphery in a dialectical relationship. Indeed, it was the observed effectiveness of the system which led the authorities gradually to dismantle it on the grounds that it deviated from the official line and usurped power. A study of the process involved is extremely valuable to any authority wishing to give real effect to reforms that are considered politically useful. Involving training centres in curriculum research, not as consumers but as producers, is a powerful means of imparting the necessary momentum and preparing the subsequent training. To be effective, the training itself must adopt the same collaborative style as the research and be based on teams of suitable volunteers who are working in the schools and are given the necessary encouragement.

A system of this kind, however, is probably incompatible with the highly-structured hierarchical system which operates in France. The Institut Pédagogique was conceived by its founder (Louis Cros) as a centre for private associations and as a form of countervailing power. The idea was healthy, but the Institute came to grief because of it.

4.3 Lastly, a fundamental problem: genuine educational research, whether theoretical or experimental, requires substantial resources (formation of teams, systematic collection of information, data-processing, publication). Is such research, i.e. research that is free to choose its targets, methods and publications, conceivable in these circumstances? The very notion of education is ambiguous as a scientific phenomenon. Education is necessarily the result of a value judgment. The decision to study a particular phenomenon necessarily follows from an interest motivated by a choice which cannot be purely intellectual. The authorities wish to have information enabling them to carry out their policies successfully. The researchers wish to acquire knowledge of the phenomena at work in order to argue more cogently in the fields which interest them, i.e. which are related to their concerns as educationalists or citizens. That is particularly clear in the case of experiments. But it is also true of theoretical research. It is no accident that research on equality of opportunity has flourished in the past 20 years. Now research on rational selection and biological determinism is reappearing. Many more examples could be quoted. The clash of power structures and political assumptions in France is merely an illustration of a basic fact which may be obscured by the different institutional situation in countries such as the United States.

For my part, I believe that educational research is necessarily a part of political strategy. In a democratic state one is in duty bound to accept that fact and to allow different approaches to be explored and different or divergent results to be published and discussed, not only to demonstrate their veracity, but to give a clearer idea of the ethical assumptions underlying them. A process of this kind is essential to democracy. But all governments dislike it, and they are the ones who provide the money!

Concise Bibliography (on French problems in particular)

CAPELLE, J. (1974). *Education et politique*. PUF.
CONSEIL DE L'EUROPE (1972, 1974, 1975). *Bulletin d'information* No. 1/1972, 2/1974, 1/1975.
GEMINARD, L. (1973). *l'Enseignement éclaté*. Casterman.
LEGRAND, L. (1977). *Pour une politique démocratique de l'éducation*. PUF.
MAJAULT, J. (1981). *Comptes, mécomptes, décomptes*. Casterman.
NISBET, J. and BROADFOOD, P. (1980). *The Impact of Research Policy and Practice in Education*. Aberdeen University Press.

CRITICISM AND DISCUSSION

Note by the editors: The feelings of the participants of the Workshop regarding Legrand's contribution were best expressed by Mitter when he said that Legrand's paper and presentation were 'highly stimulating, realistic appraisals of the situation in France'. Several topics for further research and international comparison were mentioned in the discussion. These are not presented separately, but form part of the second section where Prof. De Groot, who himself participated in the discussion, puts forward a proposal in more general phrasing.

1. Comparative remarks

Fuente Salvador (Spain) made clear that Legrand's description of the French situation fully applied to Spain as well. This is important to keep in mind since she furthermore observed that Spanish authorities normally keep a close watch on developments in France and even model their policies on them. This is not only because both countries have highly centralized systems but may also rely on the important fact that both French and Spanish speakers are using Romance languages and have relatively limited access to other literature.

Mitter expressed his appreciation of Legrand's presentation especially on the ground that 'in many respects, Legrand has not only pointed to problems existing in France, but also in other countries'. Mitter felt that the three 'purposes of decision-oriented research' as distinguished by Legrand — legitimation of existing policies, preparing and implementing innovation, criticizing existing and projected policies — could provide measurements by which the situation in many countries might be compared. As far as the Federal Republic of Germany is concerned, Mitter observed that the 'second purpose has been declining more and more in the seventies, while legitimation got a much stronger foothold'. Mitter joined Legrand in arguing for a much stronger role for 'critical research'. The workshop agreed with *Legrand* when he said that 'educational research should be considered a necessary part of political strategy in democratic countries. Democracies have a duty to finance different approaches and critical research in the course of which may be demonstrated the ethical assumptions underlying the existing policy.' He concluded that all governments disliked it despite the fact that in some countries like the US the clash between research and political values seems less apparent. Legrand suggested that these clashes do occur everywhere but that they may be obscured by the 'different institutional structures'.

The extent to which critical information is used in political systems with varying degrees of centralization was considered an interesting subject for further research.

2. A plea for more comparative research

Several speakers expressed an opinion that the existing knowledge about research contributions to policy is too fragmented and unspecified. International cooperation between the disciplines and experts was called for. It appeared that on both sides of the Atlantic this was felt to be a real need. This is why the organization of this particular Workshop and its follow-up (see Appendix D) were described as 'highly relevant, stimulating and coming at the right moment'. De Groot put forward a provisional outline for an international plan of campaign which is included here in full since it may well trigger off more concrete proposals. 'I think the remarks of Prof. Legrand suggest strongly that we are in need of an *international comparative study* aimed at comparing the environmental factors that tend to determine to a large extent what we do in and learn by our respective national research efforts.

'These factors — causes, independent variables — had better not be defined in the nationally parochial and possibly "justifying" way in which we all tend to use them when we speak of our own country. They must be defined in terms of organizational structures, extant decision procedures, the use made of expertise — Husén's safely seated professors — communication blockings, et cetera; i.e., defined in such a way that international comparisons are possible.

'The *dependent variables*, then, should not be the ultimate achievement levels but rather all those intermediary or moderating effects in between the two. I am thinking of such things as the public attitude towards educational research; the hearing and moral support it receives from governments; the quality of the work that has been done or is being done; the relative quantity of research work, in terms of money input as well as in terms of output (publications); the amount of tangible uses made of it; the amount of policy-relevant and policy-directed research; finally some measure of the amount of positively valued innovation (versus immobility) in a country. Then, ultimately, one might *also* look at the achievements of pupils – IEA's main ultimate criterion variable.

'One idea behind this proposal is that the line of intermediate links is too long to be just skipped. We had better study them, as outcomes of basic organizational factors, i.e. basic structures and procedures, political habits, extant rewards and punishments in the working and learning environment in which research is carried out.

'Another idea behind it is that in the past the most fatal errors – or, beneficial decisions – have been made in instituting structures and procedures that are now taken for granted, as a part of "the national situation".

'The third idea behind it is that these factors (independent variables) may not be as unchangeable as we tend to assume. My point is that we had better not consider them fatalistically as facts of life, as "national characteristics" that just are such and such in France and again, such and such in the Netherlands, or in Sweden. History shows that in quite a few cases extant organizational structures and political habits have changed drastically over time; compare for instance France in the thirties with France in the fifties and sixties. That implies that attempting to help them change, in a restricted area such as that in which educational research is operating, is not necessarily a hopeless enterprise.

'Fourth, if all this is so, the obvious first step to be taken is, in cases where such structures and procedures are prohibitive of a sound and fruitful development of policy-relevant or policy-directed educational research, is this step: to show by means of research, first, that this is really so, and second, by comparing the national situation with that in other, "happier" countries, that it need not be so forever. This gets us back to the research proposal.

'Fifth, such an enterprise would involve cooperation with organization experts, at the highest level available. Again, this is rarely done but possible.

'Finally, this plan may appear almost impossible to carry out with success; but then, my main argument in favour of it is that it is necessary. If we do not succeed in changing prohibitive *working and learning environments* then all our efforts at promoting the quality and the use of educational research will remain vain.'

The Sectoral Principle in Swedish Research Policy

Inger Marklund – University of Uppsala

1. The sectoral principle

In May 1979 the Swedish Riksdag passed a very important resolution on research policy the content of which can be very briefly expressed as follows.

> The central authorities responsible for development in any sector of society should be equipped with R&D resources and held responsible for R&D activities relevant to the sector concerned.
> Any research work which a central authority needs to have performed should be entrusted to university departments, and draw on the scientific competence of the universities.

The term 'central authority' requires explanation. Sweden and Finland are the only countries in which policy-making and administration are divided between two different levels. Swedish Ministries are relatively small and operate on predominantly political lines. Political decisions are interpreted and their implementation administered by central administrative boards. These boards are subordinate to the Government as a whole, although each of them operates primarily under the supervision of the appropriate ministry. The word 'sector' thus refers to the portion of society coming within a certain field of policy and covered by a central administrative authority. The school sector comprises elementary schooling, upper secondary schooling and adult education, and the National Board of Education, the NBE, which is subordinate to the Ministry of Education and Cultural Affairs, is the central administrative authority for this sector. The most important duties of a central authority include the monitoring and evaluation of reforms within its field.

The above-mentioned policy decision can be said to have confirmed a principle which had been operative in certain sectors of society, including education, for a number of years. Nonetheless, it marks the beginnings of a concerted research policy in Sweden. Accordingly, what has hitherto been regarded as good practice now constitutes an actual obligation; the central authorities responsible for R&D are now obliged to entrust their policy-oriented research to the universities, and the latter are obligated to assume the main burden of responsibility for the conduct of policy- and decision-oriented research, side by side with their traditional duties of basic (undergraduate) education and disciplinary research.

The resolution also means that responsibility in Sweden for the planning of policy-oriented research is not located at the most central political level, i.e. within the Ministries. Instead it is located at the executive, central administrative level.

Both aspects of this resolution — the administrative responsibility of the national authorities and the executive responsibility of the universities — are important. There are, however, a number of conflicts inherent in this principle of research policy, relating to the direction, quality and utiilization of policy-oriented research and its interaction with other research, which is often referred to as 'free'.

If this principle of research policy is realized as intended, it will have an important effect on the view taken of the role of research in social development. An augmentation of policy-oriented research in more and more sectors of society will most likely generate demands relating to the social relevance of research, and the use and usefulness of its findings.

2. The rationale of the sectoral principle

The motives underlying the first part of the principle — the responsibilitity of the national administrative authorities — are based on the Swedish tradition of independent central administrative boards, which was first codified in a law of 1634. This tradition is interesting in its own right, but its history is beyond the scope of the present account. The main reason for assigning responsibility for the planning and monitoring of policy-oriented research to the central administrative level rather than the central political level (i.e. within the Ministries) is a desire to avoid excessive domination of research by short-term party political interests. Another motive is the safeguarding of research planning from the political fluctuations which could follow in the wake of governmental and ministerial changes. It is also worth pointing out that the principle has not been consistently implemented in this respect: the responsibility for policy-oriented research concerning social affairs and the labour market, for example, is located at the ministerial level. School research on the other hand is planned and directed by the central administrative authority.

There are many reasons underlying the second part of the principle, i.e. the vesting of executive responsibility in the universities. One of the most important of these is economic. Sweden is a small country, and the maintenance of parallel research organizations is not considered economically justifiable. The scientific competence developed in the universities must be available for research of a more policy-oriented nature. However, this principle is not applied with complete consistency. There are in fact many fields, chiefly in science and technology, with research institutes independent of the universities. The resolution must therefore be interpreted primarily as an appeal against the establishment of additional institutes.

More significant motives for vesting executive responsibility in the universities can perhaps be found in the view taken by politicians of the role of research in the overall pattern of social development. If policy-oriented research is based on the universities, the selection of problems in disciplinary research can be broadened and a closer link thus established between university research and the community at large. It is to be hoped that a broader selection of problems will also result in both undergraduate education and research training being given a content that relates more clearly to the society in which the majority of students will be active following their graduation.

Another motive for such a link with the community is the desire at both the political and administrative levels for more exchange at the personal level between the universities and other parts of the community. This horizontal mobility of research personnel should result, on both sides, in a better knowledge among the responsible authorities of the conditions applying to research activities.

3. Codification of the sectoral principle

As has so often been the case in Swedish reform policies, an important role has been played by Government-appointed committees. Very few of the major policy decisions made in Sweden are not preceded by thorough inquiry. The most important committee connected with the sectoral principle, active between 1972 and 1977, was entitled the Research Councils Commission (FRU), a name which belies the scope of its terms of reference. The resolution on the sectoral principle passed by the Riksdag in 1978 was essentially based on the two main reports presented by this Commission, Research Councils (1) and Research Policy (2).

FRU indicated frames and guidelines for the sectoral principle. In 1978 it was followed by the Research Cooperation Committee (FOSAM), whose task has been to analyse the consequences of the sectoral principle, above all from the viewpoint of the universities, and to suggest means of facilitating the implementation of the principle throughout society and the research sector. This Committee completed its work in December 1980 (3).

Parallel to FOSAM, Swedish school research has been the subject of an inquiry by the School Research Committee (SFK), which has been primarily concerned with the portion of school research that had been planned and directed by the central authority for the school sector, the National Board of Education (NBE). The Committee was active between September 1978 and February 1980. Policy-oriented research in the school sector is probably the area in which the two components of the sectoral principle have been applied longest (since 1962) and most consistently. Parts of the work of this Committee (4) are described in (5).

All three committees of inquiry have operated within the scope of the main theme defined for the SVO workshop, and SFK was specifically concerned with school research. Let us consider some of the main ideas presented in these various investigative reports.*

4. Conflicts associated with the sectoral principle

Through the sectoral principle, light is thrown on a number of potential conflicts between the objectives and values pertaining within the scientific community and those held in respect of research in other sectors of society, above all by the political and administrative bodies concerned. The terms on which researchers work — and wish to work — frequently differ from the conditions under which political and administrative bodies work. Let us consider some of these potential conflicts.

Intradisciplinary significance — social relevance

The first committee — FRU — employed two concepts which, for better or worse, have come to dominate the debate on research policy. The following figure, based on the report (1), shows how they were presented. These criteria of classification were selected as a working device. The paired concepts were intended to characterize research activities in terms of two aspects. One of these concerned the extent to which research could influence conditions in society, taking this latter term in its broadest sense. This aspect was termed social relevance. The other aspect was concerned with the importance of research as a factor influencing the development of science itself, i.e. its intradisciplinary relevance.

---

*A certain amount of research is in progress in Sweden on the subject of research and policy-making. (See for example References (6) to (11). My preoccupation in this paper with official inquiries does not underestimate the importance of this research. On the contrary, I am convinced that research into the planning and utilization of research will come, as a result of the sectoral principle, to rank as a top priority research field. But the official reports which I have selected provide points of departure for a discussion of policy-oriented research as a principle confirmed by the Swedish Riksdag. This is why I have grouped them together under the heading 'Codification of the Sectoral Principle'.

```
                        High
                         ▲
Intradisciplinary        │
relevance                │
                         │
                         │
                         │
Imperceptible            │
or small                 │
                         └──────────────────────▶ High
                      Imperceptible
                      or small            Social relevance
```

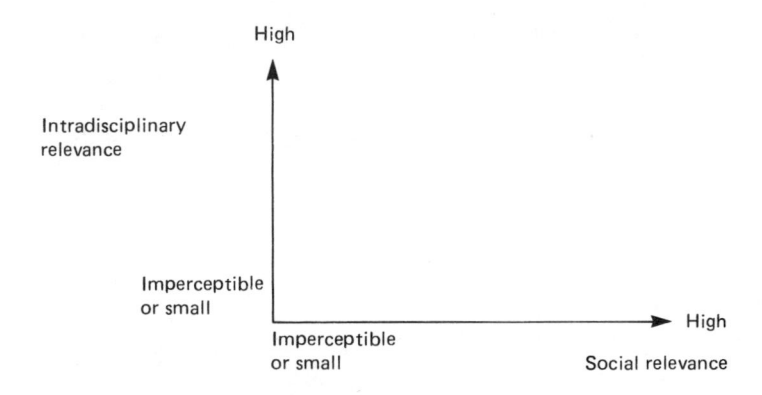

FRU organized a carefully planned discussion of the implications of these two concepts, recognizing that all research, in one way or another, is connected with the society in which it is conducted, and that there is not in principle any research which does not in some way affect society. 'Imperceptible' implies that research has little or only an insignificant *direct* influence on society, and is a key word in the figure. On the other hand, influence is never altogether non-existent.

Both these concepts have gradually acquired a different meaning, and this shift in meaning has caused participants in the debate on research policy to speak in terms of two *kinds* of research, that initiated by researchers themselves and that initiated by society, as represented by the central authorities vested with research responsibilities: This antithesis tends to be more frequently stated by researchers than by practictioners (here comprising policy-makers and administrators). In the final analysis, the antithesis relates to a difference of opinion regarding the control of research.*

To simplify matters somewhat, the attitudes of the two communities towards the two types of research can be illustrated as follows.

---

*Usage varies within and between languages. The distinction in Swedish between 'intradisciplinary relevance' and 'societal or social relevance' appears to have no counterpart in the English literature.

'Discipline-oriented research' is here used synonymously with 'research initiated by researchers' or 'basic research'.

'Policy-oriented research' is used synonymously with 'sectoral research', 'research initiated by society' or 'socially initiated research'.

'Scientific community' is used synonymously with 'research community' or 'researchers'.

'Practitioner community' is used synonymously with 'practitioners' and in this paper denotes politicians and administrative personnel. Local political and administrative personnel, and school personnel, have been intentionally excluded from the discussion.

Evaluation by the scientific community

Manner of initiation	Impact of research	
	Intradisciplinary relevance	Social relevance
Initiated by researchers	High, of prime interest	High, but not of prime interest
Initiated by society	None	High, but no research standing

The prime interest of the scientific community is in the research initiated by researchers themselves. This research is also of high social relevance, but the scientific community does not feel that its primary duty is to demonstrate this relevance. Socially initiated research is not felt to be of any importance for the development of science itself. It may be of great social relevance, but it seldom regarded as research.

Evaluation by the practitioner community

Manner of initiation	Impact of research	
	Intradisciplinary relevance	Social relevance
Initiated by researchers	High, but not immediately perceptible	High, but not immediately perceptible
Initiated by society	Not of prime interest	High, of prime interest

The practitioner community, for its part, certainly puts a high value on research initiated by researchers but finds neither its intradisciplinary relevance nor its social relevance immediately perceptible. The practitioner community is not primarily interested in the importance of socially initiated research for the internal development of a discipline. Instead, it is mainly interested in the research initiated by practitioners themselves, and this research is considered (or rather, required) to be of great social relevance. The practitioner community also assumes that socially initiated research is subject to the same qualitative stipulations as the research initiated by scientists themselves. The research community for its part seldom finds that socially initiated research provides opportunities to conduct research activities of high quality if the assignment in question is of limited duration or scope, or otherwise hedged round with conditions dictated by the practitioner community.

This discussion has been deliberately simplified. There are social sectors where the antithesis between the scientific community and the practitioner community is not as pronounced as this, but isolation of the antithesis can often provide a useful point of departure for discussing the measures to be considered with a view to reducing it.

This division into two types of research is not a specifically Swedish phenomenon, nor is it due to the sectoral principle. What is uniquely Swedish, however, is the strong emphasis placed on the interdependence of these two kinds of research, and the demand that they be conducted *in parallel within the same organization*. The two communities must be able to cooperate and to understand one another's conditions and demands, which they often find incompatible.

This is the state of affairs which has accentuated the need for a clarification of goals, which in turn has been one of the tasks allotted to the other two Government-appointed committees mentioned above, FOSAM and SFK.

Conflict analysis

There are two important starting points for an analysis of the conflicts between the values of the scientific community and those of the practitioner community. The first of these is the demand for quality. No matter how research is initiated, its conduct must meet exacting qualitative criteria. The second point of departure concerns the purposes of research. Research initiated by scientists themselves is aimed at shedding theoretical light on a given problem. Here the quest for knowledge is foremost. Research initiated by society is aimed at providing the most comprehensive insight into a given problem that is possible within the time and financial frames available, the former condition being more stringent than the latter.

Let us now proceed to isolate the conditions governing the two types of research. While school research has been taken as our particular point of departure, this characterization is probably applicable to practically any type of research field.

Again, I would stress that the conflict analysis relates to the fact that both types of research have to be performed within the same research organization, using a common pool of research competence.

Conditions of research activities

Research initiated by the sciences	Research initiated by society
Research forms part of the development of science itself and the selection of problems is governed by the interests and qualifications of the researcher	Research forms part of a wider programme of school development. It is included in a *plan* drawn up on essentially non-scientific grounds.
Research is conducted without the stipulation of a perceptible application.	Research is planned and conducted with an application in view.
Results are disseminated within the scientific community and on that community's terms. The researcher himself decides when.	The dissemination of results forms part of the research plan and must comply with the conditions imposed by both communities.
Research is evaluated by the scientific community itself.	Research is evaluated both by the scientific community and by the practitioner community.
Research is allowed a high failure risk.	Research must involve a low risk of failure.
Research is unidisciplinary in character (and by definition).	Research is often multi- or interdisciplinary.
The time frames of research are determined essentially by the researcher himself.	Time frames for research are determined by the client.

Given the first premise — identical criteria of quality — the research initiated by society is subject to more conditions than that initiated by science. No mention has been made here of financial frames, which are concerned with whether an assignment is of limited duration of involves a more permanent contract.

The second premise — the different purposes of the two kinds of research — begs a question connected with their interdependence. Can policy-oriented research, with its clear stipulations regarding implementation, be conducted without a cognitive base derived from discipline-oriented research? My answer is in the negative; it is based on two arguments. First, we are concerned, in several sectors of society, with two kinds of research; in educational research, however, the difference is more often one of degree than of kind. Second, the interdependence of the two kinds of research is such that policy-oriented research is designed to help broaden the selection of research problems in discipline-oriented research, and discipline-oriented research is designed to help deepen theories concerning the problem of policy-oriented research. Activities may take place simultaneously, but it is probably more common for theoretical developments to come earlier.

Other factors that must be considered concern the prospects of implementing the sectoral principle, and as far as the universities are concerned, the following can be mentioned.

There must be a balance between the two kinds of research in a scientific department, that is, there must be scope both for research initiated by researchers and for research initiated by society. Since the latter type of research is mainly financed by allocations of limited duration, there must be a sufficient number of permanent research appointments for the former. (This is a topic of interminable discussion in Sweden, and no solution has yet been reached).

Second, researchers must be interested in policy-oriented research and this in turn presupposes that researchers accept that the selection of problems in a research assignment is governed by other than purely scientific considerations. It also presupposes that researchers accept the stipulations regarding time and finance which are associated with a research assignment.

A third factor related to the foregoing concerns credits towards formal qualifications within the universities. Policy-oriented research initiated by society must carry the same weight as research initiated by science. This is no problem if both kinds of research are subject to the same qualitative stipulations but the qualitative stipulation applying to research initiated by society is concerned not so much with original theoretical developments as with the utilization of scientific theory and methods.

Formal qualification brings us in turn to another important factor. Within a scientific department, a researcher should be able to do both discipline- and policy-oriented research. In other words, one should avoid establishing two separate appointments for the two kinds of research. This is important not least in view of the motives underlying the resolution on the sectoral principle. Within reason mutual exchange ought to be possible at the individual level.

It is not, however, only within the universities that certain measures will have to be taken for the sectoral principle to be viable, and the following conditions need to be met by the central authorities.

A dialogue is needed between the research community and the practitioner community. In order for a dialogue of this kind to be feasible, there must also be research expertise within the practitioner community. True, this expertise can be supplied by attaching researchers to the central authorities, but this is insufficient since the central authorities are generally responsible for research planning as well as for research utilization and input documentation for decision-making; they therefore need research expertise with greater continuity than is obtainable through the temporary co-option of researchers.

The research planning activities of a central authority should therefore incorporate a balance between short-term and long-term research. The demand for practical relevance must not stipulate an immediately perceptible applicability to every given problem.

5. Alternative to the sectoral principle

One alternative to the second component of the sectoral principle – the conduct of policy-oriented research within university departments – is the establishment of separate research institutes, which may either be affiliated to the universities or completely independent.

Arguments put forward by *the practitioner community* in favour of independent institutes include the following: Institutes whose research is clearly aimed at decision-making and implementation constitute more efficient research organizations than the universities. Direct links between clients and the people doing the research are increased, and political and administrative influence can be exercised more palpably. The institute system offers clients a more flexible environment as there are no other tasks competing for the time and interest of the researcher, and this also means that an institute can undertake different assignments at short notice. The reporting and presentation of findings can also be addressed direct to the clients and tailored to their preferences.

The disadvantages of the institute system, above all the risks of research becoming isolated and stagnant, are outweighed by the advantages. (Practitioners, and even researchers themselves, are on occasion heard to argue, quite rightly, that a university department is not in itself any guarantee against the stagnation of research.) The main advantages of institutes, in the eyes of the practitioners, seem to be that the community can exert more influence, and research can be conducted more efficiently in terms of the needs of practitioners. The motives inclining the scientific community in favour of institutes are more complex. Institutes, in cases where they are presented as alternatives, are supposed to ensure the continuity of research, because the presence of a permanent research staff will foster long-term research. But the scientific community is normally unwilling to accept any form of control beyond that indicated by an institute's general field of operations. Where school research is concerned, desires have been repeatedly expressed for the establishment of 'Curricular Research Institutes'. 'Evaluation Institutes', 'Language Research Institutes' and 'Handicap Research Institutes', but these desires have always been accompanied by demands that researchers be allowed to define their own research priorities within the main sector.

As regards the alternatives for policy-oriented research, the views of the two communities thus diverge in regard to the respective degrees of *necessary* and *tolerable* control of policy-oriented research.

6. Does the sectoral principle have a future?

Policy-oriented research is aimed, by definition, at producing a comprehensive view of a given problem, and at providing documentation for political and administrative decisions. It must therefore be planned and controlled on other grounds, *as well as those* of a scientific nature. Research efforts should be selected on the basis of a total appreciation of the state of a social sector, in which the current state of knowledge within that sector is allowed to decide what points are to be elucidated by means of research, and what resources are to be allotted for such purposes. Sweden has chosen to vest this responsibility mainly in the central administrative authorities. Political influence is exerted essentially through financial and other political priorities. In this way, at least in theory, the politicians have refrained from exercising any detailed control over policy-oriented research.

One of the first questions to arise, therefore, is whether it is reasonable for the central administrative authorities to exert the decisive influence on this portion of society's research resources. Policy-oriented research might be liable to become fragmented, if society is sectoralized into watertight areas of policy, each with its own central R&D authorities. Disciplinary research on the other hand is aimed, by definition, at freely assaying and developing the theories and methods of the discipline concerned. Such research, therefore, must be planned and controlled on the terms defined by the discipline itself, and universities are the obvious agencies of this kind of research.

A second question is whether it is compatible with our views concerning the liberty of research and the independence of universities to conduct policy-oriented research.

As we have already seen, the sectoral principle presupposes that the practitioners and researchers can meet and cooperate. It also presupposes that the two groups respect each other. Researchers must accept the controlled selection of problems in policy-oriented research and practitioners must accept the researchers' selection of theory and methods in their conduct of research. In my opinion, the two communities neither can nor should have identical goals and values. It is in the very tension between the necessary control defined by the practitioner and the tolerable control defined by the researcher that I see the most important characteristic of the sectoral principle. This tension, admittedly, can still be developed if policy-oriented research is conducted independently of the universities but the other tension — that between intradisciplinary and policy-oriented research — can most fruitfully be developed in an environment where both are simultaneously present.

In their mutual interaction, policy-oriented research helps to broaden the range of problems selected by disciplinary research, at the same time as the latter helps to deepen theories concerning the problems of policy-oriented research, and this ought eventually to lead to research which is both scientifically and socially relevant. Research in the school sector has shown that there is a future for the sectoral principle. For the sake of its own development, disciplinary research needs an interlocutor in the practitioner community. This is one precondition of cognitive development, not least within research in the behavioural and other social sciences.

References

1. FORSKNINGSRÅD (Research Councils) (1975). *Report from the Research Councils Commission*. SOU 1975:26. Stockholm: Liber Förlag. (In Swedish)
2. FORSKNINGSPOLITIK (Research Policy) (1977). *Report from the Research Councils Commission*. SOU 1977:52. Stockholm: Liber Förlag. (In Swedish)
3. HÖGSKOLAN I FOU-SAMVERKAN (The Universities in Research Cooperation) (1980). *Report from the Research Cooperation Commission*. SOU 1980:46. Stockholm: Liber Förlag. (In Swedish)
4. SKOLFORSKNING OCH SKOLUTVECKLING (School Research and School Development) (1980). *Report from the School Research Commission*. SOU 1980:2. Stockholm: Liber Förlag. (In Swedish)
5. MARKLUND, I. (1981). The Impact of Educational R&D. Invited Paper for the SVO Workshop 'Educational Research and Public Policy Making'. May 20–22. The Hague.
6. PRACTITIONERS AND SOCIAL SCIENTISTS (1978). *Planning and Utilization of Social Science. Current Projects, R&D for Higher Education*. Information 1978:5. Stockholm: National Board of Universities and Colleges.
7. R&D AND PUBLIC POLICY MAKING (1980). *Current Projects. R&D for Higher Education*. Information 1980:s. Stockholm: National Board of Universities and Colleges.
8. ELZINGA, A. (1980). 'Science Policy in Sweden: Sectorization and Adjustment to Crisis,' *Research Policy*, 9 (2), April.
9. ELZINGA, A. (1980). 'Science Studies in Sweden,' *Social Studies of Science*, 10, pp. 191–214, May.
10. WITTROCK, B. (1980). 'Science Policy and the Challenge to the Welfare State,' *West European Politics*, 3 (3), October.
11. BLUME, S. (1981). *The State of Art in Science Policy Research and Implications for Policy*. A report to the Swedish Council for Planning and Co-ordination of Research. February 1981.

The Impact of Policy-Oriented Educational R & D

Inger Marklund – University of Uppsala

Background

A great deal of Swedish educational R&D in the past twenty years has been conducted within the framework of a sectorally-defined programme.*

The main responsibility for the planning of both research and development work under this programme has been vested in the National Board of Education (NBE), which is the national administrative authority in charge of elementary and upper secondary schooling, and adult education. At the same time as the Swedish Riksdag, in 1962, legislated the introduction of a comprehensive school to replace the school system then in existence, it also decided to introduce a special budgetary allocation for educational research and development. The Riskdag resolution laid down that this allocation was to be utilized for basic research at universities and other higher education establishments, and for development work both in individual schools and municipalities and by the various NBE sections responsible for curricular follow-up and the evaluation of the reform of the school system.

This allocation has increased substantially since 1962 and has come to play an important part in Sweden's overall educational research effort, but this process falls outside the scope of the present account. Before I discuss the impact which R&D activities have had on educational policy and practice, I must say a few words about the way in which the programme has been built up and the extent to which various parts of the education system have been involved in it.

1. Growth of the allocation

To begin with, in 1962, the allocation stood at a modest Skr 2 million

---

*The terms 'sector' and 'sectoral research' are discussed in Marklund, I. 'The Sectoral Principle in Swedish Research Policy', p. 141.

154   *Social Science Research and Public Policy-Making*

(roughly US $460 000). Its growth is illustrated in Table 1, which also includes data concerning total State expenditure on education in Sweden and the proportion of that expenditure comprising development costs. It should be made clear that the central and local authorities share educational costs in Sweden, and that the figures presented here refer solely to the Central Government share, which is roughly half the total volume of expenditure on schools and adult education.

Table 1: The R&D allocation in proportion to total State educational expenditure within the NBE's sphere of responsibility. Thousands of kronor. (Skr 1 000 = approx US $230)

Year	Total State Expenditure	R&D allocation	Percentage of all State expenditure	
1962/63	1 580 000	2 050	0.12	
1963/64	1 852 000	1 874	0.10	
1964/65	2 008 779	2 110	0.10	
1965/66	2 710 291	3 242	0.11	Period I
1966/67	2 992 665	3 700	0.12	
1967/68	3 494 205	5 680	0.16	
1968/69	3 831 221	9 610	0.25	
1969/70	4 918 546	13 650	0.27	
1970/71	5 219 844	18 150	0.34	
1971/72	5 520 162	20 590	0.37	
1972/73	6 457 033	22 975	0.35	
1973/74	6 845 465	24 125	0.35	Period II
1974/75	7 286 773	26 625	0.36	
1975/76	8 121 762	29 982	0.36	
1976/77	10 257 182	33 700	0.32	
1977/78	10 789 230	36 108	0.33	
1978/79	13 158 543	35 982	0.27	Period III
1979/80	14 643 045	35 982	0.24	
1980/81	17 673 389	35 982	0.20	
1981/82	20 697 100	35 857	0.17	Period IV

As can be seen, the allocation rose steeply until the mid-seventies but has remained nominally unaltered for the past few years. The relative proportions of State running costs and development costs are perhaps more interesting than the absolute figures. It is often argued that areas in process of development should be allotted at least one, and preferably two, per cent of the overall running costs for R&D. The table shows that this proportion has never exceeded 0.37 per cent, and that it declined steadily during the second half of the 1970s, so that now, in 1981, it is down to 0.17 per cent.

These, however, are not the only resources available for R&D in Sweden: the fixed resources constituted by research appointments at universities and colleges and appointments at the NBE itself for development work and R&D planning should also be added, together with other flexible resources from other central authorities and from research councils and foundations. An estimate of the total resources — subject to the uncertainties which invariably accompany such estimates — indicates that, during recent years, educational research and development in Sweden has been able to draw on about Skr 46m (approx US $10.6m.) per annum, the NBE's allocation constituting about 78 per cent of this total amount. If attention in the Swedish debate on educational R&D focuses mainly on activities financed by the NBE allocation, this is to a great extent due to the heavy predominance of that allocation as a financial source and, consequently, as a factor governing the thrust of educational R&D.

In the following pages I will concentrate on the NBE allocation.

2. R&D planning

After a brief comment on the nature of R&D activities, four periods in the history of allocations for this purpose will be discussed (see Table 1).

Policy-oriented R&D

The activities described here have been and still are distinctly policy-oriented. This was already inherent in the 1962 Riksdag resolution. There have been at least four characteristics distinguishing this policy-oriented R&D from what is commonly termed discipline-oriented or basic research.

(1) It is conducted in accordance with a *plan* which, budgetwise, covers a five-year period and, as regards detailed budget planning, spans one year. The majority of large-scale R&D projects run for three to six years. The plan is officially adopted by the NBE after consultation with a group of educational researchers.
(2) The sub-programmes within this plan are based on the *coordination of R&D*. In other words, the measures to be taken to use and apply the knowledge that research provides are often built into the activity. Hence a great deal of R&D is not educational research in the traditional sense. The development segments often involve curriculum construction and the development of teaching aids and evaluation instruments.
(3) R&D is designed particularly to facilitate the *dissemination of results*. From the very beginning, means for the transfer of information to, among other things, the in-service training of teachers, are built into

the project. This is not so much intended as a means of identifying solutions to educational problems as a way of vitalizing the educational debate on a broad front. This debate is of great importance for decision-makers on educational policy, and for the administration of the educational system.

(4) R&D of this kind is *examined and evaluated* against the goals set up for educational policy. Such examinations and evaluations are made on a number of occasions. First, the project activity is analysed by scientific observers. Second, it is assessed by educational politicians and educational administrators. Third, an Educational Advisory Council, attached to the NBE, and including representatives of the political parties and the municipalities, educational researchers, teachers and students, systematically monitors and evaluates the entire R&D programme. The Council submits an annual report to the Minister of Education.

This policy-oriented R&D has been conducted mainly on the basis of what is commonly termed the R&D model. The implication of this model is that research is conducted as basic research generating a certain amount of basic knowledge which is fed into development work. It ought by now to be clear that this model, whose premises are derived from research in the natural sciences, has not in every respect been the most suitable model for the social sciences or for educational R&D, and I shall return to this point in due course.

Four periods of R&D planning

PERIOD I covers eight years and constitutes the build-up phase of activities. 'Build-up' is a key word in this context, as a fundamental reform of the school system had been legislated in 1962. In its wake there followed a build-up of the organization of the central authority, and also of reforms in the pre-service and in-service teacher education sectors, where the establishment of schools of education had a particularly important bearing on the progress of activities. These schools were equipped with educational research departments to which the greater part of educational R&D was entrusted, and in this way the allocation came to play a very important part in the build-up of general scientific competence within these institutions.*

---

*It is worth mentioning that out of a total of 188 doctoral theses in education presented between 1962 and 1979, 22 per cent were financed entirely out of the NBE R&D allocation and 44 per cent with grants from the NBE and other central authorities or *ad hoc* Commissions. If we confine our attention to the educational research departments of the Schools of Education, the proportion of those partly or wholly financed by the NBE was 49 per cent.

The most important characteristic of this period was the increasing segregation of research and development, which came to be regarded as separate branches of activity.

Work began in the late 1960s with the aim of bridging the gap between these two portions of educational R&D. Starting in 1970/71, which marks the inauguration of Period II, activities were planned in the form of six programmes focusing on the various levels of the school system, and R&D planning acquired the following structure:

R&D concerning the problems of
    A Pre-school education
    B Elementary schools
    C Upper secondary schools
    D Adult education
    E Pre-service and in-service teacher education
    F Vertically integrated R&D

This R&D planning was built up by stages, and one of its patent advantages was the linking of research and development. Research projects and findings were more naturally integrated with the NBE's continuous monitoring and evaluation activities; development work at the NBE and in the field, in individual schools and municipalities, tended more and more to provide the basis on which priorities were defined. The process was not without its frictions among researchers, administrators and practitioners in the field.

One of the obvious drawbacks to this planning was that R&D was made to focus excessively on the different levels of the school system. Elementary school questions were separated from upper secondary school questions, and pre-service and in-service teacher education projects were quite often planned separately from projects relating to schools. Projects were demarcated according to the school administrative system, but they were not always automatically geared to the problems of a more general nature that characterize educational and psychological research.

In 1977 an effort was made to remedy this defect by designing programmes along two dimensions. During *Period III* educational levels were combined with problem areas, and these problem areas are at present as follows:

1. Documentation and analysis of the Swedish educational system
2. Educational systems and life-long learning
3. Educational planning and evaluation
4. School and the physical environment
5. In-service training and personnel development
6. Education and society

7. The 'inner work' of the schools i.e. the practical day-to-day workings of the school
8. Cognitive development
9. Communication skills
10. Socio-emotional and physical development
11. Tests and grading in educational evaluation
12. Regional and local development work
13. The linking of pre-school education and primary school
14. Subject-oriented R&D
15. Handicapped children
16. Immigrants and cultural minorities
17. Curriculum development work
18. Teaching materials

As can be seen, these problem areas are in no way mutually exclusive. The advantage of having problem areas as a complement to the stage structure lies in the subsequent anchoring of research planning in research conditions rather than in administrative conditions. In future this should continue to be one of the preferred methods for planning research projects. When current activities were audited on these lines, this planning along two dimensions also revealed how many white areas there were on the map. Above all, it was made clear that large sectors of upper secondary schooling were being omitted from systematic and long-term research and development activities, and that attention so far as adult education was concerned had focused excessively on recruitment studies, to the detriment of studies concerning the content of adult education, the educational needs of adult students, and the relevance of these to the organization of adult education.

In the past two years, owing mainly to the adverse trend in economic developments in Sweden, great importance has also been attached to priority areas. This had led to a third dimension, or perhaps rather to the identification of particularly urgent 'nodes' in the stage/problem combinations.

Apart from economic conditions, however, *Period IV*, which as the table shows commences in 1981/82, has another, more important characteristic. What has happened is that the entire fabric of R&D activities has increasingly been called in question both politically and in the field. It is the usefulness of the past eighteen years' efforts to the Swedish school system that is being queried. The period can in fact be said to have opened with the contention that 'The educational R&D undertaken so far as not been of any use to us whatsoever'. It is of course no coincidence that this should be asserted with particular vehemence in a period of economic stagnation.

It was partly on account of this scepticism that the Government, in the summer of 1978, appointed a committee to scrutinize the activities financed under the present arrangements and to propose means of bringing R&D closer to what are called 'everyday school problems' and stepping up research into the relations between schools and the community at large. The committee's work thus came to be very much concerned with the ways in which R&D planning should be transformed in order to give R&D itself greater impact.

Another factor involved here is the wave of decentralization at present sweeping across Sweden. Great changes have already occurred in several areas of the education system, resulting in the reapportionment of responsibilities between central and local authorities, and for this reason a review of educational R&D, which had hitherto been planned on a central basis, was both predictable and logical.

The committee's report* was submitted to the Minister of Education in February 1980.**

Like practically all the reports produced by Government-appointed commissions, this too was circulated to a number of interested parties within the educational sector, who were invited to give their views on the proposals it contained. In June 1981 the Riskdag took a decision on the Minister of Education's proposals in the light of the committee's proposals and reactions to these. The gist of this decision was that the previous strong tie between research and development should be loosened, in favour of a stronger link between research and long-term planning in education. The responsibility and resources for development are to be a matter of local concern, while the NBE will retain the responsibility and resources for research. All research will be performed within university departments. Research is to be more pronouncedly decision-oriented and its association with educational practice, which is to say the day-to-day work of the schools, is to be toned down.

The discussion in the present article, however, will concentrate on the analyses performed by the committee concerning the dissemination and utilization of the results of educational research.

The committee also dealt with several other points. The report thus includes a fairly exhaustive description of the structure of R&D activities and of the existing forms of political, scientific and field-based influence. The committee also analysed some of the implications for the universities in terms of their general research and the policy-oriented research derived from it. To provide documentation on which to base proposals aimed at strengthening the links between R&D and everyday school activities, a

---

*SKOLFORSKNING OCH SKOLUTVECKLING (School Research and School Development) (1980). *Report from the School Research Committee.* SOU 1980:2. Stockholm: Liber Förlag. (In Swedish).

**A brief description of the structure and procedures of the Swedish committee systems is contained in MARKLUND, I. (1981). 'Educational Research in Sweden. Reform strategics and Research Policy,' *International Review of Education,* 27, (2).

study was made of the feasibility of and impediments to local development work in three municipalities. The committee also discussed general trends in Swedish society which can be expected to have repercussions on educational R&D, and went on to consider the dissemination of educational research findings. Finally, in keeping with its terms of reference, the committee discussed ways of stepping up international exchange in the field of educational R&D. (The present author was Secretary General of the committee.)

3. The utilization of R&D results

In the committee's study of the dissemination and utilization of results the main emphasis was on a qualitative analysis of the utilization of R&D findings in seven problem areas. The analysis covered both research projects at scientific institutions and development projects at the NBE or in individual schools, muncipalities and adult education organizations.

One consistent theme of the criticism levelled against educational R&D has been the difficulties experienced, above all in the field but also at the central political level, in obtaining and using R&D results. Since educational R&D, with its clear policy focus, is aimed at promoting innovatory strategies for improving education, the question of how the results of this work are put to practical use is a particularly interesting one and it was specially emphasized in the committee's terms of reference.

The degree and nature of effects

There is no simple and unambiguous way of explaining why certain R&D results have effects on educational policy and practice. It is possible, however, to identify different *types* of effect. The commonest types of effect include the following:

arousing interest and debate
influencing attitudes
suggesting new organizational models
suggesting new administrative rules and routines
influencing curriculum design
introducing new working routines and teaching methods
supplying new teaching materials.

These effects have been ordered more or less from most general to most specific, but there is no self-evident connection between their actual impact on educational policy and practice and their degree of specificity. Every type of effect has also to be assessed according to its degree of impact, and in this respect effects can vary from those with little or no impact to those with a very powerful impact. Again positive and negative effects must be distinguished; thus, a research finding may spark off a debate on an issue of educational policy which tends to polarize various fundamental opinions rather than generate any greater understanding of the problem on which the research was intended to shed light.

Factors influencing the occurrence of effects

The conditions helping to produce effects (or preventing effects from materializing) are more interesting than the effects themselves. The term 'correlate' is sometimes employed as a collective designation for the conditions varying with the occurrence of effects.

The *nature* of effects is probably connected with the problem or problem area to which the individual R&D input refers. A project concerned with the development of teaching methods in a particular subject can have quite different effects from a project concerned with the relations between schools and the community at large. (This distinction may appear trite, but, as we shall see in due course, it only too often tends to be overlooked.) Another factor with a bearing on the nature of an effect is the question of the target group which is expected to benefit from the results. This too may seem a truism, but the importance of this aspect is not always taken into account when research findings are being dicussed.

It is not always possible to distinguish factors influencing the nature of effects from factors influencing the degree of effects. The following are some of the main factors which appear to influence the *degree* of effects:

the distinctness of the message

information dissemination routes

the existence of linkage persons and information channels (e.g. organizations, interest groups)

preparedness on the part of the recipients (in terms of knowledge, needs and interest)

the addition of new knowledge, in respect of both practical guidance and theoretical insight.

It is of course possible to identify other effects and factors to explain the occurrence of effects, and it is acknowledged that those mentioned could be defined more precisely. But I believe that the best way of elucidating the discussion so far will be to present summarily an actual case. As I have already mentioned, the committee dealt in the course of its scrutiny with seven problem areas and one of these related to the research undertaken in respect of handicapped pupils, the term handicapped being taken to refer to (1) the deaf and hard of hearing, (2) the blind and partially sighted, (3) the physically disabled and (4) the mentally handicapped or retarded. The R&D plan does not include pupils of low general ability in the handicap category.

The following is an excerpt from the relevant part of the committee's report (Appendix 1), commissioned from Professor Karl-Gustav Stukát, Department of Education, University of Göteborg.

A case study – R&D on handicapped children

A group of projects in remedial pedagogics has been devoted to the development of learning methods for handicapped pupils. This includes the Primary ADL Training project (Adjustment to Daily Life), concerning everyday skills for the mentally retarded. Method development proceeded according to principles of instructional technology and resulted in a number of training programmes. The project attracted a great deal of attention and was considered to be the first 'bread and butter' project to have been immediately translated into practice. Its practical implementation was facilitated by the compilation of NBE guides for training school and institutional staff. On the whole, however, the 'educational Zeitgeist' has been against the implementation of methods of instructional technology. The method-materials systems developed, for example, within the remedial teaching project SMID (for pupils with impaired hearing) and SISU (for low performers) have hardly achieved the practical impact expected of them, even though trials revealed positive attitudes. It is also worth noting that, in spite of the good results, many researchers later criticized the training of skills divorced from any integral context of personal psychology.

Subsequent special teaching projects have had wider aims and a greater integral emphasis. This applies, for example, to PUSS (pedagogical investigations concerning the educational situation of the blind and partially sighted), which includes both basic studies of learning and an analysis of the total educational situation. From its very inception this project has entailed close cooperation with the Association for the Blind and has been made to incorporate ideas put forward by the Association, which of course has favourably influenced the chances of the project results being put into practice. Another form of cooperation which has favourably influenced the degree of utilization has been practised in the SIF project (special pedagogics in pre-school education) where new models for activation measures and parental education in connection with children requiring special support have been tested in an experimental scheme directed by municipal study groups connected with the project. These activities have in fact continued after the termination of the project.

It can often be difficult to assess the practical effects of an individual project, while on the other hand it is easier to trace effects of total research inputs in a problem area. An example of this kind can be quoted from the teaching of the deaf and partially hearing. During the past ten years several projects, most of them forming part of the NBE R&D programme, have dealt with various aspects of language assimilation by deaf and partially hearing pupils. All of these projects have helped, from various angles, to shed light on a long disputed point in auditory pedagogics, namely the advantages and disadvantages of the manual and oral methods respectively. Manual communication takes place by means of signs and is used spontaneously by deaf persons between themselves from an early age. Its limitation is that it only works if both parties can use it. Moreover, sign language has been presumed to inhibit the learning of spoken and written language. The spoken oral language permits communication with hearing persons, but a limit is often dictated here by the difficulties encountered by a person who is deaf or whose hearing is seriously damaged in speaking and apprehending speech.

The above mentioned research projects have not yielded a conclusive answer to the question of how language learning should proceed in the case of the deaf and partially hearing, but they undoubtedly have a clear message concerning pedagogics for these pupils. The focus of the projects has varied, but they converge in the sense of undermining, in a number of ways, the arguments in favour of the dominant role of the oral language methodology hitherto. Above all, the main argument against the sign method — that it inhibits general language development — appears to lack the support of research findings. A change of methodological course would seem by all accounts to be imminent regarding language learning among the audiologically handicapped, and there can hardly be any doubt that research has actively contributed towards this development. At a conference on hearing disabilities in 1976, several representatives of Swedish pedagogics for the deaf and partially hearing clearly advocated a combination of speech and sign language and 'total communication' as distinct from a one-sided mode of communication in the teaching context. This implies a different methodological approach from that expressed in the curricular supplement so far remaining in force for special schools for the deaf and hard of hearing. That supplement is dominated by speech training, speech correction, hearing training, training in the sensory perception of speech and lip reading. It is to be expected that future methodological instructions will be given a somewhat different content.

One group of investigations which cannot really be omitted from this summary, although they have partly occurred outside the range of the NBE project programme, are the special pedagogical effect studies, i.e. the studies devoted to an evaluation of remedial class teaching.

These have had a very important effect on the educational debate and educational developments, added to which they admirably elucidate a number of important correlates of the efficacy of research. Discussion of remedial pedagogics in Sweden has above all centred round the investigations by Österling and Stangvik. The results of both these studies suggested better cognitive achievements (though possibly somewhat inferior school satisfaction) among low ability pupils continuing to attend ordinary classes, compared with pupils placed in remedial classes. These findings tallied quite well with those obtained in several international studies.

The above mentioned research findings are hardly likely to have had a decisive effect in bringing about the development towards coordinated remedial instruction which has occurred in Swedish schools during the past ten years. Demands for integration have to a greater extent been backed up with other, non-scientific arguments. But research has undoubtedly influenced standpoints and policy decisions (as for example in the case of the SIA Commission and the SIA Bill (SIA: Inner work in School.) This has been due not least to research coming at an opportune moment, i.e. during a period when there was a very great need for knowledge and information. A typical instance of the close interconnection of research information and utilization needs is provided by the research group which, at the instance of the NBE, have synthesized research findings and conclusions in their several fields; mental retardation, physical disabilities and vision and hearing difficulties. The surveys and syntheses presented in their trend report have provided the Government appointed Integration Commission with a useful source of information for its current work.*

Summing up, R&D activities in the field of remedial education can be said to have had a distinct impact in relation to educational practice and discussion. It seems reasonable to infer that the conditions governing dissemination and utilization have been propitious. Research information has been addressed to particular target groups, information has been communicated not only by researchers but also by active interest groups (associations of the handicapped), cognitive preparedness for the reception of R&D information may be presumed to be good among remedial teachers, and the projects have come at a time when there was a great need of information. There are probably several reasons for the relatively little use made of the method-materials systems of educational technology, but one of them would seem to be that the methodology was based on an excessively technological basic approach which the majority of educationalists are not in sympathy with.

*Research and development concerning integration of handicapped pupils into the ordinary school system. National Board of Education, Stockholm, 1980.

The above summary is an illuminating one. There can hardly be any other field of educational research in Sweden where the prospects for research utilization have been so auspicious. But this does *not* mean that handicap research began in these propitious circumstances or that work during the almost twenty years that have elapsed has been free from problems and conflicts. On the contrary, it would seem fair to say that the very factors that were found, in the event, to favour the efficient utilization of results were often regarded, particularly during the early years, as a great impediment to getting projects off the ground at all. Here as in all fields of research and development, time and continuity are key words. It is in the long-term context that effects can be identified, and this demands both time and continuity. Although the resources allotted for research on problems relating to the handicapped have made up a fairly limited proportion of total R&D resources (eight to ten per cent annually), there have always been R&D activities in progress. The number of researchers has also been limited, but in this connection the NBE has endeavoured to maintain and improve the special competence developed by various researchers and research groups.

The conclusions drawn by the committee on the basis of the review as regards *the degree of effects* were summarized in the following terms.

It is of course impossible to estimate the magnitude of the influence exerted by R&D projects, nor can that influence be gauged in relation to expectations. What we can say with a reasonable degree of certainty is that projects have been overwhelmingly concerned with real problems in schools and with the addition of useful knowledge to educational practice. The review of projects bears witness to a widespread aspiration to distribute information about project results to the groups and organizations concerned. It is evident from the review, and also from the project results having been translated into practical policy in various ways, that this has succeeded in no small measure. At the same time it is clear that a considered strategy for dissemination has often been lacking and that the impact of project results on actual education is less distinct than the impact of actions at the administrative level.

The fact that the clearest effects of R&D projects are observable at levels above or outside the actual educational situation can be variously interpreted, as a shortcoming or as something natural and acceptable. The first of these interpretations implies that it is unsatisfactory for project results to be applied mainly to organizational changes, the revision of statutes, curricular revisions and INSET programmes. These organizational changes are of course intended to bring about changes in teaching practice, but their direct impact on school work is less easily attested. The *second* interpretation implies that R&D results are not usually suitable for direct implementation in the classroom but need to be communicated to educational practitioners via intermediaries of various kinds. The two approaches are not mutually exclusive; if anything, they are mutually complementary. It should be a legitimate primary aim of R&D projects to shed light on problems formulated at the political or administrative level without necessarily following up those problems into the concrete school situation. At the same time the discrepancy frequently observed between reform development as manifested, for example, in curricula and observable practice constitutes a challenge to R&D activities.

4. A summary of the analysis of dissemination and result utilization

The analysis of the dissemination and utilization of results shows that the picture is by no means as gloomy as the critics have argued (and are arguing still). Within each area it was possible to demonstrate effects both on educational policy and on educational practice. But the audit material also provided a foundation for critical viewpoints, and for deliberations concerning desirable measures for future R&D planning. Some of the contexts in which weaknesses were most conspicuous were summarized in the following terms:*

... In most cases the dissemination and utilization phase is that part of the projects to which least attention is paid. Even projects which are well planned in all other respects often lack a considered dissemination strategy. It is natural to conclude that (1) the dissemination and utilization phase of a project should be included in the planning. Experience indicates that dissemination measures need to be taken early. Favourable effects have often been observed in the case of projects to which interest groups have already been attached from the beginning or during the planning phase, subsequently acting as intermediaries and channels of information for wider groups of users. (2) The forms in which project results are presented are another aspect in need of development. Discussion so far as been mainly concerned with ways of making the message available, for example through the avoidance by its sender of unnecessarily complicated language. But it is no less important (3) to adjust the information and the forms of dissemination to the needs of different groups of recipients. It is seldom likely to be sufficient for a project to be reported in one way only. Many-sided information should be aimed at instead; written and oral information, reports, articles and radio and television broadcasts, teaching materials, INSET and debates. Dissemination and utilization need to be viewed more than hitherto as the joint responsibility of the

---
*Figures in brackets and the underlined sentences which follow them indicate areas in which measures were proposed by the committee.

NBE, i.e. the sponsor or the *uppdragsgivare* and the projects. Another implication of more considered dissemination planning is (4) that the project budget should also include funds for dissemination and utilization measures.

As has already been observed, project results are mainly utilized at the administrative level, while teachers, for example, quite often say that R&D information is not particularly relevant to their everyday teaching. Even though R&D activities ought of course to a great extent to cater for the needs of administration and planning, it is not satisfactory for R&D to be considered by large groups in the education sector to be of minor importance and relevance. This problem has been touched on previously, in terms of problem selection, training and forms of dissemination. One fact to which insufficient attention seems to have been paid is (5) that it is only in exceptional cases that project results can be directly translated into practice. Projects yield information, ideas and models which need to be elaborated and adapted to local circumstances. In order for this to be accomplished, and in order for project results to be found relevant and down-to-earth, (6) there must be a certain measure of developmental preparedness within schools. Various developmental incentives are therefore needed; financial support for teacher-directed experiments, INSET, in the form of participation in experimental activities, and a link between projects and development work.

One aspect of R&D planning which is in particular need of scrutiny is (7) the relations between projects within the NBE and projects at university departments (often called 'internal' and 'external' projects). Whereas previously they were separately handled these two kinds of project are now covered by a single fabric of R&D planning. In a way this integration via common handling is more apparent than real. The plans submitted for internal projects are often so brief as to preclude any real assessment in terms of needs or quality. It is also difficult to judge the feasibility of coordinating different projects.

In future R&D planning, the same demands for exhaustively stated plans should apply to all projects. Closer coordination is also desirable in other respects. Curricular and teaching material development are principally based on internal projects, but external projects too have often influenced curricular work and resulted in the development of teaching materials which have come to be employed in teaching. Deliberate efforts to coordinate internal and external measures in these fields are less in evidence.

The external projects tend quite consistently to be research projects, albeit of various kinds. The internal projects represent a wide scale ranging from minor surveys and experiments to projects coming close to the external ones. It is reasonable for sectorial development work to include both long-term research and more immediate problem solving.

Thus educational R&D will still need in the future to include activities of various kinds. Parts of the NBE's internal project activities may come close to administrative routine. This applies above all to Government assignment or initiatives taken by the NBE itself in response to sudden problems. It is in the nature of things that internal projects like these cannot be integrated with a long-term R&D plan or even be predicted in annual budget requests. But there is a cause for a close scrutiny of internal projects in the vague border territory between development work and administrative work. (8) <u>A long-term development plan for the education sector</u> should also, one hopes, help to reduce the number of these unforeseen internal projects.

The purpose of R&D activities is to contribute towards a successive build-up of knowledge and towards the utilization of that knowledge in the education system. This purpose cannot really be achieved one hundred per cent, (9) <u>but it should be possible for R&D activities to be conducted in such a way as to make the utilization of results more effective.</u> At present surveys in the school sector often have to begin with comprehensive inquiries or research programmes and are only able to a limited extent, as a rule, to build on R&D work done previously. Naturally a survey raises questions requiring special studies, but it should be possible for cognitive preparedness to be substantially increased with the aid of the educational R&D allocation. (10) <u>This demands a planning pattern catering for the needs of coordination and long-term perspective but at the same time flexible in relation to changing requirements.</u> *Ad hoc* measures with a short-term perspective have bulked too large in R&D hitherto.

The committee's analysis of the efficacy of R&D results has necessarily, mainly due to lack of time, been limited as regards both the range of problem areas and the depth of analysis. At the same time it is clear that analyses of this kind are a very important but hitherto partially neglected field of research. Greater knowledge of the conditions impeding and promoting effective utilization of the results of R&D work would make it possible to develop alternative models and methods of dissemination and result utilization. The committee is therefore anxious (11) for <u>R&D work to be inaugurated concerning these matters.</u>

5. And still the usefulness of R&D is called in question!

The above account serves to show that educational R&D has had effects, and that these effects have had an impact on both educational policy and educational practice. Yet it has been and still is being argued that this work has been of little if any use, above all to those concerned with the practicalities of education and also to decision-makers at the political and administrative level. What is the reason for this widespread distrust? Why has it been — and why is it still — so difficult to deflate the myth of the inefficacy of educational R&D?

Perhaps the greatest paradox of all is that, at the same time as there is an ever heavier investment in R&D at the political level, confidence in the problem-solving capacity of R&D is declining. (The fact that the NBE's R&D allocation has not increased in recent years does not mean that total R&D resources have diminished, merely that they have been differently distributed.) But it is not only at the political level that expectations concerning research are expressed; expectations are voiced just as often by practitioners, with reference to highly concrete problems. The simplest form of such expectations can be found in the hope that research will solve the disciplinary problems of schools.

I would like to submit the following viewpoints concerning possible and partial explanations.

What are the aims of R&D?

One fundamental explanation for the opinions declared concerning the non-materialization of effects and the uselessness of R&D may lie in the aims defined for these activities and in the expectations thus generated.

One firmly rooted interpretation of the purposes of R&D has been that R&D is meant to help in the immediate solution of problems. This expectation rests on a belief that the problems of schools can be solved, that there is one answer and one only to given problems. This is probably where the weaknesses of the so-called R&D model are most apparent. The complex relationships involved by all human activity have been more or less disregarded. Similarly there has long been a reluctance to concede that 'everyday school life' is only a portion of the everyday life of teachers and pupils and that activities in school are not segregated from other social life.

But hopes concerning the role of research in solving problems have not been built up solely, or even primarily, by school practitioners. It would be fairer to say that the policy-makers, central administrators and researchers themselves have contributed towards these high-pitched expectations. The 1960s, when the R&D activities now under consideration began to be built up, were a period of optimism, an optimism which was by no means confined to Sweden. Efforts were made in an atmosphere of profound confidence in the ability of R&D to contribute towards the realization of the new school and against the background of a powerfully enunciated unanimity concerning education policy. Even if there is still unanimity concerning the goal, namely that we should aim at a school giving each individual the chance of developing according to his or her aptitudes, there is now far less unanimity concerning the way in which this goal is to be achieved.

One of the first things to be done, therefore, must be to discuss the purposes of R&D. All research is aimed at enhancing somebody's knowledge about something. In this respect there is no difference between policy-oriented and disciplinary research. But policy-oriented research is expected to act more rapidly in supplying new or additional knowledge about something, knowledge which can and should be translated in some way into practical activity. As I see it, R&D must continue to be aimed at solving problems. What we have to eliminate is the belief − or rather, the expectation − that R&D will provide *the* solution to *the* problem.

What are results and what are effects?

In the summary of the committee's review it was observed that investments in educational R&D and the linking of these activities to purpose-oriented development work had yielded valuable results. Where teaching materials are concerned it is common practice nowadays for the pupils' learning materials to be combined with teachers' manuals, work books and diagnostic materials. But the question is whether changes of this kind or other effects such as new syllabi, new pupil groupings and new types of test are really to be seen as improvements or merely as disruptions to the work of the school. As has already been made clear, problems in schools cannot be 'solved' through results of this kind. These results produce subsidiary effects and supporting measures, and the effect of the latter is often greatly dependent on overall aims in education. If the development of new teaching materials and methods leads to new demands for teacher collaboration or new demands concerning pupil groupings (large groups, small groups, individualized work), and if at the same time teachers oppose these things, it is naturally difficult for the results to be seen as 'practical'. Perhaps the reason for complaints that R&D results are not capable of implementation is that mutually irreconcilable demands are involved.

Preparedness for, and the acceptance of, change are a primary condition for the utilization of educational R&D. Decision-makers and 'recipients' can arrive at different valuations, inasmuch as they do not comprise identical persons or groups. The decision-maker, for example, may feel that a teacher substitute leads to better goal achievement, while the teacher, seeing his employment threatened, may be sceptical. Goal conflicts of this kind may help to explain the lack of usefulness from which educational R&D is often felt to suffer.

Direct and indirect results

Another reason for inquiring into the usefulness of educational R&D is that results and effects are often not manifest, but concealed in changes in areas not immediately associated with concrete R&D projects. Results of educational and other research in the behavioural sciences have given rise to statutory and curricular amendments and to new solutions in respect of teaching materials and facilities without the premises of these changes being directly observed or stated. Similarly, the terms of reference for committees of inquiry in the education sector have often been framed in the light of research findings, which, in this way, have been built in as the preconditions of further reforms. The effects have thus been of a long-term rather than a short-term nature, and they have often become part of a succession of interconnected development measures.

Convenient and inconvenient results

There is also another problem, namely that of the extent to which people actually benefit from and avail themselves of R&D results. In the fierce struggle which is often waged in schools between competing interests, R&D results have not infrequently been given a raw deal. Results may be inconvenient. They may say that the remedy is to be found in 'working harder' or in abandoning a working procedure which people are determined to retain at all costs. Knowledge is not used; people act as though it did not exist. For example, educational research has repeatedly shown that underachievement in schools is due more to methods and other external conditions than to deficient aptitudes on the part of the pupil. And yet people continue to teach as though the latter were the case. Pupils' aptitudes and results are still appraised according to fairly one-sided intellectual criteria, even though the importance of other bases of assessment has been frequently demonstrated.

The language of research

The language of research or of researchers is a factor often referred to as impeding the utilization of results. 'Stilted' language renders the implications of research findings incomprehensible to people outside the research community. This criticism is voiced just as often by politicians and decision-makers as by practitioners.

Undoubtedly this type of criticism is often justified and there is reason to devote more attention to the formal aspect of the presentation and discussion of results. Probably one reason why the presentation (by researchers) of policy-oriented research is hard for people outside the inner circle of researchers to penetrate is that the recipient groups are disparate and vary in terms of their previous knowledge and their motives for studying the research findings. Often the demand of the scientific community for a 'scientific' account carries more weight with researchers than the demands of other recipient groups. Policy-oriented research is mostly conducted on an assignment basis, but at the same time the researchers have a legitimate need to make a scientific name for themselves. The time available for reporting is not usually sufficient for the compilation of more than one type of account.

But the formal aspect of the presentation of results should not be overemphasized. Clear and straightforward language does not mean that the content of the message is automatically simple or guaranteed to get home. Very often the compilation of an intelligible and useful message demands a great deal of knowledge about the phenomena which have been studied. As we remarked earlier, there is a connection between cognitive preparedness and interest and needs preparedness. Without this interest in the *problem*, and not only in the solution, and without preparedness to put in the work required in order to penetrate the problem, efforts to improve the formal, linguistic aspect of presentation will be of no effect.

The R&D model as a model for R&D planning

In Section 2 I dealt with the R&D model. This model appeared in its purest form during the 1960s, above all in the development of new teaching materials. It stood for an essentially one-way process of communication:

(Basic) Research ⟶ Development Work ⟶ Large scale practical application.

This model was a more or less direct take-over of R&D models developed in the natural sciences. Both R&D programmes and individual R&D projects were planned in this one-way manner Translated into the social sciences, the model, during an introductory phase, became fundamentally a technical question. Research and the development based on it were aimed at equipping the teacher/practitioner with teaching techniques. It followed that the research problem must be limited to entities which could be handled in terms of techniques and research method. It goes without saying that in a paradigm of this kind, the overall perspective was relegated to the background. Moreover, R&D projects were for the most part initiated by researchers and administrators, and less often by field practitioners. But R&D planning in Sweden was all the time kept under some political control, the Government's general priorities being expressed on an annual basis in connection with the allocation of financial resources.

The R&D model in present-day terms is a great deal less technical and is based on mutuality between research and development. But — and this is important in the present context — it still reflects the fundamental conviction that research findings can and should be translated into practical activities.

Swedish educational R&D planning is founded on this conviction. Research, development work and INSET have gradually come to be viewed as parts of an integral programme for the development of the school system. As we saw in section 4, the committee set up to study educational R&D advocated a closer coordination of planning activities relating to R&D and INSET.

A growing realization of the interdependence of research and development has been accompanied by a debate as to the meaning of 'research' and the meaning of 'development' in the composite term 'research and development'. If research findings can and should be translated into practical activity, this is not to say that all research must focus on problems which can be expected to yield practically useful results relating to the everyday life of the schools. And it is neither possible nor desirable for all development work to take research as its starting point. There is thus a trend in favour of distinguishing between research and development.

This trend can be interpreted as a further example of scepticism concerning the usefulness of educational R&D, but it can equally be interpreted in a positive sense, as a point of departure for the revision of R&D planning. By way of conclusion I would like to touch on a number of conditions which I believe can lead to greater confidence in educational R&D and thus augment its utilization at all levels; the political, the administrative and classroom levels.

The R&D model revised

It is in the nature of things that the boundaries between research and development in policy-oriented R&D should be flexible. In fact these flexible boundaries are part of the definition of R&D; *cf* page 3. The demand for practically applicable results, however, has led to a thinning out of the research concept and of research itself. And development work has been subjected to demands which should really be made on research. I believe that it is necessary to broaden the framework of policy-oriented R&D by acknowledging more clearly the conditions and purposes of the two activities.

Research, even if it is policy-oriented, has to be conducted with a long-term perspective. This is not primarily a question of time input, but rather of the way in which research approaches problems. Not all research problems can and should be made to focus immediately on administrative measures. Practical problems which are made the subject of research often have to be redefined as subject-based problems. When the results have been obtained, the problems are 'redefined' as practical and administrative issues. This may appear circuitous, but aiming as it does at fundamental knowledge, it is often a short cut. In other words, one finds in most cases that there is nothing so practical as a good theory. Acceptance of this approach ought logically to lead to a reduction of the demands for *simultaneity* between research and development concerning a particular problem. Thus there must be scope for the elucidation of a problem by means of research without there being at the same time a 'practical' application in sight.

Another necessary widening of the research concept concerns the levels at which the research problem has to be redefined. The information requirements of practical, everyday school life are seldom the same as those existing at the political and administrative levels. True, everyday school life is ultimately determined by the frames defined by the community, but problems of educational policy are related in most cases to general social problems. The development work which can and should be prompted by research into general social phenomena must be conducted primarily at the central administrative level and be aimed at revising the frames governing educational activities. To simplify matters somewhat, I would term this 'research at the macro-level'.

Re-definition at the local level, i.e. in terms of practical, everyday school life, must primarily concern problems generated by the actual implementation of policy in schools.

Development work used to be regarded essentially as the handmaid of research. But development work as a part of current activities, without any necessary link-up to simultaneous research projects, is now being encouraged in various ways, which is a desirable development. Perhaps the main advantage in the present context is that more and more teachers, pupils and other members of the school community are taking part in school development work, and this participation can become the factor which eventually creates the best prospect for a development-minded school system. And there is *one* things on which all agree: a person who does not have a sense of participation in an activity will not ask for information as to how it can be improved.

Does this mean that I advocate a fairly complete divorce between R and D, between research and development? No, but I do advocate a broadening of the frames for R&D planning in order that R and D, when applicable, can act as a catalyst for a range of activities.

Schematically, a revised R&D model, the Interplay model, can be outlined as follows, the arrows denoting mutual interdependence in the application and use of results.

Every environment has a need for different kinds of knowledge development. The general scientific growth of knowledge within a discipline usually takes place within problem areas that are defined by the science itself, as well as within problem areas defined by practitioners.

The practitioner environment on the other hand must — regardless of whether at the central, regional or local levels and regardless of whether it

Figure 1: Interplay model of educational research and development processes

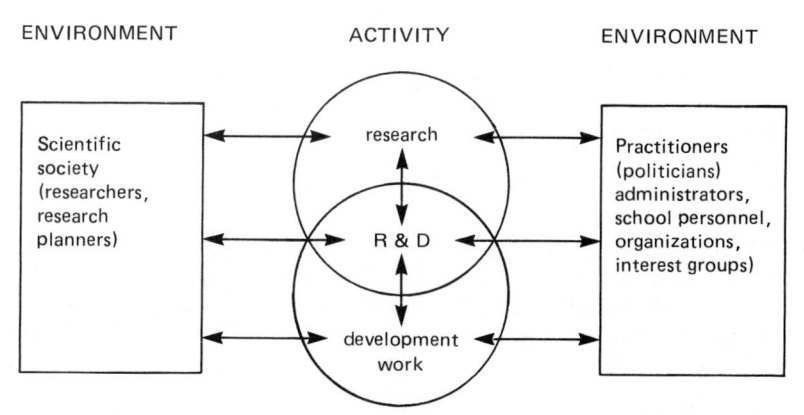

ENVIRONMENT	ACTIVITY	ENVIRONMENT
Scientific society (researchers, research planners)	research ↕ R & D ↕ development work	Practitioners (politicians) administrators, school personnel, organizations, interest groups)

is of a political, administrative or practical nature — function in interplay with research and researchers. This interplay can take place within development work that is part of the daily life of a school, in activities where research and development take place simultaneously or in basic research activities.

Such an interplay between environment and activity implies a rather different planning of R&D from that in the simpler R&D model (*cf.* page 17).

Does this Interplay model offer a better chance of R&D results being efficiently utilized? Before such a basic question can be answered, it is of use to revisit the question of what criteria should be used when considering solutions to the problems of dissemination and utilization.

The probability of result utilization will increase (according to the analysis in section 3)

> if the message is distinct, i.e. if the results are unambiguous and are lucidly presented,
> if there are established channels for the dissemination of information and findings,
> if the target group(s) is (are) clearly defined and definable, in order that the message can be addressed,
> if this target group or these target groups are interested in knowing more about something,
> if the recipient already knows a great deal about the matter in question,
> if the findings come at the right moment, i.e. when preparedness in terms of interest and needs is at its greatest and
> if the findings convey — or are felt to convey — new knowledge or confirm previous convictions.

To these 'ifs' should also be added:

if the message is adjusted to the recipient/environment.

The isolation of R&D within certain parts of a R&D-programme (or more correctly now an R(R&D)D-programme) by no means decreases the difficulties of result utilization or the redefinitions of problems at different levels. But the broadening of the frames for planning should serve as *one* starting point when planning the dissemination and utilization of results.

This Interplay model amounts partly to a change in time perspective, which means that it must be permissible for the period elapsing between research findings and 'practical implementation' to be a long one (e.g. an acceptance of the already prevailing state of affairs). And development work must be accepted for what it *also* is – part of everyday activity in the schools.

The dynamic in the interplay between environment and activity must not, however, be lost, which may very well happen if different activities are assigned solely to a specific environment or level within an environment.

The direction and scope of R&D inputs should be governed by the actual nature of the problem and the current state of knowledge. The crucial change thus lies in the formulation and specification of the problem – a process involving the initial decision as to the type of activity through which a problem should primarily be approached. And this hopefully, will offer better chances of meeting the needs established in the above-mentioned criteria.

CRITICISM AND DISCUSSION

Note by the Editors: Marklund's oral presentation was based on her two invited papers, both included in this volume.

The Swedish effort to provide each policy sector with its own research apparatus (located in the universities) in order to secure the best possible research utilization, received much attention. The general conclusions from the discussions on the Swedish case and experiences from the US especially (see section 4), are given in the first section where for brevity's sake, speakers' names have been omitted since these conclusions represent the general feeling of the Workshop participants.

Secitons 2 and 3 are elaborations on aspects of the impact problem.

The distinctions in terminology, presented in the second section, will provide a clearer picture concerning the question as to when and where one may expect impact and within how much time. As a consequence, some more remarks about the Swedish revision of the R&D model are presented in section 3, while section 4 presents the American experience in closely related matters.

1. General conclusions

In most Western countries and under a variety of labels three forms of research activity have been defined: free, policy-oriented and development. Structures for each of these have developed rapidly in the past 15 or 20 years and there is now a variety of research organizations different in pattern, function and funding. The present need is to sustain a vigorous programme of research and development through these organizations, but their level of funding is relatively low, amounting to less than half of one per cent of all educational expenditure (in the US and Sweden, for example) or slightly higher.

Teachers and policy-makers are usually unaware of research findings, even when these form the basis of their decisions. Research-based knowledge has influenced educational policy in most countries to a much higher degree than is assumed. But its effects are not fully recognized, due to the fact that research seldom has direct impact but influences policy *indirectly*, through interaction and cumulative action on public consciousness. It makes its impact by determining what kinds of questions and evidence are seen as important, and how they are seen — how people structure their perceptions of their work. In other words, research creates an agenda of concern. Often direct and clear impact is expected of forms of research (see section 2) which cannot and should not have such an effect. Recent developments in countries like Sweden, the Netherlands and the US are best understood as reflecting an over-riding concern with maximizing research impact. In the US the apparent lack of impact of (educational) research has led to a new form of evaluative inquiry, 'research on research' often presented as 'utilization research'. In Sweden and the Netherlands this led to evaluations by government-appointed committees, in 1980 and 1975. This has had some good effects by highlighting weaknesses in existing provision and practice. As a result more attention is given to dissemination of results, jargon-free communication, and frameworks for research and developments. Moreover, evaluation has now become an accepted part of innovation in Sweden and the Netherlands as has long been the case in the US.

The traditionally accepted R&D model was heavily criticized. It is considered an inadequate analysis and description of the ways in which social science research, development work and policy are related. Alternatives and revisions of this model were put forward.

The pressure for 'utilization' was considered dangerous for the further development of educational science itself: if the criterion for funding, for access and for publication is limited to short-term usefulness, then important theoretical work may be squeezed out. Despite the fact that research in education has become a nationally organized activity in most developed and many developing countries throughout the world, there is still a tendency to regard research as a dispenable luxury. However, it was felt that such an attitude is fast disappearing for research and policy-making have moved closer together. In some cases, like the Netherlands, administrators were even felt to be closing ranks in the face of research; research criticizing or challenging the existing system was becoming unwelcome or perceived as threatening.

The major questions to which answers are still sought across the modern world are how to organize and finance research in order to maximise demonstration of impact on policy and practice, what forms of research should have priority and who is to decide? One case was treated by Marklund in her paper on the 'Sectoral Principle in Swedish Research Policy'. This conscious attempt to enhance the productive impact of educational R&D received much attention during the Workshop. Marklund's attempt to review the problems of assessing impact against this background was considered a 'remarkable balance between objectivity and personal criticism' (Mitter).

The following sections give parts of the discussion in more detail.

2. Forms of research: distinctions

Mitter and *de Groot* draw attention to a terminological matter: the abundance of terms in literature dealing with research and its impact; for example, free, basic, fundamental, policy-oriented, R&D etc. *Marklund* suggested clarifying these terms somewhat along three main dimensions:

> The first dimension is the *character of research*, the second is the *functions of research* and the third dimension is *how research is motivated or initiated*. None of these dimensions is totally unrelated to the others. Yet muddling them up creates confusion in debates on research policy and research impact.
>
> As far as *character of research* is concerned the most common practice is to arrange the concepts in a linear fashion. The concepts build upon each other in a strict hierarchy as follows:
>
> Basic research ⟶ applied research ⟶ development work ⟶ practical large scale application.
>
> This linear relationship is also what constitutes the R&D model. Strictly speaking only the first two concepts refer to research. The

expression 'applied' has come to have two interpretations. Here the meaning is that research applies or uses theories and methods from basic research. But the term applied research is also often used to mean the application and use of research results for a given problem in a given context. Despite its weaknesses, this linear model occupies a key position as a means to describe research processes.

As far as the *function of research* is concerned, there are several paired concepts. One is a categorization of research function as conclusion- or discipline-oriented versus decision- or policy-oriented. The former is concerned primarily with the development of scientific theory and methods within an academic discipline, while the purpose of the latter is to provide the basis for decisions with regard to a certain issue. In discipline- or conclusion-oriented research the researchers themselves pose the questions. For decision-oriented research the questions to be investigated are stipulated by people other than researchers, or on other than scientific grounds.

A second categorization of research according to its function is conceptual versus instrumental. Simply speaking, conceptual research should provide increased knowledge about phenomena while instrumental research should provide the methods and means by which to deal with certain phenomena.

A third paired concept that has been used predominantly in Swedish contexts is the distinction between, on the one hand, that research which is of importance for the development within academic disciplines and, on the other hand, research that is more socially relevant. With this pair of concepts two of the most essential elements of research are highlighted. In the first case where it is a question of importance to the academic discipline, the primary task is to develop fundamental theories and methods where applications or uses of research are normally not yet foreseen, whereas research that is to be socially relevant is conducted with certain purposes as regards application already in mind.

The third dimension to be considered entails *motives for research*. That is, how research is initiated and motivated and often how it is financed. In the past, the most common pair of concepts used to describe research motivation has been free versus commissioned research. The former is research that is initiated by the researchers themselves and it is conducted, in principle, free from any externally imposed restrictions in selection of problems to investigate, time frames, form in which results are reported and to a certain extent research budget. Commissioned research is, as the term implies, research that is conducted under contract and it is often, but not always, characterized by certain restrictions in selection of research problem, time, form of reporting and budget.

In Sweden another set of concepts has been added to the debate:

discipline-motivated versus sector-motivated or motivated by a policy-making body. The meaning is the same as that which lies behind the distinction between free and commissioned research. The difference between these concepts is none other than a question of who initiates, and therefore finances, research. On the other hand the very selection of problems to be investigated can alter the character and function of research.

Of all three dimensions discussed so far the two which I have called character and function are closest to each other, although this is not to say that they are one and the same. The dimension that I have referred to as motivation is separate from the other two. It is in mixing up character and motivation and function and motivation that confusion has arisen. This *confusion* can be represented as follows:

Figure 1: Synonymity and dependence between research concepts

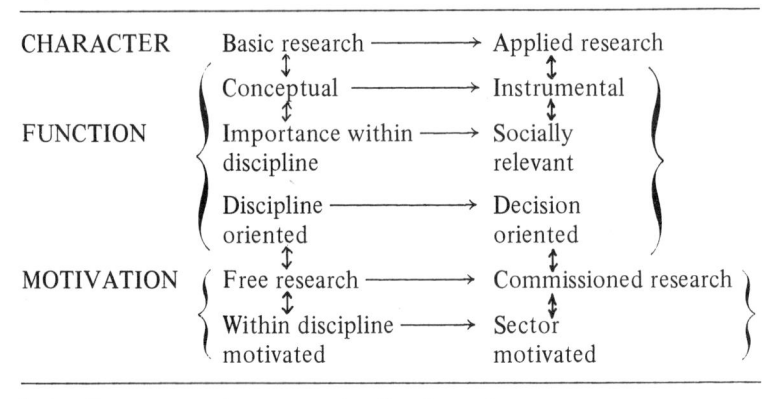

CHARACTER	Basic research ⟶	Applied research
	↕	↕
	Conceptual ⟶	Instrumental
	↕	↕
FUNCTION	Importance within ⟶ discipline	Socially relevant
	Discipline ⟶ oriented	Decision oriented
	↕	↕
MOTIVATION	Free research ⟶	Commissioned research
	↕	↕
	Within discipline ⟶ motivated	Sector motivated

↕ implies synonymity   ⟶ implies dependence

Here basic research is supposed to be synonymous with conceptual research, with discipline-oriented research and with research that is of importance to the development of an academic discipline. Each one of these four concepts is in its turn regarded as synonymous with free research and with research initiated or motivated by the researchers themselves. In other words: only discipline-motivated, free research has the character of basic research which itself is conceptual, discipline-oriented and of importance to the academic discipline. A similar simplified synonymity is assumed to exist between the concepts in the right-hand column in the diagram.

Just as it is not possible to mix an object's colour with its form so it is not possible to mix the character and function of research with its motivation.

In my view, a three dimensional figure would be a more accurate way of illustrating the interdependencies between these concepts. For the sake of simplicity I have summarized the dimensions in a table. Taking motivation as a starting point we get eight descriptions of research as possible points of departure:

Motivation	Function	Character
— Researcher motivated	discipline-oriented	basic research
— " "	decision-oriented	basic research
— " "	discipline-oriented	applied research
— " "	decision-oriented	applied research
— Sector-motivated	discipline-oriented	basic research
— " "	decision-oriented	basic research
— " "	discipline-oriented	applied research
— " "	decision-oriented	applied research

From this it follows *first* that one cannot mix character and function with motivation. *Second*, one cannot demand of sector-initiated research that it shall only be concerned with applied or application-oriented research and that it shall always be decision-oriented. Such demands would have to assume that the scientific basis upon which sector research rests would be fully developed as well as developed independently of the social and sectoral issues to which its results will be applied. *Third* one can also claim that in raising such demands, one would be completely overlooking the interdependencies between basic research and applied research as well as between research that is initiated by the researchers themselves as distinct from research that is initiated by sector organizations or policy-making bodies.

To my mind we tend to underestimate or to forget the research part of the set of concepts as far as function of research is concerned. If we stress research, does it then makes sense to demand results that are directly applicable to policy and practice, that are distinct and clearly identifiable in the decision process?

3. The R&D model revised

Marklund concluded that the R&D model — being built on an assumed linear relation between research, 'whether basic or applied, development work and an eventual practical application on a large scale — has turned out to be unfavourable for both research and development work'. In Sweden, the distinction between Research and Development work has become extremely vague. Marklund's paper on the impact of policy-oriented R&D in Sweden elaborated on that. She proposed a 'cautious separation of research and development'. However, she reported that recently the Swedish Minister of Education had introduced a new Bill into parliament, the Riksdag, in which such a *separation* was proposed in a drastic way. In brief this proposal comes down to the following:

1) The R&D funds of the National Board of Education in Sweden (NBE) should be split up into two equal halves, one used for educational research, the other for educational development.
2) NBE should be responsible for the research part, i.e. for the planning of research projects and for the utilization of the results.
3) All research projects, i.e. all research funds should be allocated to university departments on long-term and large-scale research projects.
4) Educational research should be linked mainly to long-term planning and policy questions in education. Everyday school problems, which used to be emphasized, are now relegated to second place.
5) Local school authorities are given the responsibility for the planning and conduct of development work including INSET activities.
6) Local authorities are given the other half of the funds.
7) And last but not least, NBE is given the responsibility for the follow up and evaluation of local developmental activities. The evaluation should comprise first an evaluation of whether local school developments benefit from this decentralization measure; second, research planning within the NBE should take into account any more general results from the local development work that generate researchable problems.

Marklund pointed out that this new Bill puts the Sectoral principle in Swedish research policy (see her paper on this topic) fully in effect for the first time:

> To my knowledge, no other sector of society or central administration, i.e. policy-making body in Sweden, has ever before been given research funds aiming predominantly at long-term policy-oriented research to be conducted exclusively within universities. However, this is not a coincidence, since education is that particular sector of Swedish society where the sectoral principle was already present even if in a more moderate way.

The workshop participants considered Marklund's alternative to such a drastic separation a fruitful approach. This alternative, termed the 'interplay model', is dealt with in Marklund's paper on impact, included in this volume. However, *Kallen* and *Mitter* pointed out that this model needs considerable elaboration. For example, the structure and the content of the arrows between the model's components need to be defined. The distinctions presented in section 2 were considered helpful in this context. In particular these distinctions may serve to bring to birth more realistic expectations concerning the demonstration of impact on policy-making and practice.

4. Parallel experiences in the US

Timpane gave a brief case study of the US experience, paralleling in many respects what Marklund had pointed out for Sweden. Timpane's basic assumption is

> that from the point of view of public policy, education research is mission-oriented. Not to say that it is all applied research by any means, but that its public support derives from the fact that it is intended to undergird an important social activity which is publicly supported. While it therefore relies upon a great deal of basic research in psychology, sociology, economics, anthropology and many other disciplines, nevertheless the well-spring of its public support is its impact upon a social activity which we call education.
>
> That having been said, the US has been under the almost identical urge to relate its research more closely to practice. In the US a centralized R&D activity is intended to support a decentralized political system. The improvement of educational practice has been established as a goal of the National Institute of Education (NIE) to go with its original goal of improving equal educational opportunity in the US. We required, in the past four years, that all the research planning in the agency demonstrate how it was addressing both of those goals. We did that very significantly in process terms; that is, we involved practitioners in our planning, we involved practitioners in our peer review process, we involved practitioners in our dissemination processes. In each of these cases we did this in significant numbers; we were not indulging in tokenism. In every one of these cases, while the proportion would vary with the nature of the task, we were involving practitioners as between 15 per cent and 50 per cent of our panels.
>
> There were fears that this involvement would lead to some dimunition of research quality, but rarely have researchers commented to me that that occurred. Far more often, have they commented to me that the process was enriched by the participation of the educational practitioners in it.
>
> To encompass the twin goals of equity and the improvement of practice, and to take account of the needs of researchers to pursue their inquiries, NIE established broad categories within which research programmes were carried on, so that the broad public purpose was visibly and clearly being served. At the same time, there was a great deal of latitude within each programme area, within which researchers could pursue topics of most interest to them. The programmes created

included reading performance, bilingual education, testing, desegregation, school finance, the organization and management of higher education. Within those areas, however, we moved simultaneously from directed research in the form of contract procurements, to grant competitions, with extensive peer reviews. At the same time that we focused the field substantively, we opened up procedurely and allowed the field to determine sub-priorities and a much greater measure of influence in selecting the projects. At the same time, we emphasized, both in research planning and as a function of the agency, the activities of synthesis and dissemination, so that we were conscious of the need to make translation and to make communication from the outset. We ended up doing a good deal more basic and more fundamental research than we had before, even though it was within broad topical perimeters. We ended up doing a bit more policy research. We ended up doing much less development and much less demonstration. It is a clear trade-off, and a necessary one in the US political system. Given the limited resources for centralized R and D, development and demonstration may be far better and more efficiently done at State and local levels, simply because the linkage in the policy system is more often there. I wonder sometimes whether or not States and localities will pick up the slack. Moreover, in the US at least, development has been and probably will be done in the private sector by the textbook publishing industry. Also entering that field, similarly, will be the persons who are going to be able to use telecommunications and computational technology to develop and market educational products. So, there are alternatives both in the private sector and at lower levels of government for development activity to be carried on.

All of this still operates in a research system which is at some remove from the actual practitioners, the teachers. This remains the Achilles heel of research utilization, in the US at least, and we have begun systematically to develop the protocols for collaborative research, a very important means over the long run, both to develop new methodologies for educational research, and to develop new ways to embed in the educational profession a spirit of inquiry.

Action and Knowledge from a Cognitive Point of View

Marc T. De Mey — University of Gent

It would be very discouraging if the current scepticism with respect to the utility of social science knowledge turned out to be based on the discovery of inherent limits of our capacities for creating knowledge. But apparently, no such theoretical boundary is blocking the way for social science development. The scepticism simply reflects the disillusionment of researchers and scholars who set out to use scientific methods for the construction of knowledge intended to become the basis for a social technology that would be as impressive as Space Programme technology. Compared to their efforts and devotion, the results might seem deplorable and one understands the feelings of doubt and dejection to which they give rise.

However, the situation might be less dramatic than it seems. What we witness might not be so much the erosion of social science knowledge as the erosion of a particular philosophy of science. We are moving beyond the triumphant but naive conception of the scientific method as an omnific mechanism for producing instant solutions to whatever problem that arises. This conception glorifies 'observation' and 'experiment' as indicated in Fleck's compact characterization:

> Es besteht ein sehr verbreiteter Mythus über Boebachtung und Experiment. Das erkennende Subjekt figuriert als eine Art Eroberer vom Typus *Julius* Cäsars, der nach der Formel *veni vidi vici* sein Schlachten gewinnt. Mann will etwas wissen, man macht die Beobachtung oder das Experiment — und schon weiss man es. Selbst Forscher, die manche Kämpfe gewannen, glauben dieses naive Märchen, wenn sie retrospectiv ihre eigenen Arbeiten betrachten. (Fleck, L., 1935, p. 9).

> (Observation and experiment are subject to a very popular myth. The knower is seen as a kind of conquerer, like Julius Caesar winning his

---

*This paper contains materials from introductory and concluding sections of *The Cognitive Paradigm*. © 1982, D. Reidel Publishing Company, Dordrecht, Holland.

battles according to the formula 'I came, I saw, I conquered'. A person wants to know something, so he makes the observation or experiment and then he knows. Even research workers who have won many a scientific battle may believe this naive story when looking at their own work in retrospect (Fleck, L., 1935 (p. 9), transl. 1979, p. 84).)

While still recognizing the value and importance of empirical research, we now realize that adherence and dedication to empirical methods does not automatically produce 'usable knowledge'. Several new trends in the study of scientific knowledge in philosophy of science as well as in various other 'sciences of science', in particular sociology of science, are linked to Kuhn's 1962 monograph, *The Structure of Scientific Revolutions*. It has become a symbol of the post-positivist orientation which emphasizes the role of preconceptions and social factors in the construction of scientific knowledge. For those who are familiar with Fleck (1935) it is intriguing to realize that in the same Vienna at the same time that the Vienna Circle reached its culminating point, Kuhn's predecessor presented an alternative whose relevance was perceived only decades later.

In the paper, we will try to illustrate how a newer image of scientific knowledge fits into a more general frame of thinking about knowledge: the cognitive approach. At the very same time that we are becoming more careful and modest with respect to scientific knowledge, the advance of computer and communication technology is promoting common and ordinary knowledge into a very fashionable and valuable commodity. Entailing a reconsideration of the roots and the nature of knowledge as currently explored in cognitive science, this reappraisal also leads into new perspectives on the relation between knowledge and its utilization. We will first examine what the cognitive orientation means by analyzing its momentum. In the second part, we will examine the link between knowledge and action.

The development of the cognitive view in AI

The crucial notion in the development of the cognitive view is the notion of *context*. Problems related to the application of scientific knowledge are sometimes phrased as problems of context. A solution which seems theoretically very sound and elegant might change into an awkward and inefficient scheme because in the 'context of application' new and unforeseen factors drastically alter the picture. This experience is not restricted to very complex and intricate situations. We will see that it is a central problem of knowledge and that even apparently simple and straightforward cognitive tasks are vulnerable to problems of context. This has become particularly clear from the attempts of AI (Artificial Intelligence) engineers to build computerized devices that would perform such cognitive tasks. A good grip upon the problems of context can be derived from tracing the development of a cognitive view in AI.

In the AI approaches to the study of cognitive processes as forms of information processing, we can distinguish four stages. Extending a list of labels suggested by Michie (1974), we identify them as:

- a *monadic* stage during which information-units were considered separate and independent from each other as single self-contained entities;
- a *structural* stage which considered information-units as more complex entities that are to be decomposed into several sub-units arranged in specific ways;
- a *contextual* stage where, in addition to an analysis of the structure of complex information units, supplementary information on context is required to 'disambiguate' the meaning of a message;
- a *cognitive* stage in which information is considered complementary to an elaborate conceptual system that represents the information processor's knowledge or model of the world.

When specified in terms of procedures for pattern recognition or picture processing, these stages correspond respectively to: template matching, feature analysis, contextual analysis, and analysis by synthesis. We shall describe them for the relatively simple problem of pattern recognition.

The monadic stage: template matching

Template-matching is a pattern recognition technique which uses various sets of procedures called *preprocessors* to reduce signals, in this case letters, to some form of standard representation which makes it possible to look for a match with a *template* stored in the system. An image of the signal is projected on a grid and it is described in terms of a digital representation: cells of a two dimensional array being either activated or not, depending on the way they are affected by the signal. Preprocessing might straighten up lines, eliminate blots, close up small empty spaces, rotate the signal into a vertical position, or involve a number of more exacting procedures which might require quite sophisticated mathematics. However, these procedures are not meant to be analyses of the signal. Preprocessed inputs are compared to the stored templates. Recognition consists of ascertaining a match between the preprocessed signal and a stored template. Template matching is monadic in the sense that it handles pattern entirely as isolated and monolithic units. As a pattern recognition procedure, its weakness becomes manifest with ambiguous signals such as in Figure 1.

The structural stage: feature analysis

In feature analysis the signal is decomposed and recognition involves a structural analysis of certain attributes. A pattern is defined in terms of certain features being present at certain positions. *Features* are to be thought of as elementary patterns, such as *bar, arrow, fork*, etc. The positions are parts of the figure, *top, middle, bottom* or *regions*. A pattern such as A can then be characterized by a sharp angle in the top section, a horizontal bar in the middle section and an open space in the bottom section. Feature analysis is superior to pattern matching in that it can make use of redundancies and eliminate some possible interpretations on the basis of structural anomalies (impossible figures). Nevertheless, an ambiguous signal like the one in Figure 1 cannot be 'disambiguated' through feature-analysis any more than through template matching.

Figure 1: Preprocessors are not equipped to disambiguate. Should the preprocessor close or enlarge the space at the top?

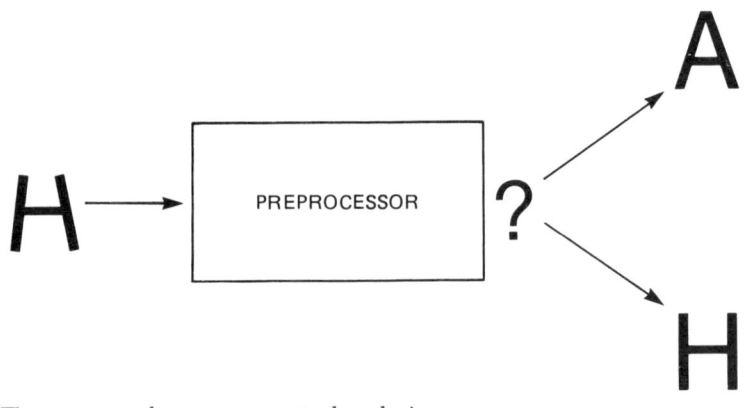

The contextual stage: contextual analysis

When a structural analysis leaves open several possible interpretations of a signal, the only way out is an analysis of the context. Making an appeal to context is not just an extension of the domain of features taken into account, but rather refers to the utilization of higher-level knowledge. In Figure 2, one can call upon his knowledge of consonant-vowel string

Figure 2: Ambiguity resolved by means of context.

TAE CAT

syntax, or simply his knowledge of words, to disambiguate characters. Thus, contextual analysis makes use of information which is not in the signal (the letter), but which belongs to a larger whole of which the signal is only a subpart. However, the problem with context is that it is so rich in possibilities, and that it has no well defined boundary. It can always be enlarged and one never knows if a sufficiently large portion of context has been checked. To elaborate the example, a phrase such as in Figure 3a receives an amplification of its 'cat'-interpretation by having a favourite cat-name in its context. However in a phrase like that in Figure 3b another

Figure 3: An alternative interpretation for part of Figure 2 suggested by another type of context.

(a) FELIX THE CHT

(b) CHT COMMISSION HYDRONIC TEMPERATURE

interpretation is suggested by the context. Although the context at the level of consonant-vowel-combination-rules suggests one interpretation, in a wider context this can apparently be overruled in favour of another interpretation.

The cognitive stage: analysis by synthesis

The next step is to introduce a well-defined context by having it supplied somewhat arbitrarily or subjectively by the information processing system itself: its *model of the world*. Recognition is guided by what the system (rightly or wrongly) considers relevant features and relevant context on the basis of its 'world knowledge'. It selects only those features which it knows are to be heeded and it analyses the signal only insofar as seems necessary to check the match between the self-generated expectations and the perceived pattern. Nothing can better illustrate this type of synthesis — experienced as analysis! — than proofreading by an author who, maybe because of his concentration on the content of his text, is apt to read misprinted words as correct. 'Analysis by synthesis' is used here in a broader sense (Neisser, 1967) to refer to a theory of perception which emphasizes the production of expectations on the basis of a world model to such a degree that intake of input can be seen as almost entirely restricted to a few points of control, and to filling in parameter values. Within such a view *perception* is, to a large extent, the product of *imagination*, the few points of intake in information only safeguarding it from becoming *illusion* by tying imagination to 'reality'. In familiar scenes much of what we see is what we know should be seen but only few things might be perceived directly.

The development of AI conceptions relevant to perception thus seems to be the expression of two tendencies:

- First, there is evolution from information in terms of *simple units* to large and *complex structures*,
- Second, there is an *increasing stress* on the *contribution* by the processor or receiver of the information; in philosophical terms, there is a shift of focus away from the known object toward the knowing subject.

Paradigms and the paradox of the cognitive viewpoint

Feldman has given an accurate synoptic description of the development we have sketched above:

> Early efforts in machine perception (and much perceptual psychology) were concerned with visual processes which operated independent of context. We studied edge detectors, pattern classifiers and algorithms for partitioning general straight-line drawings. This not only proved difficult but offered no promise of extension to typical real world scenes. There then came a concerted effort to overcome (or circumvent) perception problems by giving programs lots of domain knowledge. This has been carried to the extreme of *visual perception without vision*, viz. anything black and on a desk is a telephone (Feldman, 1975, p. 92, italics ours).

This characterization points at a confusing and even paradoxical aspect of the cognitive view. Indeed, roughly stated, the cognitive view contends that we perceive things because we expect them. But, if we only perceive what we expect to perceive, what then is the sense of perceiving? As Neiser indicates: 'There is a dialectical contradiction between these requirements: we cannot perceive *unless* we anticipate, but we must not see only what we anticipate' (Neiser, 1976, p. 43, italics in the original). This is also what makes the notion of paradigm ambivalent.

The fascinating quality of the notion of 'paradigm' in science studies stems from its link with the cognitive point of view that stresses the role of knowing subject in any act of congnition. Empiricism is just too simple to account for knowledge acquisition. The subject approaches the world and interacts with it armed with expectation-generating schemes that guide his search. The disturbing quality of the notion of paradigm stems from the same link with the cognitive orientation which seems to lock the subject up in a particular viewpoint from which he cannot escape. No way is provided to go beyond the suggestions of the scheme, break out of the accepted categories to achieve the joy of surprise in genuine discovery instead of the mixture of comfort and disappointment that accompanies the filling in of rigidly fixed boxes. Piaget's schemes are the cognitivist's schemes. They shape specific ways to interact with the world and impose boundaries upon experience. But there is an escape out of the cognitive paradox: development. Action schemes, which for Piaget embody cognitive structures, are subject to change. They are not only modifiable in the way Minskyan frames are adaptable to specific local conditions. In the course of development, they undergo substantial reorganization and systematization which opens them up for an ever extending range of new discoveries and experiences. In the idea that development overcomes the intrinsic limitations of the cognitive view lies one of Piaget's most important contributions.

Action schemes and cognitive structures

The schemes of a newborn baby constitute his cognitive capital at birth. The developmental pattern of these schemes is such that at the outset they are underspecified while in the end they become detached from their locus of origin and are cultivated on their own. The 'underspecification' means that the scheme is, at the start, very 'schematic'. The grasp reflex of a baby is awkward and ineffective. Apparently, exercise is essential for finding out and filling in specific parameter values for specific applications. In this aspect of indefiniteness, the scheme expresses its potential as carrier of newly gained knowledge since, in its adaptation to specific objects, newly discovered aspects of the external world are incorporated in the scheme. As it can be transposed to other configurations of organs or behavioural equipment, the scheme is detachable from the action in which it is embodied. Eventually it becomes reflected in consciousness where it can be cultivated on its own as a conceptual system independently of the action from which it originated. This is what Piaget calls 'reflexive abstraction'. Ultimately, such representations of action systems are organized and systematized in their own right and lead into very powerful systems for the organization and control of 'possible' actions. The formal reasoning exhibited in scientific thinking is an example of the scope of abstract conceptual systems which, however, are the end product of a development that starts with simple sensori-motor adaptations.

All this might seem rather abstract. But Piaget is able to apply these notions quite convincingly in the description of skills which children master easily and which he analyzes both as regards their performance *and* their understanding of their own performance as reflected in the descriptions they provide. Among his later works, *La prise de conscience* (1974a) in particular illustrates the importance and relevance of action as a generic source of ideas while exhibiting the link with verbal thinking in classical applications of the clinical method.

A representative example of *La prise de conscience* confronts children, ages four to twelve, with the following well-known trick. By means of the index finger, a table tennis ball is propelled away over a flat surface while receiving an inverse rotation which makes it come back on an inbound trajectory along the same path that it followed on its outbound course. A similar situation is demonstrated with a hoop thrown in such a way that it seems to be trundled through its trajectory over the floor in both directions. When shown these boyish tricks, children are interested but not impressed. When invited to try for themselves they prove in general to be quite dexterous and they reproduce the effect with the table tennis ball within a few trials. At the age of six, almost all subjects in Piaget's sample are able to perform the trick. Once successful performance has been established, conceptual understanding is checked. How do children explain the remarkable behaviour of the table tennis ball?

While the child might be perfectly able to accomplish the trick, it is quite obvious that he has at first theories about the physics of the situation which are substantially inferior to the level of his performance in practice. His very first opinions are tightly linked to the conviction that when a spherical object moves over a flat surface, it has to rotate. Thus, most children will explain the situation as due to rotation in the direction of the movement both up and down the trajectory. The annoying question is why the ball should stop at a certain location and in particular, why it should then start to roll again in the other direction without any apparent external interference. Some children arrive at ingenious ideas for saving the all-rotational model, suggesting a 180 degree turn of the ball so that no reversal of rotation is necessary. They claim to observe the rotation all along the course of the ball. This is a case of concept-driven upside-down observation where theory prescribes what can be seen. Piaget emphasizes: 'la lecture des observables est fonction de la compréhension et non pas de la perception lorsqu'il y a contradiction entre un fait et l'interprétation causale qui paraît s'imposer' (Piaget, 1974a, p. 54). Even when balls are used which have sections painted in bright colours such that the direction of rotation is easier to perceive, some children keep claiming that they *see* the rotation in the direction of the movement. The perception of the inverse rotation is obviously difficult to achieve. An observation which is apparently easier concerns the subject's own movement. Children acknowledge that the finger which produces the propulsion of the ball makes a slight but significant backward movement, i.e. down and backward. The kind of rotation this induces in the ball seems at first unnoticed. A crucial insight (or observation?) occurs when the hypothesis arises that the ball does not roll on the way up, but skims along the surface. Suddenly, the composite nature of the phenomenon becomes transparent. The outward course is due to the propelling effect of the finger moving down, thereby displacing the ball with a certain force in a specific direction. The inbound course is due to the rotation imposed upon the ball through the backward movement of the finger. It can then be seen that the two processes interact, the forward movement resulting from propulsion overcoming inverse rotation, while return is due to inverse rotation winning from straightforward propulsion.

The progression from some global 'misunderstanding' which is originally experienced as a sufficient description toward a more differentiated conceptual system that is more adequate follows specific patterns. In this simple case, Piaget attributes progress in the construction of the conceptual system to a paired elaboration of both the subject and object components involved. Being led to focus in an alternating pattern upon the behaviour of the object and his own actions producing that behaviour, the subject is forced to develop a detailed account of what specific effect goes with what specific action. In general, Piaget adheres to the principle that a process becomes conscious in some centripetal sense, i.e. we notice first the effects on the object (*observables sur l'objet*) before we take notice of our actions. In the case of the table tennis ball, the behaviour of the ball is apparently so mysterious that scrutiny is first applied to the subject's own action resulting in the 'discovery' of the dual composition of the finger movement. That does not alter the fact that the construction of an adequate conceptual system results from balancing two systems: one to account for the actions of the subject, one to account for the effects on the object. Their development is gradual and coupled: a discovery with respect to the subject's own action leads into a new analysis of the object and vice versa. This reinforces the position according to which self-knowledge is a basic constituent of genuine knowledge. Insight into the composition of actions refers to the subject and is part of self-understanding. But this gradual increase in awareness about subject-object interaction is only one aspect of the development of skills.

The book *La prise de conscience* is part of a more elaborate endeavour, the other part of which can be found in *Réussir et comprendre* (1974b). Together, these two volumes aim at clarifying the relationship between *knowing how* and *knowing that* by analyzing their developmental connections. *La prise de conscience* studies elementary skills which are easily learned. Piaget observes that elementary motor skills, such as the use of a sling, a catapult etc., are acquired on the level of performance without insight into the structure of the action. Oriented by a consciously selected goal, action apparently is self-organizing and regulates itself on the basis of unconscious sensori-motor feedback. On that level action is in advance of conceptual thinking. There is 'success' (hit the intended goal) without 'understanding' (the ballistics, or more general, the physics of throwing or shooting), *réussir* without *comprendre*. Then, along the lines indicated above for the table tennis ball, a conceptual representation is gradually built up in consciousness, mirroring in symbols what action accomplishes in fact. Conceptualization, inaccurate and irrelevant at first, catches up with action and attains the same level. *Knowing how* is now rendered accessible in terms of *knowing that* as well. But conceptualization does not stop at the level of mere reflection of action. In the second book, *Réussir et comprendre*, Piaget tends to explore more complicated tasks. To quote one example: a toy boat in a basin of water, exposed to strong wind produced by a ventilator, has to be propelled along a specific course by positioning the boat, the rudder, the sail, etc. Although, in these and similar tasks, the solution also involves some skilful sensori-motor act, success requires a detailed and complex analysis in order to 'compute' the effects of the several factors involved and to predict the result of their interaction. Action can no longer take care of itself without conceptual guidance. Conscious analysis is needed to assemble a symbolic model of the situation that allows the subject to derive, on theoretical grounds, the composite action required to reach the intended goal. Understanding has become a condition for success.

Concluding remarks

As a by-product of the advance of the computer, AI has confronted us more sharply than ever before with the problem of the nature of knowledge. While knowledge is growing into an important industrial product, static and 'eternistic' images of scientific knowledge crumble and make room for more dynamic approaches. We have seen how the cognitive view suggests an interactive and integrative model of cognitive processes instead of the one-way causal models that used to dominate behaviouristic psychology. But the cognitive orientation is bound to be caught in a paradoxical situation unless it overcomes the classical distinction between knowledge and action. Piaget's developmental model shows the intimate relationship between knowledge and action, indicating how cognitive processes are to be conceived of as gradually constructed models by means of which the knowing subject represents not only segments of the outside world but his own actions as well.

In the traditional approach where knowledge is related to 'external reality', science is for finding out about the outside world and human goals and purposes relate to subjective values that are to be determined by social processes and policies. Here a detrimental dualism appears in the guise of a distinction between the cognitive and the social. The cognitive deals with the objective, the world as it really is, the social is concerned with value, the world as the community of subjects would like it to be. Such a segmentation ignores the complex relationship between action and knowledge as we have discovered them in Piaget's developmental approach. According to that relationship, in the process of finding out about the outside world, we also learn about ourselves. Acquiring knowledge about the object goes hand in hand with learning in more detail about the action of the subject. Ultimately, when dealing with the construction of applicable knowledge, there is no way to circumvent the Socratic dictum 'Know thyself'. In the ever recurring opposition between the natural and the social sciences we currently experience the curious situation that the natural sciences are rendered suspect by their success —

reproached for begetting disruptive technology — while the social sciences are made suspect because they lack that type of success. This disequilibrium might well be related to the failure to recognize the constructive character of 'self-knowledge'. 'Selves' are made along with the external worlds we investigate and create. The difficulty of establishing or adapting to new worlds might stem from failure to recognize the self-image that goes along with a new world or from a refusal to accept it. To permit choices, these self-images should be made explicit. Some European traditions of science studies have stressed this orientation by acknowledging the importance of philosophical anthropology: the images of man that go along with certain types of science (e.g. Schelsky, 1965). It should be obvious that the notions of self-knowledge and self-analysis involved are not meant as do-it-yourself techniques of psychotherapy or eastern meditation, however worthwhile or useful such activities might be. Self-knowledge is specific and solid down-to-earth knowledge.

The elusive component in the notion of paradigm has been the *tacit* knowledge that is assumed to be guiding and directing it without being explicit. In the dual structure of subject-object world models, tacit knowledge can finally be localized and made tangible on the subject-side as self-knowledge. It is not pure coincidence that the theoretical model of man behind Schelsky's approach is Gehlen's *Der Mensch* (1940), which is similar to Piaget's model in many respects.

The simplistic model of scientific knowledge underlying social science construction of the past decades has overlooked essential components in the study of knowledge and its link with action. We might have accumulated an immense amount of knowledge in what we regard as science but we have barely begun to understand what knowledge is.

References

CARNAP, R. (1969). *Der Logische Aufbau der Welt* (1928). Translated by R.A. George as *The Logical Structure of the World*. Berkeley: Univ. of California Press.
CLOWES, M.B. (1969). 'Transformational grammar and the organization of pictures.' In: GRASELLI, A. (Ed.) *Automatic Interpretation and Classification of Images*. New York: Academic Press.
FELDMAN, J. (1975). 'Bad-mouthing frames.' In: SCHANK, R. and NASH-WEBBER, B. (Eds). *Theoretical Issues in Natural Language Processing*. Cambridge, Mass.: ACL, pp. 92–3.
FLECK, L. (1935). *Entstehung und Entwicklung einer Wissenschaftlichen Tatsache*. Basel: Benno Schwabe. Translated by F. Bradley and T. Trenn as *Genesis and Development of a Scientific Fact*. Chicago: University of Chicago Press, 1979.
GEHLEN, F. (1950). *Der Mensch, seine Natur und seine Stellung in der Welt* (1940). Bonn: Athenaum.

HALLE, M. and STEVENS, K. (1962). 'Speech recognition: a model and program for research,' *IRE Transactions on Information Theory*, 8, pp. 155–9.
KUHN, T.S. (1962). *The Structure of Scientific Revolutions*. Chicago: University of Chicago Press.
MERTON, R.K. (1938). *Science, Technology and Society in Seventeenth Century England*. New York: Harper & Row, 1970.
MICHIE, D. (1973). *On Machine Intelligence*. Edinburgh: University of Edinburgh Press.
NEISSER, U. (1967). *Cognitive Psychology*. New York: Appleton.
NEISSER, U. (1976). *Cognition and Reality*. San Francisco: Freeman.
PEARSON, K. (1892). *The Grammar of Science*. New York: Meridian, 1957.
PIAGET, J. (1964a). *La prise de conscience*. Paris: Presses Universitaires de France.
PIAGET, J. (1946). *Reussir et comprendre*. Paris: Presses Universitaires de France.
SCHELSKY, H. (1965). 'Der Mensch in der Wissenschaftlichen Zivilisation.' In: *Auf der Suche nach Wirklichkeit*. Düsseldorf.

CRITICISM AND DISCUSSION

Note by the editors: De Mey's contribution challenges deeply-rooted but fundamentally confused and confusing distinctions between internal and external factors in scientific development and tries to synthesize cognitive, action and social factors in knowledge production. This leads to new insights into the relations between knowledge and its utilization by policymakers and practitioners.

The Workshop participants considered De Mey's presentation of great value. De Mey's paper not having been reviewed before the Workshop, only the discussion following its presentation is summarized here.

SESSION DE MEY
1. An important shift in our concepts of scientific knowledge and application

De Mey's contribution to a better understanding of the complex relationships between scientific knowledge, practice and policy-making was considered highly valuable. His reconsidering of the roots and the nature of scientific knowledge as currently explored in cognitive science leads into new perspectives on the relationship between knowledge and its utilization. De Mey's recommendation to stay in touch with developments in this area — for which a Chair of Science Dynamics has been established in The Netherlands (see De Mey's contribution in Special Session Two for further details) — was considered a major impetus to continued study of a subject that is of central importance in modern society. In this context it is of interest to refer to the initiative taken by the Foundation for Educational Research in the Netherlands (SVO) in launching an international Special Interest Group which will ideally be so composed as to unite within itself various disciplines and various skills for in-depth study of this domain. In Appendix D more information about this initiative is presented.

De Mey underlined the fact that 'some of the papers that have been presented at this Workshop have provided indications of an important shift and change in our concepts of science and scientific knowledge in recent years'. Referring to Suppes 'Keynote Address' (included in this volume) De Mey felt that this Address had tackled straightforwardly the basic tenets of what has been called the orthodox or received view in the philosophy of science. The changes in conceptions of the nature of knowledge — as presented in De Mey's paper — also throw new light on the notion of application.

2. 'Context of knowledge'

De Mey has pointed out that the crucial notion in the development of the cognitive view is the notion of context. In his paper he elucidates this when he deals with the attempts of Artificial Intelligence engineers to build devices that would perform cognitive tasks while taking into account the problems of context. *Suppes* agreed with De Mey and indicated how very complex this matter really is:

As an indication of the complexity of the matter I want to cite a recent case history in artificial intelligence. There has been a very substantial effort, which will undoubtedly continue, to write computer programs that recognize spoken speech. The initial hopes were that, by taking account of the knowledge of what was said, one would be able to facilitate enormously the recognition of spoken language by a computer. The recent efforts have shown that at the present stage that is probably mistaken. There was a recent competition. (I will not try to go into the details) in which one kind of program (HEARSAY) very much emphasized context in your sense. Another (HARPY) emphasized great attention to the acoustical details of the speech, and of course you can see what I am going to say. The attention to acoustical details, rather than the extended knowledge base, turned out to be much more successful. The lesson is that there is no simple characterization of the approaches that are necessarily going to be effective. It is a lesson already well learned in educational research, but I think it is important to keep in mind, in talking about artificial intelligence, that simple, general ideas will not necessarily work. I mention this as a very good counter-example to thinking that context, in particular, the context of knowledge, is inevitably going to carry a great deal of the weight of the analysis.

De Mey pointed out that he in no way had been suggesting that there had been a progressive development leading up to a successful approach which would be the cognitive one. He feels that the 'cognitive paradox' is the major obstacle: 'What is the sense of perceiving if what you perceive is what you bring into the situation, either as a computer or as a human being on your own? So, there has been or is the need for an interactive theory of perception and for processing, going back and forth between both subject and object.' De Mey went on by explaining that he had probably been 'too systematic by indicating that this point is solved by Piaget, but I think that what the Piagetian approach shows is that these developing action schemes are the means to specify the tacit knowledge which the cognitive approach has brought into focus and has indicated as very relevant and essential for the understanding of information processing.'

De Mey's point that 'knowledge is really embedded in action' was illustrated with many examples by *Caplan* who also drew attention to an interesting development. He observed that over the years 'the cognitive psychologists tend to become more like organizational sociologists and on the other hand, organizational psychologists such as Carol Weiss who write in this area of knowledge utilization, seem to be increasingly more moving in the direction of cognitive psychology'. This tendency might indicate that the shifts in concepts of scientific knowledge and its utilization are in line with approaches such as the one De Mey described.

Evaluation Research: Political and Organizational Constraints

Jaap Scheerens — Foundation for Educational Research in the Netherlands (SVO)

Abstract

Policy-making models range from the ideal of pure rationality to what Cohen and his co-authors (1972) term a 'garbage can model of organizational decision-making'. Similarly, policy-oriented evaluation research designs vary from controlled randomized field trials to the retrospective analysis of 'black-box'-like situations.

In this paper, apart from these extremes, some 'in-between stations' are considered. In general, the strength of a given evaluation research design would appear to depend largely on the degree of rationality of the policy-making process in which it is to function. All the same, at least marginal inroads can be made on this dependency relation: intellectually, there are various options open to the evaluation researcher to escape to other levels of aggregation or even to adopt a meta-position. In practice, much will depend on the organizational setting in which evaluation research is carried out. In the present analysis, a few basic concepts borrowed from organizational science are used for the description of a number of 'everyday' organizational problems in the relationships between policy-makers, researchers and practitioners. On this basis, a broad conceptual framework is proposed that might be useful as a tool for policy analyses with respect to the functioning of evaluation research in large-scale 'experimental' innovation programmes. By adopting the perspective of 'control' — according to De Leeuw's (1974) control paradigm, i.e. by focusing on factors that are changeable and can be manipulated — the conceptual framework is given handles for its dynamic application.

The moral of the story is that identifying the major dependencies of

---

I am indebted to Professor A.C.J. de Leeuw and Professor A.D. de Groot for their incisive comments on the draft version of this paper and to Jop Spiekerman for his careful screening of the English text. My sincere thanks are due to the SVO Secretariat, who typed the manuscript.

policy-oriented research marks the first step towards controlling them so as to safeguard the independence essential to policy-oriented research.

Introduction

In the literature on evaluation research in the context of public policy-making and large-scale social intervention programmes (e.g. educational innovation projects) there seems to be a tendency to present the relationship between policy-making and evaluation research in either of two ways. On the one hand, those who advocate an experimental approach to evaluation research (e.g. Bennett and Lumsdaine 1975) tend to assume a 'natural' correspondence between policy-making, conceived as a rational decision process, and evaluation research. On the other hand, in studies which emphasize the constraints on evaluation research resulting from the policy-making process, the 'political' nature of governmental and organizational decision-making is likely to be stressed. Consequently, in the latter studies a much more modest view of the feasibility of rigorous evaluation designs is expressed (Weiss, 1975, 1980).

In this paper an attempt will be made to extend the range of 'points of comparison' between public policy-making and possible evaluation designs, by briefly describing five models (or rather classes of models) of public policy-making and exploring the constraints on evaluation research designs which each of these models is likely to have. Some attention will also be given to organizational structures that are bound to develop when evaluation research is to take place within the framework of certain forms of public policy-making. Finally, the so-called 'control paradigm' (De Leeuw, 1974) is discussed as possibly affording a more dynamic approach towards the interrelationships between policy-making, evaluation research and the organization of these processes.

Since the present discussion, apart from being a theoretical exercise, is also intended to present an analytic framework to be used in case studies in the functioning of evaluation research in some major educational innovation programmes in Holland, both public policy-making and evaluation research will be looked at from a corresponding, though fairly specific viewpoint. Public policy-making is here conceived as being at the stage where the general outline of certain (educational) innovation programmes has already been stated by the government. The discussion of evaluation research will be limited to policy-oriented evaluation research (as opposed to practitioner-oriented research).

Models of public policy-making as types of decision-making

In presenting models of public policy-making as types of decision-making a prescriptive, rather than a descriptive approach is sometimes adopted; in other words, some models of decision-making function as 'examples' or 'ideal types' for public policy-making, while others are considered to be more 'descriptively realistic'. Although it is unlikely that the full range of types of decision-making set out below can actually be observed in practice, this paper specifically seeks to avoid an *a priori* tendency to identify public policy with the most attenuated decision-making model. This position is adopted so as to present a more balanced treatment of the relationship between policy-making and evaluation research than the more or less dichotomous approach commonly found in the literature on evaluation research (see the Introduction). Since excellent and detailed overviews of types of decision-making exist in the literature on public policy-making, planning and organizational decision-making, (Dror, 1968; Faludi, 1973; Kickert, 1979), only a brief outline will be given here.

The discussion of the various models of decision-making starts out from the conception of pure rationality and successively discusses modifications that increasingly depart from this ideal. Important dimensions that distinguish these models are:

— the availability of information (on states, actions and functions that relate these two to obtain desired outcomes);
— the complexity of the decision-making process (in terms of phases);
— the inclusion of extrarational elements;
— characteristics of the goal concept.

1. The pure rationality model

This model is characterized by complete information on alternative actions, alternative states (e.g. the present state and the desired future state) and the function connecting these states of the world with the actions. Modifications of the model concern this latter function, allowing it to be probabilistic or unknown (i.e. distinguishing 'decision-making under risk' and 'decision-making under uncertainty'). A further assumption of the pure rationality model is that the decision-maker is supposed to be in a position to rank-order the complete set of states to his preference. Finally, it is assumed that the decision-maker makes, or rather computes, an optimal choice of alternatives. Essentially, the pure rationality model is a one-phase model; choosing an action, from the available set, given the preference ordering of states and varying degrees of information concerning the function that 'maps' actions upon consequences (see also Simon, 1965).

It will be clear that the pure rationality model is an unattainable ideal as far as public policy-making is concerned. But, as Dror (1964) states, its function as an example that should be approximated to as closely as possible is deeply-rooted in Western civilization. Kickert (1979, p. 45) also discusses extensions of this model involving multiple decision-makers and multiple goals.

2. Decision-making as problem-solving

'Problem-solving activity is an activity aimed at both the synthesis and evaluation of performance programmes for accomplishing desired ends' (Simon, 1978, p. 149). In situations where information about alternative actions, possible effects and action-effect links is limited, a less stringent model of decision-making (than that set out in section 1) is needed. If some set of alternatives is available, where none is both sufficient and necessary to reach a specific outcome, but only sufficient, Simon speaks of 'heuristic decision-making'. When plausible alternatives still have to be designed and tested, the definition of problem-solving activity applies. Additionally, in this model the ideal of 'optimal decisions' is replaced by a striving for 'satisficing'[1] solutions by establishing sufficient means to desired ends, with efficiency criteria concerning the search process being taken into consideration.

The problem-solving model is seen as consisting of three phases: problem identification, design and evaluation of possible solutions, and choice. (Kickert, 1979, p. 53). This scheme can be further extended by distinguishing between design and evaluation and including an implementation phase. Kickert (1979) also discusses a model developed by Mintzberg (1976) in which the temporal sequence of the phases is relaxed, allowing for interruptions, delays, and recycles.

3. Splitting up the total decision task

Faludi (1976) describes 'sequential decision-making as the breaking up of a very complex decision problem into manageable bits'. Dror (1968) refers to the sequential decision model as follows: 'If some of the information needed to succeed in an activity can be learned only during the early stages of carrying out that activity, the more promising ways to carry it out should be undertaken simultaneously, and the decision as to which is the best alternative should be delayed until the information has been learned' (p. 143). Etzioni's 'mixed scanning'[2] amounts to a differentiation between global, fundamental decisions, to be made first, and 'bit' decisions to be made next, allowing for some mutual adjustment as the programme proceeds. (Faludi 1976, Kickert 1979).

---

[1] A term first coined by Simon.

[2] 'Mixed scanning' has been proposed by Etzioni as a compromise between the rational model and the model that is to be discussed next: incrementalism.

4. Incrementalism

Lindblom criticizes the classic rational model as not being adaptable to man's limited intellectual capacities. His proposed incremental strategy has the following characteristics:

- 'it concentrates the policy-maker's analysis on familiar, better-known experience;
- it sharply reduces the number of different alternative policies to be expected;
- it sharply reduces the number and complexity of factors he has to analyze' (Lindblom, 1968).

Thus, in practice, incrementalism is associated with a 'small step' approach, where change is conceived in terms of simple extrapolations from the past.

In addition, the incrementalism model departs from the classic (as well as the satisficing) model by toning down the means-end distinction; in Lindblom's view means and ends in policy-making are closely intertwined.

Another feature of incrementalism, as pointed out by Faludi (1976), is its disjointed character, the notion that 'whatever direction the community as a whole takes, it cannot be the result of deliberate choice. Rather it is the resultant of the operation of various forces.'

While the incremental model is widely held to be an adequate description of public policy-making, Dror (1968) takes a stand against its prescriptive use, which he says might be like 'practising a self-fulfilling prophecy'. (See also Kickert, 1979, p. 48).

So far the decision-making models have been considered as rational models, characterized by a deliberate choice between available courses of action to reach more or less explicitly stated ends.

Dror (1968, p. 194) considers incrementalism as a special version of the pure rationality model. Yet the indistinctness of means and ends in incrementalism seems to make this a somewhat dubious proposition.

Kickert (1979) follows De Leeuw (1977) in stating that incrementalism is still to be seen as rational decision-making on the strength of an analysis of the goal-concept. A goal is defined as a preference ordering over alternatives. It is not necessary to have a complete ordering over all output alternatives; indeed even in the limiting case in which there are only two alternatives, the goal-concept still holds good. In practice this means that it is sufficient to have some way of evaluating the output at a certain time in comparison to the previous output for the use of the concept of rationality to be legitimately involved.

It should be noted, however, that De Leeuw and Kickert consider the goal as a concept that is attributed to the decision-maker rather than as a property intrinsic to him. I will come back to this treatment of the goal-concept later on, discussions on goal clarification are also of importance as far as the design of evaluation projects is concerned (e.g. Patton, 1978).

5. Alternative and extrarational models

More radical alternatives to the rational model of decision-making (and approximations thereof) may take the form of:

a) modifications of the (tacitly understood) 'task-relatedness' of rational decision-making;
b) putting the aspects of models of rational decision-making (means, ends, sequences) further 'upside-down';
c) referring to extrarational processes such as intuitions and implicit judgment.

sub a) Allison (1969, 1971) presents two alternatives to the model of rational policy; the organizational process-model and the model of bureaucratic politics. The organizational-process model stresses the interest of organizations and organizational units in survival, in maintaining the *staus quo* and consequently the importance of standard patterns of behaviour and routines in organizational decision-making. The model of bureaucratic politics is described as: 'bargaining along regularized channels among players positioned hierarchically within the government'. I think both models are, strictly speaking, 'substantive' alternatives in that they present two alternative 'classes' of goals (next to the usually assumed task-relatedness of rational decision-making) rather than procedural alternatives to rational decision-making.

sub b) Cohen, March and Olsen (1972) take this view of the way problems, solutions and opportunities for choice interact as elements of decision-making processes in organizations: 'An organization is a collection of choices looking for problems, issues and feelings looking for decision situations in which they may be aired, solutions looking for issues to which they might be the answer, and decision-makers looking for work' (p. 2). Not surprisingly, they call their model 'a garbage can model of organizational decision-making'.

sub c) According to Dror (1968) various conceptions of decision-making are based on a measure of acceptance of 'extrarational' processes (intuition, judgment). He calls one of the basic characteristics of his 'optimal model of public policymaking' the fact that it has both rational and extrarational components, but he also points out the limited possibilities for explicating the roles of these components.

Although the three alternative models sketched here are distinguished along different dimensions, it is quite unlikely that they are independent. In the garbage can of organized anarchies we would expect to find many intuitions towards organizational survival and a pronounced leaning towards personal ambitions, so to speak.

Organizational aspects

To recapitulate the exposé so far, various models of policy-making have been sketched so as to present a somewhat more differentiated picture of policy-making than is usually found in the literature on the political context of evaluation research. Policy-making within and with respect to social intervention programmes — the field of application of these more theoretical excursions — can be described in terms of these models and the implications of each of them for (different types of) evaluation research explored.

Before going into this any further, I will briefly dwell upon aspects of the organizational structure in which the policy-making process takes place, i.e. the organization that comes into existence as political priorities are being worked out and implemented in the form of programmes of action. In addition to the formal and substantive aspects of the policy-making process, these organizational aspects are being considered as a second class of constraints on the execution of evaluation studies in these kinds of settings. Since the scope of this paper is restricted to presenting a broad outlook, some basic concepts from organizational science can only be subjected to a cursory review.

Dealing with organizational aspects of the settings in which public policy-making and the administration of social intervention programmes take place can be seen as a straightforward extension of the abstract discussion of different models of decision-making, somewhat like picturing these models in actual, real-life situations. In doing so, we are immediately confronted with additional 'supporting' conditions for putting into practice the actions that have been chosen to attain certain ends; as Thompson (1967, p. 19) puts it: 'When organizations seek to translate the abstractions called technologies into action, they immediately face problems for which the core technologies do not provide solutions'. In discussing the design and functioning of organizations the ideal of rationality can again be taken as a leading principle. Thompson (1967) introduces the concept of 'organizational rationality' as a broader and more realistic concept than the closed systems thinking of the classical literature on scientific administrative management. 'Technical rationality is a necessary component but never alone sufficient to provide organizational rationality, which involves acquiring the inputs which are taken for granted by the technology, and dispensing outputs which again are outside the scope of the core technology' (p. 19).

Before I go any further concepts like organization, organizational structure and organizational design must be defined. Kieser and Kubicek (1977) name four defining characteristics of 'organization': goal-orientedness, durability, means of distinguishing between members and non-members and formal structure. Mintzberg (1979) defines the structure of an organization as 'the sum total of the ways in which it divides its labour into distinct tasks and then achieves coordination among them'. Pfeffer (1978) states that 'design' is commonly described as '. . . essentially the activity of constructing and changing organizational structure to achieve optimum effectiveness'. The major theme of his book, however, is 'that the problems of organizational design are concerned with control, not merely with the best way to produce more output' (p. 3).

Different authors in the field of organizational science place different emphasis on what they perceive as the main determinants of organizational structure. In turn, the importance of technological requirements (Kieser and Kubicek, 1977), environmental uncertainty (Galbraith, 1979) and the distribution of intra-organizational power (Pfeffer, 1978) is being stressed. Additional factors mentioned by Kieser and Kubicek (1977) and Mintzberg (1979) are age and size of the organization.

As regards the design and control of organizations, Kickert (1979) distinguishes two basic concepts: disjunction and coordination. Disjunction, or to use Kickert's term 'decomposition', is defined as the formation of the relevant part systems (e.g. organizational units and sub-units) of the original system and coordination as the formation of relevant relationships between these part systems (Kickert, 1979, p. 127). The issue involved is: 'On what basis should positions be grouped into units and units into larger units?' (See Mintzberg, p. 66.) It should be noted that the concept of coordination in the domain of organizational *design* should be distinguished from coordination as part of the *functioning* of the organization (see below).

Kickert's use of the term structural coordination is similar to 'structural design' in Mintzberg's use. Issues of structural design are: the design of positions, the design of superstructures (i.e. systems of formal authority), the design of a decision-making system (Mintzberg, 1979), the creation of 'lateral relations' such as staff-functions, task-forces or a matrix structure (Galbraith, 1973), the design of 'boundary spanning units' (to cope with the environment of the organization, Thompson, 1968) etc. It is beyond the scope of this paper to define the various aspects of structural design more explicitly; in a subsequent section some of them will be more closely related to the subject of this paper.

Apart from structural coordination Kickert introduces the concept of 'goal coordination' i.e. establishing consensus on goals between different sub-units of the organization. Pfeffer (1978) considers the problem of aggregating the ordinal preferences of individuals into a single ordered pattern as 'one of the major threats to the assumption of rationality in organizational design'. As we shall see later on, this problem of goal coordination can be seen as inherent in the organizational setting of research within large-scale educational innovation programmes.

On the level of organizational functioning four coordinating mechanisms are: coordination by direct supervision, coordination by mutual adjustment, coordination by plans and coordination by programmes (Keiser and Kubicek, 1977, p. 82; see also Mintzberg, 1979, Chapter 1).

Returning to the main feature of the presentation in the preceding section, a similar modification of the prevalence of the rational model can be discerned in the literature on organizational design, see e.g. Thompson, 1968 and Pfeffer, 1978. Pfeffer (1978) presents a complementary perspective in which organizations are pictured as co-optations, composed of varying groups and individuals with different demands. Social power and influence are the predominant aspects of this alternative perspective. Particularly in situations where there is a great deal of uncertainty and conflict over goals and technology the power of participants in the coalition comes to affect the decisions made. This makes it understandable why Pfeffer's view of organizational design is associated with incrementalism and *post hoc* decision-making. Thompson (1967, p. 160) comments on situations in which individual motives have successfully been translated into an organizational purpose, but where uncertainty exists about cause/effect (technological) understanding. 'Where purpose is present but patterns are vague, organizational survival becomes not simply an underlying necessity, but a conscious and pressing goal of those in the organization's power structure.'

The organization required by the execution of large-scale intervention programmes will often take the form of designing and implementing new departments and committees on the one hand, and that of coordinating different existing organizations e.g. research institutes, on the other hand. The purpose of this section has been to identify an additional source of complexities and constraints that are likely to influence the execution of evaluation research within the context of the administration of social intervention programmes. Although of necessity only a summary account of them could be given, these general concepts from organizational science may nevertheless be useful in the subsequent analysis of organizational structuring of the relationships between evaluation-researchers, policy makers, programme administrators and practitioners.

Types of evaluation research

Before discussing the implications of the political and organizational aspects of large-scale social intervention programmes for the practice of evaluation research on and within such programmes, a few types of evaluation research must be distinguished.

First of all there is the well-known, fundamental distinction between experimental, quasi-experimental and *ex post facto* research designs (Campbell and Stanley, 1963; Kerlinger, 1969). Experimental research presupposes random assignment of subjects to treatment groups and control over the independent variables (or treatment). If the first condition cannot be realized, the design is called quasi-experimental so long as the 'situation' can nevertheless be viewed as: 'any experimenter-controlled or naturally occurring event (a 'treatment') which intervenes in the lives of respondents and whose probable consequences can be empirically validated' (Campbell and Cook, 1976).

The term '*ex post facto* research' applies when the only way of obtaining evidence about relationship between outcomes and hypothetical 'causes' is retrospective inference. Recent texts on qualitative evaluation research (Guba, 1977); Patton, 1980) suggest that a hermeneutic *Verstehen* approach towards evaluation has gained some popularity in the US. Such an approach will generally be associated with *ex post facto* research.

Stufflebeam's distinction between context, input, process and product evaluation reflects the supposed sequences of phases in programme planning and execution (Stufflebeam, 1971). Stake's concept of 'congruent' evaluation seems to be particularly useful as a variant of process-evaluation: 'The data for a curriculum are congruent if what was intended actually happens' (Stake, 1967).

Finally a distinction can be made as to the length of the feedback-loop of evaluation research; if the feedback-loop is relatively short, the role of the evaluation will often be taken as formative, as opposed to a summative role of long-cycle feedback (i.e. about a 'whole' programme).

This differentiation of types of evaluation research will not be pursued any further here; elsewhere we have given a more detailed treatment of the subject (SVO, 1980). Other 'typologies' are given by House (1976) and Stufflebeam (1980).

Model of policy-making and types of evaluation research

It seems rather obvious that the type of evaluation research that is 'included' in a policy-making process which can be characterized by a certain model must be consistent with that model of policy-making. Likewise, the degree to which rigorous evaluation research is taking place within a certain policy-making process can be seen as a major indicator of the degree of rationality of the policy-making process. (In the treatment of the goal concept by De Leeuw as well as Kickert the availability of an evaluation mechanism is taken to be the decisive criterion as to whether or not one can speak of a rational process – see p. 5). Although it is useful to consider the implications of the various models of policy-making for the design of evaluation studies, the question as to whether it is somehow (to a certain extent) possible to 'break' the determination of evaluation research by the character of the policy-making process seems even more interesting. In practice, this latter approach would amount to exploring possibilities of imposing a 'stronger' evaluation design on a 'weaker' progress of policy-making. Before going into this latter subject, I will first sketch the more obvious consistencies between the models of policy-making and types of evaluation research.

In the case of pure rationality empirical evaluation research would be superfluous, since then the selection of an optimal course of action would merely be a matter of computation. The application of the problem-solving type of decision-making becomes most clearly associated with the planning and implementation of experimental innovation programmes. In this case Campbell's idea of *Reforms as Experiments* would apply (Campbell, 1969), and the obvious evaluation approach would be the use of an experimental design. Examples of 'randomized field trials' are given by Bennett and Lumsdaine, 1975, and Cook and Campbell 1976. Campbell and Cook (1976) present some ways of overcoming the practical problems connected with randomization in field studies. If there is no way of overcoming these problems the 'next best' approach, the use of a quasi-experimental design should be considered.[1]

In general, process evaluation is an indispensable part of experimental or quasi-experimental designs, if only for the purpose of identifying discrepancies between 'treatments as planned' and 'treatments as executed'.

The three approaches to 'sequential' policy-making described in section 3, (pp. 202–3) can be associated with the following three evaluation designs. Depending on the timespan between sequential cycles and the clarity in distinction and formulation of means and ends, sequential 'before-after-designs'[2] could be applied. Generally, this would lead to considerable methodological (and practical) problems, e.g. the confounding effect of 'testing' (see Campbell and Cook, 1976). Edwards and Guttentag (1975) propose an approach in which Bayesian statistics are used to 'update initial guesses as data accumulate'. Again, this approach can only be considered feasible if there is sufficient clarity about desired end states in each decision cycle.

If the policy-making process could be modelled along the lines of Dror's conception of the sequential decision model, the obvious evaluation approach would be to set up and evaluate pilot projects (because the initial learning stages of this model can be seen as alternative pilot-projects in themselves). Etzioni's 'mixed scanning' would give rise to a differentiation between large-scale global evaluations (e.g. the interpretation of administrative data in educational innovation programmes concerning pupil-

---

[1] It is beyond the scope of this paper to go into the methodological problems associated with the use of quasi-experimental designs, but see e.g. Reichardt, 1979.
[2] In other words, time series designs.

participation, absenteeism and dropout) and more detailed small-scale studies.

As for the possibilities of evaluation research within a policy-making process that is characterized by an unclear distinction between means and ends, (incrementalism, 'garbage can model'), the characterization of the goal concept as given by DeLeeuw (1977) and Kickert (1979) becomes very interesting (see the section on models of decision-making). Their treatment of the goal concept includes the following arguments:

1. The weakest version of the goal concept can be conceived as a preference ordering over two alternatives; e.g. by having a group of experts judge the state of a system at time t in comparison to the state at time t-1.
2. The goal concept is an attributed concept; goals should not be seen as intrinsic properties of individuals or organizations. De Leeuw (1977, p. 8) states that, in the context of explanation and control, goals should be seen as model characteristics.
3. Kickert (1979, p. 65) further argues that, since 'objective reality does not exist' (according to the modern methodological view), we should not be concerned with empirical confirmation of the attributed goals.

First of all it should be noted that the third argument is unacceptable as far as the statement about 'modern methodology' is concerned; it presents an overstatement of the idealistic character of modern 'post-empiricist' philosophy of science. (See e.g. Brown, 1977; Thomas, 1979.)

So, I think, we should still be concerned with empirical verification of attributed goals, which would amount to empirically testing hypothetical propositions. This point of view incidentally, would not be incompatible with statement 2 above. In situations where there exists a considerable amount of uncertainty about means and ends, I think either of two things could be done:

— opt for a 'black box' evaluation as described in statement 1, where the lack of goal-directedness might be seen as 'balanced' by the expertise of the judges;
— attribute goals to relevant audiences and verify whether these hypothetical constructs have some empirical basis.[1]

In the latter case it would be left open which relevant audiences would have to be considered (e.g. 'official' decision-makers or others) and how

---

[1] This verification could go further than merely asking for goal statements of participants, policy-makers etc.; there might well be evidence of other implicit goal-directedness.

'hard' the evidence supporting the goal attributions should be. In short, I think we cannot do without some kind of evidence about goals in the context we are dealing with; they are needed to direct the evaluation if not to provide a basis for teleological explanations[1] (Nagel, 1961).

This discussion takes us back to the issue raised at the beginning of this section, namely the degree to which the evaluation researcher is free to impose (and verify) his own theoretical model on the situation to be evaluated. The importance of this point is that decision-makers tend to be notoriously vague about goals, often in what is considered to be their best interest (See Weiss, 1978; Pfeffer, 1979, p. 196.) Hence the evaluation researcher is compelled to spend a lot of energy to obtain the information that is to be considered as the basis of his whole enterprise (see also Patton, 1978).

Clearly, when the evaluation researcher reports to programme-administrators (by whom he may even be employed) there seems to be little opportunity for a more or less independent choice of evaluation objects by the researcher. One way of obtaining more latitude might be to gear the evaluation project to a higher echelon decision-maker, although at that level similar problems might exist (see Weiss, 1975, p. 17). Another possibility might lie in the evaluation researcher's creation of his own audience. This could be less absurd than it sounds for two reasons. From recent work of Patton (1978) and Weiss (Weiss, 1980; Weiss and Bucuvalas, 1980) it appears that in policy-oriented research it is often difficult to identify the decision-makers; this would imply that the existing 'vacuum' could be used by the evaluation researcher to take matters more or less in his own hands. Secondly, it is quite conceivable that there are indeed interested audience groups, who might not have direct decision-making control, but would nevertheless have indirect influence on the eventual decision-making. Rather than impose his own personal priorities on the evaluation design, the evaluation researcher could use the issues the audiences in question find of interest. An example of this would be the direction of the evaluation of the 'Middle School' experiments in Holland towards the issues on which different professional interest groups of teachers disagree most strongly. Finally, it is of course possible (at least intellectually) for the evaluation researcher to adopt a meta-position; to step out of the circle of dependence on programme- and policy-decision-makers and conduct a study that includes the functioning of the decision-makers themselves. Audiences to which these meta-analyses could be directed are the scientific community, members of parliament or taxpayers.

Obviously, issues connected with the independence of the evaluation researcher are closely related to organizational issues, in particular the

---

[1] Teleological or functional explanations can be recognized by terms like 'in order that' or 'for the sake of'.

ways in which the relationships between researchers, practitioners and administrators are organized and institutionalized.

When the policy-making-process is consistent with the characteristics of the 'alternative' models, the evaluation researcher must make use of *ex post facto* research. (See Kerlinger, 1969 and De Groot, 1961 on the methodology of interpretation). If extrarational processes are considered to be of central importance in policy-making or programme execution, it is quite likely that policy-makers and practitioners will insist on qualitative evaluation. A case in point which illustrates this consistency is Eisner's qualitative approach to curriculum evaluation along with his emphasis on the artistic character of teaching (Eisner, 1979).

These considerations appear to lead to the following conclusion. Although the feasibility and adequacy of evaluation research designs is strongly dependent on characteristics of the policy-making process, evaluation researchers have in fact some latitude to impose 'stronger' designs than would be apparent from a descriptive assessment of the policy-making process in question. The extent to which this latitude can be implemented in practice depends on the way research and evaluation have come to be organized and institutionalized in the setting in question.

Before turning to these organizational issues once again, a few words must be said about the practical application of the general framework of relationships between types of policy-making and types of evaluation research design. In a more specified and operationalized form this framework could be used in policy planning as well as policy analysis, for instance in studies aimed at redesigning existing ways in which evaluation projects are integrated within policy-making processes. In the latter application critical variables concerning policy-making aspects would be:

— the identifiability of decision-makers;
— the degree of clarity (*v.* vagueness) and specification (*v.* generality) of goals as stated by various 'layers' of decision-makers and other relevant audiences;
— the phase of development of the process or programme;
— the time span of various decision-making cycles (e.g. the length of an experimental programme);
— the availability and clarity of technology (i.e. teaching strategies to attain educational objectives);
— the degree to which plans are global rather than specified;
— the degree to which devices for feed-back have been built into the process or programme;
— the general normative orientation of relevant audiences (policy-makers, advisers and practitioners) towards rational as opposed to extrarational modes of proceeding;
— the degree to which 'unofficial' goals and 'hidden agendas' are predominant.

Critical variables concerning the functioning of evaluation research in these settings would be:

- the exact time when evaluation researchers have been called on the scene;
- the quality and relevance of the research that has been carried out so far;
- the centrality (*v.* marginality) of the subjects to which the research projects have been (and are being) addressed;
- the degree to which technical requirements of the research system have been fulfilled (e.g. qualification of personnel, availability of facilities like supervision, documentary facilities etc.).

In the next section some organizational issues will be added to this list of variables.

The organizational context of evaluation research projects

Before relating the organizational concepts that have been described more closely to the 'execution of evaluation research in the context of policy-making', I shall give a further outline of the typical real-life situation I have in mind. As stated in the first section of this paper (see pp. 199–200) policy-making will now be considered in particular as it functions in certain large-scale social intervention programmes, more specifically educational innovation programmes. Furthermore it will be assumed that policy-making has reached the stage where the innovation programme is being executed, on a 'somewhat' experimental basis. At that stage the (e.g. governmental) policy-makers are supposed to remain involved, in that they monitor the programme and must at least be consulted if major decisions have to be taken. Other aspects of organizational functioning would concern programme administration, programme execution (i.e. teaching), development of concrete action programmes and methods (i.e. curricula), expert advisership and counselling and, of course, evaluation research.

In this particular context the following issues are considered to be of relevance for an analysis of organizational constraints on the execution of evaluation research.

a. The boundaries of 'the organization' and the distinction of relevant sub-units

All functions that have been mentioned above are likely to be organized and/or institutionalized in different sub-units. Nevertheless, we might conceive of this whole conglomerate of institutions, committees etc. as 'an organization'. In doing so, the first question that must be answered is which units (institutions, departments etc.) do and which do not 'belong' to the organization, i.e. the boundaries of the organization would be specified. Likewise, we would want to consider how to characterize the relevant environment of the organization, those sectors of society from which relevant inputs are drawn and to which outputs are to be directed.

As far as the disjunction of the total organization into various sub-units is concerned, questions about the appropriateness of the structure are of interest, particularly when various sub-units are existing organizations with all kinds of interests outside the scope of the innovational programme. To do this, criteria and standards are needed by which a 'satisficing' disjunction could be defined. One relevant question, for example would be whether researchers should be part of a team of curriculum developers or have a more autonomous position in a specialized research institute with 'independence' v. 'servitude' as a possible criterion.

b. Distinction of different phases of the process or programme

In designing an evaluation research project an important issue is that of the stage of development of the pertinent innovational programme. In this respect (a minimal amount of) agreement among the various parties involved appears to be an indispensable initial condition. If different units or different echelons of decision-makers perceive and define the programme differently — e.g., as being either in a phase of development, of experimentation or of implementation — a considerable amount of confusion in the subsequent process is certain to arise. In fact, this could be one source of conflict over the direction of the evaluation research — for instance, as to whether to apply context, input, process or product evaluation.

c. Structural coordination

Structural coordination is bound to be a problem if an innovation programme is viewed as a conglomerate of already existing institutions and newly-created committees, each with its own specific terms of reference. In such a situation, in which the respective positions and task assignments have remained largely unspecified the decision-making structure necessarily becomes quite complicated. In that case decision-making on research proposals must pass through all (weakly) coordinated sub-units in order to be agreed upon (e.g. government officials, advisory committees, representatives of practitioners etc.).

It also appears useful to specify the structure of the total organization along such dimensions as specialization, formalization,[1] configuration (i.e. authority structure) and flexibility. Of particular interest is the way in which structural solutions have been sought in order to coordinate and harmonize the activities of researchers, practitioners and administrators. Finally the degree to which the research units must be considered autonomous in certain specific professional aspects of their task e.g., the choice of instruments and data collection procedures — appears to be an important issue to be decided and agreed upon in advance.

d. Goal coordination

Particularly when the overall goals of the total organization are vague, the various sub-units can be expected to have their own and possibly divergent interpretations of these goals. In addition, vagueness of goals leaves a good deal of room for the sub-units to impose their own interests and priorities on certain aspects of the programme. Since in this case the research unit is fairly dependent on goal formulations by different audiences its problem is 'where to look' for the right directions. Goal coordination for instance, can be undertaken by using lateral relationships (e.g. task forces); or, by either adopting a 'top-bottom' or a 'bottom-up' approach. In the first instance lower echelons are expected to deduce more specific objectives from the more global goals formulated by higher echelons, in the latter case the opposite way is chosen, as in participatory planning, as described in OECD, 1974, p. 8: 'the organization of a sustained social process characterized by an increasing engagement in policy and autonomy in action for the individuals lowest in the organizational scale'.

Next to differences in goal conceptions regarding substantive issues of the programme differences of opinion about the function of research within the total process of policy-making and programme execution must also be mentioned as possible causes of conflict or confusion.

e. Power and influence

In a complex and loosely structured 'organization' of the kind that is here being considered, a complete set of formalized provisions to cover all situations where dependencies between sub-units exist through a formalized authority structure, is almost unconceivable. If, in addition, the general goals are vague and differences of opinion exist about the way certain units (e.g. the research unit) should function, then we should

---

[1] Particularly, the formalization of the relationships between policy-makers, researchers and practitioners by means of contracts is often thought to be a useful approach.

expect a substantial increase in the degree to which differences in power among the participants (sub-units) will affect the decisions made. (See e.g. Pfeffer, 1978, p. 13.)

From the host of definitions of power (see e.g. Helmers *et al.*, 1975) I adopt as usefully illustrating our purpose the following one which underlines the direct relationship between dependence and power (or influence[1]): 'The power of *b* over *a* is a function of (1) the importance of the resources or outcomes that *b* controls to *a*, and (2) the availability of the resources, actions, or outcomes from other actors'. (Emerson cited by Pfeffer, 1978, p. 19.) Evaluation researchers are highly dependent on decision-makers and practitioners. They must find ways of getting decision-makers to formulate the programme's objectives in a workable form and they depend on the cooperation of practitioners as far as data collection is concerned. As De Groot (1979, 1980) states, the former dependence in particular might lead to undesirable learning effects among researchers since they are likely to be rewarded for producing 'supportive' results regardless of the quality of the research.[2] Differences in orientations between researchers and practitioners, as described by, for instance, Caro (1975) may have analogous contaminating and/or impeding effects.

For the specific case of the functioning of evaluation research in the context of large-scale intervention programmes, the organizational issues, and ensuing variables, discussed in sub *a* through *e* are supposed to be useful analytical tools, in addition to the (general) variables presented in the preceding sections (see pp. 212–13). In policy analyses with respect to constraints on evaluation research they must be taken into account. Such policy analyses can be undertaken either for purely descriptive or for evaluative/prescriptive purposes. In the latter case an 'ideal type' model of the mode of policy-making and the organizational structuring of relationships is needed. This desirable state of affairs is then to be compared to the existing situation. The next likely step should then consist of suggestions (or prescriptions) as to how possible discrepancies between the existing and the desired state of affairs can be decreased. The important point in the latter consideration is that stating and carrying out these suggestions can be considered as an instance of control[3] — in systems theory control is defined as each and every kind of directed influence.

In the concluding section I shall briefly outline a control-systemic

---

[1] These two related concepts can be differentiated as follows: 'Power is coercive and influence persuasive' (Helmers *et al.*, 1975, p. 37).
[2] The assumption that policy-makers show little concern for the quality of policy-oriented research is supported by Patton (1978) though differentiated by the findings of Weiss and Bucuvalas. (1980).
[3] Actually an instance of *meta*-control, since we are here concerned with the control of a system in which controlled sub-systems exist.

approach. Such an approach is considered useful in two respects: first, as a conceptual tool in the characterization of procedural and structural — i.e. organizational — aspects of the object of study; second, as a tool for the characterization of the policy analysis itself viewed as a prescriptive effort to change the existing state of affairs. Other reasons for adopting this control-systemic approach are the clarity and generality of its conceptual framework — sufficient to include both procedural and structural modes of decision-making — and its flexibility as to aggregation levels to which it can be applied.

The control paradigm

The control-systemic approach mentioned in the preceding paragraph is called the 'control paradigm'. De Leeuw (1974) describes the control paradigm as a class of abstract systems, each consisting of a controlled system (CS), an environment (E) and a controller (CR). The control paradigm is usually depicted as follows:

Figure 1:

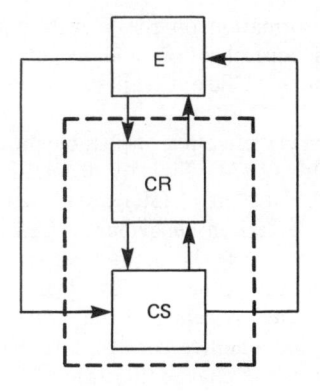

The arrows from CR to CS and from CR to E are relationships that reflect directed influence. The arrows from CS to CR and from E to CR are relationships that reflect information. The arrow from CS to E stands for the behaviour that CR wants CS to perform. The relationship between E and CS is to be seen as the influence from the environment on the behaviour of the controlled system (CS).

A further description of the theoretical foundations of the control paradigm is given by De Leeuw (1974) and Kramer (1978). This description will not be repeated here, although one central aspect concerning the goal concept should be briefly referred to. The definition of control as 'any form of directed influence' encompasses the goal concept (Kickert, 1979, p. 97). De Leeuw (1974, p. 170) states that the control paradigm reflects a vision of reality as a completely rationally structured system, 'as seen from the standpoint of the concrete system itself'. This leads to a rational reconstruction of behaviour; 'according to this rationality axiom irrational behaviour is defined away and replaced by the question of which point of view would fit a rational explanation of the behaviour concerned'. (It should be noted that De Leeuw defines rationality on the principle that only an evaluation mechanism is required to speak of goal-directedness.)

In order to apply this conceptual framework to a given case, one first has to determine the components (CR, CS and E). Next it must be examined whether the situation depicted is amenable to effective control. Kramer (1978, p. 25) mentions four conditions that must be fulfilled for effective control:

(1) CR must state a goal to be reached by CS;
(2) CR must have a model of CS, i.e. a description of the state of the system at a certain point in time with reference to relevant inputs, control actions and outputs; in other words, the model must be functional rather than static;
(3) CR must have information on the relevant parameters of the model (i.e. states, inputs, control actions and outputs);
(4) CR must possess a sufficient variety of possible control actions.

Furthermore, a general classification of possible modes of control has been developed by De Leeuw (1974). First of all internal and external control are distinguished. Internal control (IR) refers to the direct influence on CS by CR to obtain the desired behaviour of CS. Alternatively, CR could influence E in order to attain the desired behaviour of CS; this is called external control (ER). Two other modes of control are directed at the structure of the controlled system and the structure of the environment respectively; this is called adaptive control, internal adaptive control (IA) if CR uses direct influence to change the structure of CS, external adaptive control (EA) if the change in structure is accomplished by indirect influence on the environment. Finally, the system's goal could be modified (IG) or indirect control could be used to change the environment's goal (EG). These six modes of control are summarized in terms of the so called 'control characteristic' (IR, IA, IG, ER, EA, EG). Finally, the concept of meta-control can be stated in terms of this paradigm. For details of this elaborated control paradigm see Kramer (1974).

As a hypothetical example of the application of the control paradigm to the situation that has been considered in this paper, I shall picture a situation that corresponds to the way policy-oriented research with respect to central educational innovation programmes in Holland is organized. Since this is done only for purposes of illustration I will only use very broad categories. Consider a number of research teams or units as the controlled system (CS), a central organization that coordinates and supervises the work of the various research units and advises the Minister of Education and a 'partitioned' environment consisting of the Department of Education (E_1) and the scientific community (E_2) (see Figure 2).

Figure 2:

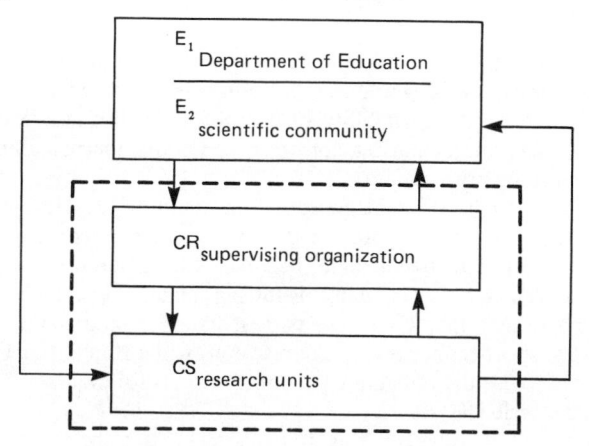

```
        ┌─────────────────────────┐
        │ E_1                     │
        │    Department of Education │
        ├─────────────────────────┤
        │ E_2                     │
        │    scientific community │
        └─────────────────────────┘
              ┌──────────────┐
              │ CR           │
              │  supervising organization │
              └──────────────┘
              ┌──────────────┐
              │ CS           │
              │   research units │
              └──────────────┘
```

The general goal of the system (CS) could be stated as: the efficient production of research results that meet requirements of utility (as defined by E_1) and scientific standards of quality (as defined by E_2). The 'behaviour' of CS could be described in terms of a function of research questions (inputs) and a coordinated effort made by the research units to obtain and process data from schools, using scientific methods. The state of the system at a certain time might be hypothetically described as follows:

— a general dissatisfaction with outcomes expressed by the Department of Education;
— a general disinterest concerning the research results as far as the scientific community is concerned;
— dissatisfaction among research units with the clarity of research questions (as posed by the Department of Education);
— difficulties concerning data collection in schools;
— lack of coordination between different research units;
— major possibilities for direct control by CR: supervision of ongoing projects;
— major inputs (from E_1): grants (i.e. the Department of Education has complete budget control) and research questions;

- potential inputs from E_2 (such as, scientific standards, supervision, training) are hardly 'coming through';
- mainly implicit and vague differences of opinion between E_1 on the one hand, and CR and CS on the other.

In order to determine the control characteristic the possibilities of the various control modes could be systematically explored:

- the effort of direct control (IR) could be increased by intensifying the process control; this would require some internal reorganization of (CR) to increase the availability of manpower for this task. Since (CR) does not have direct budget control over CS this means could not be used to enforce process control.
- the problem of insufficient coordination could be tackled by creating a task force of project leaders from the different research units (IA).
- CR could attempt to mediate between the differences of opinion about the research objective in this setting (mainly between E_1 and CS) by trying to influence CS to use part of its effort in a way acceptable to E_1 (e.g. short-term, routine-like research) while stimulating CS at the same time to use the remaining part of its efforts for evaluation projects on a larger scale (IG).
- CR could use its advisory role towards E_1 to get the Department of Education to state their research questions more explicitly. Another instance of external routine control (ER) could be an attempt to get the Department of Education to increase the power of the research units to obtain the cooperation of schools in the collection of data. Besides, contacts with the scientific community (E_2) could be used to draw more attention to the 'remote province' of policy-oriented research.
- the degree to which CR could directly control CS would increase considerably were CR to obtain direct budget control. Consequently CR could attempt to take over budget control over the research units from the Department of Education ($E_1 A$). As for the scientific community (E_2), initiatives could be taken to increase the involvement of 'outside' experts, e.g. by creating advisory groups ($E_2 A$).
- external goal control (EG) could consist in explicating the differences of opinion about the functions of research in this particular context, possibly resulting in some restatement of priorities.

Of course the feasibility of each of these control modes should be carefully examined before deciding upon specific courses of action. In any case, the present example of applying De Leeuw's control paradigm clearly shows its use in generating a, it would seem, reasonably complete set of possibly feasible ways of changing an existing state of affairs.

Conclusion

In this paper various sources of constraints on evaluation research are discussed. The general picture that emerges from this presentation appears to contrast rather strongly with the ideal of autonomous and independent research. Identification of existing constraints and sources of contamination, however, is considered a first step that must be taken in any systematic attempt at controlling them. In this way, it is hoped, the present overview and analysis may contribute indirectly to maintaining the indispensable independence of research, in particular in the case of policy-oriented evaluation research.

Bibliography

ALLISON, G.T. (1969). 'Conceptual models and the Cuban missile crisis,' *American Political Science Review*, 63, 3.
ALLISON, G.T. (1971). *Essence of decision*. Boston: Little, Brown & Co.
BENNETT, C.A. and LUMSDAINE, A.A. (1975). *Evaluation and Experiment*. New York: Academic Press Inc.
BROWN, H.J. (1977). *Perception, Theory and Commitment: The new philosophy of Science*. Chicago and London: The University of Chicago Press.
CAMPBELL, D.T. (1969). 'Reform as Experiments,' *American Psychologist*, 24, 4 (April).
CAMPBELL, D.T. and COOK, T.D. (1976). 'The design and conduct of quasi experiments and true experiments in field settings.' In: DUNETTE, M.D. (ed.) *Handbook of Individual and Organizational Psychology*.
CAMPBELL, D.T. and STANLEY, J.C. (1963). 'Experimental and quasi experimental designs for research on teaching.' In: CAGE, N.L. (ed.) *Handbook of research on teaching*. Chicago: Rand McNally.
CARO, F.G. (1975). 'Evaluative researchers and practitioners,' *Journal of Research and Development in Education*, 8, 3.
COHEN, M.D., MARCH, J.G. and OLSEN, J.P. (1972). 'A garbage can model of organizational decision making,' *Administrative Science Quarterly*, 17.
DROR, Y. (1968). *Public Policymaking Reexamined*. Scranton, Pennsylvania: Chandler.
EDWARDS, W. and GUTTENTAG, M. (1975). 'Experiments and Evaluation: a reexamination.' In: BENNETT, C.A. and LUMSDAINE, A.A. *Evaluation and Experiment*. New York: Academic Press, Inc.
EISNER, E.W. (1979). *The educational imagination: on the design and evaluation of educational programs*. New York: MacMillan.
FALUDI, A. (1973). *Planning Theory*. Oxford: Pergamon.
GALBRAITH, J.R. (1973). *Designing complex organizations*. Reading, Mass.: Addison Wesley.

GROOT, A.D. de (1961). *Methodologie.* The Hague: Mouton. English transl. *Methodology.* The Hague: Mouton, 1969.
GROOT, A.D. de (1978). *Apeliefde voor de Gamma Wetenschappen* kritiek op een beleidsnota GMG-memorandum nr. 03 78-6/019 juli 1978.
GROOT, A.D. de (1980). *Onderzoek als leerproces.* Amsterdam: B.V. Noord-Hollandse Uitgevers Maatschappij.
GUBA, E.G. (1978). *Towards a methodology of naturalistic inquiry in educational evaluation.* Los Angeles: Center for the Study of Evaluation UCLA.
HELMERS, H.M., MOKKEN, R.J., PLIJTER, R.C. and STOKMAN, F.N. (1975). *Graven naar macht.* Amsterdam: Van Gennep.
HOUSE, E.R. (1978). 'Assumptions underlying evaluation models,' *Educational Researcher*, March.
KERLINGER' F.N. (1969). *Foundations of behavioral research.* Holt, Rinehart and Winston.
KICKERT, W.J.M. (1975). *Organization of decision-making a systems-theoretical approach.* North Holland Publishing Company.
KIESER, A. and KUBRICK, H. (1977). *Organization.* De Gruyter Lehrbuch.
KRAMER, N.J.T.A. (1978). *Systeem is Probleem.* Leiden/Antwerpen: Stenfert Kroese.
LEEUW, A.C.J. de (1974). *Systeemleer en Organisatiekunde.* Stenfert Kroese.
LEEUW, A.C.J. de (1977). *Besturing en verandering van en in systemen.* T.H. Eindhoven.
LINDBLOM, C.J. (1968). *The policy-making process.* Englewood Cliffs, New Jersey: Prentice-Hall, Inc.
MINTZBERG, H. (1979). *The Structuring of Organizations.* Englewood Cliffs: Prentice Hall, Inc.
NAGEL, E. (1961). *The Structure of Science.* London: Routledge and Kegan Paul.
OECD (1979). *Participatory planning in education.* Paris.
PATTON, M.G. (1978). *Utilization focused Evaluation.* Beverly-Hills: Sage Publ.
PATTON, M.G. (1980). *Qualitative Evaluation Models.* Beverly-Hills: Sage Publ.
PFEFFER, J. (1978). *Organizational design.* Arlington Heights, Illinois: A.H.M. Publ. Corporation.
REICHARDT, C.S. (1979). 'The Statistical analysis of data from nonequivalent group designs.' In: COOK, T.D. and CAMPBELL, D.T. *Quasi-Experimentation, design + analysis issues for field studies.* Chicago: Rand McNally.
SIMON, H.A. (1965). 'The logic of rational decision-making,' *British Journal for the Philosophy of Science*, 16.
SIMON, H.A. (1967). 'The logic of heuristic decision-making.' In: RESCHER (ed.). *The Logic of Decision and Action.* University of Pittsburgh Press.
STAKE, R.E. (1967/68). 'The countenance of educational evaluation,' *Teachers College Record.*

STUFFLEBEAM, D.L. et al. (1971). *Educational evaluation and decision-making*. Ithaca, Illinois: Peacock Publ. Inc.
STUFFLEBEAM, D.L. and WEBSTER, W.J. (1980). 'An analysis of alternative approaches to evaluation,' *Educational evaluation and policy analysis*, 2, 3.
SVO (1980). *Evaluatie-onderzoek*. SVO-memorandum no. 2, 's-Gravenhage.
THOMAS, D. (1979). *Naturalism and social science*, a post-empiricist philosophy of science. Cambridge University Press.
THOMPSON, J.D. (1967). *Organizations in action*. New York: McGraw Hill.
WEISS, C.H. (1975). 'Evaluation research in the political context.' In: STRUENING, E.L. and GUTTENTAG, M. (eds.) *Handbook of Evaluation Research*, Vol. I. Sage Publications, Inc.
WEISS, C.H. (1980). 'Knowledge creep and decision accretion.' In: *Knowledge, Diffusion, Utilization*. Sage Publ., Inc.
WEISS, C.H. and BUCUVALAS, M.J. (1980). 'Truth test and utility test: decision-makers' frames of reference for social science research,' *American Sociological Review*, 45.

The Functioning of Policy-Oriented Research within some Major Innovatory Programmes in Dutch Education

Jaap Scheerens — Foundation for Educational Research in the Netherlands (SVO)

Abstract

Theoretical conceptions of policy-making processes (also involving innovatory strategies) and organizational structure feature explicitly in a description of the functioning of policy-oriented research within two major educational innovation programmes in The Netherlands, the Middle School Experiment and the Open School Experiment. To some extent, the 'incrementalistic' character of the policy-making processes and the poor structural coordination in the existing organizational pattern are seen to be reflected both in the rather fragmented picture presented by the total set of research projects and in the doubts that prevail as to the research quality and usefulness of these projects. Some suggestions are made for complementary research activities which should preferably be accompanied by an overhaul of the existing organizational structure, including incorporation of a stronger unit for coordinating research activities.

Introduction

In the first half of the seventies several major educational innovation projects were launched in The Netherlands. In 1975 a comprehensive picture of future primary and secondary education was sketched in a seminal government paper.[1] The innovatory projects focus on four areas: the integration of nursery and primary schools; the structural transformation of junior secondary education into a comprehensive or middle school system; the creation of 'open' educational facilities for adults and the restructuring of part-time education for young adults towards so-called participatory education.[2] Apart from structural reforms, these innovatory

---

The same acknowledgements of comments and assistance received are gratefully made as in Scheerens, 1981.
[1] The so-called *Contourennota*.
[2] Broadly speaking, 'participatory education' seeks to integrate working and learning.

projects also envisage fundamental changes in educational objectives and in teaching and learning strategies. Broadly speaking, these changes first of all mark a shift of emphasis towards personal growth and the realization of individual potential, with self-expression, social skills and the effective dimension of learning receiving a good deal of attention. Concomitant objectives are a closer integration of school and environment, and the introduction of forms of individualized tuition. The normative and political background of these innovatory projects is strongly associated with the ideal of equal opportunities that was predominant in the educational policy of the Socialist/Christian-Democrat government coalition of the time.

All four major educational innovatory projects referred to above were started on a fairly small scale, for a limited period, varying from two to ten years. In this broad sense they are generally referred to as 'experiments'.[1] With the 'experimental' approach came the idea of somehow incorporating research (mainly evaluation research) in these programmes. In the history of research and evaluation within the programmes a distinction has been made between policy-oriented and practitioner-oriented research; the former being generally defined on a higher level of aggregation (the total project) than the latter (specific research activities in individual schools).

The functioning of policy-oriented research in these innovatory programmes is the subject of a study in progress.[2] The present paper reports and discusses some of the major findings to date. The major aim of the study is to present and systematize descriptive material about the functioning of policy-oriented research in these programmes, so as to permit an assessment of the existing situation leading to suggestions for improvement. The assumption that the functioning of research in this particular setting is far from ideal is based on more or less articulate complaints from various relevant audiences, sceptical comments on the feasibility of evaluation research in these settings made at the outset of these programmes by various authors — e.g. Brus, 1976; De Groot, 1977 — and on personal experiences.

The increasing proportion of the total budget for educational research that the Department of Education is prepared to allocate to policy-oriented research in general has been a further incentive to undertake the study; perhaps something worthwhile can be learned from a systematic review of experiences to date.

Since the data collected as the material for the larger study are still incomplete, this paper will only refer to the 'Middle School' and 'Open School' experiments.

---

[1] To avoid confusion, the innovatory 'experiments' will from now on be referred to as Experiments or programmes and the term 'projects' will be used for research efforts undertaken with the innovatory programmes.
[2] The study is being undertaken and financed by the Foundation for Educational Research (SVO), the present author's employer.

The design of the larger study

The study attempts to describe research projects 'in their context', by explicitly taking policy-making and organizational aspects of the 'experimental' educational innovation programmes into consideration. From a methodological point of view it can best be characterized as a 'formulative or exploratory study', to use Selltiz's term (Selltiz, Wrightsman and Cook, 1976, p. 90). Although attempts have been made to improve the investigative focus by adopting an explicit theoretical framework in formulating the research problems, and by carefully selecting sources of evidence during the planning phase of the study, the limited amount of empirical data, as well as the 'broadness' of the conceptual framework, preclude stronger claims for the status of the study.

The study's conceptual framework is described in another paper (Scheerens, 1981) to be included in the documentary material for the International Workshop on Educational Research and Public Policymaking. Here the theoretical framework will therefore only be sketched in the most general terms.

For the classification of policy-making processes involved in the execution of the educational innovatory programmes, various models of policy-making, which depart increasingly from the model of pure rationality (see e.g. Dror, 1968), can be used. As such, the following models are considered: the pure rationality model, the problem-solving model, various types of sequential decision-making models, incrementalism and finally, some 'alternative' models (e.g. Allison's organizational process model).[1]

To arrive at a more systematic description of the structures that formalize the relationship between policy-makers, researchers, programme-administrators and practitioners, some concepts from organizational science are used. Key concepts in this respect are: the disjunction or 'decomposition' of organizations, coordination, organizational decision-making, and power and influence within organizations.

Research projects are described in terms of the history of the project, the degree to which the project is central to the innovatory programme, and methodological aspects. Finally, as an encompassing framework that is sufficiently broad to permit a systematic analysis of policy-making conceived as an aspect of organizational functioning (including the design and implementation of research activities), use is made of a control-systemic approach, called the 'control paradigm' (De Leeuw, 1974). Application of the control paradigm to the functioning of policy-oriented

---

[1] Thus, the sequence of models can be seen as an ordinal scale where the models placed at the bottom depart most strongly from the pure rationality model; whether or not the 'alternative' models should be referred to as rational or 'non-rational' models remains an open question.

research in the educational innovatory programs amounts to a systematic analysis of feasible ways of changing the existing 'state of affairs' with respect to standard courses of action, aims or organizational structure.

Although the overall aim of the larger study includes evaluation of certain aspects of the existing structure, I shall here in the main refrain from making evaluative comments. This position is adopted because of the inconclusiveness of the data collected and analysed so far, and also because it is beyond the scope of this paper to present a detailed discussion of the evaluation criteria and standards required for such an endeavour. Since the use of the above-mentioned control paradigm is mainly concerned with the evaluative part of the study, its application will only be sketched in the most global terms here. Nevertheless, in the final section of this paper, some ways of evaluating the phenomena observed will be discussed. Also, since describing the existing state of affairs in terms of progressive departures from the pure rationality model easily leads to attributing normative connotations concerning rationality to these descriptions, evaluative comments — including the present author's personal opinion — will occasionally creep in.

Methods

The methods used in the study are: documentary analysis, interviews with key people, and, as far as the evaluative part of the study is concerned, consultation of experts. The process of analyzing the documents was focused by specific questions formulated during the study's planning phase. The main sources for the documentary analysis have been government papers, reports of advisory committees, relevant articles in educational journals and the archives of the Foundation for Educational Research (SVO) containing documentary material on the various research projects. The findings from the documentary analysis were used to design the questionnaires for interviewing key people.[1] So far, twelve interviews have taken place with teachers, government officials and members of advisory committees.[2]

The main topics of the interview questionnaire are the function of research within the innovatory programmes, characterization of the policy-making process and innovatory strategy, opinions on the functioning of the organizational structure in question, the relevance of the research findings obtained so far and feasible ways of improving certain aspects which the interviewee himself considers problematic.

So far, 27 brief descriptions of research projects (divided over three innovatory projects, Middle School, Open School and Integrated Primary

---

[1] The major part of the data collection for the study has been carried out by an institute for marketing research, Intomart.
[2] In the course of the study, researchers will also be questioned.

School,[1] have been completed. These will appear in the larger study together with evaluative conclusions reached by applying evaluative criteria to the descriptive material, by referring to experts consulted as well as to the evaluative comments of the key people interviewed.

Discussion of results

Before presenting in more detail the results obtained so far, first a brief characterization of the two major educational programmes involved, the Middle School and the Open School Experiment, will be briefly sketched. The middle school idea is to create a comprehensive secondary school for children from 12 to 15/16 years of age, as an alternative to the current system, where different types of schools exist in parallel. Such a middle school could eventually, if Parliament so decided, replace all these schools.

The overall aims of the Middle School Experiment are stated as follows:

— Postponement of the moment of choice with respect to further education or work until children are 15 or 16 years of age;
— Provision of equal opportunities for all children to develop their individual potential;
— Increase in the scope of the educational programme (with respect to creative, technical and social skills);
— Stimulation of personal growth and social awareness.

In 1976 the experiment[2] was started in a limited number of schools. At this time, eight 'integral experiments' and 37 'resonance schools' participate in the innovatory programme. A decision by Parliament about the future role of the Middle School is planned for 1985.

The Open School Experiment is devoted to broadening and improving the general abilities and social skills of so-called underprivileged adults, defined as those with a limited level of formal schooling (up to about grade five). In 1977 the experimental programme started with about 1000[3] participants in fourteen locations widely distributed over the country. Initially, the experiment was designed for a two-year period, but since 1979 decisions to extend the programme by a one-year period have been taken twice. At present it is not quite clear on what basis or scale the Experiment will be continued.

The methods used in the Open School Experiment are called 'multi-

---

[1] For age groups four to 11, called *Baisisschool*.
[2] Usually the innovatory programme in question is referred to in the plural: experiments; here however, the singular will be used to emphasize the idea of coherence of effort between the individual experimental schools.
[3] In subsequent years the number of participants has risen to about 1400.

medial', which means that the curriculum makes use of both radio and TV as well as written material for private study and group sessions.

As a preliminary to a more detailed discussion of the organizational structure of the institutions and committees jointly involved in the decision-making, implementation and assessment of these programmes, the major 'units' of the structure will be briefly described. At the level of the Ministry of Education special departments and task-forces have been set up to prepare and support the Minister's decision-making. The so-called 'Innovatory Committees' are independent committees of experts, appointed by the Minister to advise him on the further operationalization and implementation of the general policy. To coordinate the functioning of the experimental schools, special units have been created; in the case of the Open School Experiment the coordinating unit is an independent foundation. In the sphere of policy-oriented research within the experimental programmes, the Foundation for Educational Research functions both as 'mandated principal' towards the research institutes that carry out the actual research and as an advisor to the Minister of Education on research programs and proposals. Finally special committees (the so-called Programme Advisory Committees) have been set up to develop research programmes.

In subsequent sections the results of this study will be discussed under three main headings: characteristics of the policy-making processes, organizational aspects and general characteristics of the research projects.

1. Characteristics of the policy-making processes involved

Elsewhere (Scheerens, 1981, p. 212), variables that are useful to characterize policy-making processes — particularly when the overall aim is to analyze the function of research within these processes — have been discussed. From this list of variables the following ones are used to describe the policy-making processes considered here:

— the scientific foundation of the innovation programmes;
— clarity of goals;
— articulateness of technology;
— characteristics of the innovatory strategy;
— general normative orientations;
— opinions on the function of policy-oriented research within these programmes;
— the actual stage of development of the programme;
— the use so far made of research findings in the policy-making processes.

1.1 The scientific foundation of the innovational programmes

The length of the bibliography to the second part of the overall plan for the innovatory programmes under consideration, the *Contourennota*, suggests innovatory policy-making was indeed grounded on a thorough review of the educational literature on topics like compensatory education, equality of opportunity, and experiences with large-scale innovation programmes in other countries. It should be noted, however, that this document did not appear until March 1977, when the four major innovatory programmes had already been under way for one or two years.

The reports of the committees set up to advise the government on the further development and implementation of innovatory policies, rarely contain explicit references to the relevant educational literature, although it is clear that some use of this literature has been made. The overall impression is that the scientific foundation of the innovatory policy-making, while not altogether absent, is somewhat tenuous considering the scope of the innovatory programmes. This impression is further supported by aspects of the policy-making process to be documented in subsequent sections (e.g. the vagueness of aims and technology and the characteristics of the innovatory strategy), and the fact that advisory committees sometimes explicitly say that the educational sciences are not equipped to resolve completely the problems of a particular innovatory programme (ICM, 11th advisory report p. 12).

1.2 Clarity of goals

The general aims mentioned in the introductory part to this section of both the Middle School and the Open School Experiment, have not been systematically operationalized, although some initial attempts were made to do so. In the Middle School Experiment, on several occasions some literature surveys were undertaken in order to clarify concepts like 'equality of opportunity' and 'development of social awareness'. Although these efforts provided some illumination, it is quite unclear whether the findings have been used at all (e.g. by the Innovatory Committee) to shape the innovatory process.

In the Open School Experiment an attempt was made to operationalize the goal of increasing the participants' social preparedness. Before this project — which, incidentally, like the literature studies in the Middle School Experiment, was carried out by researchers — could be completed, the project was stopped at the instigation of teachers who denied the possible validity of the instrument that was being constructed. Although three (out of four)[1] of the over-all aims of the Middle School Experiment

---

[1] The first general aim, 'postponement of choice', concerns a structural change in the existing school system, which must either be implemented or not.

are directly or indirectly concerned with dispositions and skills of pupils (or participants) which the experimental programmes are intended to stimulate or increase, at this stage vagueness prevails as to the meaning of the concepts involved.[1] Of course, in these programmes goals other than the ones to be expressed in terms of pupil dispositions or behaviour exist, but in my opinion these goals would necessarily be concerned with 'supportive' or 'lower order' conditions of the programmes. An example of such a goal is the intake of pupils; in both the Middle School and the Open School Experiment specific assumptions about the heterogeneity of the intake in terms of ability were stated; achieving the desired heterogeneity in the experimental programmes could thus be seen as the realization of a 'goal'. Apart from all this, one gets the impression that in these programmes certain 'means' come to be seen as ends in themselves. The 'experimental process' then would not constitute a systematic effort to determine which of various alternatives is the best way to attain a given end but amount to no more than the choice of a means on the basis of the attractiveness of its intrinsic characteristics, more or less regardless of whether or not the objective is achieved.

Although alternative explorations cannot be ruled out on the basis of the available facts, the predominance of the method of 'doing things in the group' in the Open School programme would seem to confirm this impression. From the interviews with key people serving on the two innovatory committees it appears that they are strongly committed to the wider implementation of the 'experimental' small-scale projects. This may not come as a big surprise, but it significantly illustrates how these key people[2] conceive the experimental character of the programmes. Statements about the wider implementation of the programmes made at a stage when evidence of the effectiveness of the programmes is absent or at best inconclusive,[3] seem to imply an attitude of non-commitment as far as defining and assessing the 'official' goals is concerned.

1.3 Articulateness of technology

The term technology will be used in a broad sense to refer to all means (methods, teaching strategies, ways of grouping pupils, etc.) that are being considered, or actually used, to attain the educational goals of the programmes.

---

[1] In the advisory reports they are referred to in the most general terms, some of them seem to be inherently vague (see Duyker on 'the ideology of personal growth', 1976), and it is quite uncertain in what way individual schools are using these general aims.

[2] Who, incidentally, must be seen as the ambassadors of the scientific community to the 'innovation province'.

[3] See also the proposal of the ICM in the 15th Advisory Report as to the implementation of a three-year Middle School on a national scale.

At the outset of the Middle School Experiment the methods by which the goals of equal opportunity, personal growth and social awareness were supposed to be attained were described in terms that were scarcely more specific than the definitions of the goals themselves. (This, however, is consistent with the innovatory strategy of this Experiment, as will become apparent in the next section). 'Individualization of tuition' and 'internal differentiation' within mixed ability groups were mentioned, but the ways in which these general principles were to be put into practice were more or less[1] left to the individual schools. Although the subsequent advisory reports of the Innovatory Committee contain descriptions of a national Middle School curriculum, these descriptions remain quite general, and again it must be said that this approach is consistent with the committee's view of the innovatory strategy.[2] It is only recently, following a memorandum from the Minister in reaction to the 11th Advisory report of the Innovatory Committee, that the Foundation for Curriculum Development was authorized to develop an Experimental Middle School Curriculum.

The Open School Experiment got off to a different start. Here a common multimedia curriculum was developed. Since this curriculum was designed as a fairly 'open' one, it still left room for all sorts of local and individual variations. After the programmes had been going for about eighteen months, a reversal of policy took place with the effect that the developmental activities were decentralized, so that there was even greater latitude for the teachers to practise local variations of the original curricular scheme.

It may be concluded that, particularly at the national level, there is considerable uncertainty about the technology of these programmes; to a large extent the question as to how to attain the 'new' educational goals is left to the individual schools or 'locations'.

1.4 The innovatory strategy

The innovatory strategy in both the Middle School and the Open School Experiment is associated most strongly with Chin and Benne's conception of 'normative-re-educative strategies' for change (Bennis, Benne and Chin, 1970). Some authors, however, have also pointed out aspects of these innovatory processes that correspond more nearly with the other two major types of strategies for change discussed by Chin and Benne, namely empirical-rational strategies and power-coercive strategies (Creemers *et al.*, 1976; Dodde, 1977).

The major characteristics of normative-re-educative strategies are: the

---

[1] The schools that take part in the Middle School Experiment have received assistance from outside educationalists.
[2] See, for instance, the Eleventh Advisory Report of the ICM, pp. 36–47.

idea that 'changes are alterations in normative structures — as well as in cognitive and perceptual orientations'; the establishment of 'collaborative relationships between researchers, educators and activists', and an emphasis on 'the client system and his (or its) involvement in working out programmes of change and improvement for himself (or itself)' (Chin and Benne, p. 43—4).

Furthermore, normative-re-educative strategies are associated with the notion of personal growth and 'release' of creativity predominant in humanistic psychology. The innovatory strategy adopted by the Middle School Innovatory Committee indeed stresses collaborative relationships between change agents and the client system (the schools). Since, however, there has long been uncertainty as to who is the change agent[1] in this programme, it has largely been left to the schools to work out for themselves the general aims of the programme.[2] While normative orientations are inherent in the notion of educational change, there are differences in the degree to which they hold sway.

In the Middle School Experiment both teachers and innovatory advisers appear strongly committed to comprehensivization. This 'movement character' of the Middle School Experiment is also reflected in the way experimental schools were selected, which was virtually on the basis of self-selection. The schools that thus came to be part of the experiment had all of them already been 'experimenting' with new approaches consonant with the Middle School aims. As appears from research reports, the experimental schools already had different orientations towards the Middle School aims at the outset of the programme. In addition, it appears that the innovatory strategy has led to a widely divergent development in individual schools.[3] I have found no instances of central attempts[4] (e.g. by the Innovatory Committee) to use feedback from schools in order to abstract common factors which could then be used to steer the developmental process of the Experiment towards convergence and greater consistency.[5]

At the same time the Middle School is seen as *an* experimental

---

[1] Probably outside educationalists qualify as such, though they seem to have played such a non-directive role that the conclusion remains the same; the burden of the innovatory activities — including developmental activities — was delegated to the schools.
[2] From the viewpoint of curriculum development, this approach has been criticized by Creemers, 1980, and Creemers and De Vries, 1980.
[3] See the reports of the *B.B. 1-project*, the *B.B. 2-project* and the *Faciliteitenonderzoek* respectively.
[4] Although the Innovatory Committee did exercise some control over the yearly approval of school-curricula by the Minister, this apparently has not led to greater convergence.
[5] Such efforts would seem necessary if one conceives *the* Experiment as one 'experimental treatment' at the national level, instead of a set of discrete experiments in individual schools.

programme with a model curriculum that must be evaluated, among other ways, through research. The first research projects set out to measure entrance behaviour, with the explicit intention of relating these measures to outcome measures at the end of the programme. This means that at least traces of a more empirical-rational approach can be detected in the Middle School Experiment.

In the Open School Experiment the innovatory strategy, although referred to as normative-re-educative, even more strongly showed an empirical-rational orientation. The Experiment was designed for a limited number of years, there was a central curricular scheme, teaching and learning materials were developed centrally and a plan for summative evaluation was drawn up. As described before, however, a policy reversal took place in this programme, which led to a more blurred, because divergent, development of individual 'schools' (or 'locations' as they are called in this programme).

If the innovatory strategies adopted in the programmes are regarded as instances of policy-making (at a more concrete level), one could attempt to classify these processes according to one (or several) of the models of public policy-making mentioned in an earlier section. The indeterminateness implied in the above discussion on innovatory strategies suggests that it would be hard to classify the policy-making processes unequivocally in terms of any one of the policy-making models alone. Nevertheless, some congruences can be detected. First of all the reliance on teachers' practical knowledge, judgment and creativity implicit in the normative-re-educative strategy bears some resemblance to Dror's conception of extrarational models of policy-making (Dror, 1968). Incidentally, it should be noted that negative connotations associated with irrationalism are totally absent from Dror's conception of extrarational processes. Furthermore, although the general ideas of both the Middle School and the Open School imply a major break with current educational practice, it is apparent from various research reports that, at the local level, no such sharp break is experienced by the teachers. They are more or less gradually pushing ahead along the lines they had already chosen before they joined the Experiments. The fact that these experimental schools and locations may nevertheless differ considerably from more 'traditional' schools can to a large extent be explained by the self-selective recruitment of experimental units.

This would imply that, although the general ideas of these innovatory programmes are too 'revolutionary' to be associated with incrementalism (which is usually thought of as a conservative strategy), yet the actual processes in the experimental schools do strongly resemble incrementalism.

Perhaps, if agreement could be reached on defining the global aims of these Experiments, while recognizing the 'small-step approach' at the local level, the total process could be identified with Etzioni's idea of 'mixed scanning'.

Finally, we might consider the policy-making processes in the light of the 'problem solving model'[1] (Scheerens, 1981, p. 3).

'Experiments' suggests the notion of trying out one or more solutions on a small scale, evaluating them and finally selecting the most satisfactory one. There are some facts that mitigate against such a classification of the policy-making processes in question. At the national level no alternative strategies have been devised to achieve the central aims of the programmes under consideration (e.g. systematic attempts to realize some of the aims of the Middle School within the existing educational structure). Also, as has become apparent from preceding sections, it is not altogether clear what goals are being pursued in these programmes and by what means; the actual situation seems to be altogether too inarticulate and too fragmented for the process to be identified with the characteristics of a problem-solving model.

In summary, it may be concluded that if we attempt to identify the policy-making processes in terms of various models of public policy-making, we find some resemblance with extrarational processes, incrementalism and perhaps 'mixed scanning', whereas 'problem-solving' appears to be too strong a model to characterize these processes.

1.5 General normative orientations

To avoid the overworked term 'ideology' with its inflated connotations I will refer to the political background of these programmes, and the value aspects of the 'philosophy' of education and educational change, in terms of 'normative orientations'.

We have seen that the political background of these programmes is strongly associated with the idea of equality of opportunity. As noted by De Koning (1977), different conceptions of equality of opportunity exist (e.g. the 'liberal' conception of tapping the reserves of talent hidden among lower-class children and the 'freedom of growth' conception, which is taken to be consonant with central ideas from humanistic psychology.[2] Do Koning further notes that these different conceptions can also be

---

[1] It should be noted that, here 'problem-solving' is conceived at a high level of aggregation, i.e. at the national level; defining 'problem-solving' at the level of individual schools would probably be more in line with the actual situation; in the national context, however, the poorly coordinated specific development of individual schools should be described as incrementalism.

Distinguishing between levels of aggregation in these programmes could ultimately take the form of two separate policy-making processes, one defined at the national level and one at the level of individual schools. Throughout this paper, however, these two processes are assumed to be mutually related in that the various lower level processes somehow correspond to the characteristics defined at the national level.

[2] See also Duyker, 1976 on 'The ideology of personal growth'.

discerned in the various ways the Middle School is conceived in The Netherlands.

It has already been observed that the normative-re-educative innovatory strategy, too, bears some resemblance to the central ideas of humanistic psychology. I think that in some, though by no means all, schools where this particular normative orientation is predominant, it accounts in the main for the teachers' resistance to 'hard' research methods, such as standardized achievement tests. Various schools opposed these tests as being irreconcilable with their philosophy of education (see also section 3.3).

In the Open School programme a similar normative orientation towards educational and innovatory processes can be observed. At the same time, feminists have a considerable say in this programme.[1] They too are generally opposed to 'hard', 'masculine' research methods (e.g. see Brunt, 1977).

1.6 Opinions on the function of policy-oriented research within these programmes

In interviews with key people serving on innovatory committees and with government officials the respondents generally mentioned 'collecting information' (in a pragmatic 'non-theoretical' way) as the major function of policy-oriented research within the innovation programmes. Particularly among government officials the idea prevails that research projects should be less theory-oriented than they have allegedly been so far and be more closely related to specific questions that the Department of Education wants answered.

Teachers generally opt for a school-oriented function of research. The Foundation for Educational Research has stressed the importance of critical evaluation research to assess the entire programme.[2]

Members of the Middle School Innovatory Committee have, on several occasions, suggested a rather limited function of evaluation research within the context of the Middle School Experiment (De Vries, 1977; Karstanje, 1979). They have particularly expressed doubts about the feasibility and necessity of comparative evaluation (comparing experimental schools with 'traditional' schools or other approaches to integrated secondary education that have developed over the years). Their 'prudent' attitude towards the scope and function of evaluation research has been criticized by Swanborn (1979), who indicates feasible ways of designing a comparative evaluative approach. Of course, the prevailing differences of opinion on the functions

---

[1] According to a news item in a local paper this has also been noted by Departmental Inspectors.
[2] E.g. see SVO's comments on the 12th Advisory Report of the ICM and SVO Memorandum no. 2, 1980.

of research among different institutions adversely affect the development and implementation of balanced research programmes.

1.7 The actual stage of development of the Experiments

The dominant feature emerging from the picture of the policy-making processes drawn in the preceding sections is their general elusiveness: vague and general goal-statements, unarticulated technology, all kinds of local variations, and normative orientations that occasionally seem almost addicted to vagueness. Another factor that adds to this general elusiveness is the indeterminacy of the stage reached in the development of the Experiments. The Middle School Experiment has been described as a 'developmental experiment' (Karstanje, 1979). Nevertheless it is to be evaluated before 1985 in order to assist Parliamentary decision-making on the future of the Middle School throughout the country. At the same time, attempts are at present being made to carry over the Middle School approach to other schools.[1] Since no clear-cut sequential distinction between a developmental phase and an experimental phase is made,[2] it is not entirely clear exactly what it is that has to be evaluated by 1985: a new educational programme that has 'emerged' and then been tried out for a few years, or a continuous process of development that has been going on for a period of about ten years.

In this respect the Open School Experiment is in a less equivocal position; although the experimental period has been extended, it is still conceivable that in the end an assessment of the entire experimental period will be made to assist in decision-making.

1.8 The use so far of research findings in the policy-making processes

In the advisory reports of the Innovatory Committees and the government memorandums published in reaction to these reports I have discovered no explicit references to research findings obtained in various research projects to date. Likewise, there is at most ambiguous evidence of major policy-changes on the basis of research findings.[3] This is somewhat surprising since in both the Middle School and the Open School Experiment research findings were obtained that seem to be at variance

---

[1] i.e. to a specific set of schools, described as 'resonance schools'.
[2] Here the distinction between 'development' and 'experiment' is thought of as sequential i.e. something is developed *before* it is tried out and subsequently compared with alternatives (experimentation).
[3] As appears from the analysis of the subsequent advisory reports, government memorandums and the response of the key people interviewed.

with some major programme intentions (and must therefore be seen as relevant to the policy-making processes).

In various research projects on the Middle School Experiment it was established that the 'integral' experimental schools had more or less gone their own way and were largely working in isolation, resulting in the disjointed pattern described before. Unless the aim of the innovatory strategy be something like 'the rediscovery of the wheel' in each and every experimental school, it comes as quite a surprise that the advisory reports of the Innovatory Committee provide no suggestions to contain this irregular growth.

As for the multimedia approach in the Open School Experiment, it has repeatedly been established that the participants (and the general public, for that matter) made hardly any use of the radio and TV programmes.[1] This led to changes in the format of these broadcasts at the beginning of the 1979/80 school year. The original idea that they should form an integral part of a multimedia curriculum has apparently been given up altogether; they are now seen as independent broadcasts within the general framework of educational programmes (Würsten, 1981). If these modifications are to be conceived as major policy changes they can only be so on the principle that 'If the mountain will not come to Mahomet, Mahomet must go the mountain' or, perhaps more fitting in this context, on the principle of 'the medium is the message'; although their use as a cornerstone of the intended multimedia Open School curriculum is given up, these radio and TV programmes are being continued, while the need to do so is defended on entirely new grounds.

1.9 Conclusion

The characteristics of the policy-making processes that emerge from the preceding sections can be summarized as follows: the scientific basis of the experimental programmes is weak considering the scope of the innovation; there is much vagueness about goals and technology; general normative orientations of relevant participants are sometimes at variance with rational empirical strategies; there is disagreement on the function of research within these programmes and, sometimes, there also seems to be uncertainty as to the actual phase reached in the development of the programme; finally, we have seen how supposedly counter-evidential research findings are neglected or rationalized in the policy-making processes. Before turning to the actual functioning of research projects in this setting, some attention will be given to the organizational structure within which the planning and implementation of research projects takes place.

---

[1] See, for instance, the reports of the media-research project.

2. Organizational aspects

2.1 Organizational structure; structural coordination

The formal relationship between the various units involved in decision-making processes about research in these programmes can be represented by the following organogram:

Figure 1:

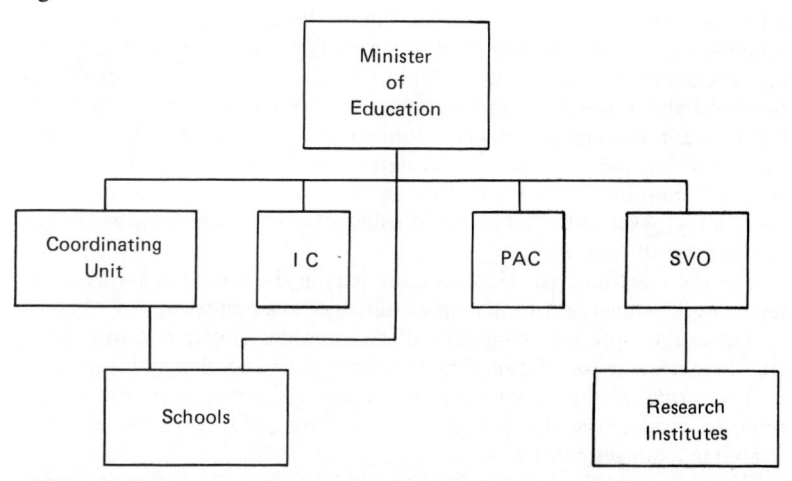

```
                    ┌─────────────┐
                    │  Minister   │
                    │     of      │
                    │  Education  │
                    └──────┬──────┘
         ┌────────────┬────┴─────┬──────────┐
   ┌─────┴─────┐  ┌───┴──┐  ┌────┴──┐  ┌────┴──┐
   │Coordinating│  │ IC  │  │  PAC  │  │  SVO  │
   │   Unit    │  │      │  │       │  │       │
   └─────┬─────┘  └──┬───┘  └───────┘  └────┬──┘
         └──────┬────┘                      │
           ┌────┴────┐                 ┌────┴─────┐
           │ Schools │                 │ Research │
           │         │                 │Institutes│
           └─────────┘                 └──────────┘
```

'Coordinating Unit' – institute, foundation or committee that coordinates the activities of schools participating in the Experiment.
I.C. – Innovatory Committee
P.A.C. – Programme Advisory Committee (these committees develop general research programs)
S.V.O. – Foundation for Educational Research.
It should be noted that the lines in the organogram do not entirely represent channels of formal authority. Characteristics of the relationships are described later on.

Before illustrating the dynamics of this organizational structure by a description of the developmental process of a research project, a brief description of the formal authority and responsibilities of each unit will be given.

The Programme Advisory Committees are set up by the Minister of Education and report directly to him. They are composed of independent experts, field representatives and observers from the Innovatory Committee, SVO and the Department of Education. Their task is to develop a general research programme and to advise on the 'policy-relevance' of specific research proposals developed within the general research programme.

Within the context of research on innovatory programmes, SVO[1] acts as 'mandated supervisor' to the institutes that carry out the actual research projects. SVO also exercises process control over the ongoing research projects and advises the Minister on the allocation of research funds, for which purpose it employs the services of external experts.

The Innovatory Committees advise the Minister of Education both on the general research programmes developed by the PACs, and on research proposals.

In each sector (Middle School, Open School, Primary School) a different kind of unit exists to coordinate the activities of experimental schools. For the Middle School this is a fairly loosely structured committee,[2] consisting of representatives from schools, the Department of Education and the Innovatory Committee. For the Open School a separate independent foundation, SPOS,[3] funded by the Department of Education was created. Although this latter construction implies a much stronger coordinating organ than in the case of the Middle School Experiment, even this foundation is subject to rigid budget control by the Department of Education.

For the experimental schools taking part in the Middle School Experiment, both budget and programme control is maintained by the Ministry of Education. For the Open School these responsibilities rest with SPOS (the independent foundation that coordinates the experimental locations).

The work of the various research institutes involved in the policy-oriented research in question, is supervised by SVO; SVO also exercises 'mandated' budget control.

We have seen that, at the Ministry of Education, various new departments have been created to advise the Minister on matters of current concern for the innovation programmes, including policy-oriented research.

I think the most important feature of this organizational structure is its heavy emphasis on advisory organs on the one hand and the relatively weak formalization of structural coordination on the other. Furthermore, this structure implies a fairly strong centralization of formal authority, residing with the Minister, i.e. the Department of Education. The mutual influence of these features is most clearly illustrated when, for example, we look at possible ways of managing problems that researchers may have in obtaining cooperation from the experimental schools. As we shall see later on, such problems are not uncommon in this setting. In this case the only unit that has the authority to arrange matters formally, is the Minister himself i.e. the Department of Education. The formal authority

---

[1] SVO (Foundation for Educational Research) is an independent foundation created by the Minister of Education; apart from the research activities which SVO itself generates, its main task is to programme, supervise and assess educational research financed by the Department of Education.
[2] The so-called 'technical committee', which replaced the earlier CLEP.
[3] SPOS = *Stichting Proefprojecten Open School.*

of SVO, as far as the enforcement of process-control by means of budget control is concerned, is limited because SVO has only 'mandated' budget control; final budget decisions still rest with the Department of Education.

Although, as far as formal authority is concerned, there is relatively little delegation from the Department of Education to the other units, and consequently government officials are actively involved in decision-making on all kinds of matters concerning these projects, it must be doubted whether the new specially designed units at the Department can handle all these tasks.[1] Consequently, frequent delays in decision-making occur. This inarticulateness of structural coordination leads to frequent negotiations between different units, lengthy advisory procedures and — in my opinion — an over-all climate of indecisiveness.[2]

2.2 Instances of organizational functioning

The consecutive stages in the developmental process of research in this setting are: the development of a general research programme by a Programme Advisory Committee, the development of specific research proposals and the actual process of carrying through research.

Programme Advisory Committees were first set up in 1977. The main motive for calling them into being was the need for greater harmony between research and the innovatory programmes. Before that time the task of coordinating the various research projects by means of general plans had been carried out by groups of researchers, but it was felt[3] that in this way research came to be programmed on too narrow a basis. Since the PACs have a broader composition, it was thought that this would improve the relevance of the total research efforts.

Although in both the Middle School Experiment and the Open School Experiment general programmes were developed, there have been some problems in the functioning of the PACs. The composition of the Middle School PAC has been changed three times. Only now have they started to develop an integral evaluation plan while in previous years the programmes essentially consisted of loosely related sets of ideas for separate research projects. The Open School PAC has gradually faded away. Since the development and implementation of the first programme (1978) attempts to construct a second programme seem to have come to nothing.

Topics for research projects are outlined in the general programme

---

[1] If only for lack of manpower.
[2] It should be noted that lack of structural coordination is most likely just one of the problematic aspects of the existing organizational pattern. In the larger study's final analysis other coordinating mechanisms will be examined and a closer look will be taken at *informal* patterns of communication and control.
[3] by government officials and SVO.

produced by the PAC. Of course, this programme has first to be approved by the Minister, who is advised by SVO and the IC. Next, various research institutes are invited to write 'project sketches' (brief research proposals). These proposals are assessed by SVO, often in consultation with government officials, and thus project-sketches are selected. Next, the research institute in question is invited to compose a fully-fledged research proposal. This proposal is evaluated by SVO, in consultation with external experts. If the proposal is approved, SVO then advises the Minister of Education to release funds for the project. In the case of the Open School Experiment this whole process took about 13 months: the PAC started work in August 1977; the first projects started in October 1978. It frequently happens that SVO 'conditionally' approves research proposals. In that case the research institute usually has to adjust the research design or submit an interim report. Indeed, in quite a few cases one or two interim reports per year have been required. Researchers tend to disapprove of these demands which they consider no more than bureaucratic.

As for the social implementation of research projects, in a majority of projects designed to collect empirical data in schools, an important element is the problems encountered in securing the cooperation of these schools. In most cases these problems are eventually solved, but not without a considerable loss of time, and often to the detriment of technical requirements of data collection. Both in the Middle School and the Open School Experiment some schools or locations altogether refused to permit certain data collection procedures (mainly tests), thus causing non-response problems. By the time the project's final report is presented the average project (among those studied so far) is about six months behind schedule.

A final aspect of the functioning of research within this setting concerns research management and the personnel available in the research institutes. Though this matter has not been looked into very closely as yet, the impression is that a relatively large number of researchers involved in these projects are fairly inexperienced.

2.3 Goal coordination; power and influence

As noted in section 1.6, some disagreement exists between different units as far as ideas on the function of research in these projects in concerned. At the level of the actual research projects this may cause some confusion as to which master should be served. However, these conflicts seem to be manifested only at this level; so far there have been very few open discussions of this important matter at higher levels in the organizational structure.

In an earlier section (2.1), where the formal authority structure was discussed, it was concluded that a considerable amount of formal authority rests with the Department of Education. At a more informal level, the experimental schools have considerable power over the researchers, who are quite dependent on the cooperation of the particular group of schools taking part in the Experiment. Since they have no formal authority to back up their arguments,[1] lengthy negotiating procedures tend to ensue. I think that there is some evidence that schools have been successful in bending research towards a form that is more useful to them and less threatening. They have succeeded in making researchers report separately on individual schools in situations where the main objective was more general, policy-oriented research. Again, since the general normative orientation that seems to have some predominance in the two Experiments under consideration — see section 1.5 — is most consonant with qualitative, participatory research, there is evidently some pressure on researchers to proceed on those lines. As will become apparent in the next section, in a majority of projects teachers are the main source of data; this too might be interpreted in terms of the schools' success in maintaining control over data-collection procedures.

2.4 Conclusion

It has been argued that the main feature of the organizational structure is its heavy emphasis on advisory units and the relative weakness where the actual structuring of coordination on the basis of formal authority is concerned.

The functioning of Programme Advisory Committees has been briefly described as well as the advisory and decision-making processes with respect to research proposals. It is the absence of attempts to coordinate goals at the higher level of the structure, the conflicting ideas on the function of research in these projects, and the apparently successful attempts by schools to control data-collection procedures which have sometimes combined to create an image of this research as a plaything bandied about between rival interest groups.

3. General characteristics of the research projects

3.1 Research topics per sector[2]

By the second half of 1980, ten[3] research projects had been carried out in the Middle School Experiment (since 1976). These ten projects covered the following themes:

---

[1] Researchers cannot fall back on explicit contracts setting out the commitment of experimental schools to research activities.
[2] i.e. the Middle School Experiment and the Open School Experiment.
[3] The so-called school-oriented studes are excluded from this list.

- description upon entrance and follow-through of the experimental school intakes in 1976 and 1977;
- five so-called partial studies, i.e. literature surveys on the following topics: description of social awareness; analysis of the problems inherent in operationalizing the general teaching aims of the innovatory programme; analysis of the problems of assessing achievement at the end of the programme; curriculum development for individual schools and instrumentation of process evaluation;
- description of characteristics of pupils' and parents' opinions at the beginning of the 1977/1978 school year;
- an exploratory study on the feasibility of recurrent assessment of the state of affairs in schools;
- description of special facilities granted to experimental schools.

At present three research projects are being conducted which seek to describe year intakes of pupils (using tests and administrative data) as they enter, go through and finish the Middle School programme. A' fourth project, aimed at describing the way schools have operationalized the general Middle School aims, is being prepared.

At the present time the major research projects in the Open School sector are still in progress. Only two 'partial studies' (descriptions of other 'Open-School-type' educational settings) have been completed so far. Since the Open School Experiment has been extended, the research projects are also being prolonged. The main topics of the Open School research programme are:

- curriculum evaluation that was started on the basis of a summative design, but has been considerably reduced in scope after the policy reversal in this experiment took place (see p. 234);
- process-description and evaluation;
- comparative description of 'spontaneous Open School groups';
- description and assessment of the use of the various media (e.g. radio and TV programmes);
- descriptions of characteristics (including motives) of people who have dropped out of the programme;
- analysis of the policy-making and innovatory strategy in the Open School Experiment;
- description and analysis of the teachers' needs for initial enlarged competence courses and in-service training.

3.2 Categorization of research projects

As a first step towards further defining these research projects the following types of research can be distinguished on the basis of an *ad hoc* classification scheme that may be a useful device for further structuring the question as to the centrality of research projects with respect to the innovatory programmes.

I Descriptive studies directed to side issues or non-central aspects of the innovation programme.
II Descriptive studies directed to more central aspects of the innovation programme which could be incorporated within a — possibly merely conjectural — general evaluation plan.
III Partial evaluation studies (i.e. aimed at the evaluation of partial aspects of the total innovatory programme).
IV Overall evaluation studies (i.e. aimed at the evaluation of the total programme; here the term summative evaluation would be appropriate).

According to this broad classification scheme presumably eight out of ten of the Middle School research projects should be classified as descriptive studies foreshadowing a general evaluation plan (cat. II). Assessment of entrance behaviour of pupils and schools; records of pupils' careers during the programme; preliminary efforts to operationalize the general aims of the programme; assessment of teachers' and parents' opinions of the programme; and the description of the provision and use of special facilities could all be seen as building blocks of a general evaluation plan.[1]

The other two projects (literature surveys on curriculum development and general approaches to the assessment of pupil achievement) correspond more closely to category I, discrete descriptive studies. Although, with a certain effort, one could thus think of the Middle School research projects as fitting into an overall scheme, it should be noted that it will not be an easy matter to integrate findings from these separate projects on a *post hoc* basis. At this moment, in the absence of such an overall evaluation plan, the Middle School research projects present a fragmented picture. A main cause of this state of affairs is the comparatively late start of a more or less coordinated research effort in this sector.

In the Open School sector, the summative evaluation project, as originally designed that is, would fit category IV. Originally, the project on the so-called 'spontaneous groups' and the study of drop-outs were closely geared to this summative evaluation design, since a comparative approach was envisaged. Although this comparison is still the object, it must be doubted whether genuine comparative evaluation can be realized to a substantial degree, since the two main projects have been greatly reduced in scope and have run into considerable difficulties over data collection. Much the same goes for the projects on process description and the use of educational media.

---

[1] In the very first research project in the Middle School sector — description of the intake situation — explicit reference is made to an overall evaluation plan.

According to the original plans, these two projects, on the 'process' side of the total programme, were to be related to the 'product' side of the evaluation, i.e. the measurement of teaching and learning effects. In terms of the general classification scheme, these two projects have therefore moved in the direction of category I (merely descriptive), whereas they started out as category II – projects, i.e. descriptive in relation to a general evaluation scheme. Since they might yield information with major implications for evaluative conclusions on the partial aspects under scrutiny, they could, after all, be said to correspond more closely to category III (partial evaluation studies). The other, relatively minor, research projects in the Open School sector should be seen as descriptive (category I) studies.

Although the information on the various research projects in these two sectors must necessarily be limited in this presentation, even the rough characterization that has been given so far, suggests a difference between the whole of the research projects in the Open School Experiment and those in the Middle School Experiment.

In my opinion the coherence in the choice of research topics is greater in the Open School Experiment. This can be explained by the fact that in the Open School Experiment more articulate attempts were made to formulate an overall research plan. In the Middle School Experiment at present the major preoccupation is still clarification of the general contours of such a plan. Perhaps at a more fundamental level of explanation this contrast can also be seen as due to the differences in policymaking and innovatory strategies between the two sectors. As we have seen, the Open School Experiment, at least initially, was more like a true field experiment than the Middle School Experiment. Furthermore, the organizational structure of the Open School Experiment has been described as incorporating a stronger coordinating unit than that of the Middle School Experiment. The Open School's less blurred innovatory strategy as well as its tighter organizational structure presumably contributed significantly to the evolution of its own coherent evaluation plan. This demonstrates that policy-making processes, organizational structure[1] and type of research all hang together.

3.3 Methodological aspects

Out of eighteen research projects in both the Middle School Experiment and the Open School Experiment referred to above, four[2] used tests

---

[1] As pointed out before, the present analysis of the organizational aspects is restricted in that other mechanisms of coordination and informal control are not systematically explored here.
[2] In these particular projects tests were not the only methods; interview and questionnaires were also used.

(i.e. standardized achievement tests, intelligence tests and attitude scales). Exclusive use of literature surveys was made in seven projects. One Open School project, aimed at the description of the educational methods and devices used, included participants' self-reports in the form of brief diaries. The project on the process-evaluation of the Open School programme mainly used (written) self-reports by teachers, unstructured talks with teachers and some unstructured observation.[1] The remaining (six) projects (including the media-research in the Open School Experiment) mainly relied on interviews and questionnaires.

It is quite remarkable that systematic direct observation techniques have not been used in any of these research projects. Since relatively little had been specified in advance,[2] and much was left to the individual schools in terms of directing and operationalizing the innovatory process, one would have expected observation techniques to be of great use in describing what actually 'goes on' in the experimental schools, providing feedback to central programme administrators and policy-makers.

In the Open School Experiment direct observation by external observers was included in the original evaluation plan, but could not be practised because the teachers strongly objected. They felt that the presence of observers would disturb group processes and be threatening to participants. In the process-evaluation project, some observation seems to have taken place on the lines of 'participatory research' with observers first having to win acceptance by the local teams through identification with their purposes.

The observers discussed their findings intensively with the teachers before writing up reports that were then discussed with the teachers again. Apparently, teachers approved of this approach to process description. On the evidence available so far it is hard to explain why in the policy-oriented research projects in the Middle School, no direct observation techniques were even proposed for any of the projects. It must be concluded that, both in the Middle School and the Open School sector, all information on actual learning and teaching processes available to date is based on loosely structured self-reports by teachers or, in the case of the Open School project, also on observation techniques that are liable to criticism for strong reactivity.

In those cases where questionnaires and interviews were used they were, most frequently, directed to teachers; in other words here, too, teachers form the main source of data. In three Middle School research projects, questionnaires were directed to parents.

In those projects where tests or questionnaires were to be administered to pupils, considerable problems of non-response have occurred in all

---

[1] Since the preliminary reports on this project have not been released, I have only limited information on this particular project.
[2] More so in the Open School Experiment than in the Middle School Experiment.

cases,[1] generally caused by teachers, rather than pupils, through their refusal to cooperate in the data-collection procedures. This source of refusal is all the more striking in the Open School Experiment where the pupils are adults. In several cases response percentages are as low as 20 per cent.[2] Also, data collection usually took place under unstandardized and uncontrolled conditions, with tests virtually everywhere being administered by the teachers.

How serious the effects of these research-technical problems are can only be established by carefully studying, case by case, an enterprise which is clearly beyond the scope of this paper. My personal view is that in the Open School Experiment research-technical problems of this nature assumed such proportions that the reliability and validity of the research findings must be severely doubted. As noted before, a major cause of these problems is the difficulty of finding teachers ready to cooperate in applying 'harder' research methods. Apart from factors like 'evaluation anxiety' and the fact that research procedures take time away from teachers who are already working to tight schedules, I think the main cause of non-cooperation is to be found in the 'ideological' clash between the dominant normative orientation of teachers and the technical rationality associated with these particular research procedures. It must be emphasized that this conflict is much more prevalent in the Open School Experiment than in the Middle School Experiment.

I think the main conclusion to be drawn from this section is that in these projects teachers have controlled data-collection procedures to a large extent, which, as we saw earlier, is in keeping with the unformalized but very real power that teachers have over researchers in this setting.

3.4 Aspects of research management

As we saw in section 2.2, research projects in these Experiments are on average six months behind schedule; preparations for these projects had as a rule taken about six months. Of course delays in the actual research can to some extent be explained by the sometimes lengthy negotiating procedures between researchers and schools about data-collection, but the fact remains that most of the projects solely using literature surveys also turned in their final reports quite late, which shows that there are other factors involved. The research reports themselves state the following causes of delay: loss of time through illness, other institutional activities, prolonged discussions with representatives of various groups (e.g. PAC, external educationists) and, in one case, the reorganization of the research institute in question.

---

[1] As appears from research reports and other documents concerning these projects.
[2] In the Open School research projects.

Since the Open School Experiment has been extended, it is difficult to form an exact idea of how badly research projects are delayed in this sector; the planning schedules of these projects have been changed several times. All the same, it is clear that some projects are more than one year behind schedule. SVO-supervisors seem to have had hardly any influence on project management in these sectors[1] and only recently has a more active policy come to be adopted. This lack of influence can partly be accounted for by a complete change of staff in this SVO department during the relevant period.

3.5 Conclusion; opinions on the usefulness of research so far

In the preceding sections topics of research projects in the Open School and Middle School Experiment have been described and classified. From this classification it appears that, as far as design is concerned, the Open School projects form a more coherent whole than the Middle School projects. This greater coherence is related to characteristics of the policy-making processes and differences in the organizational structure of the two sectors.

As far as research methods are concerned, it can be concluded that questionnaires and interviews directed to teachers apparently predominate, while systematic external, direct observation in schools is strikingly absent. Technical problems that occurred where 'harder' research methods were used to obtain data on pupils are seen to be largely due to conflicts between the normative orientations of teachers and the norms of technical rationality inherent in the research approaches.

Apart from technical quality, the next important criterion in evaluating research projects is, of course, the usefulness of research to relevant audiences. Since this issue deserves a most careful approach, as is clear from the work of Patton (1978), Alkin and others (1979), Weiss (1980), and Weiss and Bucuvalas (1980),[2] conclusions about the projects concerned will be formulated here only with the utmost reserve, the more so because the evidence consists of no more than a dozen interviews with certain key people (government officials, teachers and members of Innovatory Committees).

Asked about the usefulness of the research projects referred to above, most interviewees responded negatively. Except in the case of the (Open

---

[1] In a way this is a somewhat striking observation. Because SVO usually states all kinds of conditions to be met during the implementation of the project, one would expect to find clear instances of process control to check whether these conditions and requirements are actually being met.
[2] Generally, these authors emphasize the 'undramatic' gradual way in which findings from research projects are utilized by decision-makers.

School) process-evaluation project, which teachers approved of, respondents said they rated the usefulness of the projects in question as quite low.[1] In the Open School sector it was specifically alleged that so far hardly any evidence was available from research projects, since only a few preliminary reports had actually been produced. More definite conclusions with respect to the usefulness of the research projects must be postponed, preferably until they can be based on the opinions of a larger sample of respondents.

Apart from all this, however, there can be little doubt that the technical quality of research has a direct bearing on the usefulness of its findings and that in fact 'usefulness' is always conditional on research quality. Saying that research of poor quality can be useful makes 'usefulness' a double-edged term and lays research wide open to corruption, for instance through insistence on 'supportive' results at all costs. If we adopt this line of argument, doubts that have been expressed as to the research quality of some of the projects lead to negative predictions about the usefulness of their (future) findings.

Final conclusions: a few general recommendations

In evaluating the general picture of the functioning of policy-oriented research that has emerged so far, different perspectives may be examined. This involves choosing certain 'discrete points' on continua of policy-making models and research designs that vary in strength, and applying these models in a normative sense, taking pure rationality as the ideal.[2] Real-life situations can thus be compared to, for instance, either rational decision-making, or incrementalism, or Allison's 'organizational process model' (Allison, 1969).

These particular three perspectives will in fact be used to make some brief evaluative comments on the research situations described. Since the first perspective, rational decision-making, implies imposing the most stringent criteria, the discrepancies between the ideal type and the real-life situation will be revealed most clearly here and the need for suggesting improvements will be correspondingly greater. It therefore seems appropriate to round off the discussion of the first perspective by outlining some general ways in which improvements can be brought about.

---

[1] Teachers involved in the Middle School Experiment said they thought the 'school-oriented research', which is not being considered in this paper, was quite useful.
[2] As stated in the footnote on p. 226, the sequence of models (p. 226) can be seen as a 'rationality scale'.

Perspective 1: rational decision-making[1] as the norm

The foregoing discussion leaves little room for doubt as to the seriousness of the discrepancies between the actual innovatory processes and the ideal of rational decision-making, between the actual, poorly coordinated total research effort and the ideal of clear-cut experimental or quasi-experimental approaches, as well as between the existing organizational structure and the ideal of efficient structural coordination of the work of policy-makers, researchers and practitioners.

The most fundamental improvement would of course be achieved by a searching reorientation of the usefulness, for instance in cost-benefit terms, of the normative re-educative innovatory strategy or the specific variety thereof that is being practised in the Experiments. Since evaluative comments on the innovatory strategy are clearly outside the scope of this study, I shall restrict my suggestions to the design of research programmes and the possible overhaul of the existing coordinating structure. To suggest improvements on these two counts, while assuming that the innovatory strategies remain as they are, would be to ignore the dependencies that supposedly, and to some extent demonstrably, exist between policy-making processes (i.e. innovatory strategies) on the one hand and research 'within' these processes on the other. In other words, this would mean that at least 'marginal' possibilities of breaking these dependencies will have to be suggested: imposing 'stronger' evaluation designs on 'weaker' policy-making processes, in terms of their further removal from the pure rationality model (see Scheerens, 1981).

To return to the actual Experiments, I think such proceedings are not altogether impossible. In the Middle School Experiment there is still time[2] to develop further a comprehensive evaluation plan, in which the findings of earlier research projects could somehow be integrated. Also, attempts could still be made to operationalize the general aims of the programme (particularly those that can be stated in terms of learning effects) and to measure them, preferably in comparison with a control group of pupils in traditional secondary schools. Furthermore, research efforts might still be directed towards more objective forms of process evaluation. Since it must be regarded as out of the question at this late stage for additional research projects (including empirical data collection) to be designed for the Open School Experiment,[3] secondary data analysis could be proposed to complement the research findings that have been (or will be) obtained from the projects currently in progress. The (large

---

[1] To be more precise, the pure rationality model and the 'problem-solving model' as described in Scheerens, 1981, pp. 201–2.
[2] Since the main decisions on the programme will not be made before 1985.
[3] Because it is quite unlikely that its experimental status will be continued much longer.

number of) self-reports from teachers that have accumulated in this project may be quite useful for secondary analysis by external researchers, who have had no direct contact with the Open School Experiment. Although the basic material is probably fairly biased, perhaps the direction of the bias could be identified, and thus taken into account.

The 'control paradigm' can be used to generate systematically a fuller range of possible courses of action to improve the existing situation. Since it is beyond the scope of this paper to describe the application of the control paradigm in any detail, I will confine myself to sketching a broad outline of this control-systematic approach.

Application of the control paradigm means defining a controller, a controlled system and an environment. Three major classes of 'modes of control' are distinguished: routine control, by which the controller has direct influence on the controlled system; adaptive control, by which the organizational structure is influenced or changed; and goal control, by which the system's goal is modified. These provide three major courses of action to improve the existing situation: modification of goals, (re)design of the organizational structure and improvement of 'routine-like' actions that in the existing structure are assigned to the various units.

Goal modifications within the organizational setting with its given innovatory strategy would of necessity involve articulating and making explicit the different norms and expectations which various units (e.g. the Department of Education, SVO, research institutes and experimental schools) have about the function of policy-oriented research in the innovation programmes. Such explicit formulations could be used as a basis for seeking agreement on one or more functions and for subsequent improvements like greater consensus on the priorities within research programmes and the prevention of conflicts at the level of individual research projects. I think it most likely that the articulation of different points of view on methodological issues, like standards for designing and evaluating policy-oriented research and the methodological status of participatory research, would also be of use in coming to terms with the problem of making explicit the 'goals' of policy-oriented research in the programmes in question.

As has been implied in section 2, any new design of the organizational structure should incorporate a more powerful unit to coordinate the design and implementation of research projects.[1] This coordinating unit should preferably be included in one of the institutions that are part of the structure described in section 2, so as not to make the structure even more complicated. The greatest improvements in terms of routine control would be achieved by more 'business-like' research management (by research institutes) and a corresponding approach to project supervision on the part of SVO.

---

[1] Presumably complemented by changes in other coordination mechanisms.

Perspective 2: incrementalism as the norm

Those who stress the developmental characteristics of the Experiments tend to place a different emphasis on the function of evaluation research in these programmes than we have done so far. If, in addition, this developmental process is seen as a collection of unique processes of individual schools, the idea of summative evaluation loses much of its appeal.

If the Experiment is thus seen as a rather loosely meshed network of developmental processes going on in individual schools and, if moreover the importance of evaluation research for the 'all or none' decision at the end of the programme is put in doubt, the fragmented, and 'merely' descriptive character of the set of research projects would not be considered to be much of a problem.

Perspective 3: the organizational process-model[1]

A final perspective for evaluating the functioning of the organizational structure could be used that might at first sight appear somewhat cynical. While it is not at all certain whether the aims of the Experiments are being achieved (nor, for that matter, exactly what they are), and while it is equally uncertain to what extent research projects have succeeded in clarifying matters, there is not a shadow of doubt that newly developed departments, committees and schools have survived, that existing institutions have benefited and that a good many researchers have earned a living carrying out research in these projects. All this of course thoroughly deserves our approbation, yet, as times of plenty seem to be over, I think we need to take up more demanding evaluative positions.

Bibliography

ALKIN, M.C., DAILAK, R. and WHITE, P. (1979). *Using Evaluations*. Sage Library of Social Research.
ALLISON, G.T. (1969). 'Conceptual models and the Cuban Missile Crisis,' *American Political Science Review*, 63, 3.
BENNIS, W.G., BENNE, K.D. and CHIN, R. (1970). *The Planning of change*. New York: Holt, Rinehart and Winston.
BRUNT, E. 'Feminisme en Methodologie,' *Intermediair*, 13^e jaargang 19.
BRUS, B.T. (1976). 'Over de bijdrage van onderwijskundig onderzoek tot de realisering van een onderwijsbeleid in de geest van de Contourennota,'

---

[1] According to Allison (1969), the organizational process-model stresses the interest of organizational units in maintaining the status quo and the importance of standard patterns of behaviour and routines in organizational decision-making.

Pedagogische Studiën, 53. Contouren van een toekomstig onderwijsbestel. Discussienota Tweede Kamer der Staten-Generaal. Zitting 1974–1975. Vervolgnota. Zitting 1976–1977.

CREEMERS, B.P.M. (1980). 'Leerplanontwikkeling in het Middenschoolexperiment,' *RION Bulletin*, nr. 6, juli.

CREEMERS, B.P.M., JACOBS, W., KLEINBERGEN, P.G., RIDDERSMA, R. and WIDDERSHOVEN, W. (1976). 'Beschrijving beginsituatie Experimenten Middenschool: voorstel voor een onderzoek' RION – jan.

CREEMERS, B.P.M. and DE VRIES, A. (1980). 'Constructie en Invoering van de Middenschool.' *RION Bulletin*, nr. 6, juli.

DODDE, N.L. (1976). 'Onderwijsbeleid op langere termijn,' *Intermediair*, 12e jaargang 5.

DROR, Y. (1968). *Public Policymaking Reexamined*. Pennsylvania: Chandler Publishing Company.

DUYKER, H.C.J. (1976). 'De ideologie der zelfontplooiing,' *Pedagogische Studiën*, (53), pp. 358–73.

KARSTANJE, P.N. (1979). 'De evaluatie van experimenten in het onderwijs,' *Intermediair*, 25 juni.

KONING, P. DE (1977). Een oriënterende studie naar de afsluitproblemen van de Middenschool. Pedagogisch Didactisch Instituut van de Universiteit van Amsterdam, Dec.

LEEUW, A.C.J. DE (1978). *Systeemleer en Organisatiekunde*. Leiden/ Antwerpen: Stenfert Kroese.

PATTON, M.G. (1978). *Utilization Focused Evaluation*. Beverly-Hills: Sage Publications.

GROOT, A.D. DE (1974). 'Onderwijsvernieuwing volgens plan: Kan dat?' *Weekblad voor leraren*, 7, 15. pp. 601–11.

SCHEERENS, J. (1981). Evaluation research; political and organizational constraints. Invited paper for the workshop on Research and Public Policy Making organized by SVO, The Hague, May.

SELLTIZ, C., WRIGHTSMAN, L.C. and COOK, S.W. (1976). *Research Methods in Social Relations*. Third Edition. New York: Holt, Rinehart and Winston.

SWANBORN, P.G. (1979). 'Evaluatie van Middenschoolexperimenten,' *Intermediair* 31, Aug.

VRIES, J. DE (1975). 'Onderwijsvernieuwing en Onderzoek,' *Intermediair*, 11e jrg. 32.

WEISS, C.H. (1980). 'Knowledge creep and decision accretion.' In: *Knowledge, Diffusion, Utilization*. Sage Publication Inc.

WEISS, C.H. and BUCUVALAS, M.J. (1980). 'Truth test and utility test: decision-makers' frames of reference for social science research,' *American Sociological Review*, vol. 45.

WÜRSTEN, H. (1981). 'Radio en televisie in de Open School' *Intermediair*, 17e jrg. 8, Februari.

On the Effectiveness of Educational Research

Patrick Suppes – Stanford University

I want to begin my remarks about educational research by saying something about the character of modern science and some of the fallacies that have been held about it.

I. Character of modern science

Many of you will be familiar with Immanuel Kant's famous criticism of metaphysics. The central problems of metaphysics that Kant criticized as being impossible to solve were the celebrated triad of the existence of God, the immortality of the soul, and the freedom of the will. The metaphysic that Kant so soundly argued against has in the last two hundred years been replaced by a metaphysic of philosophy and science that has only recently been put in its proper place. Five basic tenets of this metaphysic are these:

1. The future is determined by the past.
2. Every event has a sufficient determinant cause.
3. Knowledge must be grounded in certainty.
4. Scientific knowledge can in principle be made complete.
5. The various sciences are held together by an underlying unity of concepts and methods.

I am not concerned to make the historical case as to who has or has not adhered to these tenets. They have certainly been widely accepted in much of post-Kantian philosophy and in particular in much of contemporary philosophy. It is my view that each of the five tenets is false and provides a misleading basis for discussing the nature of science and its effectiveness in society.

Determinism. Concerning the first thesis about determinism, it is easy to enter into a rather technical discussion of the foundations of physics. That marvellous period of physics running from Newton to Maxwell is also a marvellous aberration in the main tendencies of human thought. Natural theology was replaced by celestial mechanics, if a pun is permitted, and all seemed right once again with the world. But to take seriously as an account of the endless variety of natural phenomena the remarkably simple theories of classical physics, especially classical mechanics, and not to appreciate simultaneously their real inability to explain most natural phenomena is a characteristic, I should hope, of religious rather than scientific method at work.

At any given period of science, and certainly not just the present, the weight of systematic evidence has always been against a thesis of determinism, but systematic weighing of this evidence has not been a strength of either scientists or philosophers. It is easy to pick on phenomena close at hand to make the case against determinism. My own favourite is the endless babble of human speech. That anyone at any time or place could ever have been so foolish as to think that he could deterministically analyse the endless flow of talk men engage in everywhere and for most of their lives seems on the face of it ridiculous. And what I have to say applies not only to the listener or the analyst, but also to the speaker. It is unusual to formulate completely and explicitly any given sentence that we utter. In moments of complete deliberation or in an unusual state of reflection, we are capable of total preformulation, but this is exceptional. Most of the talk between human beings flows on endlessly without prior thought, and indeed, the talk and the thought are simultaneous. Even if we can paraphrase and anticipate the thought we can never predict or hope to determine the actual sequence of words spoken.

I should emphasize, of course, that I do not hold the absurd thesis that speech is wholly random. Like other natural phenomena, ranging from radioactive decay to the collisions of molecules in a gas, there are causal constraints that are not sufficient to fully determine the phenomena, but that can lead to a fruitful causal analysis.

Determinant causes. I think the proper view is that causality is not determinant but probabilistic, and consequently no inconsistency exists between randomness in nature or human affairs and the development of causal laws that are statistical or probabilistic in character. Moreover, ordinary experience as described and expressed in ordinary language is most happily analysed in terms of a probabilistic concept of cause. Research in the social sciences and in medicine could scarcely proceed if only a deterministic notion of cause were available. One of the problems for educational research and other kinds of social science research is to understand to what extent a theory of probabilistic causality can be developed in a given domain and when to accept results that are as good as can be expected. I will not attempt here to describe any serious systematic criterion of adequacy for a probabilistic theory of causality. I will remark that ideally we would like causes to render simultaneous correlated events conditionally independent, but I shall not say more about details. It is, I think, not a point that needs extensive argument in the context of a discussion of educational research that the working notions of causality are probabilistic rather than deterministic. (For a more detailed defense of this thesis, see Suppes, 1970.)

Certainty. From Descartes to Russell, a central theme of modern philosophy has been to set forth a method by which certainty can be achieved, and to find a basis of knowledge that is on the one hand certain and on the other hand adequate for the remaining superstructure. The introduction of the concept of sense data and the history of the development of the use of this concept are the history of the search for certainty in knowledge, especially in the empirical tradition, as an alternative to direct rational knowledge of the universe.

I applaud the criticism of rationalism and the justifiable concern not to accept the possibility of direct knowledge of the world without experience. But it was clearly a desire to compete with the kind of grounding that rationalism offered — and in the theological tradition that is so deeply a part of our Western experience — that the mistaken additional step was taken of attempting to ground knowledge in experience in a way that guaranteed certainty for the results.

Within this tradition of modern philosophy, there have been two kinds of knowledge about which claims of certainty have been prominent. One kind is a claim about empirical knowledge that is immediate in character. I may, for example, not be able to say that I am looking at a red apple with certainty, but I can claim in terms of immediacy and directness of knowledge that with certainty I am perceiving a red patch. By arguments of this kind, sense data have entered the picture and have played a prominent role.

The second kind of knowledge concerns logical or *a priori* knowledge. Claims of certainty have often been made about logical truths or truths of arithmetic. For example, it is often claimed that one knows with utter certainty that $7 + 5 = 12$. And also that either it is going to rain or it is not going to rain tomorrow.

Both of these views seem to me to be mistaken, but it is not very original on my part to say this. Criticisms of both the doctrine of immediacy of knowledge and the doctrine of certainty for logical truths are now widespread. On the one hand, it is claimed from the standpoint of perception that there is no such thing as immediate knowledge. The general psychological literature on perception certainly tends to support the view that perceptual knowledge is never immediate but depends upon a conceptual framework of interpretation. In a similar vein, the hope of drawing any sharp distinction between logical and empirical truths has been severely challenged, and consequently the special status classicially assigned to logical or mathematical knowledge is considered of a dubious character.

Completeness. Ordinarily accompanying the explicit doctrines of strict determinism, strict determinant causality, and asymptotic certainty of knowledge is an implicit doctrine of completeness for knowledge and science. Underlying this view are postulates like those about the uniformity of nature, which hold that the universe is ultimately totally orderly and, consequently, fully knowable in character. There are, of course, in many situations practical impediments to complete knowledge, but these impediments are only practical in character and do not exist in principle. When a strong thesis of strict determinism like that of Laplace is accepted, the concept of completeness seems otiose, because from a detailed specification of the current configuration of fundamental particles of the universe, the entire past and future of the universe is determined, and completeness of knowledge automatically follows.

In contrast, strict causality narrowly construed does not imply such completeness. For example, if the determinant cause of an event is not required to be contiguous in space and time but can act remotely, as in the case of gravitation for space or as in the case of action-at-a-distance theories of electromagnetic phenomena, then completeness may not follow from strict causality because we may be caught in a potentially infinite regress. Thus, in order to find the fully determinant cause of a given event, we must make an unbounded search of past time and outer space. Incompleteness would then be compatible with strict causality in the sense that incompleteness would follow from the unbounded character of causal connections in space and time. On the other hand, if we add to the doctrine of strict causality the doctrine of contiguity in space and time for determinant causes, then we are closer to an implicit doctrine of completeness.

The interesting things to be said about completeness are not intertwined with broad doctrines of strict determinism or strict causality, but rather with more local issues in particular disciplines and their individual character. Whatever may be our philosophical tendency to affirm broad and deep cosmological theses about determinism, it is clear that in practice our theories are more limited and partial in character, and yet, the push for completeness can still be misleading and unattainable. As in the cases of determinism, strict causality and uncertainty, the strong thrust toward completeness characteristic of so many different kinds of investigations in science and mathematics is still another theological remnant that remains from earlier fantasies of an omniscient and omnipotent God. The naive tendency in almost every domain is to strike at once for completeness and then often to be dismayed at the inability to achieve it. The proper attitude, as I see it, is to expect incompleteness and to be surprised at completeness. It is a proper task, of course, for a sophisticated empiricism to investigate the limits of completeness and to understand in as deep a way as possible why individual naive conceptions of completeness break down on detailed examination.

As the several examples considered show, in most areas of knowledge it is too much to expect theories to have a strong form of completeness. What we have learned to live with in practice is an appropriate form of incompleteness, but we have not built this working practice explicitly into our philosophy as thoroughly as we might. It is apparent from various examples that weak forms of completeness may be expected for theories about restricted areas of experience. It seems wholly inappropriate, unlikely, and, in many ways, absurd to expect theories that cover large areas of experience or, in the most grandiose cases, *all* of experience, to have a strong degree of completeness.

The application of working scientific theories to particular areas of experience is almost always schematic and highly approximate in character. Whether we are predicting the behaviour of elementary particles, the weather, or international trade — any phenomenon in fact that has a reasonable degree of complexity — we can hope only to encompass a restricted part.

It is sometimes said that it is exactly the role of experimentation to isolate particular fragments of experience that can be dealt with in relatively complete fashion. This is, I think, more a dogma of philosophers who have not engaged in much experimentation than it is of practicing experimental scientists. When I have been involved in experimentation myself I have been struck by how much my schematic views of theories applied to observational rather than experimental data also apply to experimental work. First one concrete thing and then another is abstracted and simplified to make the data fit within the limited set of concepts of the theory being tested.

Unity. Let me put the matter another way, and turn to the concept of unity of science at the same time. A common philosophical conception of science is that it is an ever closer approximation to a set of eternal truths that hold always and everywhere. Such a conception can be traced from Plato through Aristotle and onward to Descartes, Kant and more recent philosophers, and this account has no doubt been accepted by many scientists as well. It is my own view that a much better case can be made for the kind of instrumental conception of science set forth in general terms by Peirce, Dewey and their successors. In this view, scientific activity is a kind of perpetual problem-solving. No area of experience is totally and completely settled by providing a set of basic truths, but rather we are continually confronted with new situations and new problems, and we bring to these problems and situations a collection of scientific methods, techniques, and concepts, which in many cases we have learned to use with great facility.

The concept of objective truth does not directly disappear in such a view of science, but what we might call the cosmological or global view of truth is looked at with scepticism just as is a global or cosmological view of completeness. Like our own lives and endeavours, scientific theories are local and are designed to meet a given set of problems. As new problems arise new theories are needed, and in almost all cases the theories used for the old set of problems have not been tested to the fullest extent feasible nor been confirmed as broadly or as deeply as possible, but the time is ripe for something new, and we move on to something else. Again this conception of science does not mean that there cannot be some approximate convergence in a sequence of theories meeting a sequence of problems, but it does urge that the sequence does not necessarily converge. In fact, to express the kind of incompleteness and plurality I am after, we can even make the strong assumption that in many domains of experience the scientific theory that replaces the best old theory is always an improvement, and therefore we have a kind of monotone increasing sequence. Nonetheless, as in the case of a strictly monotone increasing sequence of integers there is no convergence to a finite value − the sequence is never completed, and so it is with scientific theories. *There is no bounded fixed result* towards which we are converging or that we can hope ever to achieve. Scientific knowledge, like the rest of our knowledge, will forever remain pluralistic and highly schematic in character.

II. Scientific research can be effective

All of us on occasion probably feel that there is little hope that research will seriously affect practice and thus that there should be little coupling between scientific research and the setting of public policies. Such pessimism is not historically supported by the evidence, however, and I would like to take the time to consider some examples of how great an impact scientific research can have on society.

All of the characteristic features of modern electronic communication and rapid transportation are unique products of the long tradition of science and technology. The changes that have taken place recently, for example, the widespread introduction of colour television, have especially depended on prior scientific research. Eight outstanding cases that have been studied (Battelle Report, National Science Foundation, Washington, 1973) give a good sense of the diversity of important contributions to society arising from specific scientific work. The eight cases represent developments that almost certainly would not have taken place on the basis of either enlightened common sense or bare empiricism, and they range across a variety of scientific theories and domains of application: the heart pacemaker; the development of hybrid grains and the green revolution; electrophotography, which led to office copiers; input-output economic analysis developed originally in the 1930s by Leontief; organophosphorus insecticides; oral contraceptives, which rest on relatively delicate matters of steroid chemistry; magnetic ferrites, which are widely used in communications equipment and computers; and videotape recorders, which depended upon a union of electromagnetic and communication theory with the technology of audio recording. Compared with the practical significance of these scientific and technological developments, the initial cost of research and development was relatively minor.

This list is only one that was selected by someone else for the purposes of studying the route from research to social impact, and it would be easy to add a large number of research contributions of even greater importance.

III. Social science research can be effective

Many of you will have noted that in the Battelle list I just gave only one example is drawn from the social sciences, namely, the Leontief theory of input-output analysis. In the pessimistic mood of the present — certainly in the United States where the validity and effectiveness of social science research is very much an issue — it might be easy to think that one cannot really give very many examples of social science or behaviour research that is effective. This, I think, is clearly incorrect. The best cluster of examples, especially in terms of impact on policy, are surely to be found in modern economics. As has been said in some of the papers prepared for this conference, it is not only specific results that are important but the way in which research affects the talk of policymakers and politicians in general. It is hard to think of anything that has had a more profound impact than the development of modern economic theories on the talk of policymakers. The money supply, the central bank's discount rate, the market character of exchange rates, etc., are all topics that are familiar in the daily newspaper and reflect a level of conceptual sophistication that would have been unthought of half a century ago. The detailed finetuning that is characteristic of economic efforts on the part of governments throughout the world is again very much a consequence of modern economic thought. Moreover, it is clear that there has been a definite drift from ideological attitudes toward economic problems to a much more technical and scientific attitude on the part of almost all countries, or at least almost all countries of any importance, whether their economies be capitalist or socialist in nature.

Quite different examples of effective behavioural sciences research can be found in modern psychology. Psychological theories of vision and colour, for example, have had application in a variety of training and industrial settings that I scarcely need to stop to enumerate here. Survey sampling studies on everything from the prediction of elections to the marketing of television time reflect another significant example of research that has had a major impact in society. Because I want to turn to some educational examples I shall not say more.

IV. Educational research can be effective

To a large extent, education pays more lip service to research than do other main segments of the society. Every large school system has as part of its central office some sort of research unit. The schools and colleges of education associated with institutions of higher education throughout the world are all charged with research responsibilities, some of which are specifically written into the legislative charter of the institution.

When the US Office of Education was established by federal legislation more than a hundred years ago in 1867, the first section of the Act defined the chief purpose of the new bureau, later called the Office of Education, as one of 'collecting such statistics and facts as shall show the condition and progress of education in the several states and territories, and of diffusing information respecting the organization and management of schools and school systems and methods of teaching'. There is not in this charge to the Office of Education a serious thrust of theory, and it is fair to say that most of the efforts of the Office of Education have not been directed toward the nurturing of educational theory, but rather to the more mundane and empirical matters of collecting statistics and facts and of disseminating information about the nation's schools.

For at least a hundred years there has been a serious respect for facts and statistical data about education and also for many empirical studies, often of excellent design and execution, to evaluate the learning of students, the effectiveness of a given method of instruction, and so forth. At least until recently, the empiricism of education has been more enlightened and sophisticated than the empiricism of medicine, which represents an investment comparable to education in our society.

The period running from the beginning of this century to the onset of World War II has sometimes been described as the golden age of empiricism in education. Certainly it was marked by a serious effort to move from *a priori* dogmas and principles of education to consideration of empirical results and even experimental design of inquiries to test the relative efficiency or power of different approaches to a given part of the curriculum. Detailed analysis of the nature of tests and how to interpret the results was begun, and serious attempts, especially by the American psychologist Edward L. Thorndike and his collaborators, were made to apply a broad range of results from educational psychology to actual problems of learning in the classroom.

In many respects Thorndike is the best example of an educational researcher having wide impact in education itself. The broad impact is indisputable, but even more impressive are the powerful particular ways in which Thorndike's research influenced actual curriculum and what was taught in American schools. Let me give two of the most important examples.

Teaching of arithmetic. I consider first Thorndike's impact on the teaching of arithmetic. His ideas on the teaching of arithmetic constituted a pedagogical revolution as far-reaching and as important in the history of the teaching of mathematics as the current curriculum reforms. Moreover, it is fair to say that Thorndike's proposals were more thoroughly based than these recent ones on ideas about learning, and that they involved a much more serious effort to derive changes from what was thought to be a correct theory of how students learn concepts and skills. The recent reform in mathematics curriculum has aimed to redress an imbalance created by the Thorndike revolution. The emphasis in the past decade has been on the content of the mathematics curriculum, not on the psychological aspects of how it should be taught and how students learn it. The pendulum is beginning now to swing back to a more serious consideration of the learning of students and the principles that guide that learning.

The general principles of learning worked out in Thorndike's (1913– 1914) magisterial treatise *Educational Psychology* were already applied to arithmetic in some of the experiments Thorndike cited in Volume II. Not content with these illustrative cases, he went on to complete in 1920 a systematic work on the psychology of arithmetic, which was essentially a course of lectures he gave to elementary-school teachers and others at Teachers' College. The high aims of this study and its radical new attitude toward arithmetic are best seen in the opening paragraphs of Thorndike's preface:

> Within recent years there have been three lines of advance in psychology which are of notable significance for teaching. The first is the new point of view concerning the general process of learning. We now understand that learning is essentially the formation of connections or bonds between situations and responses, that the satisfyingness of the result is the chief force that forms them, and that habit rules in the realm of thought as truly and as fully as in the realm of action.
>
> The second is the great increase in knowledge of the amount, rate, and conditions of improvement in those organized groups or hierarchies of habits which we call abilities, such as ability to add or ability to read. Practice and improvement are no longer vague generalities, but concern changes which are definable and measurable by standard tests and scales.
>
> The third is the better understanding of the so-called 'higher processes' of analysis, abstraction, the formation of general notions, and reasoning. The older view of a mental chemistry whereby sensations were compounded into percepts, percepts were duplicated by images, percepts and images were amalgamated into abstractions and concepts, and these were manipulated by reasoning, has given way to the understanding of the laws of response to elements or aspects of situations and to many situations or elements thereof in combination.

In *The Psychology of Arithmetic*, Thorndike (1922) attempted an extensive analysis of the nature of arithmetic abilities, their measurement and their structure. Using his own experiments and those of others, he analysed in detail the psychology of drills in arithmetic. He saw the psychological purpose of drill as being to strengthen the bonds between stimuli and appropriate responses. He held no overly simple view of the 'stimulus', emphasizing not only the appropriate responses to basic facts but also the strength of bonds concerning the reasons for arithmetical processes. Because Thorndike is often thought of as encouraging drill and habit formation in arithmetic, it is worth emphasizing that he appreciated the desirability of students having an understanding of the deductive theories of arithmetic and the mathematical basis of the algorithms they learned. What the pupil learns about deductive theory, he said, should 'rank among the most rather than the least permanent of a pupil's stock of arithmetical knowledge and power'.

In analysing drill in arithmetic, he moved from the general consideration of the strength of bonds to detailed and practical questions about the amount of practice and the organization of the various skills. He laid particular emphasis on the advantages of distributed practice (i.e. of spreading exercises of a certain sort over a period of time). He examined the actual distribution of practice in several textbooks, and considered how blunders might be avoided and how reasonable procedures might be instituted. His detailed proposals are more sophisticated psychologically than most current writings on methods of teaching arithmetic. In fact, as part of the swing of the pendulum mentioned earlier, the current textbooks for teachers on the teaching of arithmetic concentrate on mathematical content and spend little, if any, time on the psychology of student learning. In this respect, they resemble very closely the rationalistic texts of the eighteenth and nineteenth centuries.

In an earlier publication (Cronbach and Suppes, 1969), I have given a comparison between many arithmetic textbooks in the 1920s, after Thorndike's ideas had an impact, and earlier textbooks. It would be too much to set forth the empirical facts here, but I think an excellent case can be made that Thorndike did have a real impact on what *is* actually taught at schools and also on the general policy matter of what *should* be taught at schools. The way arithmetic is taught today in American schools and, to a large extent, in a number of other countries, reflects Thorndike's influence more than any other. The nature of this influence has been summarized by Gorman (1931) in a study of changes in the arithmetic curriculum between 1907 and 1930. With the introduction of a wider range of mathematical concepts in the school curriculum, some people consider the whole problem of teaching arithmetic trivial and unimportant. I want to emphasize how much I disagree with this view. Arithmetic continues to constitute the bulk of the elementary-school mathematics curriculum throughout the world. Thorndike's work on the teaching of arithmetic must be regarded as a major step in illumination by theoretical ideas of practical problems of teaching. Sceptics of this view are urged to review once again the unbelievably rationalistic and scholastic character of textbooks on arithmetic in the eighteenth and nineteenth centuries.

Vocabulary studies. My second example, drawn also from the research of Thorndike, concerns the impact of his studies of vocabulary on the reading curriculum. For an adequately detailed treatment the reader should consult Clifford (1978). Thorndike, along with others in the first decade or so of this century, began seriously to study the vocabularies that were used in elementary-school materials, especially the books used for teaching reading. As in the case of his work on arithmetic, he went on to write his own spellers, exemplifying his ideas about what was appropriate and proper to include in the curriculum. The book that had the widest influence was his *The Teacher's Word Book* (1921), which was imitated, criticized and widely used. His word lists were cited and used as the basis of vocabulary lists, which it is now common practice to give in the teachers' manuals or other materials accompanying readers for primary-school students. Just as the layman does not have very clear ideas about teaching arithmetic, he has even less clear ideas about the appropriate vocabulary to use when first teaching a child how to read.

By focusing on the issue of vocabulary, making extensive empirical studies, and applying those studies himself, as well as creating a framework for continuing research on the subject, Thorndike constructed a direct track from vocabulary research to the reading curriculum, substantial traces of which can still be found in current textbooks. Thorndike stands as a model for all of us concerned with educational research in ways that can have impact on our schools and our society.

V. Research problems for the future: issues of productivity

It would be easy to list a welter of promising problems for future study, but in order to attack the more serious question of how to change the underlying attitude on the part of educational researchers, on the one hand, and of policymakers on the other, that too often educational research does not have any impact and is not effective, I would like to address one central problem that we too often gingerly step around but that is central to any policy view of education. I have in mind the problem of productivity in education. The choice of this pressing issue reflects my problem-solving approach to philosophy and education. There is not much past history of analyzing the productivity of our educational systems. It is time to develop the subject with focused intensity.

Let me start my remarks with a depressing comparison of the historical facts for agriculture and education in the United States. Let us look at the data in 1870 for American elementary and secondary education and for college education and compare the ratio of students attending school or college to the ratio 100 years later in 1970. They are directly available in the *Historical Statistics of the United States* (US Bureau of the Census, 1975), and they show essentially no change over a 100-year period. In 1870 there were 4,077,000 school students and 201,000 teachers, which gives a ratio of 20.3. In 1970 there were 41,934,000 students and 2,131,000 teachers, producing a ratio of 19.7 (Part 1, pp. 375–6). In 1870 there were 52,000 college or university students and 5,553 estimated faculty, for a ratio of 9.4. In 1970 there were 7,920,000 college or university students and 729,000 faculty, for a ratio of 10.9 (Part 2, pp. 382–3). As I have done in the past, I like to contrast these data with those for agriculture. In 1870, an American agricultural worker produced enough food for 5.1 persons, but in 1970 the corresponding worker produced food for 47.1 persons (Part 1, p. 498). There is essentially an order of magnitude improvement in the productivity of agricultural workers and essentially no improvement in the productivity of teachers. From a survey of several sources and more conversations with individuals much better informed than I am, I would gather that the experience in Holland is similar, i.e., much improvement in the efficiency of agriculture and little in education, as measured by the ratios I have used.

I recognize, of course, that with the increase in productivity of agricultural workers, whether in the United States or Europe, there has been an increase in labour required in the production and processing of food once it has left the farm, and in the manufacture of farming equipment. Even when these data are taken account of, I think we must find the gains in productivity in agricultural labour enormously impressive and standing in great contrast to what has happened in education, namely, no gains at all.

Educational institutions, and especially universities, are notable for their conservatism. No doubt intellectual Luddites of a variety of types would want to say at once that there is a large conceptual difference between teaching and farming. As I have chronicled elsewhere, such Luddites are not new on the scene. They began at least with the sophists in ancient Athens, who objected to the deadness and dullness of the written word as a form of instruction (see, e.g., the strong defense of oral methods of instruction in Plato's dialogue *Phaedrus*).

I see no overweening arguments for the introduction of a sharp difference between farming and teaching. They are different, of course, and they require different skills, but such remarkable differences in productivity gains do not seem defensible on the part of teachers. But the consequences of blindly maintaining, or attempting to maintain, the status quo in our institutions of higher learning can be seen in the decrease in real terms of academic salaries in the United States in every years since 1975 (−3.6 per cent from 1972–73 to 1973–74, −4.8 per cent from 1973–74 to 1974–75, −1.0 per cent the next two years each, −1.3 per cent from 1976–77 to 1977–78, −3.1 per cent the next year, −5.5 per cent from 1978–79 to 1979–80, and most recently −2.6 per cent from 1979–80 to 1980–81 (Hansen, 1981)).

I want to conclude by surveying briefly four different ways that productivity increases in education can be approached. These four different approaches should be thought of as supplementing each other rather than as being in conflict.

1. *Use technology.* On the use of technology I would like to quote some paragraphs from an article on the effectiveness of alternative instructional media I wrote several years ago with Dean Jamison and Stuart Wells (Jamison, Suppes, and Wells, 1974).

> The key to productivity improvement in every economic sector has been through the augmentation of human efforts by technology, and we see no reason to expect a different pattern in education. We use the term *augmentation* deliberately here to set aside the notion of technology's replacing teachers; the purpose of the technology must be to make teachers more productive, not to replace them completely. The problem is not that of replacing teachers but of *successfully* using the technology to improve productivity. The overwhelming majority of the efforts devoted to developing educational technology have been directed toward improving quality with little regard for cost. We have learned much from these efforts, primarily in ITV [instructional television] and CAI [computer-assisted instruction], and now have a background of experience, program material, and evaluation that is quite substantial. Yet there has been widespread disillusionment with where educational technology is today that results, by and large, from the pattern of no significant difference findings that we have reported in this paper. Furthermore, because technology has been primarily an add-on input to enrich the individual student's experience, there are few, if any, examples one can point to where it has improved system productivity. (Technology has been more successful in providing an *alternative to* schools; successful examples here include the British Open University, the Bavarian Tellekolleg, and the Japanese NHK's Secondary School of the Air.) Technology has not yet proved that it can play an important role in American schools.

The above paragraph summarizes the somewhat uncomfortable position we are now in concerning the role of technology. On the one hand, it seems almost inevitable that productivity improvements in the schools, if they are to occur, will require the use of technology. On the other hand, in spite of very considerable expenditures on educational technology for many years, we are pressed to find an example of its use to improve productivity. What is required is a carefully designed, carefully evaluated demonstration that main-line instructional costs can be reduced without sacrificing quality – indeed it is important to attempt to improve quality – by use of a technology or mix of technologies. By introducing productivity improvement (cost reduction) as the objective of technology use instead of enrichment, we would facilitate a sharp evaluation of success and probably increase the probability of success. That so few of the attempts at quality improvement that we discussed in this paper have been successful in changing student outcomes gives hope that careful plans for productivity improvement would be successful.

The basic implication for policy of the extensive findings we have reported in this paper is, then, that we should be exploring much more systematically the potential of technology to reduce system costs through productivity improvement. We have discussed this primarily in terms of American education, but the implications are perhaps even more relevant for developing countries where traditional education demands a large and growing fraction of scarce national resources.

2. *Reduce inputs.* The extensive analysis of a variety of data in the article with Jamison and Wells shows that it is extremely difficult to get differential output results from different technologies of instruction. The robustness of teaching effects in the main has been well-demonstrated by now in a large number of studies, many of which are cited in the article referred to. For example, the traditional course in differential and integral calculus, given either at the end of secondary school or at the beginning of university education, has now been studied under many different arrangements: large lectures, small sections, small sections with presentation by television, personalized instruction, etc. There is no strong case for any one of the approaches as far as differential output, as measured by student achievement, is concerned, especially in the instruction of older students. These many studies thus argue for a greater attention to reduction of inputs, which means a continual study of how technology can be used to reduce the cost of instruction. In this connection I want to mention the great importance of using the stand-up lecturer to a large number of students whenever possible. It remains a cost-effective means of instruction where applicable.

The important policy problem, which needs to be backed up by more sustained research, is the relentless pursuit of how inputs can be reduced. It is striking to observe the different reactions of industry and institutions of education when financial problems arise. In the United States, industry is being pushed to become more productive, especially in the face of intense international competition. In contrast, the response of the educational institutions to budget cuts has been to complain about the bad effects the budget reductions will have on the quality of output. It is difficult to find even a single article by an educational official in a policy role asserting that the real way to handle the budget cuts in the United States is to face the problem of increasing productivity by reducing inputs. I feel safe in predicting that such a constructive reaction is also not to be found in European educational officials who occupy policy positions.

3. *Generate special outputs.* A third way to increase productivity is to be more responsive to the marketplace in terms of the kinds of skills needed. Educational institutions are notoriously conservative institutions. They are also often encased in large and cumbersome bureaucracies. It is not easy for them to respond to market pressures as reflected in the changing mix of skills needed in the national economy. Special task forces aimed at diverting educational resources to training in specific skills, especially specific skills in which there is clearly a shortage of labour, should receive much more focus. Every policy official able to affect such matters should ask himself how his educational organization could be more responsive to economic needs.

4. *Expand continuing education.* Throughout the world there is an increasing demand for education by populations of all ages. One of the most striking phenomena in the United States is the large percentage of adults now engaged in some form of continuing education. By reducing inputs to regular schooling, as suggested through more efficient use of technology and teaching staff, scarce resources can be diverted to increasing the proportion of the population serviced by the educational institutions of our society. Again, I want to stress that the expansion of continuing education should be at the *expense* of the ordinary cost of education, just because ordinary education should be made more efficient, and I see as the only really important way to make it more efficient, the reduction of inputs, thereby freeing resources for expansion of the educational system.

I have suggested four approaches to increasing the productivity of education: using educational technology, reducing inputs, generating special outputs, expanding continuing education. No area of educational research has a stronger relation to policy-making than the problem of increasing the productivity of our educational institutions. I hope that what I have said on these matters you will find provocative. I have tried to make it so.

References

Battelle Report. (1973). Washington, DC: National Science Foundation.
CLIFFORD, G.J. (1978). 'Words for schools: The application in education of the vocabulary researches of Edward L. Thorndike.' In: SUPPES, P. (Ed.), *Impact of research on education: Some case studies.* Washington, DC: National Academy of Education.
CRONBACH, L.J. and SUPPES, P. (Eds.) (1969). *Research for tomorrow's schools: Disciplined inquiry for education.* New York: Macmillan.
GORMAN, F.H. (1931). *Some facts concerning changes in the content and methods of arithmetic.* University of Missouri.
Historical statistics of the United States, colonial times to 1970. (1975). Bicentennial Edition. US Bureau of the Census.

HANSEN, W.L. (1981). 'The rocky road through the 1980s: Annual report of the economic status of the profession, 1980–81,' *Academe, Bulletin of the AAUP, 67,* 210–21.
JAMISON, D., SUPPES, P. and WELLS, S. (1974). 'The effectiveness of alternative instructional media: A survey,' *Review of Educational Research, 44,* 1–67.
SUPPES, P. (1970). 'A probabilistic theory of causality,' *Acta Philosophica Fennica,* 24. Amsterdam: North-Holland.
THORNDIKE, E.L. (1913–14). *Educational psychology* (3 vols.). New York: Columbia University, Teachers College.
THORNDIKE, E.L. (1927). *The teacher's word book.* New York: Teacher's College. (Originally published, 1921.)
THORNDIKE, E.L. (1972). *The psychology of arithmetic.* New York: Academic Press.

A New Federal Policy for Disseminating Educational R & D in the United States

Michael Timpane – National Institute of Education, U.S.A.

One way educational research can be made more useful to policy-makers and educators is through its more effective communication. The physical process of originating such communication has been termed 'dissemination'. The very word has changed in meaning several times in the past twenty years and is, in fact, almost a misnomer in the light of today's understanding of what it takes to insure the appropriate utilization of research. Nevertheless, 'dissemination' identifies, even when it does not define, many of the activities undertaken in the US educational research community to enhance the spread and use of new knowledge. And yet, research planning and policy-making has only begun to consider systematically the implication that requirements of effective dissemination should have upon the identification, design and conduct of research.

In 1980, taking a significant stride down this path, the National Council on Educational Research (NCER), the policy-making board of the National Institute of Education (NIE), promulgated its first explicit policy on the dissemination programme of the Institute. What follows is a brief documentary review of the policy, the analysis which led to its formulation and adoption, and the plans for its implementation.

The dissemination policy

The NCER's policy statement reads as follows:

In the statute establishing the National Institute of Education the Congress declares it 'to be the policy of the United States to provide to every person an equal opportunity to receive an education of high

---

This paper was prepared with the extensive assistance of Dr Toni Haas, NIE's chief dissemination planner, and other members of the Program of Dissemination and Improvement of Practice at the Institute; it also borrows heavily from various staff papers prepared during the process of policy development and implementation.

quality'. The Congress established the Institute to improve education by concentrating its resources on five priority research and development needs including, 'improved dissemination of the results of, and knowledge gained from educational agencies and institutions in the application of such results and knowledge'.

In responding to these broad directions, NIE recognises that many other agencies are involved in educational R&D and in its dissemination and that there are many interests to be served through work in that field. It recognizes further that dissemination is a multi-faceted and wide-ranging responsibility requiring a variety of methods to be effective. NIE's efforts to serve the many interests concerned with the dissemination of educational R&D and its choice of methods to implement its work in this field are intended to reflect the twin goals of the Institute (1) to increase educational equity and (2) to improve educational practice.

Review of NIE's work in this field by NCER suggests that special emphasis is needed on the first of these goals in the Institute's dissemination work, particularly in terms of increasing equity of access to educational research and the ability to use it to improve educational practice. While this does not imply that the choices NIE makes to provide information and to support dissemination activities should be based solely on these equity considerations, it does mean that groups, organizations, and geographic areas which often have been underrepresented in or underserved by dissemination activities must be effectively included in the dissemination activities of the Institute.

Dissemination activities which reach out to underserved groups and organizations tend to benefit the entire spectrum of education, while activities that touch on the interests of more privileged groups and organizations do not have this tendency. The Council concludes, therefore, that in the case of the dissemination responsibilities of NIE, special emphasis needs to be given to the overall goal of equity under which all NIE endeavours are conducted, and it adopts the following resolution to that end:

RESOLVED: It is the policy of the National Institute of Education to disseminate knowledge in forms most useful to educational practitioners, policy-makers and researchers, to assist them in making more effective use of knowledge, and to support research and development to improve dissemination and support of the use of knowledge in the future.

In connection with the foregoing, highest priority will be given to those who need research information and assistance in their efforts to equalize educational opportunity.

The policy development process

The adoption of the dissemination policy grew out of a year's review at

NIE of the Institute's role and function in dissemination. This review was conducted in the context of over 25 years of federal experience in the dissemination of educational R&D, but on the more proximate basis of several years of intensive national discussion of the nature and requirements of effective dissemination. The NIE policy review (from which much of the following text is adopted) identified a clear progression in the understanding of dissemination requirements:

(a) In the first federal effort to support educational research, the Cooperative Research Program started in 1954, dissemination was seen as a natural consequence of good research. The assumptions were that new research-based knowledge was the key to school improvement and research capacity was to be found in organizations external to the federal government, chiefly universities. The federal strategy was to fund research, and it was assumed that practitioners would have *access to, read* and *use* research reports.

(b) The creation of knowledge through the funding of research led quickly to a new problem: storage and retrieval. Many documents resulting from research studies were 'fugitive' (that is, not copyrighted or published), and contained otherwise unavailable knowledge. The next step, therefore, was the creation of the Educational Research (now Resources) Information Center (ERIC). ERIC was a computerized system for acquiring and exerting bibliographic control over educational resources and for archiving, announcing, and making them available to teachers, administrators, librarians, information specialists, students in education, the research community, school board members and members of the lay public who wished specific educational information. ERIC seemed an appropriate solution in terms of meeting the needs of educational researchers, practitioners and the people in whose offices the research reports were piling up, as well as being an appropriate federal function: providing a service necessary but unlikely to be provided on any other level of government. ERIC has, indeed, proven successful. The ERIC system now includes sixteen specialized content-focused clearinghouses.

(c) Though ERIC was necessary, it was not sufficient. Practitioners noted that research did not speak directly to practice. The problem appeared to be a missing transformation between research and application. Development strategies were launched, to sponsor the processing, testing and packaging of innovations. Regional laboratories and research centres were supported at the federal level; and through the 1965 Elementary and Secondary Education Act (ESEA) Title III, resources were furnished to states and localities to further developmental activities.

(d) Yet another strategy launched in the 1960s, rigorous evaluation and testing, surfaced issues of quality control and led to synthesis and interpretation activities and to systems to capture successful locally developed innovations and to diffuse them (e.g. the Joint Dissemination Review Panel (JDRP) and the National Diffusion Network (NDN)).

(e) The creation of products and the 'product pushing' state of dissemination triggered a wave of new problems: the increasing number of sources for both information and products required more coordination than any part of the system was prepared to provide. State Departments of Education, in particular, did not appear to have the capacity to provide in-state coordination of the multiplying federal dissemination activities. They also did not have the slack resources to act as the 'natural laboratories for experiment' that Brandeis suggested was their role in a federal system. Nor were they prepared to facilitate the dissemination of locally developed innovations. They did have a unique position in the education enterprise and appeared ready to undergo some very real change. Thus, five-year State Capacity Building Grants were created by NIE to increase dissemination capacity in most of the states.

(f) Building local capacity for problem solving within the existing elements of the educational enterprise was another solution. The local capacity-building approach had great intuitive appeal, and growing support from the research and evaluation literature of the 1970s. This approach was reflected in, for example, the development of teacher centres and reading improvement programmes at the federal level.

As the field of dissemination matured, a healthy modesty developed in the federal dissemination community about the ability to solve quickly the problem of using knowledge (whether empirically or experimentally based) to improve educational practice. At the same time, dissemination activities continued to proliferate. The 1976 Interstate Project on Dissemination (IPOD), conducted by seven state agencies under NIE sponsorship, identified 208 dissemination requirements in federal legislation and programme regulations. Fifty-four different individuals and agencies were identified as having responsibilities for dissemination, ranging from the President to the state and local agencies. The IPOD report recommended:

— That the education community adopt a consistent statement relative to dissemination activities and possibilities for expanding their scope.
— That roles and responsibilities of federal educational units be clearly delineated in relation to dissemination.
— That a plan for a nationwide system for sharing educational knowledge be developed and implemented.

These concerns for coordination of dissemination activities were echoed by the federal inter-agency Dissemination Analysis Group (DAG) in 1977. It determined that the appropriate role of the federal government was to 'strengthen and support existing agencies through leadership, development and demonstration programs, and research and evaluation'. DAG's management recommendations focused on needed planning and coordination at the federal level and found little fault with operational programmes on a one-by-one basis. The conclusion of the DAG report,

> that problems of dissemination are not merely technical and will not yield to a merely technical solution of reorganizing or assigning responsibilities differently. The problems are those of a lack of vision broad enough to involve all of the various actors and agencies in a coherent whole...

captured the elusive nature of the dissemination effort on a federal level. There was no single federal education dissemination policy and no realistic hope that without one any Agency policy would suffice.

As history unfolded, hopes have risen and then fallen for the possibilities that the new US Education Department would provide such unity of dissemination policy. The NIE policy, while suitable for adoption to broader purposes, is nevertheless the product of and the guidance for just one of the many agencies of dissemination.

The NIE policy review concluded with a lengthy report to the NCER. Selected conclusions of that report were that:

— The development of a nationwide educational information system, including acquisition, storage, search and retrieval functions, is well advanced.
— There has been a convergence on local problem-solving models, usually with external support and facilitation, as a major strategy of school improvement. A substantial infrastructure of organizations and services is now in place or in process of development.
— There has been a relative neglect of the use of professional development strategies, either pre-service or in-service, as vehicles for disseminating knowledge to improve practice.
— Given the proliferation of organizations, networks, projects, and programs involved in dissemination, it is appropriate to ask questions concerning coordination and efficiency.
— The most important unit of policy concern is no longer the organization or the project, but the functioning of inter-organizational networks which may involve organizations and activities funded by a variety of sources.
— The institutional system for dissemination is fragile and vulnerable to other forces of change.
— Although considerable research has been conducted on practice improvement, the phenomenon is so complex that much is still unknown. Even less is known about the factors of dissemination and knowledge use that affect equity.
— NIE should provide a balanced program of support of three perspectives on dissemination and improvement: general purpose dissemination

services, content-focused dissemination initiatives, and the use of knowledge resources for local problem-solving.

General purpose dissemination assistance activities tend to be driven by the needs of users. Problems are defined at the practice level and knowledge resources are marshalled to solve them. These general purpose strategies take two forms: *leadership* strategies and *service* strategies.

Leadership strategies include: inquiry (R&D) to strengthen the knowledge base; capacity building to strengthen field capabilities to disseminate; and coordination to provide improved use of existing capabilities (e.g. national and regional dissemination forums).

Service strategies include providing information services (e.g. ERIC), technical assistance to other service providers, sponsoring professional development efforts and sponsoring needs assessment activities.

Both leadership and service strategies are important in a comprehensive programme of general purpose dissemination assistance. A variety of output and impact indicators are typically used to determine their success. Some of these are: number of educators reached by ERIC services, user satisfaction with services, repeat users, degree of influence on decision-making, change skills and attitudes, emergence of specialized journals, and degree of Federal and field exchange on dissemination issues of common interest — to name only a few.

Content-focused dissemination initiatives represent a second major set of dissemination strategies. Energy for these tends to come from groups external to the schools and to be driven by particular substantive educational concerns. The research programmes in NIE have grappled continuously with such educational issues and developed *ad hoc* dissemination activities focused on them, in such areas as testing, school finance, desegregation, experience-based career education, the impact of declining enrolment, bilingual education and many others. Indicators of the success of these strategies have not been as clearly identified but they may include: lower-level policy changes; programme adoptions; internal programme changes; expressions of professional satisfaction (individual and organizational); and success programme demonstrations and evaluations.

The third set of strategies, those of *organizational renewal and professional growth*, represents the most far-reaching change in perspective on dissemination activities. It has so far been more the subject of research than the source of new dissemination service activities.

A growing body of research suggests that no improvement in the quality of schooling is likely unless the people in individual schools, in concert with those they serve, agree on what they want to accomplish, have the freedom to orchestrate resources to accomplish it, have access to stimulating ideas and the help of colleagues, and have the opportunity to work together over time to achieve common objectives. Again and again, research studies call attention to the importance of having fresh and sound dissemination strategies work to provide those fresh and sound ideas, and NIE supports ongoing research about dissemination to learn more about how these ideas can aid school people to renew their own organizations and to encourage professional growth. So far, however, NIE has been able to launch few new service activities. One such effort, at the seven R&D Utilization (RDU) sites, provided demonstrations and developed variants of the basic problem-solving model in a variety of local contexts. New regional and state dissemination activities (some started with but many without federal support) seem also to embody problem-solving perspectives.

Less has occurred, either by government design or by spontaneous occurrence, to invent professional development strategies as vehicles for disseminating research knowledge to improve practice. Teacher centres are the most prominent single exception to this rule; but neither schools of education nor professional associations have as yet developed many programmes of this sort.

Equity and dissemination

Furthering educational equity is a primary goal of NIE. Thus, a major task of dissemination policy development was to understand the impact that NIE dissemination activities could and should have on education equity. Eight different group characteristics that have been the basis for discrimination are specifically mentioned in NIE's mission: race, colour, religion, sex, national origin, age, handicap and social class. At least two steps are necessary to assure that dissemination activities will adequately serve educational equity:

— an affirmation of the priority of disadvantaged and unserved persons as having the most serious educational problems and thus the most urgent need for helpful information, and
— a realization that the effectiveness of dissemination efforts depends upon the goodness of fit between the information or services offered and the needs of the client.

While NIE dissemination programmes have contained many instances of special focus on the issues of educational equity, no guiding policy nor set of evaluative criteria has guided progamme development. Painfully absent is any sense of the degree to which dissemination resources and technical assistance have helped users improve educational services to equity populations.

Most recent progress has been of a procedural sort. Persons representing the perspective of disadvantaged and unserved groups serve in very significant numbers on advisory and working groups setting research and dissemination agendas, in setting programme goals and foci, in conducting the review and selection of proposals, and in long range planning. In this way, priorities, agendas and awards are all scrutinized for their contributions to the imperative that educational equity be advanced.

Lessons in policy development

The lessons we have learned along the path to this policy have been organizational, substantive and procedural.

Organizationally, the effect of devoting eighteen months to developing a dissemination policy was to heighten awareness of the issue's significance. The interest of the policy-making Council and of the Institute leadership provided powerful incentives for programme staff to think seriously about dissemination. The lead responsibility for developing the original background papers was assumed by one of three programme units, but programme offices throughout the Institute were drawn into the discussion if only because their vital interests would clearly be affected by the developing policy. Discussions about the nature of the dissemination process, the federal role in sponsoring research and development, and implications for equity were heard in offices, on elevators, and in halls, as well as in more structured meetings.

Organizational concerns in any new policy development begin with the pre-existing policies, codified or not. NIE was no exception, and one objective in the formulation of the new policy was to rationalize and protect existing practices. A second objective was the legitimation of promising new programme directions. A third was finding ways to replace practices or methods of operation that were not working. The policy development process was therefore concerned in part with deciding which programme activities fit into which of these categories, in order to provide justification for future policy and resource allocation decisions.

Substantively, the Institute's first interest was to spotlight the equity emphasis of any emerging policy. Increasing educational equity is a much more difficult concept to pin down than the other Institute goal, improving educational practice. The force of tradition, the clarity of the concept, and in some cases, the professional and personal interests of the staff could converge on agreement about what improving educational practice meant, and how to go about doing it. Equity as a concept was not seen in as clear a light. Questions were raised about levels of equity. Were we interested in equity of access? of opportunity? of outcomes? Questions were also raised about how we would decide to target our work among competing unserved or underserved groups. Could priorities be set by ethnicity? by sex? by social class? Finally, because our agency exists in a political climate and is dependent for funding on favourable opinions of our constituencies and the Congress, questions were raised about how we could divert resources from our traditional audiences to new, and in many cases, less politically powerful ones and still protect the organization. These questions, in large measure, still await definitive answers.

The other principal substantive issue was how to design a policy which would legitimate the ongoing general and content focused strategies and provide room to expand the third strategy, dissemination in the school improvement process. Each of the three strategies was a necessary but not sufficient component of a complete and effective dissemination system. The balance among them, we felt, would be dependent on situations, contexts and resources within the agency and in the field. The policy needed to provide space for adjustment and readjustment of our activity balance. Procedural matters in this policy development process began with careful attention to what we knew from the change literature. The concepts of participation and ownership were clearly central, so the process included gathering opinions widely from staff, from the research and dissemination fields, as well as from the beneficiaries of the policy, state and local educators and teachers. NIE solicited opinions from a wide variety of people, but refused to be limited to simply a measured balance of competing educational interests. Finally, NIE sought a policy which would be seen as increasing the usefulness of our sponsored work and thus, ultimately, the political legitimacy of the Institute. For this reason, NIE sought widespread understanding of our policy as it developed, not just in its proclamation.

Finally, the Institute devoted extensive attention to questions of policy implementation. Before, during and since the adoption of the dissemination policy, the burning question has been: what does it take for a new policy to change operations?

The NCER too was concerned with the question throughout the policy development process. Its policy was accompanied by a lengthy set of considerations for implementation, and NIE quickly produced a detailed implementation plan for council review and adoption.* The plan was designed to

— ensure that the equity priority contained in the policy is addressed in an active and effective way;
— improve the design and implementation of dissemination strategies employed by the Institute;
— provide resources, incentives, and accountability measures as needed to supplement current, internal practices.

---

*Executive summary attached to this paper.

Executive summary

Dissemination policy implementation plan

The National Council on Educational Research (NCER) has announced a policy resolution on dissemination activities in the National Institute of Education, (NIE). This resolution will be implemented according to the provisions of the plan described in the following pages. The plan is designed to ensure that the equity priority contained in the policy is addressed in an active and effective way. Actions are included to improve the design and implementation of dissemination strategies employed by the Institute. And, the plan provides resources, incentives, and accountability measures as needed to supplement current, internal practices. The Director has identified the equity priority in this policy for focused attention in the current programme planning cycle. The plan is presented in three sections. Section I describes actions affecting the programme planning, reviewing and budgeting practices of the NIE. These actions are designed to encourage dissemination planning for the initial stages of research programme development. Budgeting actions are included to ensure that an appropriate mix of expenditures for dissemination is achieved. Section II identifies six specific actions needed to enable staff in the NIE to more effectively work toward full policy implementation. The need for these particular actions has been identified as a result of internal analysis. As these are addressed, the Director will elicit further such recommendations for specific, internal improvements in the NIE's operations. Section III describes the resources and responsibilities for implementing the policy. Significant leadership for programme planning and development is assigned to the Associate Directors. Various staff functions within the NIE are identified to support the dissemination programme development activities. A task group established to advise and oversee implementation of the policy will continue to function over the next three years. This group will advise the Director regarding progress toward full and effective policy implementation. The Director will report to the NCER annually regarding this policy, at the opening of each fiscal year.

A summary display of actions contained in the plan is shown in the table on the following pages.

Dissemination implementation plan

Summary Display of Actions

Activity	FY 1981 Timeline O N D J F M A M J JL A S

I. PROGRAM PLANNING, REVIEW AND BUDGETING

1. *Program Planning*. The NIE program planning practices will be supplemented as follows:

   a) Forward Planning (Research Area Planning) guidance will request Associate directors to assume the primary leadership responsibility for dissemination planning, within their area of responsibility. As such, Associate Directors will be asked to prepare annual plans for dissemination activities. These may be designed for project, Research Area, Program or a mix of levels. Dissemination plans may be constructed to deal with a particular issue, or to address the information needs of a particular audience group. These plans will be provided for the Director's review according to the annual schedule forward planning. The guidance will identify dissemination priorities as they are identified in the priority setting process for forward planning. Program plans to address such priorities will be specifically encouraged. ——————X

   b) The dissemination priority in the current planning year will focus on the equity aspect of the policy. ——————X

   c) Technical assistance will be provided to NIE's dissemination planners in the form of handbooks, 'state of the art' papers, and consultation designed to enhance the quality of NIE dissemination plans. In specific, technical assistance sources regarding the equity priority of the dissemination policy will be provided. (For more detail, see Part II of the Implementation Plan.) ——————————————→

	FY 1981 Timeline
Activity	O N D J F M A M J JL A S

2. *Program Review.* The NIE programs will be reviewed annually for:

   a) Contributions to the equity priority of the dissemination policy;

   b) Need for improvements in design and effectiveness of proposed dissemination strategies;

   c) Appropriate mix of dissemination strategies.
   Forward Planning Reviews completed in the Spring, annually. _____X
   Budget Implementation Reviews completed in the Fall, annually. _____X

3. *Budgeting.* NIE budget practices will be supplemented as follows:

   a) An analysis of program expenditures proposed for dissemination activities will occur annually, prior to budget allocations based on the forward planning (research area planning) process. This analysis will define the proposed mix of dissemination strategies across the Institute, and will highlight proposals for program development addressing the equity priority in the policy. (Spring, Annual) _____X

   b) Based on the budget analysis, the Director will establish a target for dissemination expenditures. The target will take into account an appropriate mix of expenditures across strategies. The target will guide budget decisions through final budget implementation. (Spring, Annual) _____X

   c) Budget allocations for dissemination will be made at each of the following points:

   c.1) Forward Planning (based on Research Area Plans, and the Associate Director's dissemination plan – see reference in 1.a, above) _____X

   c.2) Budget Implementation (Operating Plan, established at the opening of the fiscal year during which funds are to be awarded) _____X

   c.3) Budget Implementation (Contingency Fund, to be administered throughout each budget year) X   X   X

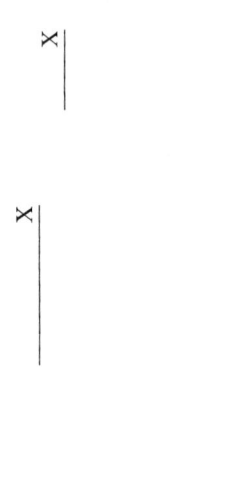

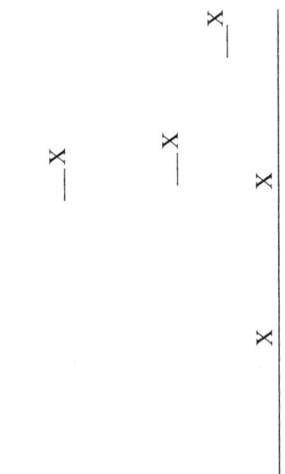

NOTE: Major needs for dissemination can be anticipated well in advance of a research program's completion. In fact, the NIE provides for dissemination planning at the very early stages of a research program, in order to ensure that the outcomes fully meet the needs of the intended audience. Therefore, we anticipate that a substantial share of the budget allocation decisions can be made at the forward planning point, based on well-conceived plans. At the same time, we find that some dissemination proposals cannot be anticipated before the research activity is near completion. Therefore, we anticipate the need to specifically review budget allocations at the budget implementation point to ensure appropriate mix of expenditures. And, we expect that unanticipated needs and opportunities for dissemination budget allocations can occur during the course of implementing a budget. For this class of needs, a Contingency Fund will be established under the control of the Director. The Contingency Fund will be allocated to the program areas on a project by project basis, as unanticipated needs and opportunities arise for advancing objectives of the dissemination policy.

4. *Laboratories and Centers: Planning, Review and Budgeting.* These activities occur within the context of long-term agreements with a set of R&D Institutions. The NIE Coordinator for these agreements will be asked by the Director to review present policy and practice, and recommend modifications consistent with the long-term agreement policy, for meeting dissemination objectives. Recommendations will be complete August 1981.

X

Activity

FY 1981   Timeline
O N D J F M A M J JL A S

II. MANAGERIAL OR 'ENABLING' ACTIONS

1. *Implementing Planning, Reviewing and Budgeting Modifications* (as shown in Part I)

   Necessary implementation instructions will be developed for implementing the modifications shown in Part I, by the concerned staff offices (for planning and budgeting functions). Instructions will be completed prior to the implementation dates shown for each action in Part I.

2. *Technical Assistance to NIE Program Staff.*

   a) In order to assist NIE program staff in planning effective dissemination program initiatives, the NIE has a need to design and offer a variety of means for conveying technical assistance regarding current 'state of the art' in dissemination practices. The Director will request recommendations from the unit on Research in Education Practice (in the Dissemination and Improvement of Practices Program) for identifying sources of such assistance, and for providing it to the NIE program staff. Recommendations will be provided by May, 1981. (Plan will place special attention on Equity priority)
   An implementation plan for the recommendations will provide for action by September 1981.

   b) Various administrative resources and mechanisms are employed by NIE program staff in meeting the objectives of the dissemination policy. A handbook on such resources and mechanisms is needed to brief program staff. The Director will request the preparation of such a handbook, by the Dissemination Policy Implementation Group, for completion by August 1981.

3. *Publications Produced Directly by the NIE.*

The NIE has resources and staff for the production of research-based publications. A publications activity has been actively supported since the NIE's creation. The Director is presently considering a set of recommendations from the senior management staff for streamlining the publications program, and increasing its effectiveness. Action on this set of recommendations will take place in February 1981. A publications committee, representing the senior management staff, will continue to operate as a source of advice and guidance regarding publications, once the initial set of recommendations have been acted upon.

4. *Mailing Lists for NIE Technical Reports and Administrative Documents.*

The NIE mails a variety of documents to the public each year. These include technical reports as well as administrative documents describing the agency, funding opportunities and particular program solicitations. Mailing lists for these various documents are maintained by the unit planning the mailing, for the most part. Work is now underway to identify efficient and effective means of ensuring that mailing lists are serving the real needs and priorities of the agency. In particular, work is focussing on ways of ensuring that equity-concerned audiences are being reached. The Director will receive status reports and recommendations from the Office of Public Affairs, and the Management Information System Working Group from time to time regarding necessary actions required for improvements in this area.

Activity

FY 1981 Timeline
O N D J F M A M J JL A S

5. *Procurement and Assistance Mechanisms.*

   a) Current contracting procedures employed by the NIE offer many opportunities for supporting dissemination. There are, however, still some very important enabling changes needed. For example, we need a way to provide funds to the creators of significant R&D products in an efficient and timely manner. We need simple models for including dissemination planning in the entire cycle of R&D, as provided for in Statements of Work. We need effective provisions governing the form and distribution of final reports. The Director will request recommendations for specific guidelines and procedures addressing these points. The recommendations will be provided by the NIE Procurement Committee by April, 1981. ———————————————— X

   b) Current regulations governing NIE grants programs are silent on needs such as those listed in 5.a, above. NIE has prepared and is recommending a clause to rectify this omission. It will be forwarded as part of the NIE Consolidated Regulations to the Department of Education for review and approval, in January 1981. Directives for implementing this clause will be developed by the NIE Procurement Committee immediately, upon its approval. ———— X

6. *Including Policy-Related Perspectives in NIE's Planning and Program Development Activities.*

   The NIE includes individuals representing a variety of policy-related perspectives (e.g. equity and practice improvement) in planning and implementing its programs. There is a need to involve in planning, procurement, conduct and review of dissemination activities individuals whose professional competence and personal experience provide a variety of perspectives and opportunities to further the goals of the policy on Dissemination. The Director will assign a staff person to develop guidelines for extending participation, ensuring the dissemination policy-related considerations are taken into account through the program. Recommendations for specific guidelines will be completed by June 1981. ———— X

III. RESPONSIBILITIES AND RESOURCES

a) Responsibilities for policy implementation will be assigned as described in Part III of this plan.

b) Staff performance will be reviewed periodically (i.e. through the Merit Pay Performance Review System) for progress in meeting the policy objectives, and the provisions of this plan.

c) The task group established by the Director to advise on implementation of this policy will oversee the implementation of this plan; will advise the Director on the need for improvements in the implementation plan; will advise the Director on the NIE's performance in meeting the policy objectives.

NCER Report.

The Director views the first three years following announcement of this policy as formative. That is, efforts will be made through the next three years – covering a full budget cycle – to improve the NIE's implementation plan and procedures. The Director will report to the NCER annually during that period regarding the status of the policy implementation.
The Director will report to the NCER in the fall of each year, corresponding to the budget implementation point at the opening of the federal government's fiscal year.

Policy Research in the Context of Diffuse Decision-Making

Carol H. Weiss — Harvard University

A distinctive characteristic of human service policies in the United States in the past ten to 15 years has been the mandate for evaluation that has accompanied them. Almost every major policy initiative in health, social services and education has been attended by formal, systematic evaluation of the effects of the policy for its intended beneficiaries. Hundreds of millions of dollars are being spent annually by the federal government to learn how well human service policies are achieving the ends for which they were designed.

The upsurge in evaluation activity and expenditures has a rational cast. The presumed purpose of all this analysis is to improve the effectiveness of policy. Evaluation, the rhetoric goes, will identify the programmes and policies that are working well so that they can be expanded, and locate the programmes and policies that are working poorly so that they can be terminated or modified. Evaluations that analyse the effects of component strategies of intervention — that indicate which components of policies are successful for which types of clientele under which conditions — will provide the basis for modifying policies and attuning them to the needs and life conditions of the participants. The enterprise, in short, is meant to use the methods and techniques of social science in the service of rational allocation of resources and the improvement of welfare policy.

American social scientists by the thousands have been attracted to evaluation and associated policy studies. Not only do they find research funds available for the study of important and interesting social and economic phenomena, but the social consequences of the work also look attractive: evaluation results will be put to work to improve the lot of the needy. Despite reservations among a few social scientists about becoming technicians for the bureaucratic welfare state, policy studies look like an ideal opportunity to combine research practice with social conscience. Researchers are able to do good while they are doing well.

The uses of evaluation and policy research

Yet by the early 1970s, after about five or six years of relatively large-scale evaluation and policy studies, it was becoming obvious that study results were not having visible impacts on policy decisions. Programmes that evaluators had found relatively ineffective, like the Head Start pre-school programme, were continued — and even expanded. Programmes that evaluators had found effective, like direct federal loans to low-income college students, were cut back. And much of the detailed advice contained in the 'Recommendations' sections of policy study reports simply went unheeded. Social scientists who had expected their work to shape future government policy became disillusioned. Not only were they not counsellors to the Prince, they were not even influential advisors to the bureau of vocational education. Given their general tendency to turn their experiences into 'findings', they began to contribute articles to the scholarly journals about the non-use and abuse of policy studies. During the 1970s there was a persistent recitation of the non-utilization tale — the resistance of self-serving government agencies to the lessons from research, the ignorance or inattention of legislators, the waste of social science wisdom, the triumph of bureaucratic routine and special-interest politics.

Recent investigations, however, provide a different interpretation of events. True, cases of immediate and direct influence of research findings on specific policy decisions are not frequent. Examples can be found, and may even be increasing, but they remain relatively uncommon. But to acknowledge this is not the same as saying that research findings have little influence on policy. On the contrary, evidence suggests that evaluation and policy studies have had significant consequences, but not necessarily on discrete provisions nor in the linear sequence that social scientists expected (Weiss, 1980b).

Rarely does research supply an 'answer' that policy actors employ to solve a policy problem. Rather, research provides a background of data, empirical generalizations, and ideas that affect the way that policy-makers think about problems. It influences their conceptualization of the issues with which they deal; it affects the facets of the issue that they consider inevitable and unchangeable or amenable to policy action; it widens the range of options that they consider; it challenges some taken-for-granted assumptions about appropriate goals and appropriate activities. Often, it helps them make sense of what they have been doing after the fact, so that they come to understand which courses of action they have followed and which courses of action have gone by default. Sometimes it makes them aware of the over-optimistic grandiosity of their objectives in light of the meagreness of programme resources. At times it helps them reconsider the entire strategies of action for achieving wanted ends (e.g. investment in compensatory education as a means for altering the distribution of income). In sum, policy studies — and social science research more generally — have made highly significant contributions by altering the terms of policy discussion.

This kind of indirect conceptual contribution is not easy to see. It is not visible to the naked eye. Sometimes it is manifested only over lengthy periods of time and after numbers of studies have yielded convergent results. For example, scores of evaluations were done of rehabilitation programmes for prison inmates, most of which concluded that counselling, education and associated services had little effect in reducing subsequent recidivism. Correctional authorities paid little attention, and efforts at in-prison rehabilitation went on relatively unchanged for a long while. However, the research results percolated through relevant bureaus, agencies and legislative chambers, and in the past few years, significant changes have been made. Not only correctional practice but also sentencing codes and judicial acts have been affected.

The state of California, for example, used to view correctional institutions as agencies of rehabilitation. Judges sentenced convicted offenders to indeterminate terms of imprisonment, leaving the date of a prisoner's release up to the decision of prison authorities on the basis of the prisoner's progress toward rehabilitation. A few years ago, the California legislature officially gave up on rehabilitation. It changed the indeterminate sentencing law, and provided instead for relatively fixed terms of sentence. The new law begins with a statement of change of goals. The preamble, in a marked shift, states that the purpose of imprisonment is punishment. Prison programmes aiming at rehabilitation continue, although more and more on a voluntary rather than compulsory basis, but the state has absorbed the lessons of evaluation: it has scaled down its expectations of rehabilitation and shifted to a different rationale for incarceration. Research results played a large part in the change.*

In similar ways, social science results and social science concepts have had effects in many fields. It is not usually a single finding or the recommendation derived from the single study that is adopted in executive or legislative action (although this occasionally happens). More often, it is the ideas and general notions coming from research that have an impact. Nor is it usually the particular 'decision-maker' for whom the study was done who uses the findings. Since few decisions in government are made by a single decision-maker or even a small group of decision-makers, and almost no decisions of sufficient scope to qualify for the category of policy, this is not the usual route to influence. Instead, what seems to happen is that generalizations and ideas from numbers of studies come into currency indirectly — through articles in academic journals and

---

*Social scientists continue to debate whether the evaluation studies that provided much of the impetus for the change were valid enough to support the conclusion that in prison programmes 'nothing works'.

journals of opinion, stories in the media, the advice of consultants, lobbying by special interest, conversation of colleagues, attendance at conferences or training programmes, and other uncatalogued sources. Ideas from research are picked up in diverse ways and percolate through to office-holders in many offices who deal with the issues.

As the ideas from research filter through, officials test them against the standards of their own knowledge and judgment. They do not uncritically accept every set of conclusions they hear about, even if the conclusions bear the imprimatur of social science. They have many sources of information other than social science, ranging from their own first-hand experience to systematic and unsystematic reports from the field. The extent to which they accept a research idea, or give it at least provisional hearing, depends on the degree to which it resonates with their prior knowledge. If it 'makes sense', if it helps to organize and make sense of their earlier knowledge and impressions, they tend to incorporate it into their stock of knowledge (Weiss and Bucuvalas, 1980).

This prevalent process of merging research results with other sources of information and ideas has two curious consequences. First, the merger often gives research results extra leverage as they shape officials' understanding of issues. Because research provides powerful labels for previously incohate and unorganized experience, it helps to mould officials' thinking into categories derived from social science. Think of the policy effects of such category labels as externalities, aptitude test scores, deinstitutionalization, white flight, intergenerational dependency.

Second, because social science is merged with other knowledge, officials are largely unaware of when and how they use research. An investigator going out to study the uses of policy research quickly finds out that respondents have great difficulty disentangling the lessons they have learned from research from their whole configuration of knowledge. They do not catalogue research separately; they do not remember sources and citations. With the best will in the world, all they can usually say is that in the course of their work they hear about a great deal of research and they're sure it affects what they think and do. They can't give specific illustrations of their use of a specific study, because that is not how they work (Weiss, 1980a).

So, if recent investigations of the consequences of research for policy leave us with greater respect for the influence of research, the influence appears to lie in affecting the shape and content of policy discourse rather than concrete choices. The nature of the effect has been called 'enlightenment': research modifies the definition of problems that policy-makers address, how they think about them, which options they discard and which they pursue, and how they conceptualize their purposes. For those who had hoped for greater direct influence on policy, it is a limited victory.

Elsewhere I have noted that even in the provisionally optimistic imagery of enlightenment, there lurk some dangers. For one thing, the research that policy actors hear about and come to accept is not necessarily the best, most comprehensive, or most up-to-date research. Sometimes they become aware of shoddy studies, outmoded ideas, and biased findings. No quality control mechanisms screen the good and relevant from the partial and sensational. The phenomenon that has been discussed as 'enlightenment' may turn out to be, in fact, 'endarkenment'.

Another limitation is that for all the potential power of shifts in policy-makers' awareness and attention, thinking differently is not the same as acting differently. While changed discourse is likely to result — eventually — in new modes of action, the process may be agonizingly slow and inexact. The policy action that finally emerges cannot be expected to correspond closely with the preferred state envisioned by the social scientist.

So much is prologue. The question to which I'd like to turn is why the use of evaluation and other social science research goes through such tortuous process. Why isn't there more immediate and direct use of research results in the making of policy? Given the fact that government agencies responsible for particular policies sponsor studies with the avowed intent of improving those policies, how come they don't put the results to use directly?

Obviously the answers to this question are multiple and complex. Some of them have to do with the inconclusiveness of the research. Many, probably most, studies are fragile guides to action, either because of limitations in the research, or the ambiguous nature of the findings, or — often most serious — the problematic relationship between the findings and any clear-cut policy recommendations. To move from data about what is, to recommendations about what should be (and how to get there) usually requires an extensive leap. Researchers who have done a painfully careful evaluation study have been known to throw caution to the winds when they come to drawing implications for action and leap to unanalysed, untested and perhaps unworkable recommendations. Other reasons for the lack of immediate adoption have to do with the nature of government agencies (e.g., their limited repertoire of available policy responses) and the imperatives of policy decisions (e.g., the overriding need to reconcile diverse interests as well as reach 'right' decisions). But one important reason has received little attention, and it is this reason that I want to talk about — the nature of political decision-making processes.

The Nature of Policy Decision-Making

Both the popular and the academic literature pictures decision-making as an event: a group of authorized decision-makers assemble at particular times and places, they review a problem (or opportunity), they consider a number of alternative courses of action with more or less explicit calculation of the advantages and disadvantages of each option, they weigh the alternatives against their goals or preferences and then select an alternative that seems well suited for achieving their purposes. The result is a decision.*

There are five major constructs in this imagery of decision-making. The first is *boundedness*. Decision-making is, in effect, set off from the ongoing stream of organizational activity. It involves a discrete set of *actors* who occupy authoritative positions, people who are officially responsible for, and empowered to make, decisions for the organization. Decision-making is bounded in *time*, taking place over a relatively short period. It is usually also bounded in *location*, with the relevant actors in contact with each other, or able to be in contact with each other, to negotiate the decision. The customary conceptualization of decision-making thus has much in common with the three unities of Greek drama.

A second construct is *purposiveness*. It is commonly assumed that decision-makers have relatively clear goals in view; they want to bring about a desired end-state or avoid an undesired state. Since Simon's seminal work (1947), it has become accepted that decision-makers do not try to optimize decisions, but rather 'satisfice' i.e. settle for something 'good enough'. Nevertheless, they are expected to have overt criteria for what is good enough and to seek a decision that promises progress toward attaining their purposes.

The third construct is *calculation*. Decision-makers are expected to generate (or have generated for them) a set of alternatives. In the past decades, scholars have recognized that no comprehensive set of alternatives is developed; limits on human abilities of cognitive processing preclude a complete canvass of options. But in the going imagery, decision-makers consider the costs and benefits of a variety of responses. Their calculation will often be informal and intuitive rather than systematic, as they proceed on the basis of experience, informed judgment or gut feeling. Their goals need not represent only properly respectable public objectives, but will usually include such unexpressed aims as bureaucratic advantage, career interests and the furtherance of electoral chances. But however mixed the objectives and however informal the assessment procedures may be, it is assumed that decision-makers weigh the relative advantages of several alternatives against their goals and their formulation of desired end-states. The alternative that registers an acceptable balance of costs and benefits

---

*There was a time when the characterization of decision-making was considerably crisper than this. In what is commonly referred to as the rational model, several additional assumptions were made, e.g. explicit goals consensually weighted, generation of all possible alternatives, explicit calculation of all costs and benefits for each option, selection of the optimal option. Scholars from the several disciplines engaged with decision-making have been chipping away at the formulation for over a generation in the light of actual organizational behaviour. The statement above is what generally remains.

will be selected. Scholars have lowered their expectations for the rationality of the calculus employed, and they have tempered their assumptions of systematic and methodical assessment of trade-offs, but they retain belief that a process of calculation takes place.

Fourth, implicit in the concept of decision-making is a construct of *perceived significance*. A decision marks a step of some moment. People who make the decision perceive the act as consequential, i.e. having consequences. When the decision involves 'policy', whichever of the many meanings are invested in the term 'policy' (Heclo, 1972), the connotations of far-reaching importance are underscored, and a 'policy decision' is doubly endowed with intimations of significance. People who make a policy decision are viewed as self-consciously aware of registering a decisive commitment to an important course of action. Scholars have noted that some decisions involve a choice to do nothing, to leave the situation unchanged. Yet even when this is the case, the choice is expected to represent a matter of consequence to those who make the decision.

Finally, there is an assumption of *sequential order*. The sequence is regarded as beginning with recognition of a problem. It proceeds to the development and consideration of alternative means for coping with the problem,* goes next to assessment of the relative advantages of the alternatives, and ends with selection of a decision.

These five constructs — boundedness, purposiveness, calculation, perceived significance, and sequential order — underlie most images of decision-making. And they capture essential elements of much of the decision-making that goes on at bureau, division and department levels, in executive agencies and legislatures, in private and public organizations. Allison's (1971) account of the 'essence of decision' by President Kennedy and his small group of advisers considering the American response to the Cuban missile crisis is an archetypical decision of this kind. Similarly, a corporation deciding whether or not to construct a new plant, the US Congress debating passage of tax-cutting legislation, an executive agency developing proposals for change in eligibility requirements for federal aid — all go through a process that may be well represented by these constructs.

Yet many policy decisions emerge through processes that bear little relationship to these descriptors. Much decision-making differs from the traditional model because one or more of the five characteristics is low, or

---

*Despite the ubiquity of the phrase 'problem-solving', most people understand that current-day government problems are rarely 'solved' once and for all, or even for long periods of time. Any solution is temporary, as likely to generate new problems as to remove the condition that it is intended to solve. And many problems, such as poverty or insufficient oil resources, are so deeprooted and intractable, that government action can at best make modest inroads. Therefore, I have selected the word 'coping' rather than 'solving' to characterize the kinds of alternatives that officials consider.

even absent. Policies, even policies of fateful magnitude, often take shape by jumbled and diffuse processes that differ in vital ways from the conventional imagery.

Government is a continuous bustle of activity, with people in many offices bumping up against problems, new conditions, discrepant rules, unprecedented requests for service and the promulgations of other offices. In coping with their daily work, people in many places take small steps, without conscious awareness that their actions are pushing policy down certain paths and foreclosing other responses. They do not necessarily perceive themselves as making – or even influencing – policy, but their many small steps (writing position papers, drafting regulations, answering inquiries, making plans, releasing news bulletins) may fuse, coalesce and harden. Over time, the congeries of small acts can set the direction, and the limits, of government policy. Only in retrospect do people become aware that policy was made.

While the people who engage in incremental adaptations are not conscious of participating in policy-making, officials at the top echelon may be equally convinced that they are not making decisions. From the top, it often looks as though they are presented with a *fait accompli*. Accommodations have been reached and a decision negotiated by people in the warren of offices below, and they have little option but to accept it. Only rarely, and with the expenditure of a considerable amount of their political capital, can they change or reject the advice they are offered. To them, the job often looks like rubber-stamping decisions already made.

Even in legislatures, the quintessential loci of decision-making, individual legislators have limited options. In the United States, committees receive drafts of complex legislative bills from the executive agencies. Committee staffs may identify controversial points in the light of legislator's general preferences and work out accommodations with agency staffs. From time to time, particularly interested and influential legislators get particular provisions amended. But when the lengthy bills come up for vote, no individual legislator can be familiar with more than a handful of provisions. By and large, he or she must either vote against the entire bill or accept it. To the participants, their own influence on policy often looks marginal.

Given the fragmentation of authority across multiple bureaus, departments and legislative committees, and the disjointed stages by which actions coalesce into decisions, the traditional model of decision-making is a highly stylized rendition of reality. Identification of any clear-cut group of decision-makers can be difficult. (Sometimes a middle-level bureaucrat has taken the key action, although she may be unaware that her action was going to be – or was – decisive.) The goals of policy are often equally diffuse, except in terms of 'taking care of' some undesirable situation. Which options are considered, and what sets of advantages and disadvantages are assessed, may be impossible to tell in the interactive, multi-participative, diffuse processes of formulating policy. The complexity of government policy-making often defies neat compartmentalization.

Alternative routes to policy

Yet policies do get made. If government often proceeds to decisions without bounded, purposeful, sequential acts of perceived significance, how do decisions emerge? Some of the undirected strategies appear to be these:

a. *Reliance on custom and implicit rules.* Officials do what the agency has traditionally done. Even if a situation is unprecedented, officials may interpret it to fall within customary procedures. In so doing, they in effect make new policy by subsuming the novel contingency within a familiar rubric.

b. *Improvisation.* Another tactic is to improvise. Confronted with an unanticipated situation, officials may exercise their ingenuity, stretching a point here, combining a few tried-and-true procedures there, adding a dash of novelty, much like a chef concocting a new recipe. Through impromptu accommodation, an agency may begin to fashion new policy.

c. *Mutual adjustment.* As Lindblom (1965) has indicated, office holders who lack any sense of common purpose ('partisans', in his term) may reach decisions by simply adapting to decisions made around them. If one office has invoked convention or made improvisations, other offices can adjust their actions to accommodate the situation.

d. *Accretion.* Once officials have extemporized under the press of events, or adapted to actions taken in other offices, they may repeat the procedures when similar — or even not so similar — situations recur. The first responses provide a precedent, and if they seem to work, they will be followed again. Over time, when numbers of cases have been handled in like fashion, or when several different contingencies have been adopted to deal with an array of exceptional circumstances, they may coalesce and rigidify. Like skeletons of millions of tiny sea creatures building up into giant coral reefs, the result can become fixed.

e. *Negotiation.* When authority is fragmented and agencies have overlapping and discrepant mandates, overt conflicts may arise. Many are settled by direct negotiation among the interested units. Threats and promises, discussion and debate on the issues, trade-offs of advantage and obligation — these are the currency of bargaining. The aim is less to reach a rational decision in the usual sense than to work out an arrangement that will at least minimally satisfy the key interests of each of the parties. Through processes long familiar in the Congress (log-rolling, horse-trading), a bargain is arranged.

f. *Move and counter-move.* If bargaining breaks down, an agency may take a unilateral move to advance its position. Other affected agencies counter with moves of their own. This kind of antagonistic adjustment is particularly likely when present policies leave some new policy territory unclaimed (*cf.* agencies' scramble to move into the turf of 'children's policy'). The series of competitive moves may continue until mutual adjustment reaches stalemate, or until resolution is shifted up to higher levels. Move and counter-move is an accustomed mode of decision in international relations.

g. *A window for solutions.* Not infrequently, the solution precedes the identification of the problem. In fact, it can be argued that unless a plausible solution is envisioned, the issue will not be identified as a problem. It will be considered a 'condition' that has to be endured, like death, the weather, and (for many centuries) poverty. Officials often become wedded to pet remedies and they seek opportunities to implement these remedies. One group may want to install a computer system, and they engage in a search for places and occasions that would justify its introduction. Another group may be wedded to the idea of deregulation as an all-purpose panacea and scour the federal system for areas amenable to regulatory rollback. These are cases where the solution is in hand, and partisans actively seek a 'window' that will provide an opening for their ready-made nostrum.

h. *Indirection.* Another route by which policy emerges is as a by-product of other decisions. In this case, policy outcomes are unintended, but because of decisions made to achieve other desired ends, they nevertheless come about. Federal guarantees of home mortgages, undertaken after World War II to help families purchase their own homes, led to an exodus from central cities and massive growth of suburbs. Federal aid to education designed to improve the quality of education particularly for disadvantaged and low-achieving students, is leading to a shift of authority over educational practice from local to state and federal education agencies. No decisions were consciously made to create such shifts, but they emerged by indirection.

This list of non-decisional processes that produce policy outcomes is probably not exhaustive. Nevertheless, it indicates a variety of ways in which major outputs can issue from government without considered review or rational assessment. In time, *ad hoc* agency actions may have to be formalized by legislation. But often the early response is decisive, and legislative action merely ratifies the decisions that have already emerged. In some areas, it is only a slight exaggeration to say that ratification of the *status quo*, and allocation of funds to support it, is a main function of legislation.

The place of research

If government policy can 'happen' without the set piece of formal decision-making, how does policy research get a hearing? When decisions take shape over long periods of time, through the incremental actions of multiple actors, and often without participants' awareness that they are shaping decisions, the opportunity for formal consideration of research information looks distinctly limited. In such situations, research data on constituents' needs, the benefits and costs of policies, effectiveness and shortcomings of programmes, seem to have little chance for impact.

Yet one of the interesting facets of the situation, verified repeatedly in empirical investigation and borne out by the record, is that United States officials value social science research. They say that it is important and useful, and they sponsor large numbers of studies. If opportunities to use research results as a guide to policy are limited by the diffuse processes of government decision-making, there must be other purposes that research serves. It seems important to identify them.

One possible reason for officials' allegiance may be that research serves as a device of control. In a federal system, federal agencies set policy and allocate resources but local agencies deliver direct services. With day-to-day control of education, health services and welfare in local hands, there can be a wide gap between federal intent and local performance. Only when the federal agency has good information about what local services are doing — their structure, the processes of service delivery and the outcomes for clients — can it begin to exercise the authority that rule-making and resource allocation allow. Evaluation and policy studies can become the mechanism by which federal agencies keep informed.

Federal education officials, intent on ensuring compliance with federal purpose, can find out whether local school districts are actually spending funds provided under Title I of the Elementary and Secondary Education Act to enrich educational opportunities for low-income and low-achieving students. Federal health officials can find out the extent to which neighbourhood health centres improve the health status of low-income clienteles. If local agencies are found to be performing poorly, the federal agency can institute stricter controls over recipient agencies — tightening up rules and even terminating particular local grants. Research results may become the basis for control — and the mere decision to undertake research can serve as an implicit threat that firmer control is possible. The United States Congress sometimes seems to write evaluation provisions into legislation for just this kind of purpose — to serve notice on agencies that it will have the capability to review the effectiveness of their operations — even if it never does.

Another possible purpose that policy research can serve is to provide support and vindication for current policies. Federal officials often expect research to justify at least some of their claims — that large numbers of people are in need of their services, that programmes do some good, that constituents like the attention and want services to continue. Even an evaluation showing little direct benefit to clients will often yield some positive evidence of this kind. The agency can use findings selectively to buttress its case for legislative reauthorization and additional funding.

If these reasons for continued sponsorship of policy research seem unduly sceptical, a third basis can be advanced. It is possible that federal officials support research because they recognize the conceptual contributions that it makes. They may have come to realize that every agency, even the most progressive, tends to grow musty and stale. It settles into a rut, taking old assumptions for granted, substituting routine for thought, tinkering at best with policy minutia rather than venturing in new directions. To overcome hardening of organizational arteries, they may welcome the fresh insights and critical perspectives that good research brings. By subjecting conventional practice to evaluation, they may seek to help the agency renew its sense of mission and adapt to changing conditions.

One may hope that some part of the reason for high levels of research support comes from motives of this latter sort. But even if the thrust for evaluation and policy studies springs from less high-minded sources, even if it is the resultant of adversarial forces (department heads checking up on the performance of bureaus, the Congress checking up on departments, agencies seeking legitimation for their programmes), even if it represents only rhetorical commitment to the norms of accountability and rational procedure, even then it has consequences. The regularized practice of evaluation and analysis has become embedded in government structures. Offices of research and evaluation exist at bureau, division and department level in many federal agencies. Their professional staffs do what evaluation and analysis staffs know how to do — continue and expand the flow of research information to the agency. Even the United States General Accounting Office, which used to serve the Congress only as financial auditor, now has its Institute of Program Evaluation. As procedures develop to transmit the results of policy studies routinely to officials through the government, an important mechanism for learning becomes institutionalized.

The importance of the inclusion of evaluation and analysis units in departmental structures should not be underestimated. They are institutionalized mechanisms for collecting, sponsoring, synthesizing and disseminating research and evaluation information. The informational function that they represent is embedded not only in the agency's table of organization but also in procedures, the flow of paper and the division and coordination of work. Members of evaluation and analysis units sit on agency committees that discuss present programmes and future policy; they prepare position papers and option statements, marshalling the evidence for and against specific proposals; reports about the information that they collect and process circulate to key officials and are discussed in meetings; their comments — and in some cases, their approval and sign-off — are built into the processes of agency work.

In many ways, the embedding of evaluation and analysis units in agency structures represents a commitment to the use of information. People with research and analytic knowledge and skills are on hand, available for consultation when issues arise, and ready to undertake new activities of research generation, knowledge integration and data-based recommendation on their own initiative. And their presence is not just happenstance, not a fortuitous occurrence that could vanish overnight — as is the occasional occupancy of legislative posts or cabinet positions by social scientists. Their jobs, with the associated skill requirements, are part of the permanent roster of agency positions. The units that they staff have specified functions and responsibilities in the line of work.

While there is no guarantee that such positions and such units are permanent (governmental departments undergo frequent reorganization), it is probable that they would be difficult to dislodge. In the late 1960s, programme-planning-budgeting (PPBS) staffs were introduced into US federal agencies, and after less than a decade PPBS was abandoned. But the people who performed the analytic tasks were retained, and in many cases they remained in — or were incorporated into — evaluation and analysis units with somewhat different focus and broader responsibilities. Their emphasis on systematic analysis still infuses federal operations.

To abolish evaluation, research, and analysis activities would go against the grain of our public rhetoric. The use of sound systematic information to guide policy-making and implementation sounds so patently reasonable that abolition of the function would carry an aura of 'know-nothingism'. If federal agencies are to have good information on what is going on in the field and the consequences of their policies, they need an evaluation capability. If they are to be accountable to their constituent groups, the elected representatives of the people and the public, they cannot dissolve the mechanisms that provide the informational basis for accountability.

Even at a time of massive cost-cutting in government, policy research and analysis should be able to survive the axe, because they can provide the evidential basis for deciding which programmes are accomplishing so little that their discontinuation is justified. Observers have noted that evaluation may in fact be better suited to a time of programme contraction than programme expansion, just because it is so adept at identifying programmes whose effects are minimal (Schick, 1971). However popular a programme may be, if good data indicate that it is not achieving much, the cost-cutters can use the data to counter the popular outcry. (Since I am writing these words before the details of President Reagan's budget cuts have been released, it remains to be seen whether the Administration recognizes the potential utility of evaluation and policy research in its cause, i.e. whether it sees research as part of the solution rather than part of the problem.)

Before I end this digression of the 'permanence' of evaluation and analytic activities in the US Government, let me note that I am not *advocating* their perpetuation or expansion as they currently exist. There is much that can be improved in the initiation, conduct and management of evaluation and policy studies in the United States, and much that should be done to enhance their contributions to policy. Nor is it obvious whether present levels of support are too low, high enough or too high. The argument for their continuance rests on their potential, and the congruence between their potential and the needs of government agencies, both for substance and for symbol, – not on any evaluation of their present contribution.

The discussion about the incorporation of evaluation personnel and units into the structure of government agencies is intended to demonstrate that the knowledge that they provide goes beyond the level of *individual* learning. It is not only individuals here and there in the agency who somehow become enlightened by the results of evaluation studies. The evaluation process is embedded in the procedures and routines, in the *dailiness*, of agency work. It represents a mechanism for learning at the organizational level. To the extent that requirements for evaluation are institutionalized (e.g. in legislation), that evaluation and analysis units perform the tasks of linking research to policy planning, and that results of evaluations are routinely disseminated and discussed, evaluation becomes a means of *organizational learning*.

With some oversimplification, it can be said that within any given political/ideological environment, policies are formulated on two bases: officials' perception of the situation and pressure from interest groups. Evaluation and policy studies, and social science research more generally, are a help on both grounds. First, they help to give officials a more accurate representation of the situation. Second, they constrain exaggeration and falsification by interest groups. As a mode of organizational learning based on independent research, conducted by numbers of outside investigators according to the canons of scientific method, evaluation and policy studies have considerable potential for vitalizing the policy process.

In the United States external developments have been reinforcing the processes internal to public bureaucracies that strengthen the role of research. The mass media are increasingly reporting the results of social science research, including evaluation and policy studies. Coverage by major national and regional newspapers and the weekly news magazines is bringing news of research to attentive publics. When the public reads evidence of failures in current policies, the demonstrated promise of alternative policies or new concepts of programming, public pressure increases on government to take account of the evidence.

In all fora of policy discussion, discourse is becoming permeated not only with social science evidence and data but also with social science concepts. Data are marshalled by proponents of all sides in policy debates to strengthen their cause. Even the Congress, rarely renowned as a champion of research, now routinely expects the case for policy to be supported with systematic and objective evidence. And the evidence is categorized and interpreted in conceptual and theoretical frameworks that come largely from the social sciences. Policies are proposed, defended, and criticized in terms that the social sciences have brought into fashion — e.g. client outcomes, implementability, inflationary consequences. Social science has become a prevalent language of discourse in the policy arena. Partisans speak the language to make their aguments convincing. But once they adopt its symbols and use its grammar, they find their positions subtly influenced by the structure of its rules.

Policy research is no longer a trivial and transient appendage to the policy-making process. It is being built into the system. In the last few paragraphs, my discussion of its place has moved from its concrete manifestations in research, evaluation and planning offices in federal agencies, to media reporting of its results, to its infiltration of policy discourse. This shift toward progressively more diffuse influences reflects the variety of indirect and circuitous ways in which research exercises its influence on policy.

Conclusion

One of the significant features of the policy process, at least on certain issues at certain times, is the diffuse manner in which decisions accrete. When policy happens without synoptic review and 'rational' choice, there seems to be little opportunity for careful consideration of relevant policy research. Officials respond to situations by hunch and experience, drawing on whatever mix of knowledge — and of course much else besides knowledge — they have at hand.

None of the traditional advice to policy researchers on how to get their conclusions heeded seems to apply. The familiar admonitions are: locate the potential user of research in advance, understand which policy variables she has the authority to change, concentrate the study of the feasible (manipulable) variables, involve the potential user in the research process, establish a relationship of trust, demonstrate awareness of the constraints that limit her options, provide practical recommendations, write results clearly and simply, communicate results in person. All of these prescriptions are directed at influencing one decision-maker; or a small group of decision-makers, to use research in making a direct, concrete, immediate choice. None fits the world of diffuse policy decisions.

But there are other ways that research gets a hearing. Officials absorb a great deal of research knowledge through informal routes. They read widely, go to meetings, listen to people, discuss with colleagues – all without necessarily having a particular decision in mind. Research information and ideas filter into their awareness, whether or not they label it research as they absorb it. This diffuse process of 'enlightenment' contributes to their stock of knowledge. When they engage in the stream of activities that aggregate into policy, they draw upon the knowledge that they have gathered from a variety of sources, including research, and apply it to their work.

The diffuse process of research use that we are calling 'enlightenment' is highly compatible with the diffuse processes of policy-making. It informs the work of many policy actors in many locations as they perform their bits and pieces of policy work. Unlike the usual notion of a single research sponsor who acquires a directed set of findings for a particular decisional purpose, it does not suggest a monopoly on research knowledge by the bureaucrat who funds the study. Many different people, with different interests and ideologies, inside and outside government, can be enlightened by research, and they can exercise their knowledge at many points, cooperatively or adversarially, as policy takes shape.

Of course, the enlightenment image represents no ideal model. When research comes to people's attention haphazardly, the process is unorganized, slow, wasteful and sloppy. Some policy actors may fail to hear about relevant research; others may fail to take the research they hear about seriously. Some people may become enchanted with catchy, faddish, irrelevant, obsolete, partial or invalid findings, or latch on to only the subset of findings that supports their predispositions and policy interests. The whole process reeks of over-simplification. People tend to forget the complexities and qualifications and remember the slogans ('the poverty programme failed', 'a guaranteed income leads to little reduction in work effort'). Diffuse enlightenment is no substitute for careful, directed analysis of the policy implications of research. Ways have to be found to improve targeted applications of targeted research as well.

Nevertheless, the fit between the diffuse processes of policy-making and officials' diffuse absorption of research is noteworthy. It seems to represent one of the most important contributions that social science research makes to public policy. The ideas derived from research provide organizing perspectives that help people make sense of experience. These ideas offer frameworks within which problems are interpreted and policy actions considered. Retrospectively, they help people understand what government has been doing and what the consequences have been. Prospectively, they help raise the possibility of alternative courses of action.

Perhaps most valuable of all, research can be a medium of criticism. Subjecting old assumptions to empirical test and introducing alternative perspectives are vital contributions. Even when officials have themselves suspected policy shortcomings or negative side effects, research crystallizes the suspicions and makes them visible to others; the review of research results provides an occasion for mapping new responses. Of course, specific findings may be questioned, and the implications that researchers single out for attention may not be accepted. Research cannot be expected to prevail over all contending influences. Yet even in cases where officials dispute the particulars, they often find themselves using the concepts and frameworks of the research to reconsider accustomed practice.

To the extent that such contributions to the public arena are important, they suggest different lessons to policy researchers from those associated with direct research application. Concern about pleasing — or at least, satisfying — the client is secondary. Being practical and timely and keeping the study within feasible boundaries may be unimportant, or even counterproductive. If the research is not completed in time for this year's budget cycle, it is no great loss. The same issues, if they are important, will come up again and again. In the enlightenment tradition, the researcher is well advised to broaden the scope of the question and take time to do first-quality research.

In fact, this lesson may be the most important implication from the recent studies of the uses of social science research in decision-making. Researchers need to be aware that the work they do, no matter how applied in intent and how practical in orientation, is not likely to have major influence on the immediate operational decision at which it is purportedly directed — at least not if policy actors' interests and ideologies are engaged. Adherence to all the traditional strictures — acceptance of decision-makers' constraints, focus on manipulable variables, timeliness, jargon-free communication, and the like — seems to increase the application of research results only minimally. When competing with other powerful factors, such as officials' concern with bureaucratic advantage, one limited study (and all studies are limited in some way) is likely to have limited impact.

But on the other hand, the stream of social science research has consequences. The generalizations, the *ideas*, that emerge from social science research help to shape the assumptions on which policy is based. Ill-conceived and slipshod research will yield conclusions of questionable value; quick and dirty *ad hoc* studies, which cut methodological corners in order to meet an arbitrary deadline or satisfy an impatient client, are more likely to muddy than to clarify the issues. To serve the longer-term policy needs of officials, research should be grounded in relevant theory and existing knowledge; it should look at issues comprehensively in all their multivariate complexity; it should be done with the greatest methodological skill that advances in research and analytic techniques have made possible.

This is not a call for retreat to the ivory tower. Researchers need to be sophisticated about the shape and contour of policy issues if their work is to be relevant to current debates. They need to recognize that decision-makers cannot wait for certainty and authoritativeness (which social science may in fact never be able to provide), but must proceed on the basis of the best knowledge available at the time. But as social scientists, their responsibility is to convince government agencies to allow them the opportunity to do the best social science of which they are capable.

The critical ingredients will be independence of thought, conceptual sophistication and methodological rigour. And, when the research has produced something worth saying, serious efforts through many channels to get its message heard.

References

ALLISON, Graham T. (1971). *Essence of Decision: Explaining the Cuban Missile Crisis*. Boston: Little, Brown.
HECLO, H. Hugh (1972). 'Review Article: Policy Analysis,' *British Journal of Political Science*, 2, pp. 83–108.
LINDBLOM, Charles E. (1965). *The Intelligence of Democracy*, New York: Free Press.
SCHICK, Allen (1971). 'From Analysis to Evaluation,' *Annals of the American Academy of Political and Social Science*, 394, pp. 57–71.
SIMON, Herbert A. (1947). *Administrative Behaviour*. New York: Free Press.
WEISS, Carol H. (1980a). 'Knowledge Creep and Decision Accretion,' *Knowledge: Creation, Diffusion, Utilization*, 1 (March).
WEISS, C.H. with BUCUVALAS, M.J. (1980b). *Social Science Research and Decision-Making*. New York: Columbia University Press.
WEISS, C.H. and BUCUVALAS, M.J. (1980). 'Truth Tests and Utility Tests: Decision Makers' Frames of Reference for Social Science Research,' *American Sociological Review*, 45 (April).

PRESENTATION

Note by the editors: The criticism and discussion results are presented after the verbatim text of Professor Weiss' presentation at the Workshop. The stipulations made in this presentation provide a valuable supplement to her paper.

WEISS: Presentation

I am delighted to be here and to have an opportunity to learn about the European experience. In fact I would like to volunteer to be that reverse Columbus that Mr. Eide recommended, because I think the US has a great deal to learn from the many kinds of organizational structures and procedures that have been introduced into your nations to facilitate the use of research in both legislative and administrative decision-making. I am very pleased to learn a little bit about it while I am here and hope to learn a great deal more.

I am also very grateful to SVO for the very good preparation of this meeting and the receipt of the critical comments from the reviewers in advance. I have never had this opportunity before and I find it extremely provocative and helpful. What I would like to do, if I may, is take the first few minutes and, in a sense, respond to some critical comments by putting the discussion in the paper in a somewhat broader framework. What I would like to do is start off with four stipulations, four points, that form a rather larger context for the discussion in the paper. I have written about most of these things elsewhere. Unfortunately the two papers that discussed these issues in detail are not available here, but I would be very happy to send them to you, if you would write to me. One of them is even available in German for those of you who would prefer it. The first application that I would like to make as background for the discussion is that policy-making in democratic governments is first and foremost a process of reaching accommodations among interest groups and ideological factions. It is a process of bargaining, negotiation and accommodation. It is designed to avoid major cleavages in the society. It is designed to insure the survival of government. That is a basic premise of political decision-making. Next, policy-making is about making wise decisions that lead to desired effects. Or to put it another way, policy making is about reaching wise decisions to realize desired objectives, within the constraints set by the need to maintain coalitions of support. It is a procedure of compromise. It is and I think it should be. Policy has to respond to diverse wants of diverse segments of the society, and thus I think is the most important constraint on the use of social science research. Political rationality must supercede scientific rationality. It is better to reach a decision around which major coalitions can rally and agree, than to reach a single best course that would lead to big divisions and major cleavages in the country. I am reminded of a conversation I had with Ray Marshall, when he was Secretary of Labour in the Carter Admini-Administration. Mr Marshall was an economist with a PhD in economics, had done research of considerable note. When he was in office, a proposal for an increase in the minimum wages was being proposed. His economist colleagues came to him with research, very good research, that almost unequivocally showed that an increase in the minimum wages would lead to a reduction in employment, to an increase in unemployment, that if you raise the minimum wages, employers would not want to pay the higher rates for unskilled workers and would do something else, like automate procedures in order to avoid the higher costs. Mr Marshall knew about the research, he believed the research and he still advocated an increase in the minimum wages law. When we talked to him about it, he said 'Yes, I know. I believe it is true, but I still support the increase in the minimum wages. Why? 1) because the labour unions very strongly advocate this increase and the labour unions are a strong bloc of support for the Carter Administration; 2) it is a matter of philosophy, a matter of equity. We believe that it is not fair to penalize the lowest paid members of the society at a time of rising inflation. So, although we believe the research, we are not going to base our policy on it. We are going to go ahead and advocate the passage of this bill.' I think this is an illustration of the point.

The second stipulation I would like to make is that social science has no monopoly on knowledge and insight. There are two parts to this argument. First, policy-makers and practitioners know a great deal, and they know things from their experience that social scientists do not know. The second part of the argument is that some research is not very good. It is methodologically weak and conceptually simplistic. All research is partial. It looks at only segments of an issue and not at the whole issue. It gives fragments of the story. Even good research well done, methodologically strong, sound, and even conceptually sensible and profound, has limitations. When studies are undertaken from different perspectives, it is not uncommon for them to produce discrepant and sometimes divergent findings. Therefore, acting on the basis of research is not always a clear-cut and obvious thing to do. It is not always obvious to a policy-maker what to make of this rather diverse body of information that social science provides.

The third point is that research is embedded with value assumptions. Even the most objective empirical research contains some tacit assumptions about desirable and undesirable states of the world. I can give you examples and I am sure you can all give me examples. Sometimes it is the policy-makers' assumptions that are contained in the underlying structure of the research; for example, when we evaluate programmes against the official objectives that the policy-makers have set for those programmes. Sometimes it is the researchers' own assumptions that are embedded in the research. I would like to, within the confines of this room, raise one uncomfortable fact that is rarely mentioned, that most social scientists tend to be liberal, reformist, egalitarian and that their value positions tend to be on the liberal left side of the spectrum. When conservative administrations are in power, they very often find the value assumptions on which research is based uncongenial and incompatible with their own points of view. That also is one of the reasons why conservative governments are less likely to make use of social science research. The fourth background statement that I would like to make has to do with the nature of the question that we are addressing here today: the use of social science research. This is a subject that I have been studying since 1974 myself and I have been thinking about it and even writing about it a little bit longer than that. The value premises embedded in my research are that social science research should influence policy-making, that we should improve the linkage of knowledge from social science to all parties, who participate in the negotiation processes of policy-making. Now, when we frame the question this way, we are like a convention of widget manufacturers who are deliberating on how to increase the sale of our widgets to the reluctant consumers. If you do not know what a widget is, that is exactly the point. A widget is anything, any product, and I think we are trying to decide here how can we get those consumers out there to buy more widgets. A different value-orientation, I think, would ask the question quite differently. I think the question might be a better question if we phrased it differently, if we said 'How can the wisdom of policy-making be improved? Can social science play a part in improving the quality of policy decisions, and if so, how?' I think that might be a rather different orientation for our discussions and for the research we do on this issue. I recognize that I am one of the offenders, one of the culprits, to take an unnecessarily restricted perspective.

Now having said that, let me get back to the business of what the paper is about. The title is 'Policy Research in the Context of Diffuse Decision-Making'. There are two parts to the argument that I have tried to make. One is that although social scientists have become rather disillusioned about how little use is made of their research, in fact there has probably been considerably more use than they have noticed. Policy-oriented researchers have been looking for immediate and direct impact of the studies that they do on specific decisional choices that policy-makers make, and they have not found very many instances of this kind. But recent research shows that there have been consequences from the research that has been done, although not necessarily on discrete provisions nor in the direct and linear sequence that social scientists have expected. Rarely is it seen that research supplies an answer that policy-makers employ to solve a policy problem. Rather research seems to provide a background of empirical generalizations and ideas that affect the way that policy-makers think about the problems. Research influences their conceptualization of the issues which they deal in. It affects the facets of the issue that they consider inevitable and unchangeable, those that are seen as amenable to policy action. It widens the range of options that they consider. It challenges some taken for granted assumptions about appropriate goals and appropriate activities. Also it helps them make sense of what they have been doing after the fact. It helps them to interpret later on, so that they come to understand what courses of action they followed, and which courses of action have gone by default. Sometimes it makes them aware of the over-optimistic grandiosity of their objectives in light of the meagreness of the resources. At times it helps them reconsider entire strategies of action for achieving wanted ends. Policy studies have made significant contributions by altering the terms of policy discussion.

This kind of indirect conceptual contribution is not easy to see, but social science results and social science concepts have had effects in many fields. When you take a longer term perspective, I think you can see the change in the nature of policy discussion that follows in the wake of research. It is not usually a single finding, or the recommendations derived from a single study, that are adopted in executive or legislative action, although this does sometimes happen. More often it is the ideas and general notions coming from research that have an impact. Ideas from research are picked up in diverse ways and percolate through to office holders in many offices who deal with the issues. Because research provides powerful conceptual labels for previously unorganized and inchoate experience, it helps to mould official thinking into categories derived from social science. I can think of the policy effects of identifying and labelling of such things as externalities, achievement test-scores, deinstitutionalization, intergenerational dependency. Some of the notions that come from social science help to structure the way that people think about policy issues. But because social science is merged with other knowledge from other sources, officials are often unaware of when and how they use research. An investigator going out to study the uses that are made of research finds that respondents have great difficulty disentangling the lessons that they have learned from research from their whole configuration of knowledge. Mr Caplan for example, found this in the empirical research that he has done. Officials find it difficult to give specific illustrations of their use of specific studies, because they merge the results of research with the information and knowledge they have gotten from other sources. The influence of research appears to lie more in affecting the shape and content of policy discourse than in determining concrete choices. The nature of the effect has been called enlightenment. Research modifies the definition of problems that policy makers address, how they think about them, which options they discard and which they pursue, and how they conceptualize their purposes. For those social scientists who had hoped for greater direct influence on policy, I think this notion is a limited victory. Even in the provisionally optimistic imagery of enlightenment, there are some dangers. For one thing, the research that policy-makers hear about is not necessarily the best, most comprehensive and most up-to-date research. Sometimes what they learn about are shoddy studies, outmoded ideas, biased findings. The phenomenon that has been discussed as enlightenment may turn out to be what I would call 'endarkenment'. Another limitation is that for all the potential power of shifts in policy makers' awareness and attention, thinking differently is not the same as acting differently. While changed discourse may result eventually in new modes of action, the process can be very slow and very inexact, and the policy action that finally emerges can be very different from what the social scientist had in mind.

The second part of the papers concerns the reasons for this state of affairs. Why does the use of social science research go through such circuitous processes? Why is there not more direct and immediate use of research results in the making of policy? Now, obviously the answers to this question are many and complex. Yesterday we talked about quite a number of them. As I have already suggested, I think some of the reasons have to do with the inconclusiveness of much research and with the nature of the policy-making process, with the overriding imperative of the political system to reconcile diverse interests as well as reach 'right' decisions. But there is another reason that has received relatively little attention in the discussions that have taken place in the field so far. Although it may not be the most salient reason, it is the one that I talk about in this paper. That is the processes by which political decisions come into being.

Both the popular and the academic literature tend to picture decision-making as an event. A group of authorized decision-makers assemble at a particular time and place, they review a problem, they consider a number of alternatives for dealing with the problem, with more or less explicit calculation of the advantages and disadvantages of each option, they weigh the alternatives against their goals or preferences, and then they select the alternative that seems well suited for achieving their aim. The result is a decision.

There are five major constructs contained in that image of decision-making. The first one is boundedness, boundedness of the number of actors, the time and the location. A second construct is purposiveness. Decision-makers have relatively clear goals in view, and they want to bring about a desired end state that they can define. The third construct is calculation. Decision-makers are expected to weigh the costs and benefits of a variety of alternatives for dealing with the problem. While their calculation may be informal and intuitive rather than systematic, it is assumed that they do go through some process of weighing advantages of different alternatives against their goals. The alternative that registers an acceptable balance of costs and benefits is the one that will be selected. A fourth implicit construct is perceived significance. A decision is assumed to mark a step of some importance, some moment. People who make the decision perceive the act as consequential. Finally, there is an assumption of sequential order, that the process starts with the recognition of a problem, that it proceeds to the development of alternatives for coping with the problem, and goes on to weighing the advantages of the different alternatives, and finally ends up with the selection of a decision. Those five constructs: boundedness, purposiveness, calculation, perceived significance and sequential order, underlie most images of decision-making. And of course they do capture important elements of much of the decision-making that goes on in government.

But I would like to suggest that many policy decisions emerge through processes that bear very little relationship to these descriptors. Policies even of fateful magnitude can take shape by jumbled and diffused processes that differ in vital ways from the conventional imagery. Those of you who are in government, I welcome your comments on these comments of mine. It seems to me that government is a continuous hubbub of activity, that there are people in many different offices going about their business all the time, bumping up against new problems, new conditions, new demands, discrepant rules, unprecedented requests, having to cope with what other offices and other ministries and other departments are doing. In coping with their daily work, people in many places take small steps without conscious awareness that their actions are pushing policy down certain paths, and foreclosing paths. Over time, the congeries of small acts taken in many different places can coalesce and set the direction and the limits of government policy. Only in retrospect, looking back, do people become aware that a policy has been made.

While the people who engage in incremental adaptations at lower levels are not necessarily conscious of participating in policy-making, officials at the top echelon may be equally convinced that they are not making policy decisions. From the top, it often looks as though they are being presented with a *fait accompli*. Accommodations have been reached and decisions negotiated by people in the offices down below, and the people at the top seem to have very little choice but to accept it or on occasion, to reject it. If they reject it, they expend a considerable amount of their political capital and time and energy. So, to them the job often looks as though they are rubber stamping decisions that have already been worked out for them. Even in legislatures, which are supposed to be the prime locus of decision-making, it often looks to individual legislators as if they have limited options. In our country for example, legislatures receive long complex legislative bills that have been drafted in the executive agencies through incremental and interactive processes of the kind that I have been describing. More interested and influential legislators can have provisions of those bills changed. But most legislators are familiar with only a small part of what is in each of the bills, and by and large, they either vote against the entire bill or they accept it. To them it often looks as though their influence on policy is marginal.

Now, of course I am overstating the case, because things are not quite as unorganized as this suggests. I am making the extreme case because I think it is not a case that has received much attention. Given the fragmentation of authority across multiple bureaus, departments and legislative committees, and the disjointed stages by which actions coalesce into decisions, it seems to me that the traditional model of decision-making may sometimes be misleading.

Yet policies do get made. If government often proceeds to decisions without bounded, purposeful, sequential acts of perceived significance, how do decisions get made? In the paper I discuss seven or eight alternative ways in which a policy can come into being. I will just go through them very briefly.

1) Reliance on custom and implicit rules. 2) Improvisation. 3) Mutual adjustment in the terms which Lindblom has discussed. 4) Accretion; just tiny build-up. 5) Negotiation. When authority is fragmented and agencies have overlapping and discrepant mandates, conflicts can come up, and many are settled by direct negotiation among the interested units. Threats and promises, discussion and debate on the issues, trade-offs of advantage and obligation, these are the currency of bargaining within the bureaucracy. The aim is less to reach a rational decision in the usual sense than to work out an arrangement that will at least minimally satisfy the key interests of each of the parties. 6) Move and countermove decisions can come about by unilateral moves by one unit, countered by counter moves by another unit. 7) Solutions seeking a window. This was mentioned yesterday. People have preformed solutions in mind and they are looking for a window, an opening, where they can put that solution into play. 8) Finally, there is the possibility of indirection. A decision made for an entirely different purpose, to achieve some other goal, has as a by-product an effect on another policy area, and essentially makes a decision for that area. For example, if we decide to spend a large fraction of our resources for teaching of handicapped children, one of the by-products of that is that we have fewer resources for some other groups. In a sense we have made policy for these other groups by shifting the allocation of resources away from them. So those are a variety of ways in which major outputs can come forth from government without considered review or rational assessment.

Now, the conclusion of this paper has to do with the place of research in this process. If government policy can happen, just happen, in diffuse ways without formal deliberation, how can policy research get a hearing? The opportunity for consideration of research information seems to be distinctly limited under the kinds of conditions that I have been discussing. So what can we do to see that research is taken into account under such circumstances? None of the traditional advice that is usually given to policy researchers on how to get their message listened to seems to apply. The familiar admonitions are: Locate the potential users of research in advance. Understand which policy variables they have the authority to change. Concentrate the study on the feasible, manipulable variables. Involve the potential users of the research in the research process. Establish a relationship of trust with the users. Demonstrate your awareness of the constraints that limit decision-makers' options. Provide practical recommendations. Write results clearly and simply, avoid jargon. Communicate well, and communicate results in person, if possible. All of those prescriptions are directed at influencing one decision-maker or a small group of decision-makers to use research in making a direct concrete immediate choice. None of them seems to fit the world of diffuse policy decisions.

But as I suggested earlier, there are other ways in which research gets a hearing. What I have called enlightenment involves the seepage of the conclusions and concepts from many different research studies into the awareness of policy-makers, through a diverse array of channels and routes, through meetings, through articles in the popular media, through articles in journals of opinion, through discussions with academics, through discussions with colleagues, through consultants from universities, all kinds of channels that bring research information to the attention of government officials. Now, the diffuse process of enlightenment happens to be highly compatible with the diffuse processes of policy-making. Enlightenment informs the work of many policy actors in many locations as they perform their bits and pieces of policy work. Unlike the usual notion of a single research sponsor who acquires a directed set of findings for a particular decisional purpose, it does not suggest a monopoly on research knowledge by the bureaucrat who funds the study. Many different people with different interests and different ideologies, inside government and outside government, can be enlightened by research and they can exercise their knowledge at many points, cooperatively or in an adversarial relationship, as policy takes shape. I do not hold that the enlightenment image is an ideal model, by any means. I hope that it is not the best that social science can do for the world of policy. There are some serious flaws in the way it works and it is a haphazard process. When research comes to people's attention haphazardly, the process is unorganized, it is often slow, it is wasteful, it is sloppy, and some people may fail to hear about important relevant work. They may hear about some very poor work. The whole process is one of over-simplification. People tend to forget the complexities and the qualifications that are embedded in the research. Researchers make clear statements about the limitations of their studies: This finding only applies under these conditions or the sample on which these results are based is limited to this population. People who hear about research in an amorphous way do not always hear about, or certainly remember, those kinds of qualifications. They tend to remember the big slogan (The poverty programme does not work). So I would like to suggest very strongly that diffuse enlightenment is no substitute for careful, directed analysis of the policy implications of research. Ways have to be found to improve targeted applications of targeted research as well.

Nevertheless the fit between the diffuse processes of policy-making and official's diffuse absorption of research is noteworthy. It seems to represent one of the most important contributions that social science is currently making to policy. The ideas derived from research seem to be providing perspectives that help people make sense of experience. Perhaps most valuable of all, research is often a medium of criticism. It subjects old assumptions to empirical test and it introduces alternative perspectives into the policy-making process.

Of course, research does not always prevail over all the other contending influences. Yet, even in cases where officials dispute the research, they often find themselves using the concepts and the frameworks of research, in their reconsideration of accustomed policy and practice. To the extent that such contributions to the public arena are important, they suggest different lessons to policy researchers than those associated with direct research application.

I will close with what I think some of the lessons might be. To serve the longer-term policy needs of officials, I think that research should take itself very seriously as research. We should ground our studies in relevant theory and in existing knowledge. We should look at issues comprehensively, in all their multivariant complexity, and we should use the greatest methodological skill that advances in research and analytic techniques have made possible. I think we should worry less about being quick and timely and feasible. We should take more seriously the unique contributions that social science research can make. The critical ingredients are independence of thought, conceptual sophistication and methodological rigour, and, when the researchers produce something worth saying, serious efforts through many channels to get the message heard. Thank you.

CRITICISM AND DISCUSSION

1. General

The 'enlightenment model' as proposed by Carol Weiss was endorsed by all participants. Her analysis of the indirect ways in which research influences policy was considered enlightening indeed. A similar reception was accorded to her analysis of the policy-making process. Several qualifying comments were made though; they are presented in the paragraphs below. A somewhat different critique was formulated by Weiler. It seems worthwhile to keep his warning in mind right from the beginning:

Weiler warns us that an 'enlightenment' role is beyond the capacity of many researchers. Disjointed and incremental as policy-making processes

may be, this fact alone fails to take into account at least two major reasons why research findings rarely have a direct impact on policy:
1. Much policy-oriented research is simply *useless*. Poor research will not be used — no matter how decisions are made. 'If the quality of policy research is generally poor, how much "enlightenment" can actually occur?', Weiler asks. He fears that in many cases 'endarkenment' is a better way of describing what happens. Furthermore, Weiler feels that it is too soon to rejoice that 'social science has become a prevalent language of discourse in the policy arena' (Weiss). It would be a mistake to assume that the ethos of science has been embraced because its language is used. On the contrary, the language and concepts of social science have been so broadly co-opted by policy-makers that the currency of research communication may have been devalued. When virtually every policy position is supported by 'research' (or its appearance), the very idea of 'systematic and objective evidence' loses much of its meaning. Weiler's conclusion has to be kept in mind when we question the degree of enlightenment that actually takes place.
2. 'Policy makers do not have great confidence in social science research. They would be unlikely to act directly on the basis of research findings even if decisions were made in the ways described by the now discredited "rational models".' The reason for this *lack of trust*, is, that researchers overpromise. Social scientists have not spoken clearly to policy-makers about the limitations of research. Naturally, policy-makers 'are inclined to ask questions that cannot be answered. They get answers to questions they did not ask, which annoys them', Weiler observes. It is on these grounds that Weiler questions the enlightenment model's 'relevance as a guide to action'.

2. Comparative findings

Kallen raised the question of the extent to which Weiss's analysis of social science utilization by policy-makers as well as her description of the policy-making processes are valid for the various European countries as well. Opinions of participants appeared to diverge only slightly, mainly as far as the description of policy-making is concerned. Weiss's view of the indirect ways in which research utilization takes place was considered to be applicable to all European countries alike, including the more centralized nations like Hungary.

An amendment, from the European viewpoint, to the description of policy-making was put forward by *in'T Veld-Langeveld*. She stressed that, in particular where the Netherlands are concerned, the picture is frequently somewhat different. 'In the US practically every major initiative in the field of welfare policy is evaluated as to its effects on the target group. The same cannot be said of European countries, where this is relatively unusual.' If this is indeed the case, considerable differences might be expected. *Ringeling*, however, indicated that, despite such a lack of evaluation-mindedness, 'everything reflects the Dutch situation'. *Lövgren* said that the same applied to Sweden. *Jobst* remarked that in the Federal Republic of Germany (and perhaps in more countries) 'calculation' — Weiss' factor number three in her list of characteristics of policy-making; see under 4 — is *always* present.

Although the enlightenment model was considered a valid description of much research utilization by policy-makers in all European countries, several speakers added riders on its application. *Weiler's* 'harder look at the model itself' is set out below. Despite the remarks presented there, participants found themselves in agreement with *Husén*, who described Weiss's model as the 'most productive conceptualization presented so far'. Husén illustrated this for Sweden with two cases where social science concepts ('ability' and 'social equality') had shaped policy-makers' thinking to a very marked degree. Drastic new policies stemmed from their new views.

An interesting, frequently overlooked fact was brought out during the discussion of how policy styles with different degrees of centralization affect the utilization potential of research. It was stressed that the scope for utilization became smaller when decisions were taken in a more centralized way. The explanation for this decrease was sought in the fewer occasions on which fewer individuals made decisions in such centralized systems. Professor *Legrand*'s paper on the French situation illustrates this finding.

Other European concerns, such as the fear of many researchers of being 'absorbed by the policy machine', as *Jenzer* put it, were shared by the·US as well. *Weiss* pointed out that in the US researchers do not want to be seen, and resist very strongly being seen, as instruments of control. They see themselves in their professional identity as being independent, autonomous, free to raise criticisms of policy and provide alternative perspectives for policy-making.

Another interesting point was made by *Knudsen*, who observed that research utilization in Denmark's educational policy was relatively minor, simply because Ministry officials have little knowledge of social science research. Up to 90 per cent of the executives have been trained as lawyers. *Vorbeck* made clear that this is the case in some other European countries as well. *De Groot*'s papers for the Workshop indicate that the situation in the Netherlands is quite different: a large percentage of government officials have been trained as social scientists (but have little experience in doing research themselves). Comparative data are lacking, however. It seems plausible that research will get a better hearing when officials come from the social sciences themselves.

It was recommended that a study should be undertaken of the many kinds of organizational structures and procedures introduced by European nations to facilitate the use of research in both legislative and administrative decision-making. *Weiss* thought such a comparative study of great importance and felt that the US might learn a great deal from it.

3. A closer look at the applicability of the enlightenment model

'The influence of research appears to lie more in affecting the shape and content of policy discourse than in determining concrete choices' is the core statement in Weiss's description of the enlightenment function of research for policy-making. *In 't Veld-Langeveld* questioned the general applicability of the enlightenment model. In particular, she wondered whether the same slow and gradual filtering through process of research implications applies to major policy initiatives which are subject to evaluative research right from the start. This point, which recurred many times in different phrasings, is dealt with in section 5. Here we focus on what was said about the fundamental indirectness of the relationship between this model and the way policy decisions are made. A note of caution was injected by Weiler: 'Too easily, policy characteristics, especially its incrementalism, might be considered the "cause" of an enlightening use of research'. After stressing that this is not the case, Weiler continued: 'In Weiss' presentation the two models are closely linked: Research is used in indirect ways *because* policies are made in a disjointed and incremental manner. If we were to agree with the "rational" models of decision-making, we should presumably expect a very different pattern of research utilization.' Weiler stressed that research *always* will be used in indirect ways: 'It always has been; *ideas* have always been influential. Whether or not such a pattern of research utilization is important, does not depend on how decisions are made, and should be decoupled from decision-making models!'

It is to be noted that in this summary no further mention will be made of the intermediate enlightenment stage in the utilization of research-based knowledge. None of the speakers explicitly reverted to the topic, although knowledge transformation was acknowledged as an intrinsic feature of research utilization (*cf.* Caplan's paper).

4. A closer look at the validity of 'diffuse decision-making'

The diffuse nature of, and the multiple participation in, political decision-making, as described by Weiss, is a point repeatedly taken up and variously commented on. Here *Weiler*'s cautionary note should be recalled: the disjointed, incremental and fragmented nature of decision-making can very easily be exaggerated. While acknowledging the disjointed/incremental model as a 'healthy adjustment' of the rational models which 'were indeed overly stylized versions of reality', Weiler commented: 'But nor is it the case that policy "just happens" in ways that are too complex to be fully comprehended'. In this context it is worth recalling *Caplan*'s point about the 'instrumental' use of research by policy-makers on middle levels in the bureaucracy. There decision-making is fairly clear-cut and geared to policy decisions of limited significance. Diffuse decision-making, on the other hand, is commonly associated with macro-level processes. However, upper-level officials, who might be expected to be regularly involved in matters where diffuse decision making is supposedly the rule, report that problems of this kind make up only ten per cent of their decision load (*cf.* Caplan's paper).

A second group of comments can best be described as minor amendments to the five constructs discerned by Weiss as underlying most decision-making: boundedness, purposiveness, calculation, perceived significance and sequential order. As we have seen, *Jobst* commented that calculation is *invariably* present in political decision-making, a point worth making since Weiss had said in her report that many policy decisions emerge through processes in which one or even more elements may be almost negligible. Jobst added that a sixth element should be distinguished: whether policy-makers regard research or research results as opportune. Especially when major policy decisions are being made, as in the German debate about comprehensivization, such an element plays an important role. Finally, with regard to the element of 'perceived significance', Jobst observed that lower-ranking officials tend to overestimate the importance and consequence of their decisions.

5. The feasibility of more direct research influence

Following up certain observations in Weiss's paper, *Ringeling* pointed out that the absence of close relations between policy and research cannot be explained merely by referring to the incremental or non-rational attributes of much decision-making. Political processes, including decisions on allocating research grants, *have another type of rationality*. Ringeling illustrated this by pointing out that even a decision on whether or not to continue a social programme of questionable effectiveness will not be arrived at on the basis of perceived goal attainment alone. This kind of decision is typically governed by political expediency.

Ringeling feels we should bear in mind that a negative evaluation outcome is only one aspect of the picture. What is generally not brought out in research reports is what the plight of the target group would have been if there had been no social programme at all. Also, the attainment or non-attainment of intended effects is usually better researched than the programme's side effects.

Recommendations for improving the relationships between research and policy have to take into account that the two parties have, and should have, their own 'rationality'.

Taking up Ringeling's line of thought, *Weiler* asked whether or not we should expect policy-oriented research to achieve more than an indirect influence on decisions. Though both types of rationality seem to occur in real decision-making, Weiler suggests that we should *not* expect greater utilization until the quality and integrity of research work improve. As things stand, research logic is obviously not appealing and persuasive enough.

Mitter pointed out that research has no monopoly in giving advice to policy-makers. Other participants agreed with him and thought that research should not even try to attain such a monopoly position. Mitter annotated his remark by pointing out that in the early seventies a tendency in that direction had been noticeable. He implied that the recent conservative, restrained attitude of policy-makers towards researchers is a consequence of that tendency.

Despite all this, research performs a service, and this service can be considerably improved. Unlike Weiler, *In 'T Veld-Langeveld* believes that a greater use of this service is feasible, especially in cases where research is drawn on for specific purposes. But this improvement will only materialize when certain conditions have been fulfilled. She specifically recommended that researchers should state explicitly what policy implications their findings have. Thus, she argued, it will no longer be necessary for policy-makers to translate the findings into terms with which they can work, with selectivity and distortions inevitably creeping it. *De Groot* wholly disagreed: he does *not* want to make researchers adopt the policy-maker's language, fearing that this will lead to a harmful role confusion. His papers, included in this volume, further elaborate this point. De Groot, like Weiss and Weiler before him, indicated that the solution can best be found in the improvement of research quality.

In T' Veld-Langeveld argued that researchers need not be afraid of such role confusion, nor of the loss of academic freedom, when they produce statements about policy options and their possible consequences within the given normative framework. She considered it perfectly possible for researchers to demonstrate the consequences of government measures, given certain normative premises. To ensure a balanced presentation, researchers are in fact bound to analyze all existing and proposed policy options on the basis of various normative premises. She added that 'action oriented research' might realize this.

In this context *Klabbers*' paper is also relevant. He presented a method which aims at the same demonstration of consequences of policy options but at the same time avoids the role confusion feared by De Groot. Klabbers' method of interactive simulation considerably enhances the mutual understanding between researchers, policy-makers and other relevant parties. That such an understanding is lacking was confirmed again by *Ringeling*, who questioned the validity of Weiss's advice that better utilization should be realized through improving the quality of research itself. Adherence to scientific rationality can block effective communication between the two parties involved. Ringeling stressed that policy-makers are not primarily interested in the conceptual sophistication and methodological rigour of such a rationality, adding that, if researchers adhered to a conceptual framework of their own, this might become a major obstacle.

Weiss highlighted an important distinction in her discussion of possibilities for greater use of targeted research: 'There is a *distinction* between policy-oriented research and policy analysis that is done within the organization by the evaluation and planning units of a government agency. These in-channel analysis units are very good places for the synthesis of available research knowledge and for applying it in assessing alternative policy options. They bring the research knowledge to bear directly on specific options that people in government are considering at the current time. Outside researchers are usually not well-equipped to do that kind of thing. People either within the government or within associated units funded by the government, who are directly and daily involved with policy issues and know the constellation of interests involved, are better equipped to aggregate the information and to interpret it in terms of the specific options being considered at the time'. Weiss stressed that it would be helpful to clarify the distinction between this kind of analysis and policy-oriented research with a broader frame, a longer time perspective, and a more independent approach to issues, and concluded with this suggestion: 'The targeted applications are perhaps better handled by the analytic staff, who know the research and the political issues and who are, in a sense, linkage agents themselves'.

Weiler made the point that we should not place too much value on the significance of embedding research and analysis units in agency structures: 'This often represents only a *symbolic* commitment to scientific decision-making. The deity of science is invoked more than science is employed. Research is part of the defensive *armamentarium* of agencies' positions.'

A final point repeatedly raised in the discussion concerned the asssumption that research would be better used if policy-making were a more rational process. *Weiss* had this to say: 'In a rational process there would be more occasions where people would weigh the consequences and, therefore, there would be more opportunity for them to examine what research has to tell them about the consequences of proceeding along different lines. I think we see that kind of use much more often in centralized bureaucratic organizations, for example private industrial organizations, where a company might be trying to decide whether to build a new plant or manufacture a new product. There is on the one hand more formal assessment of the relative advantages and disadvantages of different decisions and, on the other hand, there is a more centralized decision structure. The people holding the top positions have the authority to come to a decision and see that it is implemented. In those cases, I think we do see more use of the analytic information available. I do not say that if one had a different decision-making structure, one would automatically get huge use of research, but I think there would certainly be some difference, some increase in the attention that is paid to research and analysis.'

Special Sessions

SPECIAL SESSION ONE:

What can policy-makers and subsidizing agencies learn from two decades of social science research in a political context?

Chaired by Professor W. Mitter

Note by the editors: The first section of this chapter contains information about the format and advance organization of this special session. The second section lists the invited members of the panel and the publications circulated beforehand. Some of these publications had been written specifically for this special session.

In section three the discussion is summarized around a couple of topics which were considered of prime interest to policy-makers, research-funding agencies and research directors alike. Due to constraints of time – even though this session lasted 120 minutes – , the topics were not dealt with exhaustively. More information is to be found in the papers and other discussions. For brevity's sake, information which can be found elsewhere is not repeated. This is why some participants are quoted at greater length than others.

1. Preparations and format

Special sessions were round-the-table discussions by experts held in public. Some participating experts had been asked to write one or two papers for this special session. These are listed below. Others submitted a recent publication pertinent to the issues of this session. Both types of documents were circulated in advance. A particular effort was made to ensure that the most relevant specialisms were represented. In this case these were policy-makers, directors of national funding agencies, leading research directors and utilization experts. Moreover, the Programme Committee made sure that panel members mostly had wide experience in at least two of these specialisms. Potential role switching was felt to be of inherent importance for an effective definition of crucial problems in commissioning policy-oriented research. Authors of invited papers opened the discussion with introductory statements. Other participants of the Workshop were able to address the panel during the last thirty minutes.

2. Participating experts/Publications circulated in advance

Invited experts

1) N. Caplan; Center for Research on Utilization of Scientific Knowledge (CRUSK), University of Michigan, USA
2) W.B. Dockrell; Council for Research in Education, Edinburgh, UK
3) A.D. de Groot; University of Groningen, The Netherlands
4) L. Legrand; ex-Director of the Institut National de la Recherche Pédagogique, Professor at Strasbourg's Université Louis Pasteur, France*
5) E. Jobst; Ministerialrat, Bund-Länder-Kommission für Bildungsplanung und Forschungsförderung, Bonn, Federal Republic of Germany
6) J.A. van Kemenade; ex-Minister of Education, Professor at University of Groningen, The Netherlands*
7) E. Lövgren; National Swedish Board of Education, Stockholm, Sweden
8) J. Scheerens; Executive Staff-member of the Foundation for Educational Research in The Netherlands (SVO), The Hague, The Netherlands
9) C.W. van Seventer; Director of the Foundation for Educational Research in the Netherlands (SVO), The Hague, The Netherlands*
10) M. Timpane; ex-Director National Institute for Work and Learning, Washington, currently Dean of Teacher's College, Columbia University, New York, USA
11) D. Weiler; former member of the California Commission on Education Management and Evaluation, currently Senior Vice-President Manifest International, Berkeley, California, USA
12) CHAIRMAN: W. Mitter, Deutsches Institut für Internationale Pedagogische Forschung, Direktor des Forschungskollegiums, Frankfurt a. M., Federal Republic of Germany.

Invited publications

1. Prof A.D. de Groot — An English Summary of two Dutch Articles on: Research as a Learning Process and Policy as a Learning Environment.
2. Prof A.D. de Groot — Wanted: An Adequate Interface Between Policy and Research.

---

*Was not able to attend the session itself.

3. Prof T. Husén – Two partners with Communication Problems: Researchers and Policy-Makers in Education.
   (Draft on an unpublished article. Not included in this volume.)
4. Dr E. Jobst – Educational Research in the Federal Republic of Germany.
   (Not included in this volume; available on request at S.V.O.)
5. Drs J. Scheerens – Evaluation Research: Political and Organizational Constraints.
6. Drs J. Scheerens – The Functioning of Policy-Oriented Research within Some Major Innovatory Programs in Dutch Education.
7. Dr M. Timpane – a new federal policy for disseminating educational R&D in the United States.
8. Dr M. Timpane – Into the Maw: The Uses of Policy in Washington. *Phi Delta Kappa*, 58, 2, October 1976.
9. Dr D. Weiler and M. Stearns – The Uses and Limits of Education Evaluation at the State Level.
   In: PINCUS, John (Ed.), *Educational evaluation in the Public Policy Setting*. Santa Monica, Calif: The Rand Corporation; R-2502-RC; May 1980.

Numbers 1 to 7 were written at the invitation of the Programme Committee. Some of the nine documents have not been included due to publishing restrictions. However, they are available on request at SVO, The Netherlands.

3. Discussion

3.1 Organizational independence: a central theme

From experience with policy-oriented research in some major educational innovation projects in The Netherlands, *Scheerens* argued in favour of 'organizational conditions that guarantee a certain amount of *independence* for policy-oriented research'. Such an independence could be realized if specific attention were given to the following three points:

a) Researchers should take an active part in defining the research problems.
b) There should be less interference (by committees) with the actual research carried out.
c) Researchers must have more time and facilities for realizing an optimal quality in their work.

These three topics were dealt with extensively. The summaries below are all related to these three aspects of this central theme of independence.

Participants appeared to share the feeling that policy-making can best be served by fairly autonomous organizational structures for policy-oriented research.

Note by the editors: The distinction between 'policy-oriented research' and 'policy analysis' as made by Weiss (see section 5 of the discussion following her paper) should be kept in mind. This special session dealt with policy-oriented research only.

De Groot argued that greater independence from the policy-makers is an indispensable condition for maintaining the scientific standards without which policy-oriented research does not really contribute to the solving of problems. De Groot emphasized the point of view – expressed in his first paper – that the organizational structure in which evaluation and policy research in general are carried out, can be seen as a learning environment. Research is considered a collective and public learning process. The output of this learning process consists of 'learning effects' in the individual participants in research activities.

De Groot argued that the two systems involved – research and policy – are organizationally too much intertwined, causing 'social entropy'. Both policy-makers and researchers tend to learn the wrong things if not clearly separated. For the Netherlands in particular, a redefinition and disentanglement of the roles of policy-makers and researchers in policy-oriented research are called for. Several important shortcomings of the existing situation in the Netherlands – role confusion, inadequate types of egalitarianism, advisory committeeism, methodological alternativism, inflated notions of expertise – are discussed in De Groot's two papers and illustrated in Scheerens' description of the situation in The Netherlands. Many of these shortcomings were considered to apply to other countries, as well.

In order to decrease the social entropy in the existing organizational structure of policy-oriented research, De Groot strongly recommended that in the pertinent policy preparation, organization experts should be consulted. This might lead to a clearer separation of political and administrative responsibilities (as is the case in Sweden where the National Board of Education was instituted with this separation in mind). De Groot considers it the national Government's duty to initiate a series of measures which will lead to this separation of responsibilities and thereby promote a sound development of the social sciences.

3.2 Research and decision-making

Weiler addressed himself to the question of what could be achieved through educational research. He provided an overview of its successes and failures which might lead to a more effective development of research commissioning. In his view there are four *kinds* of decisions that decision-makers must make:

1) They have to decide what programmes to initiate
2) They have to decide what practices each programme should be required to emphasize, once a programme is initiated
3) They must make decisions about how much support, how much money, to allocate to each programme relative to all other programmes in a given budget category, and
4) They must try to find out how to regulate, manage and assist programmes.

'These are four very different decision-making functions, and perhaps we could invent other such lists, but the point of my remarks is that it is useful in these discussions, at some point, to stop speaking in a very general sense and ask what kinds of decision we are talking about, and in what respects research can be valuable to different kinds of decisions.

'In brief, my opinion about each of these areas is as follows: I think that it is quite possible for research to give very good assistance to decision-makers, when they need to find out what programmes are in need of initiation. We talked earlier about the importance of surveys, and there are I think, many examples of surveys which have pinpointed a problem, have let us know that there is an area in society where there is a deficiency, according to our values, and that some programme may well be in order to combat that deficiency. I think that sort of research has done well in education and in other social areas, and I think highly of it.

'I think it is much more difficult in education to know what programme practices to emphasize, and I think it is more difficult because this requires research about what works in education, and that is very difficult research to do. In the US at least, it has not been done successfully very often. It is expensive, time consuming, it is not done best to a legislative or agency deadline and there are a number of other reasons which I think would take too much of our time to go into.

'Perhaps the research that is least valuable, in my own opinion, is research on the issue of how to allocate support among programmes. Yet, on the face of it, this appears to be historically the research that has received the most support, and I think it is the weakest kind of research. It is very, very difficult to evaluate educational programmes in ways which will give reliable information about the relative effectiveness of that programme, compared to other programmes. Programmes are set up to do different things. That kind of research, if indeed it is to be reliable, requies some form of experimental or quasi-experimental method, which is difficult, if not impossible, under the sort of field-circumstances in which educational research takes place, and on the whole I think it has not been very successful.

'Research which can assist decision-makers in their quest for ideas about how to regulate and manage and assist programmes, I think has been more successful. This is what I would call formative research and I think it can be very useful.'

The funding mode in the US and other countries, however, is such that the strong and weak aspects of educational research are hardly taken into account. In section 3.3. recommendations for improvement are put forward. Here, it seems worthwhile to provide the context of Weiler's observations by quoting *Timpane* who gave a more historical and political perspective on educational research which might help us to compare or contrast experiences.

'While all the mistakes mentioned have been made in the US, I would suggest that the US government officials have now, in the past ten to 15 years invested in the order of two billion dollars* into educational research, and that there are no organizational or structural disabilities nor any other disability which provide educational research with any reason not to be accountable politically for the expenditure of that money. Moreover, R and D is going to be judged, politically, roughly by a linear model we all think inaccurate, called RD, D and E. While it certainly is not the case that our piece of research which ought to lead to a piece of development, ought to lead to a piece of demonstration, which should then be evaluated and looped back, I think it is absolutely fair for the political process to ask the aggregate and longitudinal questions: You have been doing all this research: What on earth has become of it? Have any of your developments produced new important features in the classroom that, at least roughly, you can tell us about? And so forth. American educational research is at that point where the questions being asked are appropriate questions for political accountability at this stage.

'The second point I will make is that educational research in the US has failed to gain strong political support. There are historical and idiosyncratic reasons which happen to be quite important to the story in the US having to do with a clash between a particular powerful congressman and particular federal officials. The only statement I make about that is that when an episode like that occurs, as it did several years ago, politicians have tremendously long memories, and a serious incident like that lives on forever in the political memory. The point is, avoid the tragic confrontational misunderstanding; it can haunt you for decades. But secondly and as significantly, educational research has failed to gain a strong constituency following. It is not highly valued by most of the actors in the politics of education in the US. It has overcome, in their view, the early disabilities.

Note by the editors: This amounts to only half of one per cent of all educational expenditure in the US. This relatively low level of funding occurs in the United Kingdom and the Netherlands as well. In some other European countries – like France – it might even be lower.

People no longer think of educational research as a laughing stock or an embarrassment to them. But they simply do not value it politically. As I was fond of saying, by the time NIE finished improving its stewardship of educational research, it had moved up to being sixth on a list of four items that the educational establishment was willing to support. It was a nice activity, but not one that anyone was ever willing to pay a political price for, relative to other interests at stake.

'These two points suggest that we should not underestimate the significance of political leadership for the research community. The research community must legitimate someone to take political leadership.

'My third point is simply that, paradoxically, educational and social science research have had an enormous impact on educational policy in the US in the last 20 years. The educational components of the War on Poverty, for example, were almost entirely based on social science conceptions. Both Head-Start, and Compensatory Education Programmes were based roughly on deficiency and remediation theories, many of them transported at the time from youth and rehabilitation projects, so that the entire structure of federal education programmes was built on social science conceptions.

'Moreover, as time went along, general applications of micro-economic theory were prominent in continuing policy decisions. The very rise of social experimentation and that of evaluation as legislative activities of the federal government were certainly derived therefrom, as were some of the substantive issues, such as vouchers and the transfer of higher education support in the US from institutional subvention to the subvention of the buying student.

'But one of these areas — evaluation — came back 'to soil the nest' with over-ambitious, premature and inappropriate use of large-scale social science methodologies to perform nationwide evaluations on these new and paltry, and unstable and unimplemented federal programmes. These evaluations produced — hardly had the programmes been initiated — a wave of reaction against them, which has persisted almost to this day.

'Gradually I think, we have begun to recover from the point counterpoint, boom-boom. We have developed painfully the building blocks for a new strategy for the use of research. Let me just give an extended example: the evaluation of the compensatory education programmes.

'The first evaluation was hastily conceived and executed, on programmes which had barely been installed under a series of very vague guidelines. Predictably, it failed to find any effect. A second evaluation undertook to remedy that shortcoming by producing the world's most perfect and elaborate regression equation which would find those effects. It was to be on a massive scale of sampling and measurement and to be longitudinal over several years time, to address all the methodological shortcomings and show what the effects were. When last sighted — and there may be more current information on that — that programme, which I believe cost

15 to 20 million dollars, was drowning in a sea of data. It was never clear that it was going to find any stronger outcome variable upon which to hang all of the other data, than had the first study. The third evaluation finally had some impact, and it did it by asking (and this is a point which is opposite to much of what has been said during the Workshop) a series of much less interesting questions from a scientific point of view, than had either of the first two studies.

'It began by consorting with the decision-makers, deeply, from the outset and continually during the study. Its design divided the operations of the programme into the distribution of the resources, the administration of the programme, the implementation of the programme and finally the effects of the programme.

'It assumed that the logic of decision-making went as follows: Did the money get there? Answer yes or no. If no, further questions are not allowed. If yes, was the programme reasonably well-administered and complied with? If no, stop and correct the situation; no further questions. If yes, proceed. Was the programme reasonably faithfully implemented in its operational setting? If yes, proceed. If no, stop and correct. Fourth, if the programme has arrived, is well complied with and faithfully implemented — if all those circumstances obtain — do those projects work? That was the logic of the decision-makers in this programme and the logic of sequential and contingent analysis. For this perspective, it did no good to know the average effect of the programme across all the projects, or even a sampling of the projects, because the decision-makers did not care. They only cared if all the "ifs" were positively answered. So, separate studies were done of resource allocations, of compliance, of implementation and of effective projects. A great deal of survey and descriptive analysis resulted and very little evaluative research. This study was used beyond the experience of any previous evaluation. It was used in the halls of Congress, in the committee rooms. When they were drafting the legislation, the lawyer who had done the compliance analysis in the study, sat at the table. This approach involved a rather fundamental accommodation between research and policy. In addition then, to our observation that there should be a balance between basic and applied research, for the overall health, vigour and quality of our research, perhaps we must — when the time comes to do a piece of applied work for the decision-makers — start with their questions and do whatever study is most appropriate to answering them, not trying to carry over into that context all of the apparatus and all of the methodological concerns which we might otherwise prefer.'

3.3 Improving the quality and relevance of policy-oriented research

The subject of 'bad research' came up on many occasions during the Workshop. In this special session, *Mitter* observed that self-criticism can be too strong, resulting in a situation where government officials refuse to negotiate with the scientific community which thus plays itself out of the game. *Timpane* felt that educational researchers unnecessarily have an inferiority complex when comparing themselves with other scientists. In his own words:

> In the US, and I suspect in many other countries, educational research labours under an inferiority complex because of the burden of the mythology of pure science. Most policy-makers and decision-makers and the public at large in the US have the idea that pure science knows how to do research and other people do not. If you asked, they would have the idea, without knowing much about it, that in physics, in chemistry, most experiments obviously show good results. I think the history of experimental science is quite the opposite; science and chemistry and biology, most of our inquiries, most experiments, fail to disprove the null hypothesis, shall we say; and it is the rare experiment, in any science, that shows a dramatic finding. Most often the findings are modest and ambiguous. Yet there is a contrast drawn and I am afraid it is a contrast in myth, more than in fact. For example, Richard Light at Harvard did a large-scale survey several years ago, comparing policy and evaluative research done in the areas of health, education and criminal justice. The person in the street in the US and certainly the person in power, would certainly have imagined that health research was both methodologically superior, and qualitatively better in execution and result, than education; and of course Richard Light found no such thing. He found that educational research, in design and execution, was every bit as good. But there is an inferiority complex, if you will, amongst educational researchers, because of this burden of science. I would be interested to know if comparable attitudes occur in other countries as well.

De Groot answered this last question for the Netherlands by observing that educational researchers in The Netherlands — both those aiming at 'pure science' and the equally numerous applied educational researchers — do not often seem to suffer from such an inferiority complex. Nevertheless, it has to be observed that the questioning by funding agents and research directors of the quality and relevance of policy-oriented research does occur all the time.

Dockrell mitigated the observation that some research is bad in the following, somewhat bantering way:

> I disagree with that. All research is bad research, in the sense that it is imperfect. Everybody is imperfect, except possibly you and me. I mean everybody else is imperfect, and so we have to live with a situation where we recognize that our own work, everybody's work, is inadequate

in some ways and has limitations. My question is: how do we handle this particular factor of human life, and to perhaps misquote Orwell, 'some pigs are more equal than others', and some researchers are more equal than others, and it is important that the status, prestige, of a researcher, does not overlay the competence of a particular piece of research. As you know, we have had a recent scandal in the UK on that particular issue and I think it is very *broadminded* of me to say the UK and not England. It was not only them, it was us it affected too. So, my question would be: how can we ensure that the sponsors, whoever they may be, are aware of the limitations and advantages of what is likely to be sound in what we have reported to them?

Having understood that 'bad research often is not so bad, after all', the Workshop participants in this Special Session turned back to Scheerens' recommendation (*cf.* section 3.1) that research should have a more active part in defining the questions it should tackle. *Caplan* elaborated on this when he pointed out that research had often been focused on the *wrong issues*. 'There has been a lesson learned, in that there is a missing link . . . between the programme as conceived and planned and allegedly put out to be carried out, and the programme that actually will be evaluated. . . Once out in the field, a programme takes hold in many different ways, and unless one — in addition to having an impact assessment — also follows, assesses and evaluates the implementation of the treatment and the programme, you may find that later on you are under the impression that you have evaluated one thing, and in fact you really have not.' This *broadened conception* of evaluation is difficult to get funded, though. As *Weiler* set out before, the funding mode (in the US) is such that most money that comes for the funding of evaluation is money that comes with the programme. It is almost always part of the programme appropriation. Because of this close association with the programme itself, the research dollar must nominally be spent for the narrow aims of programme evaluation. 'And yet I have maintained that those are the aims which are least likely to be filled successfully by research in the present state of the art.' Weiler underscores that decision-makers need to know about the workings of a particular programme, and while they need to know that, they need to know other things as well, and primarily they need to have much more profound knowledge, than knowledge about how a particular programme works. They need knowledge about how schools really work, how change takes place, about how growth occurs in these very complex social organizations that deliver educational services. They need to know what the role of local agencies can be in promoting that kind of change and educational improvement.

'It has been my experience that government agencies rarely ask these questions directly. They are more likely, as I have noted, to ask questions about the specifics of a particular programme, to ask whether a program works or not. I think that is a mis-specified question and that it is up to the research community very often to enter into a dialogue with decision-makers to see if the question cannot be asked in a vein which will yield much richer results than can be yielded if the focus is kept too narrow.

'I want to close by speaking directly on an issue from my own experience, that illustrates this point and I think it may be of interest to Dr Scheerens also. There was an experiment begun in the US with what are loosely called education vouchers. It would take us too much time to elaborate the various versions of that. Suffice it to say that an experiment was begun and as usual there was confusion between the initiative that the government took as an experiment and the intiative as a demonstration. Dr Scheerens talked about that confusion to some extent.

'It was in fact not an experiment in the classic sense, but an attempt to demonstrate that vouchers could be successful in a school district, so that the programme could be enlarged. I was charged with the evaluation of this demonstration and I began by mis-specifying what was happening. I treated this and conceived of what was happening as a test of the effects of a treatment. And it only gradually dawned on me (those were days when I was a good deal more innocent, I like to think) that this was a totally wrong way of conceiving what was going on. This was not in fact a treatment. A treatment is something that can be described very concretely and specifically. It is a particular set of activities under circumstances where you are aware of or can control all other possible sets of activities that could influence an outcome, and you are able to make some approximation at least, of the effects of that intervention of the results. In the situation in a school district, a government programme in this case, as in other cases, is a sum of money and a loose agreement about how it is to be spent. That is not a treatment and it could not be studied like that. So there was originally a complete misunderstanding, based, I think – to pick up a notion of Dr Timpane – on a misapplication of scientific method, of what exactly was happening, and it was more to the point to try to understand the total process of implementation and the role of local factors in influencing that outcome, as well as the very limited role that the federal agency was able to play. Since that time, much research in the US, some of which I have participated in, has found over and over again, that this is true.

'So I think it is terribly important, again, to broaden the question, and that if policy-makers are not in a position to fund the kind of research that will give them insight into the kind of changes that take place in social systems, then I think it is up to the research community to insist that that is the kind of question that needs to be asked, and as has been noted before, to save a little part of the pie to do that, or better yet, take a very large part of the pie and do it anyway.'

3.4 Case studies and generalization

Dockrell suggested inserting a fourth question for administrators into Weiler's list of kinds of decisions that policy-makers must make (*cf.* section 3.2 above), and that is: 'What did actually happen? Dockrell explained his point with reference to the middle school project:

> We can in fact provide descriptive case studies of what actually went on in particular, in our case in schools, or in institutions of various kinds....
> 'The fact that they all would be different, makes them more valuable . . . and makes them more valuable as case studies and provides more information. It is a kind of research that we have been doing more and more of in my own (Scottish) council for the last ten years. I do not want to go into details of this but it does refer back again to the keynote address, to Suppes' point about the generalizations. What kind of generalizations can one make and especially about human behaviour, where it is so variable and where it is influenced by many factors? It seems to me – since the kind of generalizations we can make are always probablistic as Suppes said – that generalizations can better be used on case studies than they can on other kinds of data, perhaps even survey data.

Several speakers considered this a valuable suggestion, but also drew attention to the danger of exaggerating the use of case studies, despite the fact that educational researchers – as *Weiler* put it – 'have been at a disadvantage compared with their brethren in history, when it comes to case studies'. Weiler thinks that we are at some point in a cycle of reaction against quantitative research, and 'it would be too bad if the necessity to support and argue on behalf of good qualitative research, blinded us to the continuing necessity for good quantitative research to go hand in hand with good case studies'. *Timpane* concluded 'We have, especially for policy research purposes, greatly underestimated the significance of careful and perceptive descriptive analysis, both quantitative and qualitative'. He furthermore stressed that 'good descriptive analysis can reveal many of the elementary issues of fact without which the decision-maker is unwilling to proceed to what we might think of as the more elegant questions of cause and effect. At stake here is the question of 'adequacy', adequacy in tackling the pertinent problem.' In the previous section we have seen the 'right issues' in evaluation matters are difficult to get by. More use of descriptive analysis might improve that situation.

3.5 Basic and applied research

The issue of the balance between basic and applied research cropped up on many occasions. *Husén* though that 'at least on this side of the Atlantic, we have learned to keep a proper balance between research conducted within the close framework of policy-making and research that is more fundamental and basic'. This becomes clearer when we keep in mind that in certain countries like Sweden research funding has been organized in such a way that much research can be carried out — mostly within University settings — without policy demands or any interference from outside. *Mitter* pointed out that such a division of funding need not necessarily lead to two kinds of research. Furthermore, it has been proved that 'fundamental' research can become 'policy-oriented'. Mitter illustrated this with the German case of 'oriental studies' (like Turkish language and literature) which became all of a sudden very relevant for policy-makers when the influence of Turkish migrant workers called for better understanding of these people's way of life. In the case of the United Kingdom even a percentage of the funds available for policy-oriented research is reserved — in principle at least — for carrying out research to which no strings are attached. As *Dockrell* put it:

> The research in Britain, both physical science and social science, is supposed to be based, I think still, on the Rothschild report. One of the recommendations is that practical projects should be commissioned, but provision should be made in the budget for ten per cent to permit the particular kind of studies that allow the researcher to carry out studies which he himself finds of interest.

But this idea does not seem to live amongst researchers. Dockrell said: 'I have yet to find a research proposal that has that ten per cent written in'.

The Workshop participants felt that the critical function of research was best safeguarded within the context of research that is carried out on the basis of researchers' interest in particular phenomena. However, the existence of an infrastructure of what Husén termed 'safely seated professors who are in a position to be critical' does not mean that this has necessarily an effect on policy and practice, said *de Groot*. He feels that 'in the Dutch situation such an infrastructure does exist, but is not consulted, not listened to — maybe to a large extent because of the fact that it does not speak'. According to de Groot, government appears hardly to be interested in promoting the development of such a critical scientific 'forum' while many academics lack interest in matters that are 'contaminated' by politics.

SPECIAL SESSION TWO:

Research into the interplay between social science research and policy making in the 1980s: inventory and prospects

Chaired by Professor T. Husén

Note by the editors: The first section of this chapter contains information about the preparation and format of the special session of the Workshop. The second section lists the invited members of the discussion panel and the publications circulated in advance. The special session on current and future research into the interplay between the social sciences and policy-making was used predominantly as an opportunity for the panel members to amplify the brief position statements they had submitted. The main points made by each of the panel members are summarized in section 3. The proposals arising from the panel's discussion with the CCC delegates and other experts are also recorded there. Please note that the panel members did not deal with the planned 'inventory' aspect of this session. However, a selective list of current research in this field had been prepared by the host organization SVO and was distributed at the Workshop. The list and some relevant bibliographies prepared for the Workshop (see Appendix C) are available on request.

1. Format

The Special Sessions took the form of public round-the-table discussions by invited experts. A particular effort had been made to ensure that a range of specialisms were represented: philosophy of science and science dynamics, utilization research, policy studies, and methodology of the social sciences. Chairman of these sessions were selected for their broad knowledge of developments in the fields of educational research and policy making in their widest sense. Some recent publications relevant to the topic of the Special Session and written by the invited experts were sent to participants in advance of the Workshop. Brief position statements served as guidelines for the discussion itself.

2. Participating experts/publications circulated in advance

Invited experts:

1) N. Caplan; Center for Research on Utilization of Scientific Knowledge (CRUSK), University of Michigan, USA.
2) J.H.G. Klabbers; Futures Research Unit, Dept. of Social and Organizational Psychology, Leiden University, Leiden, The Netherlands.
3) Inger Marklund; Secretary of the Swedish Governmental Commission on Educational R&D, University of Uppsala, Sweden.
4) Marc De May; Associate Professor in Science Studies, University of Gent, Belgium.
5) Martin Rein; Dept. of Urban Studies and Planning, Massachusetts Institute of Technology (MIT), Cambridge, Mass., USA.
6) A.B. Ringeling; Political Sciences, Erasmus University, Rotterdam, The Netherlands.
7) Patrick Suppes; Institute for Mathematical Studies in Social Sciences of Stanford University, Stanford, Calif. USA.
8) Carol Weiss; Sociology of Knowledge Application, Graduate School of Education, Harvard University, USA.
9) CHAIRMAN: Torsten Husén; Institute of International Education, University of Stockholm, Stockholm, Sweden.

Publications circulated in advance:

1) Prof H.H.G. KLABBERS *et al.* (1980). 'Development of an Interactive Simulation Game; A Case Study of DENTIST.' In: KLABBERS *Simulation & Games.* Vol. II, No. 1, March, 59–86.
2) Dr M. de Mey (1980). 'The Interaction between Theory and Data in Science; Exploring a New Model for Perception in an Application to Harvey's Discovery of the Circulation of the Blood.' In: KNORR, Karin D., KROHN, Roger and WHITLEY, Richard (eds.) (1980). 'The Social Process of Scientific Investigation.' *Sociology of the Sciences*, IV, 3–23.
3) Prof M. REIN. (1980). 'Methodology for the Study of the Interplay between Social Science and Social Policy', *Int. Soc. Sci. J.*, XXXII, 2, 361–368.
4) Prof. C.H. WEISS. (1980). 'Knowledge Creep and Decision Accretion.' In: *Knowledge: Creation, Diffusion, Utilization.* 1, 3, March, 381–404.

3. Summaries

WEISS:

Weiss considered it somewhat premature to suggest future directions for research on knowledge use. Commenting on the Workshop, she explained: 'I feel that I have learned so much in these past two days that I have not yet digested'. However, she suggested that it would be useful to collect cross-cultural information and mentioned three possible lines of research:

1) The difference between the use of research by people in political and administrative positions, and its use by people who are engaged in direct delivery service, those actually implementing social programmes. She explained: 'It seems to me that there may be other ways in which teachers absorb research knowledge and integrate it into their experience and their practice, but which we do not yet fully comprehend. ... Some research on the differences between doing research that is practice-oriented and doing research that is policy-oriented might be useful.'

2) The development of methods of empirical inquiry into the uses of social science research that do not depend on immediate and direct applications of research results to decision-making. Weiss clarified this suggestion, which had also been proposed by Caplan in his paper, as follows: 'As we understand more about the diffuse uses of research, where the impact is not on the decision but on the frame of discourse, the terms of understanding, the re-definition of the problem, and other such diffuse kinds of impact, we need new methods to study the consequences of research for policy action'.

3) Undertaking a study of the consultant structures in different countries, specifically of the use of social scientists as consultants. This was felt to be a fruitful direction for future research because much might be learned by comparing the structural arrangements through which different countries bring in experts during the consultative processes that precede government action.

DE MEY:

De Mey was strongly in favour of keeping in touch with, and actively cooperating in, developments in the area of what has been called 'science dynamics'. In the Netherlands this is a 'most relevant development' which has been going on for some time and which is shortly to be formally recognized through the establishment of a Chair of Science Dynamics. De Mey stated that 'the recurrent discovery is that the utilization of knowledge is closely connected to its construction'. He clarified this by reference to the background paper which he had submitted for this special session (see section 2 above). This background paper, while dealing with 'the "old" case of Harvey', explored one aspect of the new philosophy of science that is now developing. In particular, it analysed an interactive and integrative model of perception that incorporates the subject's contribution in any process of knowledge acquisition. At the same time, a new theory of perception is only one aspect of the new model of knowledge production. Current developments in what is called 'science studies' or social studies of science' emphasize the socially constructed nature of scientific knowledge. Scientific specialisms, rather than disciplines, are the focus of attention here. Knowledge claims are related to the 'invisible colleges' that explore and cultivate a particular scheme or line of approach.

De Mey went on to discuss the decline of the 'orthodox' or 'received' view in the philosophy of science, referred to in several papers and considered by Suppes in his keynote address in terms of the basic tenets of the metaphysics of philosophy and science. This decline in the orthodox view, combined with the expansion of the sociology of science as an alternative approach, gives rise to the possibility of developing a genuine 'science of science' which might be better suited to assessing the applicability of scientific knowledge.... The Advisory Council for Science Policy in the Netherlands (RAWB) had recognized the importance of this trend towards a new model of science. . . As this new model challenges deeply rooted but fundamentally confused distinctions between internal and external factors in scientific development, cognitive versus social factors, it may be hoped that it will also lead to new insights into the relation between scientific knowledge and its utilization. What is involved is a new conceptualization of the notions of knowledge and 'use'. The new field of science dynamics could be important, not only in providing revealing case studies, but also by proving that, with regard to knowledge use, it is once again true that 'there is nothing as practically useful as a good theory'.

REIN

Related to De Mey's recommendations for a science dynamics approach was Rein's suggestion that before new research proposals were designed the traditional utilization question should be rephrased. To make such a redefinition possible, Rein introduced two concepts to help elucidate his ideas. The first, in his own words, was: 'I think we need a concept called the "frame", which does the following: it brings together and integrates theory, facts, values, interests and action...

I would argue that the field of policy is really a debate about multiple frames for alternative courses of action. But it is also the case that research itself is about multiple frames. Research does not ride above frames, but it, too, is imprisoned in them. So, one could talk about practice frames which grow out of the policy debate, but also about disciplinary frames which are tied to interests and action.'

The second concept Rein proposed for redefining the utilization problem was 'discourse'. He made a clear distinction between this concept and 'dialogue': 'It is possible to have a dialogue within a frame in which you and I agree on the action implications. But I believe that the most important question is not dialogue, but discourse. What I define as discourse takes place when you are dealing with conflicting frames in which the action implications and the inquiry processes are subject to different action positions.' The relationship between inquiry and policy 'has in fact to do with discourse across frames. So, if one wants to understand the role of policy and the role of research, it has to be done within the framework of what I would call discourse.'

Another of Rein's points deserves mention here: the role of the mass media, a topic which has not yet been studied in detail in knowledge utilization research. Rein believes that 'the media play a critical role as a nexus in generating communication between individuals that are engaged in this frame discourse. . . . Every important policy question must affect established interests and hence is politically controversial. If policy research enters this arena, the question it poses, the methods it uses and its findings are also likely to become politicized. This can be seen when, for example, disagreements among experts can be traced to their different purposes and interests. The media play an important role, making public the exchange of the views and the different interests, including the disagreements among experts. To improve the utilization of policy research we must better understand this process of politically engaged discourse.'
Note by the editors: The role of the media was also discussed by Caplan in relation to the conceptual use of knowledge by top policy makers (*cf.* Caplan's paper).

Klabbers

Klabbers pointed out that the method 'interactive simulation games' developed by himself and others could be used for organizing the 'discourse across frames' proposed by Rein. All interested parties, policymakers, practitioners, researchers and so on, 'come in with their own world models, their own frames, in a setting in which knowledge is in action'. Klabbers believed that in this way a highly relevant contribution could be made to improving the interface between research and policymaking since research proposals put forward as one of the outcomes of a 'frame game' would be more relevant for policy than those formulated in the traditional way. Also, a more direct use of research results might thereby be realized. Klabbers proposed that one of the directions to be pursued by utilization research in the 1980s should be a systematic study of knowledge use through interactive simulation games.

Ringeling

Ringeling made no specific recommendation for directions in utilization research but suggested a series of points which should be borne in mind in carrying out policy-oriented research and research on the interplay between policy and science. Ringeling emphasized the following main points:

- policy makers cannot be localized as such (*cf.* Weiss's 'boundedness' in her analysis of decision-making);
- it might be worthwhile to inventory the reasons why policy-makers and practitioners accept or reject research outcomes;
- both the policy world and the research world have the characteristics of a market; the commissioning of research should be understood against that background;
- a number of trends in the development of organizational structures for policy-oriented research should be inventoried and analyzed (e.g. the bureaucratization of research in the Netherlands);
- it would be worthwhile for policy-oriented researchers to project themselves every now and then into the role of policy-makers and, on the other hand, to adopt the perspective of pure, fundamental research.

Caplan

Caplan observed that 'conceptually an enormous amount of progress has been made at this conference' and time was needed to digest this. He recommended that researchers should make far greater use of case studies, and that they should abandon the 'semantic ordeal' going on in the field and seek international agreement on important terms. Also, researchers should in the future 'accentuate the positive more than has been done in the past... I think that we know a great deal more than we allow ourselves to admit, and we often equivocate and are apologetic about how little we know.' Finally, Caplan stressed that the distinction he had drawn between instrumental and conceptual utilization should be kept in mind.

Marklund

Marklund drew attention to a distinction which was often lost sight of: the influence that research use has on policy must not be confused with policy-oriented research, that is research specifically undertaken in the context of policy-making. Either type of research may or may not be commissioned, and care should be taken over the distinction between the two types in planning utilization studies.

Like several other participants of this Special Session, Marklund urged that cross-national studies and case studies should be undertaken. Furthermore, she argued that the 'decision maker' is not always the same person as the 'policy-maker'. More attention to the policy-making processes and their implications for utilization research was required. Also, utilization studies too often overlook the fact that research too is a process – perhaps even as diffuse as policy-making itself. More systematic attention should be given to the genesis, growth and finalization of research proposals, and to how these are carried out and the results communicated.

Discussion with other participants

Husén said that he himself was conducting a study of the way researchers related to the policy communities in four countries, West German, the UK, Sweden and the US. *Van Seventer* suggested that it might be useful to include the Netherlands as well.

Mitter — like Legrand before him — recommended that more explicit attention should be given to practitioners and organizations like parents' associations in dealing with policy analysis and utilization matters. He also made a case for bringing in a wider variety of disciplines, such as history and linguistics, in research dealing with educational policy making and policy analysis.

Weiler pointed out that 'the research community is in the habit of presenting formal findings on structured research to the policy community, and the debate then takes the form of asking the question 'how does the policy community make use of formal findings? Do they act on them directly? Do they absorb and use them in some more indirect way? etc".' Weiler said that among the research and evaluation community in the US there was strong resistance to breaking down the barriers of formal interaction between the two communities. More attention should be paid to this and attempts made to bring researchers and policy makers closer together.

Sandbergen proposed that a comprehensive study should be undertaken to analyse the different types of research which might be applicable to various stages of decision-making processes. Ingrid *Eide* emphasized the need to pay more attention to some important sectors of policy-making, namely political parties and their programmes, which policy-oriented researchers in education had so far ignored. She also observed that universities, even more than policy communities, were guilty of ignoring educational research outcomes.

De Groot felt that social and behavioural scientists — in particular educational researchers — should attempt to conduct research in a similar way to colleagues in the 'hard' sciences. He referred in particular to the need to construct 'a body of basic knowledge, formulated in standard terminology'. The social sciences seemed systematically to worsen their communication with the general public and target groups such as policy makers: 'Every theoretician uses his own, or at least his school's technical terms . . . and younger theorists and researchers are rewarded when they are "original" enough to create new models, new concepts and coin new terms'. De Groot therefore proposed that a start should be made towards 'some agreement on a few basic conceptualizations, and towards standardizing a few basic terms internationally'. He added: 'This proposal may seem very pedestrian and to involve laborious and uncreative work, and it can hardly be called a research proposal. But for the sake of communicating more fruitfully with audiences, we have to do something about what I consider to be the main ailment of our sciences: the lack of diachronic and synchronic coherence and consistency in our theory and conceptual production.'

Marklund added that the standardization of terms should lead to a multilingual thesaurus of 'core concepts' to enable researchers also to employ the correct terminology when using another language.

Weiss, Rein and others expressed the hope that the conference would 'institute a mechanism for further exchanges so that the very fruitful discussions that we have had during these few days can be continued in an organized context'. The Workshop participants therefore unanimously welcomed the initiative of the Foundation for Educational Research in the Netherlands (SVO) to launch a Special Interest Group as a future communication channel.

APPENDIX A

Address Directory

(Full addresses of all participants are listed in section 8)

1) Organizer

The workshop was organized by Drs Gerard B. Kosse with the assistance of Drs H.C. Wagenaar, both executive staff members of SVO, with the technical assistance of the Ministry of Education and Science, under the auspices of the Secretary General of the Council of Europe and the Foundation for Educational Research in The Netherlands (SVO)
Address: Pletterijkade 50, 2515 SH The Hague, The Netherlands
Correspondence: P.O. Box 19050, 2500 CB The Hague, The Netherlands
Telephone: (070)824321
Director: Drs C.W. van Seventer

2) Authors of invited papers

Caplan, Dr N.; Center for research on Utilization of Scientific Knowledge (CRUSK), University of Michigan, Ann Arbor, Michigan, USA
Dockrell, Dr W.B.; Council for Research in Education, 15 St. John Street, Edinburgh EH8 8JR, United Kingdom
Groot, Prof A.D. de; Middenstreek 7, 9166 LL Schiermonnikoog, The Netherlands
Klabbers, Dr J.H.G.; Oostervelden 59, 6681 WR Bemmel, The Netherlands
Legrand, Prof L.; 5, Rue de la Fontaine des Joncs, 91380 Chilly-Mazarin, France
Marklund, Prof L.; University of Uppsala, P.O. Box 2109, 750 02 Uppsala, Sweden
Mey, Dr M. De; University of Gent, Blandijnberg 2, 9000 Gent, Belgium
Scheerens, Drs J.; Zandpad 36, 3601 NA Maarsen, The Netherlands
Timpane, Dr M.; Columbia University, 525 West 120th Street, New York, NY 10027, U.S.A.

Wagenaar, Drs H.C.; Victorieplein 47^{II}, 1078 PD Amsterdam, The Netherlands

Weiss, Prof C.; Graduate School of Education, Gutman Library, Appian Way, Harvard University, Cambridge MA 02138, USA.

3) Critics/discussants

Eide, Dr I.; Grefsenkollvn. 12A, Leil 403, Olso 4, Norway

Groot, Prof A.D. de; Middenstreek 7, 9166 LL Schiermonnikoog, The Netherlands

Heene, Prof J.; University of Gent, Henry Dunantlaan 2, 9000 Gent, Belgium

Husén, Prof T.; Institute of International Education, University of Stockholm, S-106 91 Stockholm, Sweden

Jobst, Dr E.; Ministerialrat, Bund-Länder-Kommission für Forschungsförderung, Friedrich-Ebert-Allee 39, 5300 Bonn 1, Federal Republic of Germany

Kemenade, Prof J.A. van; Jonkerlaan 57, 2242 GB Wassenaar, The Netherlands

Lövgren, Esse; The National Swedish Board of Education, S-106 42 Stockholm, Sweden

Mitter, Prof W.; Deutsches Institut für Internationale Pädagogische Forschung, Postfach 90 02 80, 6 Frankfurt am Main 90, Deutsche Bundesrepublik (FRG)

Rein, Prof Martin; Massachusetts Institute of Technology, 77 Massachusetts Avenue, Cambridge, Massachusetts 02139. USA

Ringeling, Prof A.B.; Erasmus University Rotterdam, Rondo 8, 2925 AD Krimpen a/d IJssel, The Netherlands

Timpane, Dr Michael; Columbia University, 525 West 120th Street, New York, NY 10027, USA

Veld-Langeveld, Dr H. in 't; Advisory Council on Government Policy (WRR), Plein 1813 nr.2, 2514JN, The Hague, The Netherlands

Weiler, Dr D.; 11969 Woodbine Street, Los Angeles, California 90066 USA

4) Programme committee

Kallen, Prof. D.; 257, Rue St. Martin, 75003, Paris, France

Kloprogge, Drs J.J.J.; Ministry of Education and Science, Willemstraat 77, 2514 HL The Hague, The Netherlands

Kosse, Drs. Gerard B.; Foundation for Educational Research in the Netherlands (SVO), P.O. Box 19050, 2500 CB The Hague, The Netherlands

Vorbeck, Dr. Michael.; Council of Europe, 67006 Strasbourg-Cedex, France (Chairman)

5) **Delegates of member states of the Council for Cultural Co-operation (CCC) of the Council of Europe**

Alonso, Dr I; Instituto Nacional de Ciencias de Educacion (National Institute of Educational Sciences), Diudad Universitaria, Madrid-3, Spain

Eide, Dr K.; Director General Research and Planning Department, Ministry of Education, Box 8119 Dept., Oslo 1, Norway

Fuente Salvador, Dr C.; Ministry of Education and Science, Departamento de Prospeccion Educativa (Department of Educational Research), INCIE – Ciudad Universitaria, Madrid-3, Spain

Goldschmidt, E.; Deputy Permanent Secretary, Ministry of Education, Frederiksholms Kanal 21, DK 1220 Copenhagen, Denmark

Hoellinger, Dr S.; Bundesministerium für Wissenschaft und Forschung (Ministry of Science and Research), Minoritenplatz 5, A-1010 Vienna, Austria.

Jenzer, Dr C.; Erziehungsdepartement des Kantons Solothurn (Department for Education of the Kanton Solothurn), Rathaus, 4500 Solothurn, Switzerland

Kari, Prof J.; Head of the Institute for Educational Research, Yliopistonkatu 9, 40100 Jyväskylä 10, Finland

Kvalbein, Mrs I.A.; Research Director Research and Planning Department, Ministry of Education, Box 8119 Dept., Oslo 1, Norway

Lampinen, O.; Ministry of Education, Aleksanterinkatu 15B, 00170 Helsinki 17, Finland

Mitter, Prof W.; Deutsches Institut für Internationale Pädagogische Forschung (German Institute for International Educational Research), Schloszstrasse 29–31, 6000 Frankfurt am Main 90, Federal Republic of Germany

Partisch, Dr F.; Ministerialrat, Bundesministerium für Unterricht und Kunst (Ministry for Education and Art), Minoritenplatz 5, A-1010 Vienna, Austria

Peaker, G.; Staff Inspector (Research), Department of Education and Science, Elizabeth House, York Road, London SE1 7PH, Great Britain

Plough, Olsen, Prof T.; The Royal Danish College of Educational Studies Emdrupvej 101, Copenhagen 2400 NV, Denmark

Schorb, Prof A.O.; Staatsinstitüt für Bildungsforschung und Bildungsplanung (Government Institute for Educational Research and Planning), Arabellastrasse 1, 8000 Munchen 81, Federal Republic of Germany

Smith G., University of Oxford, Department of Social and Administrative Studies, New Barnett House, 28 Little Clarendon Street, Oxford DX1 2ER, Great Britain

6) **Honorary committee**

Brenningkmeijer, Dr G.; Netherlands Universities Council (AR), P.O. Box 590, 2270 AN Voorburg, The Netherlands

Bueren, Prof H.G. van; Advisory Council for Science Policy in the Netherlands, P.O. Box 18524, 2502 EM The Hague, The Netherlands

Dees, Drs D.J.D.; Standing Committee on Science Policy, Lower House of Parliament, Binnenhof 1 A, 2513 AA The Hague, The Netherlands

Gaay Fortman, Prof W.F. de; Netherlands Organization for the Advancement of Pure Research (ZWO), P.O. Box 93138, 2509 AC The Hague, The Netherlands

Hermes, A.J.; State Secretary for Education and Science, P.O. Box 20551, 2500 EN The Hague, The Netherlands

Jong, Prof W.A.; The Netherlands Organization for Applied Scientific Research (TNO) P.O. Box 297, 2501 BD The Hague, The Netherlands

Karasek, Dr F.; Council of Europe, 67006 Strasburg-Cedex, France

Lieshout, Ir. W.C.M. van; Foundation for Educational Research in the Netherlands (SVO), P.O. Box 9102, 6500 HC Nijmegen, The Netherlands

Moor, Prof R.A. de; Netherlands Social Science Council of the Royal Academy of Arts and Sciences (SWR), Herengracht 410, 1017 BX Amsterdam, The Netherlands

Ooijen, D.A. Th, van; Standing Committee on Education and Science, Lower House of Parliament, Binnenhof 1 A, 2513 AA The Hague, The Netherlands

Quené, Ir. Th.; Advisory Council on Government Policy (WRR), P.O. Box 20004, 2500 EA The Hague, The Netherlands

Trier, Dr A.A.Th.M. van; Minister for Science Policy, P.O. Box 20601, 2500 EP The Hague, The Netherlands

Waterschoot, C.Th.A. van; Standing Committee on Education and Science, Upper House of Parliament, Binnenhof 1 A, 2513 AA The Hague, The Netherlands

7) **Other participants**

Please refer to the next section where all participants are listed.

8) Address directory of all participants

All participants in alphabetical order:

Aarts, Dr J.F.M.C.
University of Nijmegen, Dept. of Education, P.O. Box 9102, 6500 HC Nijmegen, The Netherlands

Akker, Drs E.M.
Ministry of Education and Science, Dept. for Innovation of Primary Education, Dr. H. Colijnlaan 341, 2283 XL Rijswijk, The Netherlands.

Al, Drs G.J.A.
Director Studycentre OTO (Higher Education Policy), P.O. Box 16759, 2500 BT The Hague, The Netherlands.

Alonso, Dr I.
Director National Institute for Educational Sciences, Ciudad Universitaria, Madrid-3, Spain.

Beintema, Dr K.A.
University of Leiden, Dept. of Education, Stationsplein 12, 2300 RA Leiden, The Netherlands.

Berg, Drs A.H. van den
Director Centre for Educational Research of the University of Amsterdam, P.O. Box 3753, 1001 AN Amsterdam, The Netherlands.

Bernaert, Dr G.F.
Association for Research and Development in Higher Education in The Netherlands (CRWO), Graaf Willemlaan 151, 1141 XG Monnikendam, The Netherlands.

Boissevain, Drs E.M.
Central Institute for Catholic Education, Bezuidenhoutseweg 275, 2594 AN The Hague, The Netherlands.

Branger, Dr J.D.C.
University of Leiden, Dept. of Educational Sciences, The Netherlands.

Brenninkmeijer, Dr G.
Chairman Netherlands Universities Council (AR), P.O. Box 590, 2270 AN Voorburg, The Netherlands.

Bruggen, Drs J.C. van
Foundation for Curriculum Development, P.O. Box 2041, 7500 CA Enschede, The Netherlands.

Buis, Dr P.
Central Bureau for Research on University Education, P.O. Box 590, 2270 AN Voorburg, The Netherlands.

Caplan, Dr N.
Centre for Research on Utilization of Scientific Knowledge (CRUSK), University of Michigan, Ann Arbor, Michigan, USA.

Creemers, Prof B.P.M.
Director Northern Educational Research Institute, Nieuwe Stationsweg 5-9, 9751 SZ Haren, The Netherlands.

Dirkzwager, Dr A.
  Free University, Dept. of Psychology, De Boelelaan 1115, 1081 HV Amsterdam, The Netherlands.
Dockrell, Dr W.B.
  Director of The Scottish Council for Research in Education, 15 St. John Street, Edinburgh EH8 8JR, Great Britain.
Eide, Dr I.
  Parlementarian.
  Grefsenkollvn 12A, Leil 403, Oslo 4, Norway.
Eide, Dr K.
  Director General Research and Planning Department, Ministry of Education, Box 8119 Dept., Oslo 1, Norway.
Floor, Dr P.
  University of Leiden, Dept. for Educational and Research Policy of the University Administration, Stationsweg 46, 2312 AV Leiden, The Netherlands.
Fuente Salvador, Dr C.
  Ministry of Education and Science, Dept. for Educational Research, INCIE-Ciudad Universitaria, Madrid 3, Spain.
Goldschmidt, Mr E.
  Deputy Permanent Secretary, Ministry of Education, Frederiksholms Kanal 21, DK 1220 Copenhagen, Denmark.
Greef, Prof J.A. de
  University Institute Antwerp, Universiteitsplein 1, 2610 Wilrijk, Belgium.
Groeneweg, Drs Ph. C.
  Project Manager Foundation for Educational Research in The Netherlands, (SVO), P.O. Box 19050, 2500 CB The Hague, The Netherlands.
Groot, Prof A.D. de
  Professor of Methodology of the Social Sciences, University of Groningen, Middenstreek 7, 9166 LL Schiermonnikoog, The Netherlands.
Haatjes, Drs J.
  Adjunct Director, Foundation for Educational Research in The Netherlands, (SVO), P.O. Box 19050, 2500 CB The Hague, The Netherlands.
Heene, Prof J.
  University of Gent, Henry Dunantlaan 2, 9000 Gent, Belgium.
Hermes, Mr A.J.
  State Secretary for Education and Sciences, Nieuwe Uitleg 1, 2514 BP The Hague, The Netherlands.
Hoellinger, Dr S.
  Bundesministerium für Wissenschaft und Forschung (Ministry of Science and Research), Minoritenplatz 5, A-1010 Vienna, Austria.
Husén, Prof T.
  Director Institute of International Education, University of Stockholm, S-106 91 Stockholm, Sweden.

Hutjes, Dr J.
   Institute for Applied Sociology, Graafseweg 274, 6532 ZV Nijmegen, The Netherlands.
Jenzer, Dr C.
   Erziehungsdepartement des Kantons Solothurn (Ministry of Education of the Kanton Solothurn), Rathaus, 4500 Solothurn, Switzerland.
Jobst, Dr E.
   Ministerialrat, Bund-Länder-Kommission für Forschungsförderung, Friedrich-Ebert-Allee 39, 5300 Bonn 1, Federal Republic of Germany.
Jong, Drs D. de
   University of Leiden, Interdisciplinary Centre for Educational Research, Stationsplein 10, 2312 AK Leiden, The Netherlands.
Kalle, Drs P.H.
   University of Utrecht, Dept. of Educational Science, Heidelberglaan 1, 3584 CS Utrecht, The Netherlands.
Kallen, Prof D.
   Professor of Educational Sciences, University of Paris VIII 257, Rue St. Martin, 75003 Paris, France.
Kallenberg, Dr A.G.
   Head of the Documentation Dept., Foundation for Educational Research in The Netherlands, (SVO), P.O. Box 19050, 2500 CB The Hague, The Netherlands.
Kari, Prof J.
   Head of Institute for Educational Research, University of Jyväskylä, Yliopistonkatu 9, 40100 Jyväskylä 10, Finland.
Kate, Drs N. ten
   Adjunct-director, Directorate of Educational Support Structure, Ministry of Education and Science, P.O. Box 20551, 2500 EN The Hague, The Netherlands.
Kemenade, Prof J.A. van
   Professor of Sociology, University of Groningen (Minister of Education and Science for a second term at the moment this book appears), Jonkerlaan 57, 2242 GB Wassenaar, The Netherlands.
Klabbers, Prof J.H.G.
   Head of the Social Systems Research Group, University of Nijmegen; head of Futures Research Unit of the Dept. of Social and Organizational Psychology, University of Leiden, Oostervelden 59, 6681 WR Bemmel, The Netherlands.
Kloprogge, Drs J.J.J.
   Ministry of Education and Science, Division for Educational Research of the Directorate of Educational Support Structure, P.O. Box 20551, 2500 EN The Hague, The Netherlands.
Korsten, Dr A.
   University of Nijmegen, Institute for Political Science, Section Public Administration, Van Schaeck Mathonsingel 41, 6512 AN Nijmegen, The Netherlands.

Kosse, Drs G.B.
Executive Staff member Foundation for Educational Research in The Netherlands (SVO), P.O. Box 19050 CB The Hague, The Netherlands.

Kronjee, Drs G.J.
Advisory Council on Government Policy (WRR), Plein 1813 no. 2, 2514 JN The Hague, The Netherlands.

Kvalbein, Dr I.A.
Research Director, Research and Planning Dept., Ministry of Education, Box 8119 Dep., Oslo 1, Norway.

Lampinen, Mr O.
Ministry of Education, Aleksanterinkatu 15B, 00170 Helsinki 17, Finland.

Legrand, Prof L.
Professor Louis Pasteur University, Strasbourg (ex-Director of the Institute National de la Recherche Pédagogique), 5, Rue de la Fontaine des Joncs, 91380 Chilly-Mazarin, France.

Lövgren, E.
Director, National Swedish Board of Education, S-106 42 Stockholm, Sweden.

Marklund, Prof I.
University of Uppsala, Department of Education, Box 2109, 750 02 Uppsala, Sweden.

Mentink, Drs D.
Adjunct Director, Foundation for Educational Research in The Netherlands (SVO), P.O. Box 19050, 2500 CB The Hague, The Netherlands.

Mey, Dr M.T. De
University of Gent, Institute for Logic and Epistemology, Blandijnberg 2, 9000 Gent, Belgium.

Mitter, Prof W.
Deutsches Institut für Internationale Pädagogische Forschung (German Institute for International Educational Research), P.O. Box 90 02 80, 6 Frankfurt am Main 90, Federal Republic of Germany.

Moncada, Dr A.
Director, Institute of Education, University of Madrid, Pilar de Saragossa 3, Madrid 3, Spain.

Moor, Prof R.A. de
Chairman of the Netherlands Social Science Council (SWR) of the Royal Academy of Arts and Sciences, Herengracht 410, 1017 BX Amsterdam, The Netherlands.

Mottier-Holtz, Drs I.
Ministry of Education and Science, Directorate of Educational Support Structure, P.O. Box 20551, 2500 EN The Hague, The Netherlands.

Neave, Dr G.
Times Educational Supplement, 55 Calabria Road, London N5 1HU, Great Britain.

Noordenburg, Drs H.V. van
  Director, Union of Local and Regional Educational Support Centres, Noordeinde 94a, 2514 GM The Hague, The Netherlands.
Nijhof, Prof W.J.
  Twente University of Technology, Dept. of Educational Technology, Akkerweg 62, 3972 AC Driebergen, The Netherlands.
Oosterom, Drs W. van
  Ministry of Education and Science, Dept. for Innovation of Secondary Education, P.O. Box 20551, 2500 EN The Hague, The Netherlands.
Ooijen, Drs D.A.Th. van
  Chairman Standing Committee on Education and Science, Lower House of Parliament, Binnenhof 1A, 2513 AA The Hague, The Netherlands.
Oijen, Drs P. van
  Leiden Institute for Social Policy Research (LISBON), Stationsplein 242, 2312 AR Leiden, The Netherlands.
Partisch, Dr F.
  Bundesministerium für Unterricht und Kunst (Ministry for Education and Art), Minoritenplatz 5, A-1010 Vienna, Austria.
Patijn-Stroink, Drs E.A.
  Project Manager Foundation for Educational Research in The Netherlands (SVO), P.O. Box 19050, 2500 CB The Hague, The Netherlands.
Peaker, Mr G.
  Staff Inspector (Research), Department of Education and Science, Elizabeth House, York Road, London SE1 7PH, Great-Britain.
Plough Olsen, Prof T.
  The Royal Danish College of Educational Studies, Emdrupsvej 101, Cophenhagen 2400 NV, Denmark.
Puts, Drs H.
  Head of the Project Control Dept., Foundation for Educational Research in The Netherlands (SVO), P.O. Box 19050 CB The Hague, The Netherlands.
Rein, Prof M.
  Dept. of Urban Studies and Planning, Massachusetts, Institute of Technology (MIT), 77, Massachusetts Avenue, Cambridge, Mass. 02139, U.S.A.
Ringeling, Prof A.B.
  Professor of Political Science and Policy Analysis, Erasmus University Rotterdam, Rondo 8, 2925 AD Krimpen a/d IJssel, The Netherlands.
Rottländer-Meyer, Drs C.
  Director Institute of Social Research on Policy, Nassauplein 17, 2485 EB The Hague, The Netherlands.
Sandbergen, Dr S.
  Ministry of Education and Science, P.O. Box 20551, 2500 EN The Hague, The Netherlands.

Sheerens, Drs J.
  Executive Staff member, Foundation for Educational Research in The Netherlands (SVO), P.O. Box 19050, 2500 CB The Hague, The Netherlands.
Schorb, Prof A.O.
  Staatsinstitut für Bildungsforschung und Bildungsplannung (Government Institute for Educational Research and Planning), Arabellastrasse 1, 8000 München 81, Federal Republic of Germany.
Seventer, Drs C.W. van
  Director, Foundation for Educational Research in The Netherlands (SVO), P.O. Box 19050, 2500 CB The Hague, The Netherlands.
Sixma, Prof J.
  University of Utrecht, Dept. of Educational Science, Heidelberglaan 1, 3584 CS Utrecht, The Netherlands.
Smith, Dr G.
  University of Oxford, Dept. of Social and Administrative Studies, New Barnett House, 28 Little Clarendon Street, Oxford OX1 2ER, Great Britain.
Snellen, Dr I.Th.M.
  Director, Institute for Social Research, Hogeschoollaan 225, 5037 GC Tilburg, The Netherlands.
Spiekerman, Mr J.A.A.
  Director ACADEME, Complete English Language Service, Prins Mauritslaan 144, 2582 LZ The Hague, The Netherlands.
Strien, Dr H.M. van
  Executive Staff member, Foundation for Educational Research in The Netherlands (SVO), P.O. Box 19050, 2500 CB The Hague, The Netherlands.
Suppes, Prof P.
  Director Institute for Mathematical Studies in the Social Sciences, Ventura Hall, Stanford University, Stanford CA 94305, USA.
Swanborn, Prof P.G.
  University of Utrecht, Institute of Sociology, Heidelberglaan 2, P.O. Box 80. 108, 3508 TC Utrecht, The Netherlands.
Thio, Drs K.D.
  National Institute for Educational Measurement (CITO), P.O. Box 1034, 6801 MG Arnhem, The Netherlands.
Timpane, Dr M.
  Former Director of the National Institute of Education (NIE) and the National Institute for Work and Learning; at present Dean of Teachers College, Columbia University, 525 West 120th Street, New York, NY 10027, USA.
Veld-Langeveld, Dr H. in 't
  Advisory Council on Government Policy (WRR), Plein 1813 no. 2, 2514 JN The Hague, The Netherlands.

Veld, Prof R.J. in 't
Professor of Public Administration, University of Nijmegen; advisor to the Minister for Science Policy, Valkenier 7, 6581 AZ Malden, The Netherlands.

Velzen, Dr W.G. van
Catholic Pedagogic Centre, P.O. Box 482, 5201 AL 's-Hertogenbosch, The Netherlands.

Vorbeck, Dr M.
Head of the Section for Educational Research and Documentation, Council of Europe, 67006 Strasbourg-Cedex, France.

Voster, Dr W.
Director, Directorate of Educational Support Structure, Ministry of Education and Science, P.O. Box 20551, 2500 EN The Hague, The Netherlands.

Vrijenhoef, Mr H.H.
Head of the Information Dept., Foundation for Educational Research in The Netherlands (SVO), P.O. Box 19050, 2500 CB The Hague, The Netherlands.

Wagenaar, Drs H.C.
Executive Staffmember, Foundation for Educational Research in The Netherlands (SVO), P.O. Box 19050, 2500 CB The Hague, The Netherlands.

Weiler, Dr D.
Senior Vice-President Manifest International, 11969 Woodbine Street, Los Angeles, California 90066, USA.

Weiss, Prof C.H. Graduate School of Education, Gutman Library, Appian Way, Harvard University, Cambridge MA 02138, USA.

Westerlaak, Dr J.W. van
Director, Institute for Applied Sociology, University of Nijmegen, Graafseweg 274, 6532 ZV Nijmegen, The Netherlands.

Wieringen, Dr A.M.L. van
Ministry of Education and Science, Directorate for Secondary Education, P.O. Box 20551, 2500 EN The Hague, The Netherlands.

Winkel, Dr H.W. te
Ministry of Education and Science, Directorate General for Higher and University Education, P.O. Box 20551, 2500 EN The Hague, The Netherlands.

Wolff-Albers, Dr A.D.
Ministry of Education and Science, Directorate for Science Policy, P.O. Box 20601, 2500 EP The Hague, The Netherlands.

APPENDIX B

About the Editors, Invited Authors and Critics

1) Editors

DENIS B.P. KALLEN is Associate Professor of Education at the Department of Educational Sciences of the Université de Paris, VIII Vincennes-Saint-Denis. He is also extra-ordinary Professor of Educational Policy in a Comparative Perspective at the University of Amsterdam. He is a member of the editorial board of several educational journals, e.g. the *European Journal of Education* and *Western European Education*. Denis Kallen is President of the Francophone Association of Comparative Education and past President of the Comparative Education Society in Europe. He is also a Board member of several internationally oriented bodies such as the Institute of Education of the European Cultural Foundation. His international outlook is reflected in several publications of which he has been co-author or editor, such as *Development of Secondary Education: Trends and Implications* (OECD, 1969), *Recurrent Education: a Strategy for Lifelong Learning* (OECD, 1973). Professor Kallen has held research positions with the University of Münster's Social Science Research Institute, the International Study of University Admissions and the European Cultural Foundation's Institute of Education in Paris. He has for many years been a senior staff member of OECD's Directorate for Scientific Affairs and of its Centre for Educational Research and Innovation, and held the chair of general and comparative education at the University of Amsterdam. He was also a long-standing member of the Council of Europe's former Project Group on The Development of Adult Education.

JO J.J. KLOPROGGE (1948) graduated in sociology. He has been Head of the Educational Research Department of the Dutch Ministry of Education and Science since 1978. This department's major task has been the commissioning and funding of policy-oriented educational research via organizations such as the Foundation for Educational Research (SVO) in The

Netherlands and independent research institutes. He represents the Ministry on SVO's Board of Directors, chairs the Ministry's Co-ordination Group for Educational Research, is a member of the Standing Interministerial Conference on Social Science Research in The Netherlands and other national committees in this field. Before coming to his present post, he was a senior researcher of the National Agricultural Economic Institute dealing with social science research programmes for national agricultural policies and the development of economic indicators for agricultural inputs and outputs. His publications appear in Dutch and deal with future plans for students in agriculture, career changes of farmers, and inheritance and management problems in the Dutch agricultural sector. He is working, with his staff, on the analysis of national educational policy for priority setting purposes.

GERARD B. KOSSE (1945) trained as a teacher and organizational psychologist. In 1975 he moved into educational research planning and since 1979 has been one of the two executive staff members of the Policy Planning Unit of SVO, the major sponsoring and policy-making body in the field of educational research. Within the Policy Planning Unit, which is responsible for developing and monitoring SVO's overall policy, his main task concerns the assessment of research needs on which he, with others, has published in Dutch, e.g. *Strategies and Methods for the Inventory of Society's Educational Research Needs (1980)*. He is a member of several governing boards of national and international humanist institutions such as, the Post Academic Training Centre and the Foundation for the Enhancement of Social Science and Philosophy which supports a number of Chairs at Dutch universities. His interest has focused on problems of ethnic and other minorities and he has undertaken policy-oriented consulting assignments for Third World aid organizations such as Foster Parents Plan, and municipal minority organizations. An important focus of his other consultancies has been the policy relevance of national research programmes on tolerance, and public image improvement. In 1975 he published two studies on the characteristics of a small ethical group, the humanists, and an assessment of their influence on national welfare policies entitled *Characteristics of Dutch Humanists and their Social Influence.*

MICHAEL VORBECK has been Head of the Council of Europe's Section for Educational Research and Documentation since 1978. Within this international context he has taken many initiatives for the promotion and coordination of educational research within the 23 countries which are members of the Council for Cultural Co-operation.

Among other things, he has been responsible for the organization of educational research workshops and the further development of the multilingual computer-based European Documentation and Information

System for Education (EUDISED). He is trained in law and his dissertation 'Wesen und Inhalt gemeindlicher Nutzungsrechte' dealt with aspects of Bavarian common law still alive in rural areas. He has also written articles on European cooperation in higher education as well as in educational research.

He previously served as an administrator in local authorities and then with the Ministry of Education in Bavaria, one of the States of the Federal Republic of Germany. His responsibilities included the planning of higher education and research (arrangement of meetings of the Higher Education Committee of the Standing Conference of German Ministers of Education), legal aspects of educational planning, educational cooperation with the other States of the Federal Republic and the Federal Government, international educational cooperation (UNESCO, OECD, Council of Europe) and East-West relations in education. In 1968 he joined the Council of Europe's Division for Higher Education and Research and from 1971 to 1977 he acted as Secretary to the Council of Europe's Committee for Higher Education and Research.

HENK C. WAGENAAR (1950) trained as clinical psychologist but has since moved into the policy studies area as an executive staff member of the Policy Planning Unit of the Foundation for Educational Research (SVO) in The Netherlands, the country's major sponsoring and policy-making body in the field of educational research. His responsibilities include the planning of the Foundation's long- and short-term research policy and the promotion of research management in the institutes sponsored by SVO. His major field of interest is the relationship between social science research and public policy making and his publications (mostly in Dutch) include *Commentary by SVO on the Medium-term Plan for Social Research and Policy of the Minister of Science (1979)* and *The Organization and Financing of Educational Research* (1980). His contribution to this volume *A Cloud of Unknowing* appeared also in Dutch and French. He has remained in close contact with psycho-therapy and national health and welfare programmes, and in this area he carried out an investigation of the psychological and social-economical factors which led to the current legal status of disability (1976). His continuing interest in the planning, evaluation and management of national social programs has focussed on the unobtrusive but decisive role played by diverse values. His recent *Review of: Governments Commissioning of Research. A case Study* (by M.N. Kogan *et al.*) is an example of this.

2) Invited authors

NATHAN CAPLAN (1930) is Professor of Psychology, University of Michigan and Program Director of this University's Center for Research on

Utilization of Scientific Knowledge. His early publications primarily dealt with intellectual functioning, juvenile delinquents and ghetto phenomena. In 1974 he published with others *Social experimentation for evaluation and planning*. In the same year he presented a paper at the OECD/Dartmouth Conference on Social Research and Public Policies: the frequently cited *The use of social science information by federal executives*, and published *Factors affecting the utilization of social research in policy making at the national level*. The utilization of social science knowledge by policy-makers is an important theme in all his work since then. Among his publications are: *The use of social science knowledge in policy decisions at the national level: a report to respondents* (together with A. Morrison and R. Stambaugh, 1975), a paper presented at the Institute for Advanced Studies in Vienna, Austria, entitled *Emerging theoretical possibilities in utilization (1980)* and *Social psychology and social problem solving* (chapter 9 in SPSSI-sponsored Social Psychology test). Since 1975 he has been consultant to the OECD. Other consultancies include the Government of Finland (since 1978), and the General Accounting Office (1977). He is a member of the American Association for the Advancement of Science's Advisory Committee to the Office of Science and Technology Policy (1978-present), member of the Committee on Program Evaluation in Education of the National Research Council (1980-present), and editor of *Knowledge: Creation, Diffusion, Utilization*, a journal published by Sage.

WILLIAM BRYAN DOCKRELL (1929) is Director of the Scottish Council for Research in Education. Before he was appointed to this post in 1971, he was Professor of Education at the Department of Special Education and Director of the Educational Clinic, both of the Ontario Institute in Education (1967–1971), and served as Associate Professor of Educational Psychology and director of the Educational Clinic of the University of Alberta (1958–1967). Special honours include fellowships at New York University, the University of Chicago, the Educational Institute of Scotland and others. He also holds a First Class Merit Certificate in Psychology (Edinburgh, 1952) and was a Senior Imperial Relations Trust Fellow at the Institute of Education, University of London, 1966–67. Among his wide range of addresses and papers special mention is made of *Negotiated Research* (1975), *Educational Research Crossnational, Multinational, International* (1980) and *Educational Research – an International Perspective* (1980). Achievement and ability are dealt with in a wide range of publications. Together with H.D. Black he published *Diagnostic Assessment* (four volumes, 1980/81). He is a member of the Standing Committee of the International Association of the Evaluation of Educational Achievement, Chairman of the Consultative Committee on the Impact and Take-up of Schools Council Projects, member of the Executive Committee of the International Association for Educational Assessment, and a member of the Policy Committee for Education and Training of the City and Guilds of London Institute.

ADRIAAN D.DE GROOT (1914) is Professor of Methodology of the Social Sciences at the University of Groningen. Over the years his interests have included cognition, various fields of applied psychology and research methodology, and educational measurement and evaluation. He has been active in various capacities related to education: as a pioneer in educational research in The Netherlands, as co-founder of the Foundation for Educational Research in The Netherlands (SVO), and the Dutch National Institute for Educational Measurement (CITO), as a government adviser on educational planning, and as a theorist on educational objectives, systems, and policy.

He is and has been a member of many national research and planning commissions and was a Member of the Board of the Netherlands Organization for the Advancement of Pure Research (ZWO). From 1971 to 1979 he held a personal Chair at the University of Amsterdam where he was a full professor before that time. Professor De Groot's honours include a fellowship at the Center for Advanced Study in the Behavioral Sciences, Stanford, California, an Honorary Doctorate from the University of Gent, Belgium, and a Membership of the Royal Academy of Sciences (KNAW). De Groot has published numerous research reports and articles, mostly in Dutch. Books published in English as well are: *Thought and Choice in Chess*, (1965) 1978. 2nd edition (translation of *Het denken van den schaker*, 1946), *Saint Nicholas, a psychoanalytical study of his history and myth*, 1966 (translation of 'Sint Nicolaas, patroon van liefde', 1949), and *Methodology, Foundations of inference and research in the behavioral sciences*, 1969 (translation of 'Methodologie', 1961). Together with N.H. Frijda he edited *Otto Selz. His contribution to psychology* (1981). In press is a book on Higher Education, Science and Policy, written in Dutch.

JAN H.G. KLABBERS (1938) is a Professor at the University of Utrecht and Special Professor Futures Studies, University of Leyden, The Netherlands. His early work deals with principles of systems. He also studied at MIT's Sloan School of Management, and the Systems Research Center, Case Western Reserve University, Cleveland, where he took part in Prof M.D. Mesarovic's 'Lake Erie Ecosystem Project' and the 'Mesarovic-Pestel World modelling Project'. He is General Secretary of the International Simulation and Gaming Association (ISAGA), and member of the Editorial Board of *Simulation Games for Learning* of the Society for Academic Gaming and Simulation in Education and Training (SAGSET, UK). He has extensively dealt with gaming as an aid in policy formulation and implementation. His publications include *Human computer decision-making. Notes concerning the interactive mode* (1974), 'Energy policy assessment using an interactive model package' (1978, with H. Bossel and others) in A. Straszak and J. Owinski, eds. *New trends in mathematical modelling* and *Development of an interactive simulation game: a case study of DENTIST (Dental health care system Interactive Simulation Tool)*, 1980 (with J. van der Hijden and others).

Professor Klabbers has been invited speaker at numerous conferences on model-building processes and analysis of social systems.

LOUIS LEGRAND (1921) is Professor of Educational Sciences at the University of Strasbourg and was until recently Director of the French National Educational Research Institute (INRP). Besides being one of France's leading educational scientists he is known for his political insight. His awards include a prestigious Officier d'Académie, a Chevalier de l'Ordre National du Mérite, a Chevalier de la Légion d'Honneur and the Prix Jean Zay. He has published in French only. Some of his frequently cited books are *Psychologie appliquée à l'éducation intellectuelle* (1961), *Pédagogie fonctionnelle pour l'école élémentaire nouvelle* (1973, with T. Nathan), 'Les grandes orientations de la pédagogie contemporaine' in: *Textes de pédagogie pour l'école d'aujourd'hui* (1974), and *Pour une politique démocratique de l'éducation* (1977).

INGER MARKLUND is the Head of the Research Planning Unit of the Swedish National Board of Education. Since she accepted this post in 1975, she has also been the Secretary-General of the Government-appointed Committee on Educational Research and Development (1978–1980) and Professor of Education at the University of Uppsala (1980–1981). After publications on increasing the rate of return in postal surveys (1970), she primarily dealt with research planning, assessment of foreign language needs in industry and trade, multi-language teaching, teaching of mathematics, and social science's role in policy-making. Since she has only published on these topics in Swedish, no titles are mentioned here.

Ms. Marklund has been a guest lecturer at several universities, e.g., the University of Melbourne, of Canberra and of Brisbane. For the Council of Europe she participated in the development of the computer-based European Documentation and Information System for Education (EUDISED). She is a Member of the Swedish Committee on Co-operation between Universities and Society, and a winner of the 1974 Academy Award of the Department of Social Science from Lund University.

MARC T.M. DE MEY (1940) PhD Psychology and Pedagogics, is Director of the Institute of Logic and Epistemology of the State University of Gent, Belgium. He is a winner of the Lauréat du Concours universitaire, the Frank Boas Award, and had a Fulbright Scholarship at the Harvard Center for Cognitive Studies (with Professor J.S. Bruner) and MIT. Among his former posts was an Associate Professorship in Science of Science and Methodology at Tilburg University in The Netherlands. He is a co-founder of *Communication and Cognition* and its editor since 1968, a founder member of the Society for the Social Study of Science, Ithaca, NY, a member of the Study Group for the Social Psychological and Subjective Aspects of Science, Worcester Polytechnic Institute, Mass., the Association for Computational Linguistics, the American Association for Artificial Intelligence, the History of Science Society and several other distinguished professional societies. With L. Apostel, A. Phalet and F. Verdamme he has published the results of a four-year project *Cognitive science and the analysis of representation of knowledge in logic compared to the results of empirical studies of knowledge processes* (1980). At present he is working on a three-year project 'Science dynamics as an integration of philosophy of science and science of science in relation to new ideas on history and theory of scientific methods'. Among his extensive list of invited papers and presentations at conferences the following deserve special mention: *The cognitive paradigm in science studies* (Harvard University, Society for the Social Study of Science, 1977), *A ninety degree turn in thinking about perception and new ideas on the interaction between theory and data* (Netherlands Institute for Advanced Studies in Wassenaar, International Conference on Knowledge and Representation, 1979), *Beyond figure-ground and context* (Vienna, Austria, Institute for Advanced Studies, conference in honour of Paul Lazarsfeld: The Political Realization of Social Science Knowledge and Research: Toward New Scenarios, 1980) and *Note on citation tracing of key publications as a bibliometric indicator of the cognitive dynamics of a scientific specialty* (OECD Science and Technology Indicators Conference, 1980). Some of his frequently cited articles are Incommensurability of Theories and Untranslatability of Languages, in Pinxten, R. (Ed.), *Universalism and Relativism in Language and Thought* (1976), From behavior to action, *Communication and Cognition (1976)* and The Relevance of the Cognitive Paradigm for Information Science, in Harbo, O. and Kajberg L. (Eds.) *Theory and the application of Information Research* (1980). His latest book *The Cognitive Paradigm* will appear in 1982.

JAAP SCHEERENS (1946) graduated in pedagogics (1974) and psychology (1982). He specialized in methodology of the social sciences. At present he is an executive staff member of SVO, the major Dutch sponsoring and policy-making body in the field of educational research. His main task concerns the organization and control of the review system of the SVO, in particular the assessment of research quality and of the social relevance of commissioned research proposals and reports. He has published in Dutch on curriculum evaluation and evaluation research. A particular interest of his has been the policy and organizational context of evaluation research, on which he is to publish a book this year.

PATRICK SUPPES (1922) PhD Columbia University, is one of the most influential and respected philosophers in the United States. He teaches logic, philosophy and education at Stanford University and is the Head of the Institute for Mathematical Studies in Social Sciences. He is the President of the Division of Logic, Methodology and Philosophy of Science of the National Academy of Education, was awarded with the Columbia Teachers College Medal for Distinguished Service, and was elected member of the National Academy of Sciences in 1978.

He has made outstanding contributions in many areas. In the series *Profiles: An International Series on Contemporary Philosophers and Logicians* (published by Reidel, 1979) volume 1 classifies Suppes' research and publications into the following major fields: 1. foundations of physics; 2. theory of measurement; 3. decision theory, probability, and causability; 4. foundations of psychology; 5. philosophy of language; 6. education and computers.

He has published extensively and to pick out particular titles for special mention is inevitably somewhat arbitrary, but particularly relevant in the context of the International Workshop are *Impact of Research on Education: Some Case-Studies* (1978) which he edited and his forthcoming book in the philosophy of science *Set-theoretical Structures in Science* of which mimeographed copies have been fairly widely circulated.

P. MICHAEL TIMPANE (1934), MPA Harvard University 1970. At the present Dean of Teachers College, Columbia University, New York. Until recently he was Director of the National Institute of Education (NIE), the Federal Government's principal educational research and development agency. He represented the agency in appearances before Congress, in Administration councils, and in numerous meetings with professional associations and the public. He also executed the agency's plans for reauthorization and appropriations, and maintained oversight of all aspects of programme management and administration.

From 1977 to 1979, he was the Deputy Director of NIE in charge of the planning and execution of the Institute's research programme, which spends $80 million per year in grants and contracts. He also had special responsibility for NIE's participation in the broader educational policy development processes of the Department of Health, Education and Welfare (HEW), and the Executive Branch, including the amendment of the Elementary and Secondary Education Act, the Higher Education Act, and the development of proposals for a Department of Education. Previous professional experience includes the Washington Office of the Rand Corporation where he served as Director of Studies for the Aspen Institute of Humanistic Studies' Program for Education in a Changing Society, a two-year review of emerging issues in national educational policy. In the Department of Health, Education and Welfare he was Director of Education Planning from January, 1971 to November, 1972, directing policy analysis, programme planning, and evaluation planning. For this service he was given the Department's Distinguished Service Award. His special professional activities have included membership on the National Academy of Education's Task Force on Collective Bargaining and the National Academy of Science's Panel on Methodology for Statistical Priorities (which produced *Setting Statistical Priorities*, 1976) and was leader of the US educational research delegation to the People's Republic of China. His publications include *Limitations of the HEW Policy Process in Using Educational Research* (1973), *Youth Policy in Transition* (1976, principal investigator), and 'Federal Aid to Education: Prologue and Prospects', Chapter I in *The Federal Interest in Financing Schooling* (Timpane, ed., 1979).

CAROL H. WEISS PhD Sociology, Columbia University, where she held several posts, among them Senior Research Associate at the Center for Social Sciences (1977–1978). Since then she has been Senior Research Associate and Senior Lecturer at the Graduate School of Education of Harvard University. Much of her earlier work deals with Evaluation Research and she published a text book with this title (Prentice-Hall, 1972). Her work on evaluation research in the political context includes a paper of this title in *Handbook of Evaluation Research,* Vol. 1 (1957, E. Struening and M. Guttentag, eds.) This publication was also translated into German as *Planvolle Steuerung gesellschaftlichen Handelns* (1975). Her more recent works also deal with social science research and policy-making but focus more on utilization aspects. Her many papers and monographs in this field are considered of outstanding quality and relevance by scholars and policy-makers all over the world. Among her forthcoming publications are 'Knowledge Utilization in Decision-Making: Reflection on the Terms of the Discussion' in Ronald G. Corwin (ed.), *Policy Research in Education,* vol. 3 of *Research in Sociology and Socialization,* 'Measuring the Use of Evaluation' in James A. Ciarlo (ed.), *Utilizing Evaluation: Concepts and Measurements Techniques* (Sage Publications), 'Three terms in Search of Reconceptualization: Knowledge, Utilization, and Decision-Making' in Hermann Strasser (ed.), *Proceedings of the Vienna Conference on Political Realization of Social Science Knowledge* (Physica-Verlag), and 'Use of Social Science Research in Organizations: the Functions of Information', in Herman D. Stein (ed.), *Organization and the Human Services* (Temple University Press). Some of her most noteworthy recent books are *Social Science Research and Decision-Making* (1980), *Making Bureaucracies Work* (with A.H. Barton, 1980), and *Using Social Research in Public Policy Making* (1977). Professor Weiss is a member of several editorial boards of journals: *Annals of Public Administration, Educational Evaluation and Policy Analysis, Policy Analysis, Knowledge: Creation, Diffusion, Utilization, Evaluation Studies Review Annual,* and *Public Opinion Quarterly*. Her consultancies include the National Institute of Mental Health's Network of Consultants on Knowledge Transfer, the Office of Technology Assessment, the General Accounting Office, the National Science Foundation, Rand Corporation, the Urban Institute and many university, non-profit, and profit-making research organizations. She was the winner of the 1980 Myrdal Award for Science from the Evaluation Research Society.

3) Critics

INGRID EIDE (1933) is a member of the Norwegian Parliament and a former deputy-minister of education. She is also Assistant Professor at the Institute of Sociology of the University of Olso. She has published extensively in Norwegian on Consumer Affairs, International Cooperation and Conflict, Development Aid, Evaluation, and Sociology of Education. She is co-founder of the Institute of International Peace Research in Oslo (PRIO).

JOHAN A.P. HEENE (1940) obtained his PhD Psychology and Pedagogics Summa Cum Laude, at the University of Gent, Belgium, where he is now Associate Professor in Didactics. One of his former posts was lecturer at the municipal Institute for Advanced Social Studies, Gent, where he read genetic psychology and differential psychology. From 1968–72 he was Belgium's National Technical Officer in the International Association for the Evaluation of Educational Achievement. Many of his invited addresses and papers for international conferences deal with creativity, on which he has published extensively in Dutch, French and Spanish. He is chairman both of the Dutch-Belgium Committee for Documentation and Information for Educational Research and of Belgium's National Committee for Continuing Education for the Employed. His latest book is *'Creativiteit en Didactiek'* (1980) which appeared in Dutch only, as did his 1978 book on achievement testing in biology. Heene is co-author of the Dutch edition of the *Multilingual Thesaurus for Information Processing in the Field of Education* of the computer-based European Documentation and Information System for Education (EUDISED) (1977). He is Senior Editor of *Pedagogisch Forum/Tijdschrift voor Opvoedkunde*, and contributor to an authoritative encyclopedia of Education, the *Standaard Encyclopedie voor Opvoeding en Onderwijs*.

TORSTEN HUSÉN (1916) was appointed to the first Chair in Education at the University of Stockholm in 1953. He held a professorship at the Stockholm School of Education (1956–1971) where he directed a comprehensive research programme related to Swedish school reform. As Chairman of The International Association for the Evaluation of Educational Achievement (IEA) for some ten years he was closely involved in evaluations of national systems of education in 20 countries. In 1971 he was appointed to a Chair in International Education established for him at the University of Stockholm, of which he has been Director since that year. He holds honorary doctorates of several universities, including the University of Chicago, the University of Rhode Island, the University of Glasgow, Brunel University, the University of Amsterdam and the University of Joensuu, Finland. His awards include the Columbia University Medal for Distinguished Service. He has been a member of the Scientific Board of the Max Planck Institute for Educational Research in Berlin since 1964, consultant to the Organisation for Economic Co-operation and Development (OECD) in Paris since 1968, member of the Board of Trustees and the Executive Committee of the International Council for Educational Development since 1970, Member of the Royal Swedish Academy and of several Royal Committees within the Swedish Ministry of Education.

He is author of some 30 books, among them *Talent, Opportunity and Career* (1969), *Social Background and Educational Career* (1972), *The Learning Society* (1974), *Talent, Equality and Meritocracy* (1974), *The School in Question* (1979), and *The Future of Formal Schooling* (1980). He is on the Editorial Board or Board of Consulting Editors of a number of journals, such as *Scandinavian Journal of Educational Research, Comparative Education Review, Western European Education, Teachers College Record*, and *Sociology of Education*.

Furthermore, he is a Member of the International Advisory Board of the *World Book Encyclopedia*, the Editorial Advisory Board of the *Encyclopedia of Higher Education*, and Co-editor-in-Chief of the *International Encyclopedia of Education: Research and Studies*.

BERNHARD JOBST (1938) is a top administrator in the German Federal Committee for Educational Planning and Advancement of Research in Bonn. There he is the Head of the Planning Group. Former positions include a post as Assistant-Professor at the California Institute of Technology, and a lecturership on educational planning at the University of Bielefeld. Forthcoming is a book on Didactics for Higher Education on which he worked for the Federal Committee.

Dr Jobst's earlier publications deal with German opposition to Hitler and economic policy trends in European thought. Later articles and invited addresses concern public policy-planning and adult education, the long-term development of higher education and the employment of highly qualified manpower. Most of his publications are in German.

ESSE LÖVGREN is the Head of the Division for Administration of Educational R&D of the Swedish National Board of Education. His major publications deal with teaching of geography, history and civics, the central school administration of Sweden and the R&D policy of the

Swedish National Board of Education. Since he has only published on these topics in Swedish, no titles are mentioned here. He represented the National Board in appearances before Government and in numerous meetings with professional associations and the public, and took part in major educational policy debates and research programmes.

WOLFGANG MITTER (1927) is Director of the Research Board of the German Institute for International Educational Research in Frankfurt a.M. He is considered one of the leading experts on Soviet and East European educational systems and policies, about which he has published numerous articles and papers in German and English. The research carried out under his direction in this field is described in *Research into Soviet and East European educational systems at the German Institute for International Educational Research* (1978).

Special mention should be made of 'Marxist-Leninist Pedagogics. Links between Marxist-Leninist and Western Pedagogics, in *Marxism, Communism and Western Society. A Comparative encyclopedia* (1971).

Professor Mitter is a member of the German UNESCO Commission, acting editor of *Bildung und Erziehung,* President of the Comparative Education Society, Europe and editor of *The International Review of Education.*

MARTIN REIN (1928) PhD Brandeis University 1961. His present position is Professor of the Department of Urban Studies and Planning, Massachusetts Institute of Technology. He is also a visiting Professor at the School of Education, Harvard University. His honours and fellowships include Contemporary Authors 1980, the Guggenheim Award 1978, a fellowship at the Center for Advanced Study in the Behavioral Sciences in Palo Alto, California, and a Senior Research Fulbright award at the London School of Economics and Political Science. One of the recent research grants he has been awarded is the Ford Foundation grant for a comparative study of the Welfare State in Europe and the United States (1979–81) (with Lee Rainwater). He is a member of the Governor's Committee on Children and the Family in Massachusetts, the International Advisory Board of *Policy Sciences,* the Executive Committee of the Joint Center for Urban Studies of Massachusetts Institute of Technology and Harvard University, and has served as a consultant to such institutions as the General Accounting Office, the Office of Child Development, the Office of Program Planning, Research and Evaluation, the Department of Health, Education and Welfare, and the Ford Foundation's Social Development Program. Forthcoming publications are *Economic Well-Being in the Welfare State: a Study of Family Income in Sweden, Great Britain and the United States* (with Lee Rainwater and Joe Schwartz) and *From Social Policy to Practice* (M.E. Sharpe Publication). He has written many articles dealing with public policy issues and the utilization of the social sciences in policy-making. Special mention is made of 'Methodology for the Study of the Interplay between Social Science and Social Policy', *International Social Science Journal*, Volume XXXII, No. 2, 1980 and 'Social Science Knowledge and Social Work Practice', *Sourcebook on Research Utilization* (Allen Rubin and Aaron Rosenblatt (eds.) 1979). Professor Rein is one of the most frequently cited authors dealing with the welfare crisis and social service problems.

ARTHUR B. RINGELING (1942) is Professor at Rotterdam's Erasmus University in The Netherlands. He has a full professorship at the Department of Political Sciences and Policy Analysis and is Deputy Chairman of the Department of Administrative Sciences of Nijmegen University. He is a member of the board of the Netherlands Universities Joint Social Research Centre (SISWO), editor of *Beleid en Maatschappij* and of *Lokaal Bestuur*. From an extensive list of publications, special mention is made of the articles 'Administration of the Dutch policy for option-regretters' in K.C. Davis *et al.*, *Discretionary Justice in Europe and America* (1976), and 'Administrative Discretion', *The Netherlands Journal of Sociology*, 1980. Most of Ringeling's publications are in Dutch and deal with decision-making in politics and administration, bureaucratization, and the dynamics of planning and implementation.

H.M. IN 'T VELD-LANGEVELD (1926) PhD Sociology. Since 1973 she has been a member of the Dutch Advisory Council on Government Policy (WRR). Before this she held a post as Professor in Empirical Sociology at the Erasmus University of Rotterdam, The Netherlands. She has published extensively on the relationships between research and policy, family sociology, emancipation, and the fine arts and the public. Although some of her articles and other publications have been translated into French and German, most of her work is only published in Dutch, thus no titles are mentioned here.

DANIEL WEILER is Senior Vice President of Manifest International, Berkeley, California. In addition to his corporate management duties, he is currently directing a two-year statewide policy evaluation for the State legislature of the California School Improvement Program. Until 1980 he was a senior staff member of the Rand Corporation's Education and Human Resources Program. Mr Weiler was principal investigator on a study of the relationship between changes in educational systems and school-community relations, consultant to the UCLA Center for Computer Based Behavioral Studies on studies of political gaming, served as a Resident Consultant to the Rand Corporation, and has extensive research experience dating back to the early 1960s. From 1976–1980 he was a member of the California Educational Management and Evaluation Commission, an advisory body created by the State legislature to work with the State Board of Education, he has served on the Education Committee of the Community Relations Conference of Southern California, and is presently a Director of the Martin Luther King Legacy Association, an affiliated organization of the Southern Christian Leadership Conference of which he has also been a Director. His honours include Pi Sigma Alpha of the Political Science Honor Society and the Pi Gamma Mu of the Social Science Honor Society. Invited presentations deal with legislative uses of evaluation, and the politics of evaluation. Some of his publications are: *The Uses and Limits of Educational Evaluation at the State Level* (1978, senior co-author), *A Public School Voucher Demonstration: The First Year at Alum Rock* (1974, 4 vols; study director), *The dissemination of Educational R&D Projects: Research and Policy Issues for the Federal Government* (1973). Forthcoming are: *Vouchers in Alum Rock: A Retrospective Analysis* (The Rand Corporation), and *A Study of Alternatives in American Education, Vol. VII: Summary and Policy Implications* (The Rand Corporation).

APPENDIX C

Bibliographies, Unsolicited Papers and French Texts

Per address one copy of each document can be obtained free of charge. This offer is valid until December 1983.
Please write to:
Foundation for Educational Research in The Netherlands (SVO)
Information and Public Relations Dept.
P.O. Box 19050
2500 CB The Hague
The Netherlands

1) Bibliographies

Foundation for Educational Research in the Netherlands (SVO)	Education in the member states of the council for cultural cooperation (CCC): structure, policy, innovations, research and evaluation. A bibliography of publications published between 1975–1981 Prepared for the international SVO Workshop 'Educational Research and Public Policy-Making', The Hague, The Netherlands, 20–22 May 1981.
Foundation for Educational Research in the Netherlands (SVO)	Social science research and public policy making: a bibliography prepared for the international SVO Workshop 'Educational Research and Public Policy Making', The Hague, The Netherlands, 20–22 May 1981 Recherche en sciences sociales et politique gouvernementale: Une bibliographie preparée pour le 'SVO-Atelier international sur les relations entre la recherche et la politique en matière d'éducation', La Haye, Pays-Bas, les 20, 21 et 22 Mai 1981.

Foundation for Educational Research in the Netherlands (SVO)	SVO Workshop 'Educational research and public policy making', The Hague, The Netherlands, 20, 21 and 22 May 1981. List of sponsored ongoing research related to the theme of the workshop.
Advisory Council for Science Policy in the Netherlands (RAWB)	SVO Workshop, 'Educational research and public policy making' A concise bibliography listing empirical studies of the utilization of social science research by policy-makers; The Hague, The Netherlands, 20–22 May 1981.
Centrale Directie Documentatie Ministerie van O. en W.	– Foreign language publications on education and science policy in the Netherlands Bibliography 1976–1980 – Publications en langues étrangères (sauf le Néerlandais) consacrées à l' enseignement et à la politique scientifique aux Pay-Bas. Bibliographie 1976–1980 – Niet-Nederlandse publicaties over onderwijs en wetenschapsbeleid in nederland. Bibliografie 1976–1980

2) Unsolicited papers

Husén, Torsten	Two partners with communication problems: researchers and policy-makers in education. Paper written for the SVO Workshop 'Educational Research and Public Policy Making', May, 20–22, 1981.
Jobst, Eberhard	Educational research in the Federal Republic of German. Background paper for the SVO Workshop 'Educational Research and Public Policy Making', May, 20–22, 1981.
Vall, Mark van de and Bolas, Cheryl, A.	External versus internal client oriented researchers in social policy formation: a comparative evaluation. Leiden, Leiden Institute for Social Policy Research University of Leiden, 1981.
Vall, Mark van de and Bolas, Cheryl, A.	Utilizing social policy research for solving social problems: an empirical analysis of structure and functions. Leiden, Leiden Institute for Social Policy Research/University of Leiden, 1981.

Kursten, Arnold, F.A. Summary prepared for the SVO Workshop 'Educational Research and Public Policy making', 20, 21 and 22 May, 1981.
Analysis of conventional and 'new' thinking about utilisation of social science results in public policy making in the Netherlands, in comparison with some other countries.

3) French versions of invited papers

All contributions have been translated into French. The translations are available upon request.

APPENDIX D

Special Interest Group (SIG)

During the Workshop SVO proposed the setting up of an informal Special Interest Group (SIG), provisionally named 'Social Science and Public Policy-making' to cover all aspects of the complex relations between social science research and policy-making. In view of the broad scope of the problem area the membership of this SIG should reflect a variety of different disciplines and expert skills. One of the SIG's main features would be its international character combining inputs from both sides of the Atlantic which could make it an excellent communication channel in its sphere of interest and study. The output of the Workshop, in particular the special session 'Research on the interplay between social science research and public policy-making in the 1980s: Inventory and Prospects' could be taken as the starting point for defining the SIG's terms of reference.

The projected Special Interest Group would have the following objectives:

— Scientific communication: to form a scientific communication network for the study of social science and public policy-making, e.g. by circulating pre-publications among SIG members.
— Exchange of information: to publish a regular SIG newsletters. (The first issue will include more information on the decisions reached.)
— Documentation: to compile and publish each year a selective up-to-date bibliography and a list of ongoing research and to ensure that publications by SIG members are circulated to relevant documentation centres.
— Organization of symposia relevant to the problem area.
— Translation into English of important published studies in the field.

Following preliminary soundings at the Workshop, the following persons expressed interest in becoming involved in the informal SIG network. Addresses can be found in Appendix A. Where members mentioned their special field of interest this is also listed.